Dear Debra, my Friend —

I hope this Book will be
a Blessing For you & a
Daily Inspiration As you seek
To get Closer To Jesus Each
Day. He Will NEVER leave
or Forsake you.

        With love —

            Bert Logan

a special gift

_____

presented to:

_____

from:

_____

date:

"Create in me a clean heart, O God;
And renew a right spirit within me."

—Psalm 51:10

RENEW

The Women's Devotional Series

To order, call 1-800-765-6955.
Visit us at www.reviewandherald.com
for more information on other Review and Herald® products.

RENEW

Ardis Dick Stenbakken, editor

REVIEW AND HERALD® PUBLISHING ASSOCIATION
Since 1861 | www.reviewandherald.com

Review and Herald® titles may be purchased in bulk for educational, business, fund-raising, or sales promotional use. For information, e-mail SpecialMarkets@reviewandherald.com.

The Review and Herald® Publishing Association publishes biblically based materials for spiritual, physical, and mental growth and Christian discipleship.

The author assumes full responsibility for the accuracy of all facts and quotations as cited in this book.

This book was
Edited by Jeannette R. Johnson
Copyedited by Judy Blodgett
Designed by Michelle C. Petz
Cover art by thinkstock.com
Typeset: 10.5/13.5

PRINTED IN U.S.A.

15 14 13 12 11   5 4 3 2 1

Library of Congress Cataloging-in-Publication Data
Renew / Ardis Dick Stenbakken, editor.
    p. cm.
1. Seventh-Day Adventist women—Prayers and devotions. 2. Devotional calendars—
Seventh-Day Adventists. I. Stenbakken, Ardis Dick.
  BV4844.R46 2011
  242'.643—dc22

                                        2010041816

ISBN 978-0-8280-2571-3

There is an aspect of this book that is unique.

None of these contributors has been paid—each have shared freely so that all profits go to scholarships for women. As this book goes to press, 1,748 scholarships have been given to women in 115 countries.

For more current information, or to contribute to these scholarships, please go to http://adventistwomensministries.org/index.php?id=60. In this way you too can renew the dreams of some woman—or even your own—in seeking a higher degree.

Cool Resolution

For I resolved to know nothing . . . except Jesus Christ and him crucified.
1 Cor. 2:2, NIV.

WHILE WORKING in my language-impaired Phase II classroom, I'd been given the job of preparing a large bulletin board for the new year. With the help of *The Mailbox* magazine I went to work. The board featured a background sky of vivid blue, and piles of fluffy snow covered the bottom half. A bright-red border set off the caption "Cool Resolutions."

I explained to the children the meaning of "resolution," and they began the task of writing their resolutions on a snowman that would be put up on the board. First they struggled to think of an idea, a goal. Then they struggled to put it into words. Finally they struggled with spelling those words. At last their resolutions were written on their snowmen. After reading and talking about their resolutions one more time, we finally stapled them on the bulletin board.

The next few hours were spent on the spelling and reading lessons, but as we continued through the morning I watched those children break all their resolutions! Every one of them! Jaymes had written quite simply: "I will try to be good." Well, somehow that just didn't seem to be on his agenda for that morning. Deon had promised to "work very hard at school," but Deon was hardly working. Terrence had said he was going to get all his work done in class. He really didn't have a clue as to what that meant. And so it went, right down to the last child. *Well,* I thought, *make 'em and break 'em.*

Later that day, as I had more time to reflect on the events of the morning, I had to admit that those children were really no different than anyone else. Who has not made a New Year's resolution and then proceeded to break it a few days (or maybe even hours) later? Perhaps there is only one resolution that we really need to make. As we begin this year, we simply need to resolve to spend some significant time with Jesus every day to get to know Him better. And as we learn to know Jesus, He will work in us "to will and to act according to his good pleasure" (Phil. 2:13, NIV). The other goals on your list will come in time, one by one, as you and Jesus get better acquainted.

So this new year let's resolve to know Jesus. That, indeed, will be a cool resolution!

Sharon Oster

Divine Interruption

I am the vine, you are the branches; he who abides in Me and I in him,
he bears much fruit, for apart from Me you can do nothing.
John 15:5, NASB.

I DON'T DO RESOLUTIONS. I've observed two things: that humans have an in-defatigable drive to fix themselves, and that it is utterly futile and fruitless. The only good that comes from our self-fixing is that some of us finally learn it's impossible.

Observe every world religion other than the faith of Jesus. Each proposes a method whereby lost souls may ascend to God. Whether they depend on endless meditations or prayers, there is an intended incline from earth to heaven, fueled by human effort—endless resolutions to do better, to aim higher, to improve, to achieve, to arrive.

In sharp contrast is the faith of Jesus. The most essential path of this religion isn't the *ascending* path of the God-follower, but the *descending* path of God, stretching from heaven to hell, and only ascending after its initial, heroic descent. Jesus, equal with God, became a servant, a man, an outlaw, and, finally, sin itself on our behalf (Phil. 2). Then God "made us alive together with Christ" and "raised us up with Him" (Eph. 2:5, 6, NASB). Alleluia!

Consider evolution versus biblical creation. Evolution features the same ascendency (in this case a biological one) from ape to human. Creation features a divine interruption in which God spoke and it was. God came down to earth to form the man out of dust and the woman out of the man. We didn't achieve God-likeness as a result of millennia of self-development; we were made in God's image by His own tender touch.

God is still touching people with something called grace. It comes to us via the same heaven-to-hell path that was carved out by the incarnate God more than 2,000 years ago. It's a divine interruption, a supernatural interposition, and the only means of truly elevating us out of our stinking, boring, hellish existence.

Maybe you're at a point in life where you realize that attempts at self-improvement have yielded little. Realize one more thing, then: it's not over! There's this amazing thing called grace, and it saturates the atmosphere. The great thing about failure is that your deep sobs create within you more room for the exhilarating air of grace. Take it in. It's what's been missing.

Jennifer Jill Schwirzer

Seeing the Big Picture

*We know that all things work together for good to those who love God,
to those who are the called according to His purpose.
Rom. 8:28, NKJV.*

FOR MANY YEARS I've been a published writer. In college I took courses to sharpen my writing skills: learning more about the surface story, what lies deeper, and seeing the small picture versus "the big picture." Even so, I had some difficulty understanding today's text. But God was about to use one of our cats to help me with that.

We had four cats. Chocky, our Himalayan tabby, at nearly 11, was our oldest. He was rather delicate, with more health problems than the other three. I had to squirt liquid antibiotic down his throat for his urinary tract infections. I needed to apply ointment and wipe his eyes clean for his sore eyes. He didn't enjoy taking nutritional supplements or shark collagen to help his arthritic joints, either.

He could see only the here and now ("This isn't fun!"), and he didn't understand the whys. But he was always happy when he started feeling better.

I began to see that at times my relationship with God resembles how Chocky's was with me. When God allows some problems and trials to chip some rough edges off my character or personality, I squirm, protest, and ask, "Why? Why me? Why now?" Like Chocky, I may not fully understand what's happening to me. For with my finite mind I can't see the complete picture and don't know what all of God's plans are for me.

Chocky has led my husband, Carl, and me on some real chases until one or the other of us finally caught him and picked him up. Once caught, Chocky submitted with as much grace as he could muster, and we were able to do what was necessary for his well-being.

Hebrews 10:31 says, "It is a fearful thing to fall into the hands of the living God" (NKJV). That may well describe the feelings of anyone who doesn't know God well enough to fully trust Him.

Will you pray this prayer with me? "Lord, like a cat, or like the prophet Jonah, I often want to run and don't trust You enough to willingly fall into Your hands. Help me to slow down and let You catch me so that You won't be hindered from guiding my life and doing what is best for me. Amen."

Bonnie Moyers

The Simple Life

For I have learned in whatever state I am, to be content. Phil. 4:11, NKJV.

MY HUSBAND, JOE, AND I had an opportunity to visit a certain country a few years ago. We had heard on the news how difficult life was there. We'd seen the pictures of their suffering and living conditions. But we experienced the "simple life" while visiting them. I recall that the food was strange (many of the vegetables we did not even know), but the dishes were so tastefully and well prepared that I found myself asking for recipes so I could try them myself with other vegetables.

The one thing that amazed us was how contented our brothers and sisters were. They knew their needs, and I'm sure they would have liked to have more comfortable lives, yet they did not walk around looking stressed or burdened. They had an outlook on life that I longed to have. With all the conveniences of the Western world, we also have all the stresses. Then I realized that the simplicity of their lives and their attitude of contentment is one of the blessings of their life.

On returning home, Joe and I had much time to talk on our long flight. We talked about how we could simplify our lives and seek God's contentment whether we had little or much. In the months that followed, we made some major changes. Oh, we still have the stereo and the television and other such conveniences, but we let go of other things and think twice before we buy more. We have changed our diet to one that is more healthful and natural. Now when I shop in the supermarket my cart is filled with food that comes from the ground and not from a can or package. I've learned to taste my food and to taste life.

Paul continues in Philippians 4:12: "I know how to live on almost nothing or with everything. I have learned the secret of living in every situation, whether it is with a full stomach or empty, with plenty or little" (NLT). And that is what we should all be striving for—contentment with life that brings peace and joy. Joe and I aren't quite there yet, but we aren't where we used to be, either.

As we face this new year, let's ask God to give us the peace and joy that contentment brings, and to take away the restlessness and selfish desire for more and more things that cannot bring peace or joy.

Heather-Dawn Small

Love Kindness

O man, what is good; and what does the Lord require of you but to do justice, and to love kindness, and to walk humbly with your God? Micah 6:8, ESV.

OH, MARY!" Linda pleaded, obviously disturbed. "Would you pray for me?"

"Absolutely!" My response was quick as I listened to Linda share her story. She shared her overwhelming feelings of inadequacy as I did my second round at the gym where I work out five days a week.

As I listened to Linda, I quickly remembered feeling that same way a few years before, and I empathized with her. "Linda," I asked, "when I pray for you, do you have something really specific I can pray for?" I'd known Linda for about three years and had developed a friendship with her over that time. I knew she might feel uncomfortable if I prayed for her with people around. As she continued to share her concerns with me, I prayed that somehow God would open up a way for me to pray with her before I had to leave. Putting the concern aside, I concentrated on my listening skills with more intensity.

Briefly sharing with Linda how I understood her desperation, I counseled, "Do remember, Linda, that God will never place you somewhere without equipping you."

I had less than half a lap to complete when suddenly all the other women left. (It didn't come to my attention until later how God allowed all this to transpire.) As I finished up my workout, the Holy Spirit convinced and convicted me: "Pray for Linda before you leave, Mary."

On the way toward the door I responded to the Holy Spirit by saying, "Linda, would you feel comfortable if I prayed with you before I leave?" She responded eagerly. After my brief prayer, I hugged Linda and left.

The next day when I saw her, she ran over, beaming. "I told my husband about what you did, and he said God sent an angel to me. I have such peace and confidence in God that I'm not overwhelmed anymore. I can't thank you enough for taking time to pray with me!"

As I reflected on this divine appointment I realized that when we take time to show our "love kindness" to those with whom we become acquainted, this is God's method of evangelism—learning to love to be kind.

Mary L. Maxson

Before Arriving in Malta

But now I urge you to keep up your courage, because not one of you will be lost; only the ship will be destroyed. Acts 27:22, NIV.

ONE DAY DURING my devotional time I read the Bible story of the shipwreck involving the apostle Paul when he went to Rome to be judged by the emperor. I saw a parallel between this story and my life when I face "storms" and problems.

As the story unfolds in Acts, days before the storm hit, the ship passes by a small place. Paul suggests that they wait out the winter there because it will be very dangerous to sail during that time of the year. However, the crew and passengers don't want to follow his advice. The ship continues its journey and, days later, the sea becomes rough. Waves hit the ship with great force, and the rain is torrential. For several days they remain afloat, subjected to the violent sea. (I face terrible storms in my life at times because I don't follow God's counsel. I spend days surrounded by darkness. Fearful, I cry to the Lord for salvation.)

The sailors begin to throw the cargo overboard—it was now unnecessary. (The dark moments of life cause me to evaluate what is prohibiting me from giving myself completely to the Lord, and doing away with everything that isn't from the Lord. I undo the baggage of anger, resentment, discontentment, lack of forgiveness, pride, arrogance, self-will.)

One night God appears to Paul, saying that all on board will be saved. The following morning Paul gathers everyone together and reveals his dream. He instructs the passengers and crew to eat, since they haven't eaten because of worry. (In my own difficult moments I also need to nourish myself with God's Word and to pray so I can be strong when the winds whirl around me.)

With an island in sight, they abandon the ship as it begins to break up from the force of the waves. It must have been frightening to throw oneself into the sea with fierce waves. (Likewise, it is frightening to trust in God when I don't see exactly what is in front of me. However, I need to trust and place my life in God's hands so that He may take me safely to the Malta of His plans.)

I have decided to trust fully in the Lord and to throw myself into an unknown future, knowing that I will find the Island of Malta where I will find all that I need.

Iani Dias Lauer-Leite

Fabric by the Meter

As surely as I valued your life today, so may the Lord value my life
and deliver me from all trouble. 1 Sam. 26:24, NIV.

LAST WEEK I MADE a trip to IKEA, a Swedish furniture store, with my daughter to buy something in the fabric section. While I looked at a piece, my daughter said, "Look! There's Hannele!" When I looked blank, she pointed. "Look at that fabric, the turquoise one . . . Over there. And you can even get it in white."

I saw two bales of fabric labeled "Hannele." It is a well-known fact that IKEA gives all its products Scandinavian names, but I had never come across a Hannele. I looked at the fabric with interest. It looked good and had a nice pattern. But at the moment I had no use for Hannele.

The Hannele fabric cost €4.60 per meter, and since then I've been brooding over the question of whether or not I could calculate my own worth in euros: length times price = €7.18. What worries me about this calculation? That the sum is so cheap? And if the material had been an expensive brocade with golden threads? The result would have been considerably higher.

Of course I know that my thoughts were ridiculous. I am no fabric to be bought by the meter, neither beautiful cotton nor brocade. I am a human being whose worth cannot be calculated in this way. And yet I was somehow hurt. My well-hidden insecurity had once more come to the surface. What is my worth?

We all want to feel valuable, in spite of our faults. The Bible tells us that King Saul was pursuing David and wanted to kill him. One night David could have killed Saul (1 Sam. 26) but didn't because he considered the king's life to be valuable. David did not want to act on his own behalf but waited for the Lord's plan to work out to make him the new king. He knew that he was called to this position, and this knowledge gave him mental balance in the difficult situation. Thus he was able to say, "So may the Lord value my life." This was no self-exaltation but an insight God gave him. In God's eyes he was valuable and precious.

The same applies to me: In God's eyes I am not just fabric by the meter but a unique piece of art, made by the hands of God, who makes me to be just what He wants me to be. He is still working on me. I am looking forward to seeing what the finished product will be like!

Hannele Ottschofski

Order My Steps

Noah was a righteous man, blameless among the people
of his time, and he walked with God. Gen. 6:9, NIV.

So Moses and Aaron went to Pharaoh and said to him, "This is what the Lord,
the God of the Hebrews, says: 'How long will you refuse to humble yourself
before me? Let my people go, so that they may worship me.'" Ex. 10:3, NIV.

EVERY DAY I ASK the Lord to use me in His service in all that I do or say. Recently, while my husband and I were shopping at a club warehouse for motor oil, we passed by the office supply section. We didn't need any office supplies, but some 9" x 6" envelopes caught my eye. As I placed them in my basket, I noticed there were 150 in the box. Samuel asked me why these particular envelopes, and why so many. I replied, "I don't know, but I will find a use for them." When we reached the checkout the cashier asked if I needed postage stamps; I said yes without thinking about what we did or didn't have at home. Later, in the car, my husband asked again about this particular purchase, and again I told him I didn't know right then but would think of something.

A few days later we received a delivery of some books about the Ten Commandments for use by our church for community outreach. I was impressed that some people could not do the door-to-door outreach but might be interested in a mailing program. Now I knew why I had bought the envelopes and the first-class stamps!

I presented the idea to the personal ministries leader at church, who was very happy about promoting my idea and pledged to mail five books per week. Others offered to help as well. I was impressed to use the telephone book to make labels, and others decided they would stuff the envelopes and add a Bible study card inside. The plan was to make the books available to every home in the community.

Out of our first mailing of 50 books, 20 came back for various reasons. We prayed especially for the ones who received the book. This united effort has given each of us a feeling of working together in the Lord's vineyard.

Every day I ask the Lord to use me in His service. You never know how He will do this.

Betty G. Perry

The Perfect Interpreter

For we know not what we should pray for as we ought: but the Spirit itself maketh intercession for us with groanings which cannot be uttered. Rom. 8:26.

I MIGRATED TO THE United States from the small island country of Haiti. I was 17, and I didn't speak English. For many years I dedicated time and effort to learning English, which has served as a passport to this English-speaking society. I learned enough to earn degrees, and with the increasing ability to handle the language, I felt an obligation to reach out to others. So I signed up as an interpreter.

One day I was assigned to interpret in court for a young woman. As a rule, I'm not supposed to speak to her. So I was a bit stumped when I exited the restroom stall to find the woman standing in front of the bathroom sink. She stepped next to me as we washed our hands and whispered a timid "Thank you." I nodded and returned a quiet "You're welcome" without looking into her eyes. We were perfect strangers, bound by a common language. I had just interpreted for her in a serious matter, and she felt that she needed to thank me.

I hadn't done much. I had simply lent her my voice. I interpreted from her native Creole to English her concerns and part of her life story, and I interpreted the questions, comments, and findings of the English speaker to her. Communication was possible because I was there, and for that she thanked me.

As I thought of that young woman, I recalled with overwhelming gratitude that very often I also need a voice. At times life's struggles knock me off my feet, and I'm perplexed, frightened, distressed. All I can do is sigh, cry, or moan. Then, as if by miracle, my joy is restored, my hope renewed, and my wish granted. Someone lends me a voice when my words fail and when my heart falters under the weight of this life.

Somebody speaks for me! The Holy Spirit interprets my moanings and groanings to the Father who delivers me. Communication between the Father and me is possible with the Spirit's presence. Many times I shout "Thank You!" But once in a while, as I realize the miracle of it all and the grandeur of His love for me, I whisper a timid "Thank You! Thank You, Holy Spirit; thank You, Spirit of the living God—the Perfect Interpreter."

Rose Joseph Thomas

The Ladder

Let not him that eateth despise him that eateth not; and let not him which eateth not judge him that eateth: for God hath received him. Rom. 14:3.

WHEN I WAS TAKING my baptismal lessons, Pastor Collier explained that when I entered the church I wasn't to see a room full of pews; I was to see a room full of ladders. And instead of being seated in a church, every member was standing on a rung of the ladder.

Each ladder had the same number of rungs. Each ladder reached into heaven—the goal of every person in the room. Every rung of the ladder had the name of one of the fruits of the Spirit on it. But no two ladders had the rungs in the same order. The name of the rung each was on was the lesson in life that they were learning from the Holy Spirit at that time. I would have no idea what order of learning had been assigned to my neighbor.

Let's say that everyone in church is on the third rung of the ladder. I am on the rung labeled "love." The life lessons I am learning from the Holy Spirit are how to love my fellow beings as Christ does. I have already learned the first two lessons, and come up the first two rungs, which are "peace" and "joy."

But the third rung of the ladder that the person on my left is standing on might be named "peace." The two steps she has learned from the Holy Spirit were named "joy" and "love." And the third rung that the person to my right is standing on might be "joy." The two steps she has learned from the Holy Spirit were named "love" and "peace."

God addresses flaws in our personality one at a time, and He works with us as we are able to learn. I judge God and His methods when I judge a brother or sister by my standards and demand that they follow the path that has been laid out for me rather than acknowledging they have their own valid path to follow (or, rather, ladder rung on which to stand).

We have a wonderful promise in Luke 6:37: "Judge not, and you shall not be judged. Condemn not, and you shall not be condemned. Forgive, and you will be forgiven" (NKJV). So today I challenge myself—and each reader—to accept ourselves and others as Christ accepts us. At the same time we can thank Him for accepting us as we are, and for working with us to bring us into alignment with the image of Christ.

Darlenejoan McKibbin Rhine

Your Driver Today Is . . .

I will instruct you and teach you in the way you should go;
I will counsel you and watch over you. Ps. 32:8, NIV.

I FELT ANXIOUS and stressed as I stepped onto the shuttle bus that ran from the long-term airport parking lot to the terminal. It was still early in the morning, but I'd been up a couple hours putting last-minute items in my suitcase, getting my water bottle filled—well, you know how it is just before you leave on a trip. As usual, I wished I had at least another day to get everything ready to leave home. I had driven the hour to the airport, parked the car, and gotten my suitcase, carry-on bag, purse, and papers gathered up and transferred. What had I forgotten? Would the security lines be as bad as they'd been last time? Would I have time to get something to eat before I needed to board my flight? So many concerns!

But now I settled into my seat on the shuttle and looked around. And then I saw it. There, above the windshield, was a small sign that read: "Your driver today is: Jesus."

I smiled, took a deep breath, and relaxed. Jesus was my driver. I didn't need to be stressed anymore. Now, I know that Jesus is a common Hispanic name, and the sign really had nothing to do with my Lord and Redeemer. However, it did remind me that if I let Jesus, my God, be my driver, be in control of my day and my life, I could relax. My blood pressure could return to normal, and I could enjoy my day. When I let Jesus take control, I can know that what happens is something that God wants, or allows, to happen.

I find this promise of how it can work so reassuring: "May the God of peace,...that great Shepherd of the sheep, equip you with everything good for doing his will, and may he work in us what is pleasing to him, through Jesus Christ, to whom be glory for ever and ever. Amen" (Heb. 13:20, 21, NIV).

How about you? Is Jesus your driver today? As we begin a new year it is so important that I allow Jesus to be my driver. Not only must I let Him be my driver—I must also let Him pick the destination and how I will get there. Handing over control can be so hard, but so rewarding!

I think it is time for me to move out of the driver's seat and let Jesus take over permanently—and no backseat driving!

Ardis Dick Stenbakken

The Pits

He lifted me out of the slimy pit, out of the mud and mire;
he set my feet on a rock and gave me a firm place to stand. He put
a new song in my mouth, a hymn of praise to our God. Ps. 40:2, 3, NIV.

GOD CALLED ME to walk with a new friend through a time of great hardship. She is a single mother with a debilitating health condition and an inadequate income. When she had pneumonia early in our friendship, I took groceries to her. But God impressed me that her needs went beyond paying her rent and bills. Her situation needed to change, and that would have to be God's doing.

I assured Missy that I would pray for her, and I encouraged her to look to God for direction and that she needed to attend church where she would also find supportive friends. I once loaned her money, but reluctantly concluded that additional financial help was unwise. I ached for her as days and weeks passed and God didn't perform a miracle—though she didn't go hungry, and the rent money did materialize. *What more can I do?* I wondered.

Then I read about an intercessor who would rather spend half an hour silently praying for a friend in need than an hour in conversation with her. I could hardly imagine such a thing! Spend an entire half hour in silent petition for Missy's need? What would I say to God? Surely I wasn't supposed to just cry "Help her!" again and again!

Baffled, I found myself opening the book of Psalms. The cries for deliverance pulled me in, and I spent half an hour reading one psalm after another, holding Missy before God.

When I closed the Bible, my heart was calm. I reflected on literal and figurative pits. Getting out requires help, and it isn't easy. I remembered the state penitentiary where I once taught. Getting out of that "pit"—even as staff or visitor—is similarly complicated. Going in or out, it's a succession of clanking doors, hallways, and more clanking doors. You don't just open a door and walk out.

I don't have the keys to release Missy from the prison of her present circumstances. But I can pray with her, help strengthen her faith, and walk with her through the grim hallways, sharing my confidence that eventually she will exit the last clanking door into the freedom of a new life.

Dolores Klinsky Walker

Facing Life's Challenges

I can do all things through Christ which strengtheneth me. Phil. 4:13.

I AWOKE THIS MORNING, legs stiff and painful. I don't know how it is possible to go through another day of pain and relearning to walk yet one more time. I don't even want to try. I feel like giving up before the sun has peeked over the horizon, but I don't.

I tell myself, "Dorothy, you can do this! The promise is there. Christ will give you strength to get up, dress, wash, get breakfast, exercise, and do everything that needs doing today."

I will admit that life has not been fair to me these past three years: two rounds of chemo, lymphoma twice, breast cancer, mastectomy, radiation, left knee operations three times, and right hip operation once. The struggle has been long and hard. Each time I nearly reach recovery I get knocked down again. But by God's grace and strength I have been able to get up and keep going. God is good and has sent so many blessings my way in the midst of all of these challenges.

I'll never forget the first time I claimed today's promise. I was a freshman at a church boarding high school. I had piano lessons with Miss Soper and was ready to perform in a recital. She had me on stage the afternoon before the program to run through my piece. I was scared. "I can't do this!" I moaned. "Take my name off the recital list."

"Yes, you can do it," my teacher replied. "Go to your room and read Philippians 4:13 and memorize it. When you have to play, just remember God will be with you to give you courage and strength."

I did as she said, and I managed to play my piece perfectly that night. "Oh, thank You, Jesus!" I said. Since then I have claimed that promise many times.

With God's help and that verse I found that I could do so many things I never dreamed I could do, such as lead a cooking school, run Vacation Bible School, speak at a women's retreat, teach school one year with no textbooks, start an orphanage, finish college after marriage, learn to adjust to a new culture, write 27 books, begin Adventist Child Care India to care for thousands of poor children, lead out in women's ministries, and the list goes on.

So today's challenges are something that can be conquered by God's grace and strength. He has not let me down so far. He will not forsake me now.

Dorothy Eaton Watts

God Knows Best

A man reaps what he sows. Gal. 6:7, NIV.

ON SATURDAY, January 13, 2007, my sister Gerry died. The Tuesday before she died I had the most overwhelming sense that I literally had to drop everything I was doing and go to the hospital where Gerry had been admitted a few days before. When I arrived at the hospital, I knew why—Gerry and her husband, David, had just been told that she had only days to live. It was a strange day, trying to keep my emotions under control, as I struggled to support them.

I remember sitting with Gerry alone as she sobbed that she didn't want to die. She didn't want to leave her sons, 23-year-old Luke and 12-year-old Joe, and her husband. She half laughed and cried as she said she didn't want to miss my fiftieth birthday party that she and my family had been planning for the summer. She looked at my face as she shared that she was scared. But then she said, "If this is what God wants for my life, then it is OK."

One of the things I had to do later that day was tell my other three sisters and Dad about Gerry's condition. Mom was too upset to tell them. Shortly after that, two of my sisters were back at the hospital. Gerry had begun her journey to leave this world. When I reentered her room, she asked me, "Did you tell Dad? What did he say?"

I told her that Dad had said, "Gerry has suffered enough in her life, and God knows what is best for her. If this is the way that He wants to stop her suffering, then that is OK."

"Tell Dad thank you. I needed to hear that," she said, and from that moment Gerry faced her death with peace.

For the first time in my life I saw new meaning to today's verse. My parents have a strong love for God. In that love they surrendered everything to God, and so they have been able to trust Him with their lives and the lives of their daughters. It was common, as we grew up, to hear Dad say, "God knows best"—especially if some crisis came upon us.

The way we parents trust God, the confidence we display in Him, influences the way our children trust God. Gerry was able to say, "God knows best."

Today, think about what your relationship with God is saying to others, especially to those you love the most. Then spend some time thinking about whether, like Gerry, you too believe that "God knows best." Talk to God about what you discover.

Mary Barrett

Be Still

Be still, and know that I am God. Ps. 46:10.

I HAVE A REMOTE control for my car. It has many purposes. It will start and turn off the motor. It will lock and unlock the doors. It will open the trunk and, when it is triggered, the car's horn will blow continually until I turn it off. Maybe there are even more uses of which I'm unaware.

One day I discovered a strange thing about remote controls. I came out of a store into the large parking lot and realized that I had no idea where my car was. I headed off in the general direction that I thought it was, only to discover it wasn't there. So I headed another direction. To my dismay, it wasn't there, either. I stood in the middle of the parking lot wondering what to do. Then I remembered that the car horn blows when I press a button on my remote. Because of the traffic noise, I had to tune in and listen carefully to hear the sound of my particular horn. I had to be still. I finally heard it in the far distance and headed that direction.

When I still couldn't locate my car, I pressed the button again. This time the sound came from behind me. This continued for a few times. I got the giggles thinking about it as I kept wandering around the parking lot following the sound of the horn—back and forth, back and forth. How could I be hearing the car but not seeing it? Finally it dawned on me what I had done wrong (to my great relief). I had purchased a new car a few days before. It was totally different from the one I'd been driving for four years—even the color was different. I had heard the right car all the time but was looking for a car of a different color.

Is the mind our Creator gave us tuned in to the right things? Are our eyes deceiving us? What voices do we hear in our lives? Are they the right voices? Are our ears tuned into hearing what God has to say to us? Do we immediately head in that direction, as I did in response to the horn on my car? And do we recognize His leading when we see it? That is God's desire for our lives, you know.

Jesus Christ is waiting for us to be still and listen carefully to Him and His teachings, to look at the beauty He has in store for us, and to know in our minds what it is we're looking for. Again, we are invited to be still and know that He is God!

Vidella McClellan

The Lost Book

Be careful for nothing; but in every thing by prayer and supplication with thanksgiving let your requests be made known unto God. Phil. 4:6.

IT'S WONDERFUL TO know that we can come to God with all our sorrows and wishes at any time. We can tell Him everything—He is always listening.

Can we ask for something and say "thank You" at the same time? Isn't it better to ask and wait to see how things turn out before thanking God for His intervention? No! As far as God is concerned, we can be sure that He will help us. No matter what, He won't let us down.

If we are prepared to bring our requests to God, we must also be prepared to accept His help, in whatever form it turns out to be. God will not ask us to hold the line indefinitely. However, God expects us to be patient since He picks the right moment in our life for His solution. To ask is easy, but to thank God is important. Often it's easier for us to tell Him our wishes than to offer Him our thanks for all the good things we have already received.

My little daughter Selina was able to experience how important it is to ask and to give thanks. She had lent a book to someone, a book that was important to her. Then she forgot to whom she had given it. For days and weeks we racked our brains about where it could be. Teachers and classmates were asked to help in the search for the book. We even asked our neighbors. Nobody knew. One evening when Selina was already in bed I proposed that we ask God to help us. We prayed, "Heavenly Father, please let us know where the book is, and we thank You already that we will have it back soon!" Since we were sure that God would help us, we could say our "thank You" at the same time.

We had been looking for the book for two weeks. But at the moment we asked for God's help it was as if lightning had struck and I knew where the book was: it was at the cousin's house! It was fantastic! It was like a miracle! Such experiences help our small children to trust in our great God—and help us as well.

Everything does not always work out so quickly, but we can be sure that God is listening; we can approach Him with all our cares. God's ears are always open to hear our prayers. Let us thank Him.

Sandra Widulle

Friends Till Death

A man of many companions may come to ruin, but there is
a friend who sticks closer than a brother. Prov. 18:24, NIV.

MICHAEL BECAME OUR friend the first day we met in the Sabbath school Bible class at the Newbold College church. When he realized that we are Africans, he told us of his experience in Africa as a Navy officer during World War II. He met our children later and came to love them as if they were his own grandchildren. He made sure he talked to us every Sabbath, and he became very close to my family.

After graduation we said goodbye and left for missionary work in The Gambia. We kept on calling Michael, and he never stopped sending us news, greetings cards, magazines, and pictures from Newbold. We also sent him pictures about our missionary life. He loved the baptismal pictures so much that he asked the church administration for a corner of the main bulletin board and posted our pictures there with the words: "The Kweis' missionary work in The Gambia." He wrote to tell us about it and how happy he was for students and Newbold church members to see his African friends working for God.

Michael was already old when we met, so we were not surprised when his wife, Brenda, wrote to tell us that he had lost his eyesight. Soon she told us not to try to talk to Michael on the phone, as he couldn't hear well anymore. We were sad, but my husband visited him whenever he went to England, and Michael never forgot us.

A few months later we got a phone call from the Newbold church pastor telling us that Michael had peacefully gone to rest in the Lord. We learned that he wrote in his will that $900 (£550) should be given to us for our missionary work in The Gambia.

See how Michael stuck to us like a brother till death? That is what Psalm 133:1 says: "How good and pleasant it is when brothers live . . . in unity" (NIV). We even felt his love after his death. What a friend! He reminds me of Jesus, our true heavenly friend who never gives up on us. Even if we go astray, He waits patiently and makes sure we come back. Thus the hymnist wrote, "What a friend we have in Jesus/All our sins and grief to bear."

Do you need a friend forever? Try Jesus.

Mabel Kwei

When You Least Expect It

Before they call, I will answer; and while they are yet speaking, I will hear.
Isa. 65:24.

I WISH I COULD do something for You, Lord. But I don't know what to do, I silently prayed as I sat in the back of the Sabbath school Bible class. The teacher was sharing stories of regular people doing things for the Lord, encouraging the class to get involved and do more for the cause of Christ. I was a new Christian and had been attending that church for only about six weeks. I was shy and didn't really know anyone very well, but that morning the Holy Spirit spoke to my heart, and I wanted to do something for the Lord.

The bell rang, signaling time for dismissal. I got up from my seat and was headed for the door when someone called, "Emily!" I was surprised. I had spoken to so few people that I was taken aback that someone remembered my name. I turned to see my son's Sabbath school teacher. "Would you be interested in helping teach some lessons in the earliteen class?"

I was in shock! I had no idea that the Lord could—or even would—answer so quickly. I didn't know what to say. There was no denying that it was a direct answer to the prayer I had whispered not 10 minutes earlier. Somehow it was just not what I was expecting. I'd never thought about teaching.

Actually, I'd never thought much about anything I could do. But God had. I said, "Yes."

I was unbelievably nervous and unsure of myself. And to make matters worse, my son was in that class, which didn't make a difficult job any easier. Even though I had no experience doing that work before, the Lord helped me beyond measure. I am glad that He knows what we should be doing, even when we don't.

And I can praise Him today because I know that when I call, He will answer. As a matter of fact, He declares that "before they call, I will answer; and while they are yet speaking, I will hear" (Isa. 65:24). What a promise that is! He's already worked it out. Before you can even tell Him the desires of your heart, the answer is already on its way.

Do you have something you want to do for God? Let Him know about it. He's just waiting to use you. He's been waiting all your life. And He knows just where to place you in His perfect plan.

Emily Felts Jones

A Modern-Day Miracle

Oh, give thanks to the Lord! Call upon His name; make known
His deeds among the peoples. Ps. 105:1, NKJV.

AFTER OUR BUS TURNED over on the way to the youth conference in Surinam,
I suffered with backaches for many years. I had constant pain in my shoulder and
back, and like the woman with the issue of blood, I had gone to many doctors and
found no cure. Nearly every doctor I saw after moving to Maryland five years later
wanted to perform surgery on my back. I was hesitant, so I refused. I had to exercise
daily to prevent the excruciating pain.

There were many things that I couldn't do with my right side. Besides the injury, I had scoliosis in my back that hadn't been treated. I began to pray daily for
healing. It would be 21 years before I would be healed.

I walked with a limp, and I couldn't hold back my right shoulder because of the
permanent dislocation on my right side. My arm seemed to be getting shorter as the
years went by.

One day my older sister came to visit. I continued exercising, as usual, but the
pain appeared to be getting much worse. I wondered why, because my routine had-
n't changed. When my sister inquired about my distress, I told her about the pain
I'd had ever since my accident. She thought for a moment then told me that she
knew someone who could help me in St. Thomas, Virgin Islands. I had plans to go
there for a wedding in June, and she promised to make the arrangements for me to
see him. I felt a small ray of hope.

It required almost 10 visits to this young man. First, he measured my legs. The
right side was three fourths of an inch shorter than the left! He moved my ligaments
and veins back to their original positions. Next, he worked on my back and legs,
putting them in place. After he finished, he asked me to stand and hold back both
of my shoulders. I did it with ease.

I felt like a new person; I felt healed, and the pain disappeared! The doctor told
me to take it easy because the bones had been out of place so long—it was easy for
them to slip back out. I jumped for joy and rejoiced for the miracle of healing. I can
now imagine how that woman felt when she was healed by Jesus Himself.

Irisdeane Henley-Charles

What Do You Want?

"What do you want me to do for you?" Jesus asked him. Mark 10:51, NIV.

ONE OF JESUS' favorite questions is "What do you want?" Many times we don't know what we want, and Jesus challenges us to clarify.

Years ago I had eye surgery. In the middle of the procedure the doctor said, "Raquel, there is a problem, and your right eye will be affected." Leaving the hospital that day the desire of my heart was to meet Jesus and hear Him ask, "What do you want me to do for you?" Have you ever been in such a situation, when your heart looked for an answer?

When I read the story of blind Bartimaeus, I find it fascinating that Jesus asks him what he wants. I think the answer is so obvious: the blind man would want to see! Don't you think that was obvious to Jesus? Receiving his sight also meant a total lifestyle change for Bartimaeus. He would have to change everything—no more begging, a real job, and his eyes opened in many other ways. But why does Jesus ask the obvious? I can think of two reasons: (1) to energize faith and cause it to be vocalized, and (2) to help the person determine what he wants from Jesus.

When God asked Solomon what he wanted, he chose wisdom. This was bigger than wealth, loads of wives, or favor among all the other kingdoms around him. But he ended up with all those things in addition to the wisdom.

I expect Bartimaeus served as a tremendous encouragement to others. When newcomers asked about Jesus, the disciples pointed to Bartimaeus and said, "Jesus healed him of blindness, you know!" Full of praise to God, Bartimaeus brought glory to Jesus.

Bartimaeus' healing is a powerful example of how it pleases Jesus for our faith to see its opportunity, grasp it, and refuse to let it go until we receive what we need from God. Who would have thought this beggar would become a giver? What can your faith help you become?

What about letting God ask you that same question: What do you want Me to do for you? Search your heart of hearts. What do you really want God to do? Tell Him; trust Him!

If we come before God as the broken beggars we are, we can trust that Christ will restore our vision, and, like Bartimaeus, we will see God. As you face this day, remember that Jesus is near. He asks you today, "What do you want Me to do for you?" Do you have the answer?

Raquel Queiroz da Costa Arrais

People Who Change the World

These that have turned the world upside down are come hither also.
Acts 17:6.

WHEN WE THINK of those who have changed the world, we think of famous and powerful people. We often forget the ordinary people who contribute to changing society for the better. As a nurse for the aged, I hear numerous stories that are a blessing to me. I treasure these, especially because health professionals in my country are forbidden to discuss their religion at work.

Anita* needs 24-hour-a-day care because she is developmentally delayed. She was born at a time in my country's history that people with severe disabilities were isolated from those considered "normal." It was also the era during which teenage girls had their babies stolen from them because some believed that it was "best" for the teenager and the baby.

When I met Anita's sister, Lee, she told the story of how Anita was a much-wanted daughter. She spoke of how Anita was named before birth, and about a little blanket her father made before she was conceived. As I listened to the story my thoughts turned to our heavenly Father, who knew us before we were conceived and who had made preparations for our salvation before it was required. Anita was born apparently normal, but then without reason things went wrong, and it became obvious that she had a severe disability. Anita was isolated from her family and grew up in institutions. Lee expressed remorse that she and her siblings were denied contact with Anita. Even as an adult, Lee begged her parents to let her meet Anita, but they refused. Then an amazing turn of events changed her parents' mind, and Lee found Anita in our nursing home. Lee expressed feelings of guilt about how Anita was treated by her family. I used the opportunity to explain that in those days people believed they were doing the "right thing," and that it's people like her who change society by undoing the mistakes of the past, bringing about a society that includes all individuals, regardless of their age, color, disability, or gender.

Lee later told of her Christian faith and said she never understood why Anita was disabled. She shared her new understanding of John 9:3 about the man who was born blind so "that the works of God should be revealed in him." She never knew of my Christian faith, much less of my difficulty with understanding that verse. I praise God for Anita and Lee and how society has been turned upside down by people like her.

Bridgid Kilgour

*Names have been changed.

Empty Vessels Made Full

May the God of hope fill you with all joy and peace as you trust in him, so that you may overflow with hope by the power of the Holy Spirit.
Rom. 15:13, NIV.

FROM TIME TO TIME I need some kind of vessel—maybe pots and pans, a basket, a bucket, or an urn for flowers.

To find just the vessel, I want I go shopping. There are different sizes, colors, and shapes at different prices to choose from. They are all empty.

It takes time and money, decision-making, and follow-through to accomplish my goal. Once this is done I can fill my vessels with anything I choose.

God asks us to be empty vessels; empty of selfishness, pride, envy, strife, jealousy, or anything else we have allowed the enemy to put in our hearts. When we are empty of these things He, through the Holy Spirit, can fill us with His characteristics, such as love, joy, peace, gentleness, meekness, and goodness. He can also optimize the talents and abilities He has given us to bring glory to His name.

Of course, the emptying process is not something we can do ourselves. When we attempt to do it through our own efforts, failure is sure to result. It is the Holy Spirit who softens and sensitizes our hearts and minds that we may be changed and filled.

The emptying of self is a daily process. God's blessings are fresh every morning. To receive them, we must be rid of the thoughts, attitudes, and a spirit that builds barriers that blocks them. God will not intervene against our will. There is nothing He values more than our free choice. But He invites us to ask that we might receive.

And when God is doing the filling we can be sure He has our best interests in mind. He wants our joy and peace to be complete; He will go to any length to give us the fullness of life He desires for each of His children.

Are you God's chosen vessel? Each day do you invite Him to fill you with the attributes you will need that day to stay close to Him and be a blessing to others? Do you welcome the nudging of the Holy Spirit to guide you? Today we can ask God to fill us with all those attributes that will reflect His character in us.

Marian M. Hart

No More Pain

There will be no more death or mourning or crying or pain. Rev. 21:4, NIV.

MY EYES FLUTTERED open and focused. Gradually I gained conscious awareness. The glistening recovery room wrapped around me. The odors of blood, anesthetic, and antiseptic enveloped me. My first thought was *The pain is gone!* Yes, I could feel the fresh incision, muscles protesting at being poked, prodded, and stretched, and bones complaining at having been sawed, drilled, and pounded. That discomfort I could handle. There was no pain!

Next to coming to terms with my own mortality, which seemed of late to be rushing toward me at the speed of light, the surgery dilemma had been the most difficult. Multiple physicians had opined that unless I had a hip replacement, sooner or later I would be in a wheelchair. On the other hand, if the tricky and complicated surgery failed, I would be in a wheelchair. Either way—not much in the way of options.

Over the nearly five years of increasingly sharp and unrelenting osteo pain in a hip that was already congenitally malformed, I started to identify with Jeremiah when he asked, "Why is my pain unending?" (Jer. 15:18, NIV), and with Isaiah, who had declared, "My body is racked with pain" (Isa. 21:3, NIV). Eventually enough was enough. It was time to take care of the problem. I put myself in the hands of God, along with a carefully selected pair of Christian orthopedic surgeons and their team of dedicated ortho nurses and physical therapists. And now here I was. No more pain!

Scripture often comes alive only after one experiences personally what the passages address. As a lifelong nurse, I wanted to believe that through the years I'd exhibited empathy toward patients under my care. But truth be told, I had possessed little concept of the "unrelentingness" of chronic pain and its all-encompassing impact on one's life—until I had lived with it myself.

During the weeks of recovery, as I learned to walk again, today's promise in Revelation took on fuller meaning. I sensed at a much deeper level how millions of earth dwellers over the centuries have held onto those hopeful words and longed for their fulfillment.

Don't you, too, want Jesus to come quickly, so there will be no more pain?

Arlene Taylor

When Something Is Stronger, Don't Fight It

The Lord is my shepherd; I have all that I need. Ps. 23:1, NLT.

I REMEMBERED as I awoke that my friend's 10-month journey through leukemia was over. I couldn't say the fight was over, because she didn't fight.

That was the lesson she'd taught me. When something is stronger than you, such as death, don't fight it, because when it wins, you'll feel as if you've lost. But if you accept it, you win. And she'd won!

I began repeating Psalm 23 and seeing the parallel to Judy's experience. Truly the Lord was her Shepherd. Daily she recommitted to following her all-wise Shepherd on the path laid out for her. She chose to rest in the green pastures and by the still waters, and in this way He could restore her soul. She determined to walk in the paths of righteousness for her Shepherd's sake, rather than wander in the paths of self-pity.

As she walked through the valley of the shadow of death, she did not fear this evil; she knew her Shepherd was with her. She had immersed herself in the Scriptures and now leaned on this staff for comfort and used the rod of humor to cheer us up. She partook of the table of promises set before her in the presence of the great enemy death.

The elders anointed her with oil. At the last she grasped the running-over bitter cup and drank it because she confidently knew that because of her Shepherd's love, somehow this, too, was part of the goodness and mercy she had seen follow her through all her days.

You might say she died alone in her hospital room, but I think she would say that she died in the loving arms of her Shepherd, knowing that in the blink of an eye, at the resurrection, she will come forth to dwell in the house of her Lord forever.

At the funeral parlor, during her viewing, I whispered, "Thank you, Judy, for showing me what it is like for a Christian to truly die in the Lord with hope." At her memorial service Psalm 23 was printed in the program with this explanation: "The twenty-third psalm was Judy's first introduction to the Bible. She learned it from her grandmother at the age of 4."

Yes, the seed of the Word had been planted, and for 50 years the roots had grown. When the raging winds of suffering and death whipped through her soul, the plant proved strong enough to endure.

Lana Fletcher

Giving and Taking

Now to him who is able to do immeasurably more than all we ask or imagine, according to his power that is at work within us, to him be glory in the church and in Christ Jesus throughout all generations, for ever and ever! Amen. Eph. 3:20, 21, NIV.

THE ROAD OUTSIDE our church has space for less than a dozen cars. By 10:00 on Sabbath morning all the parking on nearby streets is usually gone. After that, unless you want a $100 (£60) fine, using the car park several streets away is your only option.

It was after 10:00 by the time I left the house. I'd been asked to take part in the program and was running behind schedule, so I decided to head straight for the car park. But even as I made that decision I "heard" a voice say to me, "I have a space outside the church for you."

During the next few minutes I debated whether or not God really would give me a parking space. My prayer every morning that week had been "O Lord, bless me indeed!" and He had blessed me—every single day, spectacularly and unexpectedly. Yet the nearer I got to the church the less confident I became that this particular blessing would be part of the package. As I turned the last corner I blurted out, "I believe; help my unbelief."

As I drew alongside the church, a row of cars stretched from one side of the building to the next. But right there, just before the start of the no-parking zone, was one empty space. I couldn't believe it! In fact, I drove straight past it, telling myself that it had been left empty for the pastor. My space would be in the next street.

In the next street I tried to park in a gap between two vehicles, but found myself partially blocking an access way. I inspected two more streets. The spaces in them were so far away from the church that I decided I might as well go to the car park. As I doubled back past the church, my eyes were drawn to that one empty space right outside. Suddenly it hit me—*that* was my parking space! That was the space God had promised me.

I turned my car around and slipped into the spot. It was a perfect fit. Sadly, by that time I'd missed my slot in the program and disappointed a lot of people simply because of my refusal to accept what God was offering. We focus so often on rationalizing life's miracles that we miss out on God's gifts—not because He doesn't give, but because we don't take.

Avery Davis

Patiently Waiting

I waited patiently for the Lord to help me, and he turned to me and heard my cry. He lifted me out of the pit of despair. . . . He set my feet on solid ground. . . . He has given me a new song to sing. Ps. 40:1-3, NLT.

AS I READ today's verse it gave me new courage. You see, I had vehicle problems, and then furnace expense. Both situations were unavoidable.

I'd been praying for extra work to help me sort out the problem. Since the debt was not of my making, I thought that the help would come quickly. When help didn't come as I had expected, I began to fret about the what ifs.

What if I didn't get extra teaching work? What if something happened to delay my pension payments? What if my husband should not be able to meet the monthly bills? The concerns went on and on. It was beginning to keep me awake at night.

It was at that point that I read a comment in one of my devotional books: "When you are in difficulty, wait patiently and prayerfully." Instead of fretting and lying awake, worrying, I began to refuse to allow myself to dwell on the issue. Instead, I chose to use the time giving thanks for the way the Lord had led in the past. Lately I've been sleeping better.

Then this morning, as I was studying God's Word, I came across today's verse. I have even more proof that God will hear and lift me from any lingering despair. He will set me on solid ground once more.

It would be so great if I could always keep this promise in front of me. But too often I let my earthly concerns take over my peace of mind, and then I'm caught once more in despair. I have to remind myself that this is Satan's goal. He wants to keep us so focused on our problems that we take our eyes off God and His ultimate goal for us—heaven and the earth made new.

The financial issue has not gone away. But my God owns the cattle on a thousand hills (Ps. 50:10). My good health and the countless other blessings He sends my way should be reminders that He will take care of this situation in His time. "Beloved, I wish above all things that thou mayest prosper and be in good health" (3 John 2) is the promise that I shall cling to as I wait patiently and prayerfully for His answer.

Patricia Cove

A Way Out of No Way

But my God shall supply all your need according to his riches in glory by Christ Jesus. Phil. 4:19.

IN THE 1980S my cousin's daughter, Audrey, was completing her premed course at Boston University, where she faithfully attended the weekly interdenominational services and fellowship sponsored by one of the deans. Being blessed with a beautiful spirit, without being asked she graciously assisted in the setting up and tidying up after the events.

On one such evening the dean and other faculty members engaged her in what she thought was small talk about her parentage, her homeland, and her plans for the future. Among other things she told them that her great-grandfather had been a Methodist preacher in Guyana, South America, in the early 1900s. They wished her success and parted for the evening.

A few weeks later she put in a somewhat subdued but frantic call to her mother, many states away, who was just about to leave home for work. "Mom, I need $2,500 by tomorrow to apply for my final exam."

"Twenty-five-hundred *what*? Child, I don't have 2,500 cents, but you've given me a great idea on how to spend my suppertime."

At suppertime Gwen, Audrey's mother, slipped into the chapel at her job and prayed, "Lord, this child is not mine. I gave her to You a long time ago. If there is anything You want me to help You with, please let me know; otherwise, the problem is all Yours."

Before the end of her shift Gwen was paged for a phone call. This time there was excitement as Audrey announced, "Mom, I got a Jessie Durrell Scholarship! And guess for how much, Mom? *Exactly $2,500.* Isn't that great?"

"And who is Jessie Durrell?" her mother wanted to know. The Jessie Durrell Scholarship was founded for the education of descendants of Methodist preachers in the New Hampshire area. The deans had secretly submitted an application for Audrey, unsure as to whether it would apply to her since she came from Guyana. "Well, praise the Lord, and thank Jessie Durrell!" Gwen exclaimed. Papa Mac's work did indeed follow him (see Rev. 14:13), and today Audrey is the medical director of a hospital in Pennsylvania.

Vashti Hinds-Vanier

You in a Hurry, God?

But the Lord replied to her by saying, Martha, Martha, you are
anxious and troubled about many things; there is need of only one. . . .
Mary has chosen the good portion, which shall not be taken away from her.
Luke 10:41, 42, Amplified.

SHE ENTERED THE office in a whirl. In seconds she turned on the computer and took off her coat while taking messages from the answering service. She answered the phone with a smile in her voice while continuing to dust the computer and file. She managed her family and personal life the same way. She could drive the boys to football practice, shop for groceries, and attend a baby shower in the hour between leaving work and starting dinner. I envied her. If only I could be that efficient! I was impressed and felt very fortunate that she chose to work for our company!

Then I noticed that the first words out of her mouth each morning were "Oh, I'm so behind!" Throughout the day she would say to herself, *Oh, I'm so behind!* I began to feel more pity than envy. I wondered, *Was God ever in a hurry? What was Jesus like as a carpenter?* There's a hint in the book *The Desire of Ages*. When clients came into His shop and tried to rush Him, He began to sing. Soon they would be singing too.

Like most Americans, I'm also afflicted with "hurry sickness." I liked it that Karen did three things at a time in the office. I did it too. But I read that we are to carry only the burdens the Lord has placed upon us. We are not to take upon us burdens the Lord has not placed upon us. Could part of my hurry sickness be because I have taken upon myself burdens He never intended me to carry?

One day my heart began to skip, my chest hurt, and I found I couldn't push as much into the day as I thought I needed to. After a little research I discovered that one of the treatments for cardiac symptoms is meditation. The book said that one should find a quiet spot and relax and meditate on breathing in and out. They recommended a whole hour of this activity—or inactivity, as the case may be! Then it hit me: I could be using that hour every day to meditate on God!

And what about God's handiwork? I've never been able to hurry the tide or rush the hatching of a barn swallow egg. What do you think? Is God in a hurry?

Elizabeth Boyd

Fellowship, Sharing, and Giving

That which we have seen and heard declare we unto you, that
ye also may have fellowship with us: and truly our fellowship
is with the Father, and with his Son Jesus Christ. 1 John 1:3.

EVERY SO OFTEN I am invited to lunch with friends or associates, or I am presented with opportunities to share time and goods or give food baskets. I feel good after such fellowship, and I'm happy to help meet the needs of others. Getting together in groups and socializing is an enjoyable form of fellowship. Somehow life seems drab and boring if a person is alone all the time.

Sometime ago I was privileged to be part of a team that planned a retreat at one of our island's simple and secluded hotels. The planning took all our strength, so we were happy when the arrangements (except for a few glitches) fell into place. The north coast scenery was calm and inviting, beckoning us to rest. We spent quiet moments among the many spirit-filled and educational activities shared and enjoyed time to dip and dive among the rolling waves on the seashore. Sometimes we simply sat under the pounding water that streamed down from the rocky fountain into the pool below. It was added pleasure just to relax and enjoy the meals that we were spared the effort of preparing.

Fellowship comes in many forms, and spending time together never seems complete without food and eating together. A table spread with an array of foods of different colors and styles is a welcome sight and holds great promise for the taste buds. The moments we shared were just for a time, and all too soon we were on our way back to our regular schedule. Individuals could be heard asking, "When can we do this again? This moment is great!"

It makes a difference when we take time out to fellowship together, to share, and to give to others. We form relationships and bonds in our times together, and we feel cheerful and receive companionship. Fellowship, sharing, and giving helps us determine the social and fulfilling way we desire to live. Inviting the Lord to tabernacle with us in these special moments is an even greater blessing.

"Let us not give up meeting together, as some are in the habit of doing, but let us encourage one another—and all the more as you see the Day approaching" (Heb. 10:25, NIV). And as we fellowship we want to remember to invite Jesus to be our special guest.

Elizabeth Ida Cain

Thank God for Color

Purge me with hyssop, and I shall be clean: wash me, and I shall be whiter than snow. Ps. 51:7.

"BUNDLE UP! Snow storm warning, high winds, and near-zero visibility." As the meteorologist announced the forecast one morning in January I looked out the window. The ground was already covered with eight to 12 inches of snow as a result of two days of constant snowfall. Despite this severe weather prediction, I ventured out on the icy roads to attend a workshop.

Later that afternoon I picked up David, my son, from his band practice. On the way home we talked about our day, the weather, and the icy road conditions. I told him about the accidents I'd seen on my way to my workshop, and he told me about his day at school, and his plans to start playing bass trombone in a band.

As I pulled into our driveway David blurted, "Mom, look at that!" He pointed to our front yard. "I like to see the snow like it is on the ground over there." Looking at the pristine coverlet of snow, I agreed. "When no one has walked on the snow, it's so white and beautiful it gives me a sense of purity. It reminds me of what God can do for us when we sin."

My mother's heart was touched as I heard him explain.

After a short pause David added, "Footprints and tire marks make the snow dirty, but a good snowfall will cover all that dirt so it will be all white and clean again. God does the same with us when He washes our sins away. We become whiter than snow, and we are renewed by Him when we ask Him."

I think about a sermon I read from a long time ago: "Sins, no matter how deep the color, will be made white as snow. We are to be clothed with white raiment, our scarlet sins to be changed and our filthy stained garments to be changed like wool, white as snow. When we ask to have our sins taken away it is asking to be cleansed. What does it mean to be made white as snow? That is the garment that is to be put upon us—whiter than any fuller can make them. This is the blessed promise" (Alonzo T. Jones, "Five Sermons on Righteousness," presented at the Ottawa, Kansas, Institute and Camp Meeting, May 1889).

Surely this is God's promise to us because He loves each of us.

Margo Peterson

Mother's Casket

But my God shall supply all your need according to his riches in glory by Christ Jesus. Phil. 4:19.

JUST THREE YEARS before my mother passed away she asked me to take her to a local funeral parlor to arrange for a prepaid funeral plan and to pick out a casket. We giggled as we walked around the casket room, and she said it seemed rather odd to be choosing the box she would be buried in, but she knew exactly what she wanted. Almost everything was more expensive than she desired. And then, there it was. It was pink, with pink satin lining, and it was the least-expensive one of all. She turned to me and said, "This is it! Be sure I am buried in one just like this. I want it to be pink, lined with pink satin."

By the time Mother passed away we had moved to a different town, and when we went to the mortuary to make plans for her service we were told they didn't have the casket she wanted, nor anything at all like it. What to do? I knew Mother would never know, and yet it was very important to me because it had been so important to her to have that very one.

The funeral director was a very kind and caring woman and said she would make some phone calls to see what could be done. First, she called the funeral home where Mother had chosen the casket. They no longer stocked it, but they told her of another place she might call. After two more calls she was able to locate one. Mother had passed away on Wednesday, and her service was to be on Friday afternoon, so time was of the essence. The place where the casket was located was many miles away, but they promised they would have it delivered by Friday morning. I also learned that it was the last available casket like that.

As I walked into the chapel that Friday afternoon and saw how lovely Mother looked in her very special pink casket, I cried. They were not only tears of sadness for the loss of my wonderful mother, but tears of joy. God cared enough to work through a funeral director to find just the casket that Mother had wanted, and through some miracle it was delivered in time for her to be buried in it.

I pray it will not be long until Jesus returns to awaken Mother, who is now taking a little nap in her pink casket, and takes us all to heaven. There will be no more need for caskets!

Anna May Radke Waters

God Is Sovereign

Thine, O Lord, is the greatness, and the power, and the glory, and the victory, and the majesty: for all that is in the heaven and in the earth is thine; thine is the kingdom, O Lord, and thou art exalted as head above all. 1 Chron. 29:11.

And Jesus came and spake unto them, saying, All power is given unto me in heaven and in earth. Matt. 28:18.

MORE THAN ONE person has likened me to a modern-day Job because the past 20 years have been fraught with hardship. Despite Satan's attempts to convict me, I know that I did not bring these problems upon myself. I also know that God wouldn't allow me to continue in this prolonged crucible year after year if He didn't consider me worth preparing and perfecting for eternal life with Him. I may be obtuse regarding what I am supposed to learn, or release, or I may not recognize the witnesses who are being blessed as I deal with my trials, but even so I have been able to glean a few truths amid my day-to-day challenges.

My sovereign God is in control, and He knows my past, present, and future. Furthermore, although at times I have questioned whether He expected too much of me, He has never asked me to bear more than He can carry me through. Having already lost nearly everything that a human can lose, I am able to travel lightly through the remainder of life. With no immediate family, no permanent income, and few material assets, I can go wherever God next leads me.

I have been cured of my former habit of worry, for God has been all things to me as He has provided everything that I truly need. While I have been "broken" and no longer have any tolerance for stress, I find that I can wait and rely on the Lord instead of becoming frustrated. Assuming that I am still alive when our world's final time of trouble arrives, I already will be accustomed to unwavering trust in my sovereign God. He who is my Creator, Savior, best friend, guide, provider, and great physician will be with me to the end.

My experience with trials allows me to strengthen and encourage others who undergo testing. I have learned the joy and peace that only God can give because He has proved Himself worthy of my gratitude, love, commitment, and faith. Christ in His sovereignty has kept His promise to give me a peace that the world neither knows nor understands.

Heidi Vogt

BMW Welt:
Theater of the Universe

We have been made a spectacle to the whole universe, to angels as well as to men. 1 Cor. 4:9, NIV.

I COULD NOT resist a visit to BMW Welt (BMW World) when I visited Munich, because I like to drive German cars. Everything about BMW Welt says quality, from the design of the buildings to all the activities and displays within. You can even buy BMW-branded clothes, BMW infant seats, BMW bikes, and authentic BMW bicycle locks that snap shut with satisfying precision. Hungry? Dine in the restaurant overlooking the empire, or linger under sun umbrellas at the outdoor café. BMW is not just a brand; it's a lifestyle!

But the real drama at BMW Welt is the reality show unfolding on center stage, suspended in the air for all to see. Access to this stage is restricted to buyers. After being wined and dined in the restaurant, the fortunate check in as if boarding an airline flight. They are escorted to the stage through locked elevators. Soon the longed-for car magically appears in another large glass elevator and glides out and around a track rimming the perimeter and parks on a rotating disk, chrome and paint glittering as it turns. Then the smartly dressed attendant provides a guided tour to the wonders of this new driving machine. At last the keys are handed over, and the new owner takes a victory lap before descending the stage down an arched ramp. Concealed doors at the end of the ramp noiselessly slide open, and, blinking into the sunshine, the driver exits. Onlookers whistle and applaud as the doors slide shut on retail theater at its best.

Each of us has a role in a show in which the stakes are not merchandise but lives. As at BMW Welt, it's not about a single choice. It's about an entire lifestyle and a pattern of choices. A missed line or flubbed scene is not the whole show. It is a lifestyle of faith that matters.

Some of us have had difficult parts to play, with trials, setbacks, or physical disabilities. Perhaps we've had to watch helplessly as those we love suffer. We've tried to act intelligently and with courage, but sometimes we despair that the scene will never change.

But look! The curtains are already closing. They will reopen to the spectacular finale in the theater of the universe. Soon God will be vindicated forever, along with all who place their confidence in Him, and the final scenes of eternal joy defy the imagination.

Lisa M. Beardsley

The Parking Place

Hear, O Lord, and have mercy upon me: Lord, be thou my helper. Ps. 30:10.

ONE EVENING MY son-in-law Shannon noticed a strange bulge in his left groin area after showering; he called my daughter Julie to look at it. They came to the conclusion that he might have an inguinal hernia. Their family doctor confirmed their fears and arranged a consultation with a surgeon. After examination, the surgeon told him that he had not just one but three hernias: two inguinal and one umbilical. Surgery was scheduled for the following week.

On the morning of the surgery I drove to the hospital to be with them during the procedure. I prayed, "Dear Lord, You know I am bad with directions; please find me a parking place near the entrance to the hospital." Suddenly my cell phone rang. Julie said, "Mama, the parking here is just horrible; I had to park blocks away. Don't feel bad if you can't make it before the surgery. Be careful; I'll see you when you get here." I turned off the interstate and drove to the hospital. As I fearfully entered the parking garage I spied a woman walking through the garage and rolled down my window to ask her if she was leaving. She nodded her head, and I circled around, only to realize that I was headed in the wrong direction. I backed up and proceeded through the next levels. My faith wavered as I scanned the sea of parked cars. When a man emerged from the hospital door, I slowed down and watched as he hurried to his car. He backed out, leaving the space for me to pull into. Through the falling rain I could make out the sign: St. Joseph's Hospital Outpatient Surgery Waiting Room. I stared at it in disbelief. This was exactly where I was supposed to be! I was in such a state of awe and thanksgiving that I could only whisper, "Thank You, Lord; thank You, Lord!"

Soon I found the room where Shannon and Julie were waiting. The surgery had been postponed for an hour, and I was able to share my parking experience. They, too, felt that the Lord had directed me to find the perfect parking place that He had arranged for me. We all held hands and thanked Him for His guidance, asking Him to be in the operating room during the surgery. The surgery went well, and Shannon is fully recovered.

Does the Lord really care about answering even our smallest requests, uttered in times of concern and stress? My answer is "Oh yes, He does! I've experienced it firsthand."

Rose Neff Sikora

Honey From the Honeycomb

For God is not unjust. He will not forget how hard you have worked for him and how you have shown your love to him by caring for other believers. . . . Our great desire is that you will keep on loving others as long as life lasts, in order to make certain that what you hope for will come true. Heb. 6:10, 11, NLT.

TEARS WELLED UP in their beautiful eyes (and mine too) as I said my goodbyes. "It's been my pleasure meeting you, and sharing my faith, and serving you these past 14 months."

They responded, "We'll miss you; you are so kind." Then we shared something priceless: the kindred spirit smile. You know the one I'm speaking of—the glimpse of hope, trusting that everything we experience will work out for good because we do love God.

When asked why I was leaving, I told some the painful truth. There had been a confrontation with management regarding my holiday pay, which ultimately led to a choice: either stop sharing my personal faith with coworkers and customers or be fired.

This spiritual battle left me paralyzed. I didn't have the strength to get up from my chair and leave the room without bursting into tears. I bowed my head, closed my eyes, and prayed silently, *I love my job here, but Lord Jesus, I love You most; what shall I do?* Again and again I silently repeated this prayer until I found the courage to get up. As my hand touched the door I remembered a letter in my purse. That letter gave courage, honey from the honeycomb.

In obedience to the Holy Spirit I went to my locker and got the letter and gave it to management to read. It had arrived in the mail just one day before this unpleasant ordeal began. The letter was handwritten by a saintly 80-year-old gentleman who had personally witnessed my life's journey for the past 40 years. In his letter he describes me as a mother of Israel, doing a good job, sharing the love of Jesus around the world.

For me this blessed letter is equivalent to a holy kiss from the King of the universe, giving me needed strength for the journey ahead. It's affirmation from heaven above that I am what I profess to be: a Christian cheerleader in Jesus' campaign to tell the world of His soon return. As I face any challenge today I say thank You, to Jesus, and I look forward to Paradise with Him. I pray you will taste the same honey from the honeycomb as needed today.

Deborah Sanders

Before I Called, He Answered

Before they call I will answer; while they are still speaking I will hear.
Isa. 65:24, NIV.

THE ONE-WAY rented trailer held the last of my belongings. It was dark, and I dreaded the long drive from San Francisco to my mother's in San Diego. Pushing past my feelings, I climbed into the little Chevy and headed south. Tears often filled my eyes, blurring the curvy mountain road. *What if I were to run over the side? Would anyone care?* I wondered. "Why did it all happen at once?" I cried. My husband was gone, my children were gone; my job and home were gone, and my furniture given away. Many weary hours later I reached Mother's. "Call on God," she encouraged.

I heaved a sigh. "I just wish I could believe that He cares." After a few days I looked for work. The interview was unsuccessful (which was not a surprise). I was depressed. Later that week my former employer in San Francisco called to say that my old job was open again. I drove back, still numb.

I found a tiny room downtown near the office. After working a week, I had no money for food, but was embarrassed to request an advance. *What should I do?* I thought while waiting after work for the traffic signal to change. The flower man on the corner interrupted my thoughts by handing me a flower. When I thanked him, he grabbed it and, without a word, shoved a whole bouquet at me. "Oh!" I gasped. Reaching my room, I found a check from my San Diego interviewer for travel expenses. *Maybe God cares?* I dared to hope.

That same night I drove to the church where I had attended years before. From the empty foyer I heard the speaker. He was telling about a depressed woman, emotionally trapped in a room with no doors or windows. He said to her, "Write on a card 10 things for which to be thankful each day for 10 days and call me every three days." She called once saying, "I have windows now." Two weeks later she called to say, "I'm babysitting, and my psychiatrist tells me I'm healed." I hurried out of the church thinking, *I'll try that!*

The next morning I could think of only two things to be thankful for. I left for work, discouraged. While walking down Bush Street, I cried, "Lord, if You care, please show me that there is nothing between us!" Then my eyes were drawn up high between the skyscrapers. The fog was gone! I smiled. What a beautiful blue!

Marjorie Ackley

Awakened by an Angel

The angel of the Lord encamps around those who fear him,
and he delivers them. Ps. 34:7, NIV.

SINCE MY CHILDHOOD I was taught to say my prayers before I went to sleep at night, to thank God for the blessings received during the day and to ask His protection during the night. Many times I would lie on the bed, sleepless. Then I'd remember that I hadn't prayed. And today it is the same.

One day I slept in a friend's house. She lived alone with her three children. I arranged the pillow and blanket, and I turned in bed to try to get to sleep. Then I saw the door of my bedroom open, squeaking on its hinges. It was dark, and I saw only a little light, seeming to be a minilantern.

Without understanding what was happening and supposing that it was someone from the house, I said, "You can turn on the light; I'm awake." Then I listened to some words that I could not understand, and the person left, running through the hall and going down the stairs.

Questions tumbled through my mind. *Was the person still around? Why did someone come into my room?* I gathered all my courage and left the bedroom to call my colleague in her bedroom, where she slept with her children. I saw that everybody was there, so it couldn't have been any of them. Who, then, was the person who had tried to enter my bedroom?

When everybody was awake, we tried to find a clue and noticed that some objects were missing. Someone had invaded the house to rob us. We called the police, who inspected the place with gun in hand, but they didn't find anyone. The thief had run away.

What if I hadn't awakened at the right moment? Where would the invader have gone? What could he have done? Would he have entered my bedroom and approached me? Imagine the dread of waking up at night and having someone you don't know in your bedroom!

I believe that on that night I didn't simply wake up—I was awakened. The Lord sent His angel to wake me up. To this day I am sure that "the angel of the Lord encamps around those who fear him, and he delivers them."

Darlen Cibeli Martelo Bach

Kindness Makes a Difference

And forgive us our debts, as we forgive our debtors. Matt. 6:12.

MUSIC APPEARS TO have become an ever-present part of life. When we're shopping at the mall, it's music. At the grocery store, it's music. At the bank, and even when we're placed on hold during a telephone business transaction, it's music, music, music! I love music, but there are times I prefer not to hear any.

Recently I went out of town by bus to visit a friend. The bus drivers of this particular company always request that passengers listening to music keep the volume turned down so that only the person listening to the device will be able to hear it.

I struggled to place my luggage on the overhead rack midway back in the bus. I chose an aisle seat, made myself comfortable, and closed my eyes. Oh, how I welcomed the idea of spending serene, quality time of tranquillity and peacefulness on my four-hour journey.

About 45 minutes into the trip I noticed a young man sitting two or three rows behind me, on the opposite side of the aisle, listening to hip-hop music. He was wearing earphones, but the volume of the music caught my attention. The sound was most annoying, and by the end of the trip I had made up my mind to let him know what a nuisance he had been and that I didn't appreciate listening to his music for more than three hours. I was fuming!

I waited until the bus came to a complete stop, then I rose from my seat, turned, and saw him reaching for *my* luggage. "I believe this is yours, isn't it?" he said softly as he smiled and handed me my luggage.

I immediately thought of how I must sometimes agitate our heavenly Father, not intentionally, yet He still looks down and smiles as He continues to reach out to hand me blessings and to meet my needs. "I believe these are yours," He whispers softly.

This young man may not have had a clue that he was disturbing those around him. I, on the other hand, could have handled the situation in a more Christlike manner, not allowing anger to overwhelm me. This was a lesson well learned; a lesson worth learning. Today, through the power of the Holy Spirit, I want to be more aware of how I am affecting people around me and be Christlike in my actions.

Cora A. Walker

God Hears

This is the confidence we have in approaching God: that if we ask anything according to his will, he hears us. And if we know that he hears us—whatever we ask—we know that we have what we asked of Him. 1 John 5:14, 15, NIV.

ANOTHER BIG EMOTIONAL change had come into my daily life. It was time to move our 7-month-old out of our bedroom! But this time it was much easier, because I already had done this with our older son. The only struggle now was that both sons would be sharing a room, and both have different bedtimes. (There seems to be no end to the dilemmas that moms and dads face.)

On this particular night my older son went to bed late because he'd had a late-afternoon nap. I climbed onto his bed, as we did every night, and read him a story, prayed with him, and sang his favorite song, "I Love You." Normally he stands on the bed and does the actions and sings out loudly; and that's what he began to do. So I gently tugged his hand to sit down, then I whispered in his ear that he was singing too loudly.

Of course the 4-year-old asked, "But why, Mommy?" I reminded him that he was now sharing a room with his brother, who was already sleeping, so if he sang too loudly he would awaken his brother, who would begin crying.

Looking at his face after I said that to him, I realized he looked very sad. "But Mommy," he said, "God won't hear me if I sing so low." I smiled at how innocent his little thoughts were.

"God will hear you at any time, whether you speak loudly or quietly," I assured him.

From that night on, my son whispered his prayer to God. That night he prayed, "Jesus, bless Mommy, Daddy, and Patric; and please hear me when I am quiet. Amen."

God hears us when we pray, as small as we are on this planet. God hears our prayers whoever we are. God hears the true prayers of His people. God cares about all of us sinners as we accept His forgiveness and promise of a new life.

Let's remember that He hears us. When we come to know that God hears us, a miraculous power from God flows down into our hearts and lives, and we begin to understand that we are not invisible to Him but are fully known, fully heard, and fully loved by Him. When we speak, Jesus hears.

Shelly-Ann Patricia Zabala

Kind of a Miracle

I will fight those who fight you, and I will save your children. Isa. 49:25, NLT.

PERHAPS YOU'VE experienced the pain of seeing a child "crash" in one way or another. A horrified mother once watched her 19-year-old crash into an ice rink wall as he was practicing for a skating competition. J. R. Celski lay on the ice, blood pouring from the gaping wound his skate blade had made when it sliced across his left thigh.

Because my children have taken an occasional nasty spill on life's skating rink, I took special notice when this young man won his first Olympic medal just months later because he really shouldn't have been there. But then again, he had a mother rooting for him!

Amazingly, Celski managed to compete in the Vancouver Olympics 1,500-meter short-track speed skating final. He held a dismal fifth-place position on the last turn. Television cameras briefly panned to the stands to his mother's tense face as she cheered him on.

Suddenly, for no apparent reason, the skaters in the silver and bronze positions crashed, and young J. R. Celski whizzed across the finish line in third place—an Olympic medalist! "Kind of a miracle" is how one sports reporter described the skater's unexpected finish.

The Originator of miracles is still working in response to mothers' prayers—especially when it comes to bringing their children across heaven's finish line. No matter how badly our kids crash, we can still cheer them on by claiming promises of blessing as in today's text.

For years a friend of mine, whom I'll call Sonny, crashed repeatedly—morally, physically, spiritually. Until the moment of her death, however, Sonny's mother claimed promises for her son's salvation. Years later Sonny met and accepted Jesus Christ as Lord of his life. That's kind of a miracle too, isn't it!

Sonny likes to describe what the next reunion with his mother will be like. He says, "When I cross that finish line stretched between heaven's pearly gates, my mother will see me. Her first words will be 'Praise God, Sonny—how on earth did you get here?'" And my response will be "By the grace of God, Mama, and because of your prayers of faith."

Let's fight for all our kids on our knees before God's open Word. Let's cheer them on when they're doing their best. And finally, let's trust God to work His last-minute miracles in their lives.

Carolyn Sutton

Before They Call I Will Answer

And it shall come to pass, that before they call, I will answer;
and while they are yet speaking, I will hear. Isa. 65:24.

MY MOTHER WAS living on the island of Antigua, and I lived in New York City when I got word that she had had a massive stroke. I went to her as soon as I was able to secure a flight, but when I arrived, she was in a coma. The doctor didn't hold out very much hope for recovery, but he allowed her to remain at home and visited her daily. I found a group of women attending her and administering their local remedies. They had a small dish with a mixture of lime juice and salt at her bedside. They had tied a kerchief around her head and were soaking it with the mixture. Whenever she began to twitch, and it appeared that she was about to have a seizure, they would quickly soak the kerchief, and the twitching would cease. Meanwhile, they rubbed her with a very strong British-made ointment called Fiery Jack to stimulate her nerves.

Mama remained in the coma for weeks. Then one day she opened her eyes. Another day I saw her move one big toe very slightly. I was overjoyed and reported this to the doctor. He smiled, thinking I was imagining what I hoped to see. But to his astonishment (and that of many others) Mama improved dramatically and was able to walk with aid. She no longer needed to be rubbed with the Fiery Jack. Since there was no further sign of seizure activity the application of the salt and lime mixture had been discontinued as well.

Then the unexpected happened. I was alone with Mama when she began to twitch. I looked around for the saucer, but it was dry, and there was not a lime in the house. I began to pray loudly as only one in deep distress can pray: "Lord, save my mama!" Suddenly there was a knock on the door. I ran to the door to find the postman there, holding a crate of limes that had been mailed to us from the island of Nevis days before. I can't remember how I got that crate opened, but I did. I quickly squeezed the lime juice over the salt in the dish and applied the mixture to my mother's forehead. Immediately the shaking stopped.

Before I called, God had answered. He knew the moment those limes would be needed and impressed someone to ship them to us ahead of time, and while I was yet speaking, they arrived.

H. Elizabeth Sweeney-Cabey

The Appointment

I will call to you whenever I'm in trouble, and you will answer me.
Ps. 86:7, NLT.

I LIVE ON a small island where certain specialized health professionals, such as dentists, are few. Subsequently, it's very difficult for the islanders to arrange appointments. It's not unusual to wait months to get in for a routine cleaning. Therefore many people opt to have their routine elective care done outside of the island.

I was having trouble with a tooth and was told by a dentist that I needed to have a root canal; however, I couldn't get an early appointment. As the weeks dragged on, so did my periodic pain, an excruciating pain that interrupted my daily life. I cried bitterly because of its intensity.

One night at church someone gave a testimony of how the Lord provided an early appointment for her at the island's only hospital after she prayed. It was this testimony that I remembered during one of my painful episodes. I cried to the Lord and reminded Him of how He answered the prayer of this individual and begged Him to work for me in like manner. I got off my knees and called the dental office. The courteous receptionist apologetically informed me that there were no openings but that she would call me if there were any cancellations. I hung up the phone, resigned to continue suffering, and again sent up a silent prayer. Within an hour the phone rang. It was the dental office, calling to see if I would be able to come in the next day.

This experience occurred some months ago, but as I reflect on the relevance of prayer I'm reminded of the following which was written years ago by an unknown Christian author: "Prayer is the answer to every problem in life. . . . So often we do not pray in certain situations because from our standpoint the outlook is hopeless, but nothing is impossible with God. . . . Whatever we need, if we trust God He can supply it. If anything is causing worry or anxiety let us stop, rehearse the difficulty, and trust God for healing, love, and power."

Jesus said in John 14:13, 14: "You can ask for anything in my name, and I will do it, so that the Son can bring glory to the Father. Yes, ask me for anything in my name, and I will do it!" (NLT). I have tested this, and God has answered in wonderful ways. Thank God that He still hears the cries of His children.

Tamar Boswell

A Pink-and-White Kiss From Heaven

You are precious to me. You are honored, and I love you. Isa. 43:4, NLT.

IT STORMED YESTERDAY; life-giving showers refreshed the parched, dry countryside in our little corner of Australia. So this morning everything was exceptionally clean and fresh. The world was beautiful! I went for my morning walk, rejoicing with all of nature at the miracle of the regenerating rain and mindful of the obvious spiritual applications before me.

How beautifully falling rain washes away all the dust and stain of life, leaving everything cleansed. And not only does it cleanse—it refreshes. The trees, the grasses, patchworks of pastureland, birds on the wing, and the resting cattle—all are somehow transformed. And especially my soul! Vitality is restored; new life springs forth. Oh, how I love the miracle of rain, the transforming beauty of the water of life!

As I walked, all around me birds were singing out their joy, regaling me with a symphony of sound and sight, delighting my senses. I just couldn't help it; a spontaneous song of praise and thanksgiving burst forth from the depth of my own soul, and I joined with theirs.

Then suddenly I saw it. There, on the road before me under a big gum tree, lay a fresh, clean, fluffy, pink-and-white galah feather. It was perfect: downy-soft white below, crowned with a smooth, rosy, pastel-pink dome above. So delicate and—maybe—romantic?

It was the soft pink of gentle love and tenderness. My heart swelled with awe and joy as I recognized what it really was—God's kiss from heaven to me! A private moment of intimacy between Creator and created, Father and child, made known through a tiny pink-and-white feather. It was as though I could audibly hear Him speaking soft and low: "My sweetheart, this is just for you to tell you how much I love you!"

I stooped and picked up that tiny treasure and clasped it to my breast in awe. Awareness washed over me as to just how precious I really am to my God. How honored and blessed to have received such a gift! How loved!

It just blows me away that the God of the universe makes time to take such a tiny thing and make it so special, that He would do that for me! But He did. And the rest of my day was beautiful because of it.

Lynette Kenny

The Awesomeness of God

O Lord our Lord, how excellent is thy name in all the earth! who hast
set thy glory above the heavens. . . . When I consider thy heavens,
the work of thy fingers, the moon and the stars, which thou hast
ordained; what is man, that thou art mindful of him? Ps. 8:1-4.

MY DAUGHTER, Sam, and I looked forward to meteor showers. We would set our alarms so that at the precise time we would awake to see the celestial event. Cold, and in the wee hours of the morning, we thought we were the only ones in our neighborhood staring into the night sky, watching and waiting. Finally we would see the first one shower, then more—and more—and in our excitement we thanked God for the moment. "Did you see that?" "Look over there!" "Not there; over there!"

Those who were driving by probably wondered what we were doing, wrapped in blankets, sitting on bar stools in the middle of the night, pointing to the sky. We chuckled at their wonder, because in their place we were sure that we would have been wondering the same. The star showers subsided, and once again it was time to go back to bed to prepare for work and school.

Sam is now 21. I know that when she hears of meteor showers she thinks of those cold nights in the side yard with Mom.

While sitting in the cold night and thanking God for the privilege, I was in awe at the magnificence of it all, the grandeur and splendor of the night sky, and the mystery of what lies beyond. Zillions of stars appeared to be in the heavens, and everything was moving in its order. The universe, genuinely created by the Master Craftsman, is a mass of order and design, with everything knowing its place and time without interference from the call of man.

And another marvel: with the multitude of life's daily productions that our Savior tends, He makes time for me. He knows me by name. He tends to me personally as if I were the only one in existence. He knows when my heart aches and He comforts me, speaking to me in the night season when I'm too busy during the day to hear Him. He directs me, counsels me, and defends me in times of trouble. My trust is solely in Him.

As I read Psalm 8 in its entirety I am reminded of His majesty, His mighty power, and the awesomeness of His existence. O Lord, our Lord, how excellent is thy name in all the earth!

Sylvia Bennett

My Valentine Message

We can rejoice, too, when we run into problems and trials, for we know that they help us develop endurance. And endurance develops strength of character, and character strengthens our confident hope of salvation. And this hope will not lead to disappointment. For we know how dearly God loves us, because he has given us the Holy Spirit to fill our hearts with his love. Rom. 5:3-5, NLT.

VALENTINE'S DAY IS not a happy time for a college student who has just had her heart broken for the first time right before Valentine's Day. Her friends had received a rose at vespers the evening before. On Sabbath everybody anticipated the special Valentine's program. She was happy for them, but she thought, *Do I need to put myself through this? I know I'm going to feel hurt.* With a heavy heart she walked toward the church. People around her talked excitedly, and the decorations in the sanctuary were beautiful. Her heart raced as she entered. She definitely loved her friends—they were so precious, and she wanted to be surrounded with loving friends—but it still hurt. Friends greeted her with love, so she put a smile on her face.

The back row was her ultimate desired seat so she could dive back into her misery. Surprisingly, against her will, she found herself walking to the front seats. She noticed that each seat had a heart with a message inside. She sincerely wanted to take that piece of paper and rip it into tiny shreds. *Surely there can't be a Valentine's message appropriate for me—nobody knows how I feel,* she thought.

With trembling hands she decided to open the heart. She stared at the message in astonishment, disbelieving: "Jesus knows you are hurt." She instantly closed the card then reopened it with tears in her eyes. *How could this be possible? I want to hug Jesus right now!* Then she thought to herself, *Valentine's is a happy occasion. Who would write such a message for Valentine's Day?* Hesitantly, she checked other hearts in the room. There was not one heart in that room that had a message similar to hers.

Many hearts are broken each day because of abuse, betrayal, and death. Satan has gotten ahold of our relationships. On that tearful, agonizing Valentine's Day, as I chose to walk toward Him, He chose to be my valentine and heal me eternally. There is nothing in this world that can hurt me again. Let Him help you walk those few steps in reaching out to Him.

Suhana Chikatla

Saying Goodbye

So teach us to count our days that we may gain a wise heart.
Ps. 90:12, NRSV.

HUMAN BEINGS NATURALLY seem to hate to part, even when it's for a good purpose—children going off to school, friends or relatives moving away to pursue career opportunities, or simply going on a vacation. Given life's frailties and uncertainties, we know the possibility exists that we may not see each other again in this life. The worst parting is the one that comes through death. Even sincere Christians, whose theology is firmly grounded in the belief that death is merely a long sleep, still find it difficult to say goodbye.

Recently a staff member shared the news that a prominent lawyer, who appeared before my court on a regular basis, was ill. His diagnosis was unknown at the time. This vibrant, healthy-looking man was in the prime of his life. Don was as popular with his colleagues as he was with his clients, court staff, and the judiciary because of his pleasant and professional demeanor. Within three weeks he was confined to a wheelchair because he was too weak to stand or walk. He was diagnosed with inoperable cancer of the lungs and liver and given six months to live. Because he was a nonsmoker it was presumed that these were not the primary source of the malignancy.

On Friday I received an open letter, sent on Don's behalf. In it he asked us not to be sad about his leaving. Even in this difficult situation he found the energy and will to make the situation easier for those he would leave behind.

The question for today is this: How would you spend the rest of your life if you knew you had only six months to live? Most of us would choose to be kinder, gentler, and far more gracious and caring to those around us. We would spend less time chasing material things and fussing and arguing over inconsequential matters.

On the cross Christ took time from His pain and sorrow to grant salvation to the criminal who repented (Luke 23:39-43). He took time to ensure that His mother, Mary, would have her physical and emotional needs met by giving John, His disciple, to her as a son (John 19:26, 27).

By God's grace let's live each day as best we can. We never know when we will have to say goodbye.

Avis Mae Rodney

Trust God Through Disappointments

And we know that all things work together for good to those who love God, to those who are the called according to His purpose. Rom. 8:28, NKJV.

WHEN YOU ARE a Christian there is no such thing as luck or coincidence. When you walk with the Lord daily, He guides you and works things out for your good. I have discovered this many times; however, the incident that riveted this truth in my mind happened when I was completing my master's degree. During my final semester I was scheduled to complete my student teaching in Canada. My supervising professor, a Canadian, offered to drive me the eight hours to the school, as he was going home to visit relatives.

As we reached the United States-Canadian border, I showed my documents to the officer and expected to be waved across the bridge. However, the immigration officer sent us back to Detroit to the U.S. Embassy, saying I needed a work permit. Ironically, the officer in Detroit had said I needed a Canadian Student Visa. After going back and forth for several hours, I was finally told I could not complete my training in Canada!

I was deeply disappointed. All the way back to Berrien Springs, Michigan, I asked God to take control of the situation. Even though I prayed, I didn't see how the Lord could change this situation, or bring any good out of it. But I was yet to see how a mighty God works! For two days my professors tried to get me into another school. On the third day I got a call saying that I had been placed at a small boarding church school in Holly, Michigan. I knew nothing about this school, but at this juncture I had no choice but to go.

In spite of my initial trepidation, I quickly warmed up to the school, its students, and Patty, my supervising teacher. I soon discovered that there was an unexpected blessing to being close to my university. Another student teacher from there had been assigned to the same school, and she made frequent weekend trips back to the campus. I also had a male friend on campus and enjoyed our frequent visits. It was on one of those trips that my friend surprised me with a proposal of marriage! Had I gone to Canada I am convinced that events would have unfolded differently. I have now been married to that friend for 27 years. The Lord worked things out for our good.

Lynn C. Smith

The Box

I thank my God in all my remembrance of you, always offering prayer with joy in my every prayer for you all. Phil. 1:3, 4, NASB.

BECKY'S FRIEND WAS RETIRING, probably at too young an age and too soon. Her retirement would also mean moving from her familiar place to another state, where she would be close to her granddaughter.

Becky was disappointed and grieved that her dear friend would be moving far from her, but wanted to reassure her that she would never be far from her heart. Becky bought a simple yet beautiful box and put in it 12 letters, each one marked with a month of the year. In each of the letters Becky shared expressions that reminded her friend how precious and gifted she was to her, and what a gift her friendship was.

The move happened, and Becky's friend found out it was lonelier than she ever could have imagined. Her husband, a salesman, was often away. Her granddaughter was a delight, but when she wasn't with her, she felt so abandoned—except for the box. The gift box is kept in her kitchen. Each month she opens her monthly letter and remembers the good times with Becky and her former home. She is encouraged and strengthened as she reads the letters again and again. It takes all her determination not to open all the letters at once, but how she looks forward to opening the next month's letter! And she writes Becky, sending a letter every month to tell her how important she and the box are in her life. Becky feels as though she has received the greatest blessing from the letters and notes of appreciation, and all because of the simple gift of a box.

God's Word to us is like that box. Each promise is a love note, reminding us how precious and special we are to Him. He tells us of His love, forgiveness, joy, and His longing for us to be in His presence for eternity. With hope we look forward to our reunion with the Creator God, our Friend, who is so far away but so close to us in His Word. And when we return to Him our prayers of thanksgiving, He is then most blessed.

Today I thank the Lord for His loving care to us, whatever our circumstances. His Word continues to be our strength and comfort as we look longingly toward our homecoming. It is my prayer that we will all be there together.

Wanda Grimes Davis

God Cares About the Details

O give thanks unto the Lord, for he is good: for his mercy endureth for ever.
Ps. 107:1.

I cried with my whole heart; hear me, O Lord: I will keep thy statutes.
Ps. 119:145.

IT'S AMAZING HOW little details make a very big difference. It may be a single dot or line in a work of art, or a comma in a sentence—very small and simple things. But they change the meaning of that sentence or the beauty of that work of art. The same is true when we work on something that's important to us. God takes care of the details in our lives because we are important to Him. And when we strive to obey God in the details, the big things will come easier.

Life as a young woman is not always a breath of fresh air or a bed of roses; it has its thorns, and the devil knows where to put them. But I have learned that just because we don't see the immediate results or benefits of obeying God, it doesn't mean they aren't there.

One situation that could be considered a detail by some is the temptation to enter into a relationship with a man who is not of our faith. We see that as something simple and small, and some may even say that as long as we don't marry, it doesn't matter. The same could be said for any relationship: she decides to give in to her feelings (or maybe peer pressure). Later on, to please the other one, she may give in to something else. Maybe the detail could be missing going to church, or going to certain places one wouldn't ordinarily go to. Because these things are small, it may seem that one time shouldn't make a difference. But it is God's plan that we be with a person who will help us grow spiritually, a person who can be there to offer advice or spiritual comfort in time of need, a person with the same values and the same convictions.

The same way a mother knows the needs of her child and does all possible to take care of those needs, our loving and caring heavenly Father knows what is best for us and supplies our needs—but in His time, the time He knows is best. God cares about things as small as our cooking, if we get to work on time, or if we feel sad or tired. He cares about every single thing, but He is waiting for us to confide in and to trust in Him.

We are His sentences, His works of art, and He will take care of all the dots and lines, all the commas, in our lives.

Yvita Antonette Villalona Bacchus

Hugs

Fear not; for thou shalt not be ashamed: . . . For thy Maker is thine husband;
the Lord of hosts is his name; and thy Redeemer. . . . For the Lord
hath called thee as a woman forsaken and grieved in spirit . . .
when thou wast refused, saith thy God. Isa. 54:4-6.

SEPARATION AND DIVORCE is a hard thing. It rips at your insides and causes you to question everything. I learned this lesson firsthand during the years 1999 through 2002. I found myself in the middle of a separation that later became final and absolute. It was hard enough dealing with the fact that my marriage didn't work out, but the acrimony and bitterness experienced because of it was even more painful. My husband had been my best friend, and now that was over.

I was a Christian single mother, active in my church, and wondering what was wrong with me, wondering if God loved me. My husband had said that he had never really loved me, so why should God?

I tried to put up a brave face, but ended up crying all over the place to the echoes of "you are not the first, and you will not be the last." I felt I needed at least to be strong for my 4-year-old daughter; instead, she was the one comforting me. I felt ashamed, rejected. There was no one I could turn to; there was no one who understood. The emptiness was like a yawning hole that sucked at my insides and left me drained and defeated.

One night in desperation I cried out to God, telling Him how lonely and hurt and confused I was. I just needed a hug; to know that someone was there in my corner, and not just discussing me behind my back. In the midst of my tears I felt a Presence there in the room, and arms literally reached out to me and held me. Peace and assurance were mine. I was neither forgotten nor discarded. The Lord reminded me of His promise to me that He would be my husband when my own deserted me; He would accept me when the world turned away.

In the years since I have grown stronger and wiser. I now know that God's love is mine, and I cannot be separated from it. "Neither height nor depth, nor anything else in all creation, will be able to separate us from the love of God that is in Christ Jesus our Lord" (Rom. 8:39, NIV).

I've gotten many hugs, but none can rival the hands of God holding me. Why not ask God for a hug today? He's always there, willing to give it.

Greta Michelle Joachim-Fox-Dyett

Emergency!

Watch therefore, for ye know neither the day nor the hour
wherein the Son of man cometh. Matt. 25:13.

IN MY WORK AS an administrative assistant I am approached almost daily with
"emergencies." "I forgot to reserve a conference room for my meeting." "I need a
conference call set up for 10:00 a.m." "Oh, by the way, I'll need 50 copies of that for
my meeting in 30 minutes." And so it goes, day after day. This was mentioned on
my most recent performance review at work. And this is what my manager said:
"Angèle's only area of opportunity would be to better convey her ability to think on
the fly. She does this very well, but as she seeks to identify information she needs to
do her job, especially on projects with short-to-no notice, she can occasionally
come across as resistive."

I was shocked and hurt! I'm an organized person, and people who wait till the
last minute do tend to throw a wrench in my day. One of my favorite sayings (that
I wish I could post on my desk at work) is: "The lack of planning on your part does
not constitute an emergency on my part."

Of course, being a Christian, I can relate this to our spiritual walk and our
preparing for Christ's soon return. In fact, as I type this, knowing that the devotional books are planned a couple of years in advance, I wonder if this devotional
will ever make it to print. And I wonder this because I truly believe that Christ's second coming is very near.

As frustrated as I get on my job with those who wait until the last minute, I am
saddened because I know that there will be many who think they can wait till the
last minute to give their hearts to the Lord, only to find out that time has run out.
There won't be an administrative assistant to run to in that "emergency." And
praise the Lord He never becomes frustrated with us! Yes, I know; that's something
I need to work on.

So if this devotional makes it to print and Christ has not returned, don't view
it as "Oh, I have some time." No, you don't! Today is the day! As Paul wrote: "I tell
you, now is the time of God's favor, now is the day of salvation" (2 Cor. 6:2, NIV).
Plan now to spend eternity with Him.

Angèle Peterson

Trusting God in All Circumstances

Trust in the Lord forever, for the Lord, the Lord, is the Rock eternal.
Isa. 26:4, NIV.

SEVERAL YEARS AGO I was diagnosed with Ménière's disease, an inner ear disorder that causes vertigo and hearing loss. Although Ménière's is not a life-threatening illness, it was the first time I had been faced with a health issue that couldn't be cured.

Right after I was diagnosed I looked on the Internet to find out more about the disease. When I discovered that the vertigo gets so bad in some people that they literally can't function for weeks or months at a time and that others go totally deaf in both ears, I panicked. All I could think about was that I live alone, I have to travel to earn my livelihood, and that if I lost my hearing and couldn't communicate with people I would lose my job.

One day I mentioned my fears to a small group of wise, godly women. One of them pressed me and asked, "And what would happen if you lost your job?"

"I would starve to death because I have no one to take care of me," I said.

"You aren't trusting God to take care of you," she replied, reminding me that nothing can happen to me for which God has not already made provision.

She was right. I had totally forgotten that God has always taken care of me. I had been through much tougher situations than Ménière's disease and had always felt His presence in a very real way. But I had allowed fear to rob me of the peace God intended for me. I thank the Lord for godly friends who were willing to help me confront the real issue—lack of trust. Isaiah 30:15 tells us: "In repentance and rest is your salvation, in quietness and trust is your strength" (NIV).

Quietness and trust mean not whining and asking "Why me?" when things go wrong. Paul had plenty of reason to whine and complain when he was imprisoned on trumped-up charges. Instead, he trusted God and was able to use his time productively while in prison. Some of his most encouraging Epistles to the young Christian churches were written from prison.

And by trusting in God's ability to take care of us in all circumstances, we too find the strength we need to cope with the trials that we all experience. As I have learned to trust God with my illness, He has indeed been more than faithful to enable me to do everything I need to do for my work and for living on my own.

Carla Baker

Rocked in the Cradle of the Deep

*I will lie down and sleep in peace, for you alone,
O Lord, make me dwell in safety. Ps. 4:8, NIV.*

FEW EXPERIENCES ARE more thrilling than living on an ocean liner for at least a day or two. Seven miles beneath you lies the floor of the emerald sea, and for countless miles around the rippling ocean rolls. During the day, while you're involved in the busy activities aboard ship, with fine dining, picture taking, and entertainment, somehow the environment doesn't seem ominous. You are relaxed, happy, unconcerned. You're having fun. Then comes the night, and darkness descends. The engine quietly hums, the waves crash, but somehow you are still able to lie down, close your eyes, and enjoy a peaceful sleep.

What trust! What faith! You have confidence that as you rest someone is at the controls, directing this huge vessel in the pitch darkness. While you can see nothing, not even a star in the sky, you trust the one who does. When forked lightning splits the sky and the thunder rolls, you turn over and continue your gentle snoring, confident that there is someone in charge—a captain in a sparkling white uniform who has promised to take you through the dark unknown to your destination.

In the morning you awaken to the warm glow of the rising sun. Forgetting the darkness of the previous night, you arise to the brightness of a hope-filled new day. How exciting to look ahead and see the outline of a distant shore! You're almost there! As you approach land, the view becomes clearer. Soon you can see houses and vehicles. Yes, you're almost there.

In the dark nights of our own lives do we remember that Someone is at the helm, and that He knows the way through the dark, through the storms, and through the tears? Do we remember how He guided us through the darkness of a previous night when we thought day would never come, through the terror of the wind, and through the frightful thunder? Can we trust Him to take us safely home?

Our Savior is still at the helm. Don't lose faith. We may not see Him, but we know He is there. The same Pilot who guided our vessel through the past, through the dark channels of challenge and doubt, is still at the controls today. He does not sleep, and He does not slumber.

Be at peace. All is well.

Annette Walwyn Michael

The Official's Daughter

No one can snatch them out of my Father's hand. John 10:29, NIV.

THIS YEAR I AM privileged to be homeroom teacher to Dee,* the daughter of a high government official. She's a delightful 16-year-old with special educational needs. Although she doesn't participate in my classes, I'm still in charge of taking her down to the daily prayer assembly in the school's courtyard and of making sure she gets back safely to the classroom. Her legs are misshapen, which causes her to walk unsteadily. Because of this, she needs somebody to hold her hand, especially when walking in a crowd or up or down stairs.

From time to time her tutor is there to help her to the courtyard for morning meeting. More often than not I walk with her. When the bell rings, I stay back a few moments to usher the tenth graders out of the room, and then Dee and I walk together. But it's not very often that she waits for me. Being a teenager in search of independence, she runs ahead; but she doesn't get very far before I catch up with her. By that time she's usually exhausted from trying to keep her balance, and she's grateful to grab hold of my hand.

One morning, as usual, Dee ran ahead. A few minutes later some students informed me that she had vomited in the hallway. I finally found her walking with another teacher. I took her to the nurse's office, where she was taken care of. For the next few days Dee made sure to wait for me. But it wasn't long until she started yearning for autonomy again.

On more than one occasion she has gotten all the way to the courtyard alone, then becomes confused and ends up standing with the wrong group. As she spins around, desperately trying to find her classmates, I walk up to her and lead her to the right queue.

Sometimes on our way back to the classroom she tries to let go of my hand. If the door is close by, I let her go because I know she's safe.

My daily interactions with Dee remind me of my relationship with God. More often than I care to remember, I run ahead, trying to do things my way. This never ends well. I'm thankful for God's strong arm that leads me back to the right pathway. I'm thankful for the people God places in my way to hold my hand and guide me through life's journey. I can rest assured that God has made provision for me to be taken care of. Praise this awesome God!

Dinorah Blackman

* The name has been changed.

Quenching Your Thirst

As the deer pants for the water brooks, so pants my soul for You, O God. Ps. 42:1, NKJV.

HAVE YOU EVER had such a longing for something that unless you fulfilled that longing you would not have any peace? The psalmist expressed his deepest longing for the Lord in today's passage of Scripture. A deer's natural desire for water is necessary for his survival. Our survival is also based on our need for the water that only Jesus Christ can give. This water is a refreshing for our soul. The desire to be in communion with the most high God was placed in all humans at the foundation of the world. We can't satisfy this God-given desire with anything other than a close personal walk with the Lord.

When we learned about the condition of our economy and what motivated those who committed unspeakable acts of greed, we saw the results of what happens when we try to fill the Christ void in our lives with manmade idols. There is only one Lord, and His name is Jesus. He loves us so much that He gave His life for us. If there were only one person to accept Jesus as Lord and Savior He still would have come for the sake of that one soul. Think about it: the King of glory laid down His divinity, His place in the heavens where His every word is followed reverently, without question and with praise, in order to put on human flesh to fulfill God the Father's plan to pay the price for our sins. He paid the price that no one else could pay without insisting on His own rights or way.

Why, then, do we seek after things that will not quench the thirst that we have? Consider this for one moment: We are afraid that if we give our lives over to this God we don't see, don't understand, and, in many instances, don't trust, we will miss out on something. As the psalmist says, "I would have lost heart, unless I had believed that I would see the goodness of the Lord in the land of the living" (Ps. 27:13, NKJV). No one, and nothing but Jesus, can fill the God-ordained void that we have in our soul. That is just how we are wired!

If we open our heart to Him, He will come in and give us the living water that comes from Him alone. The water that He gives will not only quench our thirst but will cleanse us from all our sins and iniquities. Take time today to enter into fellowship with Him and receive the refreshing that your soul needs and longs for. It has brought healing and peace to my soul.

Eilean L. Greene

Weight Capacity

Pile your troubles on God's shoulders—he'll carry your load, he'll help you out.
Ps. 55:22, Message.

Come to Me, all who are weary and heavy-laden, and I will give you rest.
Matt. 11:28, NASB.

HAVE YOU EVER been in an elevator, on a bridge, or in a multistory building and noticed that there's a weight capacity? It's a warning that whatever you're in, or standing on, is built to handle only so much weight. This means that if the weight capacity is exceeded, the elevator, bridge, or floor may collapse.

It is natural for women to multitask. Some of us juggle married life, children, careers, education, siblings, elderly parents, health, and church all at the same time. And once we've served everybody and everything else, what are we left with? Where is our sanity? We have weight capacities, too, but unfortunately our breaking points aren't labeled anywhere on our bodies as they are on manufactured structures. Yet we know they are there, but we ignore them because we're driven to serve. My mother has told me on several occasions, "You can't do everything."

Has God asked us to bear the weight of everything? No! Psalm 55:22 says, "Cast your burden upon the Lord and He will sustain you" (NASB). I also like how the Message puts it in today's text.

Aren't you glad that God doesn't have a weight limit? He's able to handle your finances, family, fluctuating weight, and marital problems—and He still has room for more. He's able to deal with your health, housing, and vehicle breakdowns—and He still has room for more. He can handle insecurities and addictions—and He still has room for more. Legal trouble, employment needs—and He still has room for more. Relationships, children, and sexual abuse—God has room for more. Death and depression, prison, and recession—God still has room for more! So He says in Matthew 11:28: "Come to Me, all who are weary and heavy-laden, and I will give you rest." This is such an encouraging promise! If we come to God and trust Him to take care of the things that weigh us down, He promises us rest.

We serve an awesome God! He has no weight capacity limit because there's no problem that He can't fix. "Pile your troubles on God's shoulders—He'll carry your load."

Tina Carriger

I Saw an Angel

Then shall thy light break forth as the morning, and thine health shall spring forth speedily: and thy righteousness shall go before thee; the glory of the Lord shall be thy rereward. Isa. 58:8.

LISTENING TO THE Lord's call, we went to work at a church newly born, located about 300 miles (500 kilometers) from São Paulo, Brazil. I taught and helped my husband in his ministry. The work was arduous. Besides the construction of the church, we had 600 people to nurture and confirm in their faith, and meetings to conduct.

Satan was very angry with us, attacking us with diseases and suffering. On one of these occasions I had to undergo surgery in São Paulo. As our meetings were scheduled for Sunday evenings, my husband took me to the hospital early Sunday then drove the 300 miles home to take care of his responsibilities. He planned to return Monday morning to be with me as I had the surgery, and left our 12-year-old son as my companion. However, very soon after I was taken to the surgery center, I felt unbearable pain. I called the nurse, who checked my intravenous line, and reported that it was flowing normally. "Your pain will soon pass," she assured me.

I waited for a long time, and my pain became worse. I called her again and said, "I can't bear this pain anymore. Please, call my doctor!" When she came back, she told me, "The doctor informed me that I can't give you painkiller for six hours." I became desperate, but I didn't want to cry in front of my son, who didn't understand what was going on. As it was near lunchtime, I asked him to go to eat lunch.

As soon as he left the room I began to cry loudly. Looking up at the ceiling, I prayed, "I know, my Jesus, that You suffered much more on the cross of Calvary. However, if You don't come to relieve me now I will die because of this pain." I was still talking when suddenly the door opened. I saw a Being enter, wearing clothes as white as snow. I immediately covered my face. He came close to my bed and put His hand on my shoulder. I peeked at Him through my fingers, looking at His profile. So beautiful!

Almost immediately I slept, not waking until the next day. I didn't know when my son or husband came into the room. The following day I was discharged—completely well.

How wonderful is our God! Surely He will support you, too, when you call to Him.

Neusa Bueno Targas

February 27

The God of the Impossible

*And Hezekiah received the letter of the hand of the messengers,
and read it: and Hezekiah went up into the house of the Lord,
and spread it before the Lord. 2 Kings 19:14.*

I WAS VERY HAPPY when we found out that I was pregnant, and especially happy because I was expecting a girl (we already had a beautiful boy). My husband was especially enjoying the fact that he would be the father of a girl. Then in the sixth month of my pregnancy we got a not-very-pleasant surprise. The doctor said I had acquired a virus, and that virus could cause defects in our baby's hearing or eyesight.

I have always heard people say that when they passed through a bad experience they had felt as if the floor had opened beneath them. I had difficulty imagining that until that day in the doctor's office. We were totally caught by surprise. After scaring us, the doctor told us that maybe the laboratory could have made a mistake. All the exams were repeated in two laboratories, confirming the presence of the virus. The doctor suggested that he shouldn't perform the tubal ligation that we had asked for until after we knew the status of the baby's health. That worried me further.

Then Rosely, a great friend of mine whom I consider a woman of prayer, called me and said that she had arranged an appointment with a doctor who was connected with our health plan, and she begged me to go for a consultation. Before I consented, however, I remembered King Hezekiah's prayer and put my case before God, begging for a miracle for my daughter and me. The week previous to the consultation I prayed a lot. I made a list of how I would like the new doctor to act so that I could feel calm. I even asked that she be a Christian, but then I removed this request, saying I was asking too much.

The day of the consultation came. The doctor looked at all the exams, then examined me. When I asked if she saw evidence of the virus, she reviewed the exams again and said that everything had been a mistake by the laboratories. (I had forgotten about my request about the doctor being a Christian, but I found out later that she was.)

Today I have a beautiful 7-year-old girl. She is smart, intelligent, and healthy, to the honor and glory of God who loves me so much and can do the impossible—for each of us!

Érica Cristina Pinheiro de Souza

God's Spoiled Little Girl

Though my father and mother forsake me, the Lord will receive me.
Ps. 27:10, NIV.

ALTHOUGH THE YOUNGEST of three, I never experienced the pleasure of getting a lot of attention or of being spoiled. My siblings and I are so close in age that I guess we were all being babied at the same time. I would say, however, that my brother, the oldest and the only boy, not only got a lot of attention but usually what he wanted. My sister, being the middle child, learned how to draw some attention to herself and how to get her way as well.

My brother and sister are 10 months apart in age. My mother admitted to me that when she was pregnant again (with me) before my sister even turned 1, she got a lot of criticism from people, teasing that she was a baby-making machine. It caused her to be somewhat depressed as she carried me.

My parents loved me, I know that, though I may not have always felt it. I thank God that my position and experience as a last child taught me to be independent. I praise God also that my parents raised us as Christians, and I learned that I could (and needed) to depend on God for all my needs. As I grew and developed a close relationship with God, I eventually stopped feeling sorry for myself.

Looking back over my life now I can see that God has supplied all my needs, and He's done it with perfect timing—His. I really came to see this one Friday evening after a very rough week at work and dealing with personal family matters. Two things that had kept me up, worrying late at night, were resolved by God. I saw, too, that they were things I wasted time worrying about—God had been in control all along.

I went up to my room as the sun was setting and, oh! what a magnificent view! I realized also that through the other window, on the opposite side of my bedroom, I often had a wonderful view of the sunrise. This was actually an answer to a casual prayer I had prayed quite sometime in the past, to live in a home where I could get a clear view of these two daily events. This brought back memories of all the other serious and casual prayers God has answered. It gave me faith that God will take care of me through future struggles. As long as I try to live according to His will, the blessings flow. These blessings I must share with others.

Mirlène André

February 29

Mixed Blessings

Be still, and know that I am God. Ps. 46:10.

WHEN MY MOM came to visit me, I decided I would take her to visit friends and family in Birmingham, England, where my dad's cousins (who were originally from Montserrat) reside. We were having a pretty good time until I began having pain in my right hand.

By that night it was swollen and more painful, and we had to keep a watchful eye on it. Around midnight it was so swollen and painful I couldn't sleep. I cried, waiting and praying for daylight to come so I could go to the hospital or contact my family doctor. My mom couldn't sleep because of my crying, so she got up and tried to assist me. She put an ice pack on it, which helped briefly. When I was able to think, and there was some relief from all the pain, I prayed and cried for longer relief.

Morning finally came, and it was time to get ready to go home. I decided to visit the pharmacy for more pain relief until I could get to my own doctor at home, since it could take a long time to get to the emergency room. The trip was grueling; however, we finally made it.

My doctor sent me to have an X-ray at the hospital to eliminate carpal tunnel syndrome, which he had diagnosed previously. While waiting to be called in for my X-ray in the waiting room, I sat reading a book by Susan Wales, *Standing on the Promises*. The passage I read was about waiting for results in a waiting room. I just had to laugh at how God is so instrumental in our lives, even guiding me to read that particular book to be reminded of that message. When we are unwell God doesn't always heal us physically—it's also about our spiritual healing.

All this caused me to reflect on what was happening at work and how I was becoming more preoccupied with that situation than with the God who was molding and making me while taking me through the situation. He wanted to cleanse me spiritually so that I could serve the purpose He intended. I needed to remain focused. Proverbs 3:5 and 6 came to mind: "Trust in the Lord . . . and lean not unto thine own understanding."

I also want to remind you to trust God, for we all need encouragement to remember Him in all circumstances. "Be still, and know that [He is] God."

Susan Riley

Perfect Timing

And it shall come to pass, that before they call, I will answer; and while they are yet speaking, I will hear. Isa. 65:24.

I RECEIVED A LETTER stating that because I was a college student I could present the letter to any car dealership that had a logo that they pictured—and I could buy a car. I didn't think much about it, because I already had a car that got wonderful gas mileage. Some of my family teased me about how swiftly I got about in my cream-colored Dodge Omni. I had traveled to work and out of town in that car. My cousin and I had transported wedding cakes to receptions in my car. It wasn't a new car (I had bought it from a used-car dealer), but it suited my purpose to get me from point A to point B—or even point Z. I was just starting out as a teacher, and I didn't have much money for a new car.

However, my mother didn't like riding in the back because it was a hatchback, and she thought that her head was too close to the wires that had an automatic release to open the hatch. One time my grandmother and I were traveling on the highway when the engine cut out as we were in the passing lane, and a semitruck was coming. But the good Lord allowed it to go around us, and finally I was able to restart the car.

Before this incident I really had never had any problems with the car until the night my car threw a rod. I had to have it towed more than 50 miles to get it home. I didn't have the money to have it fixed and was told that it probably would be best to get a new car instead of putting more money into this one. I said, "Lord, what am I going to do? I need a car."

Then I remembered that envelope that had been sent to me. I told my mother about the letter, and we went to a dealership and presented the letter. We had no problems! The Lord knew that I needed a car before I did. He definitely has perfect timing! Hallelujah!

Not only does God listen to our needs and knows what we need before we even know it, but He is also faithful in His response. As Isaiah says, "O Lord, you are my God; I will exalt you and praise your name, for in perfect faithfulness you have done marvelous things, things planned long ago" (Isa. 25:1, NIV).

Bertha Hall

Faith in All Things

And we know that all things work together for good to them that love God, to them who are the called according to his purpose. Rom. 8:28.

LONG BEFORE MICHAEL JACKSON was an international icon, he sang with his brothers. In 1984 the Jackson brothers, including Michael, had one last tour together, the Victory Tour. I was away at college and wanted badly to see this concert, but the logistics seemed too challenging. Surprisingly, my mother called to say a family friend in the entertainment journalism industry had received two choice tickets for the concert in Chicago and would be willing to let her have them so I could attend. This was the best news ever! In addition, my mother offered to fly me home for the occasion. It would be a birthday gift. After the excitement settled down, there were two huge issues: I had to be back for a final exam at Oakwood College (now Oakwood University) in Huntsville, Alabama, the morning after the concert. The concert was in Chicago, and all the return flights were booked. I could get a flight only as far as Nashville, Tennessee.

My excitement evolved into conflict. The details weren't working out. But I wanted to go! I was a good student and realized I was being rewarded by my mother and our family friend for that. After weighing the costs and benefits, I decided I would step out in faith. This meant going to Chicago with no confirmed way back to school in order to take my final exam.

We usually think of having faith in times of crises, but I decided that if God had worked out the details so far He would work out the rest. I went to the concert and had a wonderful time! (My brother used the other ticket.) I took a red-eye out of Chicago and made it to Nashville. I stopped at a pay phone to let my mother know I had arrived at that point safely. (This was before the day of cell phones.) As we were discussing my dilemma, I heard a familiar voice on the pay phone next to me, outlining his travel from the airport to the Oakwood campus. I assured my mother I would be all right and approached the other caller, a faculty member, and explained my dilemma. He was gracious and said he'd be happy for me to catch a ride back to campus with him.

I made it to the final exam and received an A on it. I have never forgotten that God cared enough about me to work out the details of something that I really wanted to do by putting the right person in the right place at the right time.

Kimberly N. Sutton

Limited Blessings

Ask, and you will receive. Search, and you will find. Knock, and the door will be opened for you. Everyone who asks will receive. Everyone who searches will find. And the door will be opened for everyone who knocks.
Matt. 7:7, 8, CEV.

I IMAGINE THERE are other women who do the same thing I do when it comes to shopping. There are some shops on which I don't waste my limited time (or money) even browsing in because I already have a preconceived idea that they are way out of the reach of my budget. So I don't even step inside.

One early spring day I had gone to a conference. When the last session ended a bit earlier than I had anticipated, I had extra time on my hands. I felt like indulging myself in one of my favorite pastimes: window shopping. As I headed to one of my well-known stores, I arrived first at one that I had always seen but never had the nerve to enter. So I took a detour and went in. As I began browsing, I saw some items that I liked and took a closer look, daring to look at the price tag. The price of the first item seemed particularly attractive. *Well*, I thought, *that must be a mistake.* But it was clearly marked. I checked several other items in turn and could hardly believe my eyes. Yes, they were having a sale of out-of-season items, and I was able to get several things at a good bargain price.

And I returned to that store more than once in the succeeding months. Interestingly, I also noticed that occasionally there were advertising flyers from that store in my mailbox, and I wondered if they had been there before and I had simply overlooked them, thus limiting my blessings.

More recently I reflected on that situation. I asked myself whether at times I've been acting the same way in my spiritual life as I have done in my shopping life. Do I limit the blessings I could give and receive by not daring to launch out into the untried areas that my heavenly Father has waiting for me? My prayer today is that God will open my eyes to new possibilities, and that I will not limit what He could do in and through me. He has invited us to knock at His storehouse; He can show us the way out of our timidity and unbelief. I invite you to join me in doing that!

Doreen Evans-Yorke

March 4

Deliver Us From Evil

Lead us not into temptation, but deliver us from evil. Matt. 6:13.

HAVE YOU EVER THOUGHT about what the Lord hates? The first time I read a passage in the Bible about hate, it shocked me. Hate is a word that catches my attention. The dictionary defines it as "dislike intensely," "extreme aversion," "abhor," "detest," "loathe," "abominate," "despise." The Bible says there are six things the Lord hates, seven that are detestable to Him. These are listed in Proverbs 6.

First are *haughty eyes*. I think this means a proud look, arrogance, and would include those who try to show off their knowledge. Next is *a lying tongue*. Lying is hateful to God because He is truth. Satan is the father of lies. God does not accept a lying tongue in the mouth of His children.

Hands that shed innocent blood are the third thing God hates. This implies cruelty. Murder. But we might be guilty of judging someone on hearsay and being critical of someone who is really innocent of the supposed wrong. The real truth is we're not to judge anyone.

Fourth, God hates *a heart that devises wicked schemes*. Wicked plans come from a wicked heart; the blood of Christ makes a heart pure. His desire is that we hide His Word in our hearts. The fifth thing God hates are *feet that are quick to rush into evil*.

Did you notice that the first five things the Lord hates mention parts of the body: eyes, tongue, hands, heart, and feet? There seems to be a progression to evil. If we find ourselves in an evil pattern, or a bent toward sinful activity, we need to forsake it and cause our feet to run from it.

Another hate (related to the second) is a *false witness* who pours out lies. This is the sixth hate. God is truth, and He expects His children to tell the truth and to be an accurate witness to the best of their ability. And last is *a person who stirs up dissension among brothers or sisters*. The body of Christ needs all of its members to live in harmony. "Behold, how good and how pleasant it is for brethren [and sisters] to dwell together in unity!" (Ps. 133:1, NKJV).

If our desire is to please God, why don't we try every morning to commit ourselves to Christ? Each morning, when the world is still quiet and dark, we can consecrate ourselves to Him and His glory, asking that we not displease Him in any way.

Emma Lutz

God Puts Us in Places for a Reason

Trust in the Lord with all thine heart; and lean not unto thine own understanding. In all thy ways acknowledge him, and he shall direct thy paths. Prov. 3:5, 6.

ALL THE EMPLOYEES were summoned to the cafeteria for the surprise news that the hospital would close in three months because of the buyout, or takeover, by another local hospital. Administration informed us so that we would not be alarmed to hear about it by the headline news the following day.

It took us by surprise. It felt as if the rug was being pulled out from under our feet. We had thought that we'd be able to stay together and see our children graduate from high school, move on to college, and even marry—in short, go through life's passages together. Instead, together we went through a myriad of emotions, from wondering if, and where, we'd work to how we'd be able to pay our bills. We found out that the new hospital wouldn't accommodate all of us. After working at the hospital for 22 years I was facing the possibility of finding another job because of the takeover.

During this emotionally stressful time I had the opportunity to witness to my friends and coworkers regarding the precious promises of God. I encouraged them—and myself—to put our trust in God. At the same time hospital management found ways to easily eliminate jobs: by requiring that we reapply for our current positions. This caused many experienced workers to lose their jobs because even though they had many years of work experience, they lacked the degrees behind their names. As a result, many were asked to take positions that paid far less, and when they refused because the pay was not enough to cover their current expenses, they were terminated on the grounds of their refusal. Many lost the benefits they had accrued over the past years. We shed many tears together as we said farewell.

Finally my turn came, and I was informed that I would be one of the fortunate workers to be retained by the new hospital. I realized that God had prepared a way for me long before the entire ordeal. He had placed me there so that I could point others to His comforting arms in a time of crisis. He had also allowed me to keep up with my certification and stay abreast with changes in my field. He had directed my paths, and I feel Him still leading.

Priscilla Charles

Banana Revelation

But the Lord said unto Samuel, Look not on his countenance,
or on the height of his stature; because I have refused him:
for the Lord seeth not as man seeth; for man looketh on the outward
appearance, but the Lord looketh on the heart. 1 Sam. 16:7.

BANANAS ARE NOT my favorite fruit. So why do I eat a banana every day before I go to work? Because it's a healthy practice that I began more than a year ago.

As I got into the habit of reaching for a banana each morning I began noticing things about bananas. Some were big, some were small. The peelings on some were yellow without blemish and they were firm, while the peelings on others were spotted and soft to the touch. I would instinctively reach for those bananas with unblemished exteriors and firm to touch, anticipating that when I peeled back the covering the inside would be whole and untainted. To my dismay, often the inside would have dark spots in different places, and those places would be soft and mushy; or the dark spoilers would be throughout. Not being able to salvage any part of the banana for eating purposes, I would quickly discard it.

Having no recourse, I grudgingly would then reach for one of the bananas that had a blemished exterior and were soft to touch. To my surprise, after peeling back the covering, I found the inside to be unblemished and ripe and perfect for eating.

What a lesson! Don't you see? We sinful human beings often judge people by what they look like on the outside versus getting to know a little about their life's story and then making our decisions about them. Just think about the many blessings we miss either in helping, serving, or learning from others, when we judge from the outside.

What have you learned about bananas? Have you had any revelations as you consider them? More important, have you learned any lessons about judging other people or actions before looking inside the peeling?

I'm so happy we serve a compassionate, loving, and just heavenly Father who looks on the inside of all of us, not only to judge but to uplift, cleanse, and daily renew a right spirit within each of us. God doesn't discard us as I did the unblemished bananas that were spoiled on the inside; rather He purposes to save us by His grace and His Son's shed blood on Calvary.

Cynthia Best-Goring

Showers of Blessing

Bring ye all the tithes into the storehouse, that there may be meat in mine house, and prove me now herewith, saith the Lord of hosts, if I will not open you the windows of heaven, and pour you out a blessing, that there shall not be room enough to receive it. And I will rebuke the devourer for your sakes, and he shall not destroy the fruits of your ground; neither shall your vine cast her fruit before the time in the field, saith the Lord of hosts. Mal. 3:10, 11.

MY CLOTHES SEEM TO LAST for so many years, and also it seems I don't have to buy shoes for a long, long time. Yet when I wear my old clothes people often think they are new and express joy at seeing me in them. It's the same way with my husband's clothes. For many years now he hasn't purchased new ones and is also blessed with new clothes as gifts. We count these gifts as blessings and return God's tithe faithfully, because we didn't have to spend money to buy them.

Just imagine how much money we've saved because God has preserved our clothes and shoes! What we return as God's share is so little, and God returns such abundant blessings, that there's no room to receive them. This experience reminds me of God's people in the wilderness. Their clothes and shoes lasted for 40 years. God supplied all that they needed.

God loved them so much that He provided shade so that the sun wouldn't cause them discomfort. He gave them light at night, and even warmth. Sometimes I wonder why we calculate only our income so we can return a faithful tithe, as if that were the only blessing we receive. What about the solar power, the fresh air, and fresh water?

We thank God for our fruit trees in our small garden. We enjoy sharing with others around us. We would never find that much joy if we were to sell them. We don't forget, of course, the Lord's share. The more we give, the more the trees yield, and it is so amazing to watch how God fulfills His promise as stated in today's text.

As we begin to count God's blessings, the list goes on and on: the blessing of fellowship, love, and trust we get from our family, friends, and church. There is good health that spares us medical expenses. Good sleep at night, with our faithful guardian angel by our side, is a blessing. The joy, the laughter, the sunrise and sunset, the beautiful nature around us. . . . We can only recognize our faithful Lord and Savior who lavishly pours His blessings upon us.

Birdie Poddar

Safe Haven

Let us hold fast the confession of our hope without wavering, for He who promised is faithful. Heb. 10:23, NKJV.

WHEN I WAS growing up in Queens, New York, my dad kept bird feeders in the backyard. Faithfully, he fed what he fondly called "his chickens" in the morning and evening. My dad could look out the small window in our kitchen to see all the birds. Each one was unique, and Dad would point out the things he learned from watching them. We girls grew to enjoy watching these birds as well.

Believe it or not, even though we lived in a large city a big hawk came into our backyard every now and then. When it spotted food from above, it came zooming down into our yard. Hawks are beautiful and powerful but frightening to the little birds, who quickly hid in the bushes. One time after a hawk had left the yard Dad was able to go outside and actually hold a trembling bird. He picked up the still-frightened little bird from one of the bushes. As long as the birds stayed hidden, they were completely safe. A hawk couldn't penetrate the tight branches of bushes, so it used scare tactics to get a bird to leave its safe haven. The hawk would fly from one side of the bush to the other side. Sometimes a bird would just fly out, and that was the one the hawk caught.

This has a spiritual application and an important lesson. God has given us a church, a place of safety where we can be nourished and can grow. But the enemy does not want any of us to stay within God's fold and is constantly inventing ways to get us to leave. The enemy uses all kinds of tactics—fear, conflict, discontent, gossip, et cetera—and some people then decide it's better to leave—exactly what the enemy wants. Unfortunately, members who leave the church are usually taken far away from God's fold.

So the lesson for all of us is that God's church is the best place to be and the place God wants us to be. Although things may not be perfect, we should not allow the enemy to shoo us out of God's remnant church; instead, we should hold on tighter to what God has provided for our safety. As it says in Revelation 3:11, "Behold, I am coming quickly! Hold fast what you have, that no one may take your crown" (NKJV).

Rosemarie Clardy

A Promise to Overcome Temptations

The temptations in your life are no different from what others experience. And God is faithful. He will not allow the temptation to be more than you can stand. When you are tempted, he will show you a way out so that you can endure. 1 Cor. 10:13, NLT.

SHORTLY AFTER MY HUSBAND and I decided to say goodbye to our church family in Kohala, Hawaii, the president of Mission College in Thailand invited us to join their faculty and staff. He would be the senior pastor for the college church, and I would be an English-as-a-second-language teacher. We had thought we'd retire completely, but then we counted it an honor and privilege to continue working for the Lord, even as volunteers. So we arrived on the beautiful campus of Mission College. What a joy it was to be back to Thailand after being away for 22 years! Right away we were engaged with our respective jobs. And how I relished being back in the classroom.

One day a distinguished gentleman came to visit us after he and my husband and a rich donor finished distributing some personal necessities and other goods to the indigent people in the nearby area. As the first gentleman sat and talked with me, he commented, "You speak very good English." He was stepping down as president of a well-known institution and had accepted an offer to be the administrator of a newly established international school. Then he offered, "If you will teach in our school, you could easily be given a salary of 70,000 baht." At that time the exchange was one U.S. dollar to 38.50 baht, or $1,818.18. What a huge amount of money!

In Thailand the cost of living was very low, so 70,000 baht was enormous. And to think that I could be paid so much compared to teaching (volunteering) at the Mission College was a big temptation. However, I didn't even say "Let me think about it."

Instead I said, without hesitation, "Thank you, sir, but I don't think I can accept your offer. My husband and I have a contract for two years at this college, and we want to honor that."

The Scriptures say, "He will not allow the temptation to be more than you can stand. When you are tempted, he will show you a way out so that you can endure."

Have you ever been tempted to do something you knew was not God's will for your life? How have you handled it? Have you turned to God for leading and strength? He is faithful!

Ofelia A. Pangan

The Hurtful Words

A word aptly spoken is like apples of gold in settings of silver. Prov. 25:11, NIV.

IN MY LAST YEAR of high school I participated in a cotillion. I had to compete with other girls to raise funds for scholarships, participate in preliminary meetings, and perform in a talent show. I had sung many times in a small choir and a teenagers' gospel group at my church, doing numerous solo parts. I felt ready to sing on my own. Since I was quiet and timid, this would be a major accomplishment for me, but I told the coordinators I would sing. At the same time I planned to wear a matching dress and hat outfit that I had made in sewing class at school.

Several weeks later one of my great-aunts, who had been helping with the cotillion, was at a practice session. I became very nervous while waiting, but when my turn came I sang my song and was approved to sing it for the talent program. I was quite proud of myself. As I packed up my things my aunt came to me and said curtly, "Iris, you really should stick to sewing. Singing is not for you." My feelings were deeply hurt, though I tried not to show it.

In spite of my wounded spirit, I sang my song in the talent show and was pleased with what I had done. I wasn't any of the others, only myself; and I knew that I had overcome a lot to feel confident enough to sing. Coronation evening was a nice event. Each girl wore a lovely white dress and was escorted by a young man, preselected for the occasion. I was pleasantly surprised to find that I had won second place at the coronation because of the substantial money that friends and family had helped me to raise. I was awarded a modest scholarship, which helped with my first year of college.

It's been more than 43 years since those hurtful words were said to me, but I still feel the sting. My aunt's words discouraged me when I was beginning to feel that singing just might be one of my talents. I didn't sing another solo for more than 16 years. In my mid-30s, however, I again had the desire to sing and to use other talents I had developed. Through the years people have asked if I have a CD out. "Your voice is so mellow!" others say. "Are you still singing?"

And so I ask you, are you still singing, or speaking, or sewing, or volunteering in a ministry about which you are passionate? God has a special plan for you, and He will give you what you need to accomplish it. As you have occasion, take time to encourage someone. Your words could make the difference.

Iris L. Kitching

Good Plans

"For I know the plans that I have for you," declares the Lord, "plans for welfare and not for calamity to give you a future and a hope." Jer. 29:11, NASB.

EVER SINCE I was a girl my mother told me it was important to study to become a professional. Although she never studied, she had the right to say this because she was trying to give the best to her five children. So when I was 23 years old I became a dentist. At my graduation one of the most exciting moments of my life happened at rehearsal. The woman who was leading us asked me to go up front because I was the first in my class. In that instant I praised the Lord and vowed that all the achievements of my career would be first for Him.

After that I gladly returned home, but then my mother insisted I was not complete without a master's degree. She said it would be easier for me to study than if I were married and with kids. Wise words! So very soon I started searching universities inside and outside my country for master's degree programs. I decided on one and completed all the applications and studied all the material they asked for in the entry examination. To my disappointment, after months of research and nights of study, they published that the day of the test was to be on a Sabbath. During all my collegiate work I never had an examination on Sabbath, and this was like a trial of my faith. Immediately I called to see if it was possible to have the test on another day. The woman laughed and said it was absolutely impossible.

So I had to change my plans, but not before asking God to guide me. Many people told me I was crazy to waste that opportunity, but I was firm in my decision. I wouldn't take an examination on Sabbath.

After eight months my father visited another university that offered the same master's degree. Once again I sent in all the application forms, and they called to inform me that the entrance test was on a Thursday. I did my best on that test, and in a group of about 80 persons who applied, I was finally selected for a course in pediatric dentistry.

All this happened eight years ago, but I still remember how God guided my life in crucial moments. He opens doors when they look closed to us. We have to trust in Him with all our heart and be faithful.

María Gabriela Acosta de Camargo

Unexpected Delay

If we confess our sins, he is faithful and just to forgive us our sins. 1 John 1:9.

MY HUSBAND AND I had just enjoyed a wonderful vacation on St. Thomas, Virgin Islands, and were at the airport for our flight home. We had arrived early, so we hadn't needed to rush as we made leisurely but steady progress toward our airline kiosk. After checking our luggage, we were directed to the security line. Since September 11, 2001, extra security measures have been in effect in an effort to mitigate the possibility of other terrorist attacks. We had to remove belts, shoes, watches, loose change, and other items as directed by security.

After we completed this routine, the "magic wand" was waved in front, behind, and on both sides of us. We assumed we were all clear until a security officer called us to the side. He asked, "Have either of you been injected with any dye recently?" I had had a thallium stress test about a week before our trip during which a very small amount of dye was injected to determine if there was any cardiac blockage as I had been experiencing chest pain. The test proved normal, and we agreed that a vacation was "just what the doctor ordered" for us.

The officer instructed us to go to an area off to the side because the "magic wand" had detected something unusual, and they wanted to be sure I wasn't carrying some form of contamination. Once there, two other officers asked questions, waved the wand again, and explained what had happened. Highly sensitive technology used for security had detected the dye, even though it had measured less than a half teaspoon. Unknown to me, it was still in my system, posing a potential security risk.

This reminded me that we are constantly under God's watchful eye, and the sophistication of His detection system isn't to be compared with any human-made device. Will I be "cleared" for my trip to heaven on that day, or will I be turned away because of some unforsaken, unforgiven sin, undetected by the human eye—perhaps sin even I don't realize I'm still carrying?

I thank the Lord that He gives us the strength to confess and forsake all known and unknown sin, and that He forgives all so that there may be no delay when we approach the gates of heaven.

Gloria Stella Felder

Do I Really Want to Go Home?

But as it is written, Eye hath not seen, nor ear heard,
neither have entered into the heart of man, the things which
God hath prepared for them that love him. 1 Cor. 2:9.

I RECENTLY HAD the privilege of visiting the island of Puerto Rico, the place of my childhood. It's still as beautiful as ever. It was amazing to hear the rooster sing at the crack of dawn and the night song of the *coqui* (a native relative of the frog), and to see chicks responding to the feeding call of the mother hen, flowers that grow among palm and almond trees, and so many other beautiful things. I delighted in the luscious green scenery, the mountains, hills and valleys, the ocean view, the sound of rain dancing on rooftops, and the smell of banana leaves and native spices in the kitchen. It seemed like a dream. To hear folks sing to a long-lost love throughout the day pulled at my heart. The warm air embraced my skin, waking my senses to a whole new world. Yes, it's a totally different world on the island.

To see the rainbow after the afternoon rain, to enjoy the starry sky at night, to view the valley from the mountaintop—these are just a few of its pleasures that I enjoyed once again. To slowly savor the *guarapo* (freshly squeezed sugar cane juice), the *carambolas* (starfruit), and many other native fruits was a treat.

The different tones of green against a bright-blue sky is enough to take your breath away and make you fall in love with this tropical paradise all over again.

Do I really want to go home? I understand that while the island is indeed a delightful place to visit, it is no longer my home. Its charms and pleasures shouldn't dissuade me from returning home to my family.

Although this world is marred by the effects of sin, it still offers many fascinating views and places. It also offers countless temporary pleasures. It would be effortless for someone to get used to it and attached to it. But once I accepted Jesus as my Savior this world was no longer my home. I am just a passerby. I am going to my heavenly home and must not let my senses succumb to the enchantments of this world. All its pleasures cannot compare to what my Father has in store for me.

As our text makes clear, we cannot even imagine heaven's sights, sounds, smells, and beauties. Do I really want to go home? You bet!

Rhodi Alers de López

Moving Again?

Do not let your hearts be troubled. Trust in God; trust also in me. . . .
I am going there to prepare a place for you. John 14:1, 2, NIV.

WE ARE MOVING to Greenville, South Carolina, after having lived in our nation's capital for about six years. Our family has moved five times while serving in the U.S. Navy for 25 years. The children have adjusted and have fond memories of the places where they've spent their childhood. We've been stationed in San Diego, California (twice); Guam; Corpus Christi, Texas; and Washington, D.C. My husband, Jun, has traveled all over the country and the Pacific, on land, air, and sea during those 25 years. Hopefully, this will be our final move following his retirement. We have to decide what to take and which things to give away. After 25 years of accumulating things from different places, it takes a lot of courage to part with stuff you hold dear to your heart! The packers are moving our household goods in a few days.

Moving has always been an adventure for us—seeing new places, meeting people and making new friends, finding a new job and a new school. At one place we helped to establish a church school so our children could enjoy a Christian education. Moving also meant looking for a place to call home and selecting a church that would meet our spiritual needs. God has led and blessed us throughout this journey, and we are grateful for His guidance and providence.

We're excited about moving to Greenville and look forward to the change of pace after the big city. We've lived through the terrorists' attacks of September 11, the fear and terror of the sniper attacks in 2002, and the ongoing Iraqi war. We had to deal with the anxiety of using the subway system after the London subway bombing incident. Yet we learned how to go on with our lives, trusting in our heavenly Father, knowing that He would take care of us.

As we continue this earthly journey we are just as excited to know that Jesus is coming soon. We are looking forward to our permanent home in heaven. No more packing and moving. No more moving stress or fear. We don't even have to sort through our earthly belongings—Jesus has done everything for us and has prepared a home for us. Do we get to choose what kind of house we want to live in for eternity? It doesn't matter; we know the Builder, and He knows what is best for us.

Rhona Grace Magpayo

Preparation for the Appearing in the Sky

And then shall appear the sign of the Son of man in heaven: and then shall all the tribes of the earth mourn, and they shall see the Son of man coming in the clouds of heaven with power and great glory. And he shall send his angels with a great sound of a trumpet, and they shall gather together his elect from the four winds, from one end of heaven to the other.
Matt. 24:30, 31.

IT SEEMED THAT all the life in the lake had suddenly come alive. More than a thousand ducks made quacking noises, and the frogs sounded their tunes to provide the needed harmony. I sat by the lakeside and observed and listened. It was late afternoon, and I had come to watch birds and be blessed by nature.

Then the noise suddenly went silent. Every duck in the water climbed out on the bank until the whole bank was black with ducks and the water was clear. I suspected that something would happen. They seemed to be anticipating something. The sky slowly darkened. I quickly gazed at the horizon and was rewarded by seeing the greatest flock of flying ducks that I had ever witnessed. They covered half the sky and were flying right toward me. These birds flew in an organized arrangement almost triangular in shape. I made no movement; the ducks on the lakeside then struck another tune so sudden and loud that it shocked me.

As the flying ducks approached the lake, I could hear loud and happy duck noises and the flapping of wings by the great multitude of ducks. Half of the flying ducks flew down and landed in the spacious lake water recently vacated by the ducks already on the ground. The remaining flew on, and then half of them landed from the eastern side of the lake while the others flew on farther still in that triangular formation to the next lake over the hill.

I was amazed at how these ducks knew and prepared for the arrival of the coming host. There was joyful noise when the flying ducks eventually arrived, and they were welcomed into the prepared space.

This experience reminded me that the Lord one day will appear in the clouds of heaven. Am I ready and prepared? Am I busily announcing His arrival and preparing all those around me to receive Him? I learned a wonderful lesson from the ducks that day about preparing and waiting to receive our coming King Jesus. Let us each be ready!

Fulori Sususewa Bola

Unprepared to Enter

Instead, they were longing for a better country—a heavenly one.
Therefore God is not ashamed to be called their God,
for He has prepared a city for them. Heb. 11:16, NIV.

VIETNAM IS A PLACE that was often in the news when I was in school. It was a nightmare to find out that someone had been drafted and had to go there. However, it has been said to be a nice place to visit these days. So I planned a beautiful vacation in Hanoi to do some touring.

With all the modern technology now available, one thing I decided to do in preparation for my trip was to apply for my visa online. The procedure was simple, the price was inexpensive, and I felt so proud of myself for taking care of business without going to the embassy. Then the day arrived for me to leave. My luggage was packed, and I had my ticket. I had a long layover in Thailand, with a late flight to Vietnam in the evening.

Well, I arrived at the Hanoi airport and went immediately to the visa desk to retrieve my visa paperwork with the necessary stamp—only to find that I didn't have everything I needed. I had failed to check for all my papers online before leaving Seoul, and the visa was not processed and could not be processed. Suddenly I realized how unprepared I was for my trip. The hotel was paid for, the pickup service was outside of the airport waiting for me, but I couldn't leave the airport. After all the preparations I had made, I couldn't enter Hanoi. The officials checked and rechecked, but my records were not even in the computer system.

I learned a great lesson that day. What if this had happened while I was on my way to heaven? I wouldn't be able to enter in through the gates. I couldn't get angry at anyone but myself because I was unprepared.

I decided that I don't want this to happen to me on my journey to heaven. How about you? Are you prepared to enter heaven? Is everything in order? I wasn't prepared to enter Vietnam, and I'm glad it was Vietnam and not heaven. God is so gracious with His grace and mercy. Unlike some earthly governments, He gives us chance after chance when we make mistakes. Let's pray that we have everything in order when it's our time to meet our Maker. Let's be prepared!

Bessie Russell Haynes

God of Many Names

When we tell you these things, we do not use words that come from human wisdom. Instead, we speak words given to us by the Spirit, using the Spirit's words to explain spiritual truths. 1 Cor. 2:13, NLT.

BEFORE GOING TO bed one night, I decided to catch up on my Bible reading. It wasn't a particularly difficult or exciting time that I was going through; rather everything seemed quite calm for a change. I wasn't rushed as I often was when I did my devotions. I read through the Bible every year, and this year I was reading the Old and New Testaments simultaneously. I didn't realize that I was actually a bit ahead when I finished reading. After reading several other devotional items, I realized it wasn't even as late as I had anticipated.

Around midnight I found myself wide awake with the urge to pray. I thought perhaps it was because I had forgotten to pray, but the Holy Spirit had other plans. So I got up, and as I closed my eyes a miraculous thing happened. The prayer I was going to say took off on its own. In the salutation names for God popped into my head, one after the other. It was a fantastic experience! The prayer continued on its own accord—just a few sentences. I remember that it seemed to come out of the book of Revelation. Some went something like "To God be all honor, glory, and power."

I sat in solemn silence while contemplating my experience and the names for God. Some were traditional, some were new, and some seemed to be way out in left field. I turned on the light and wrote some of the names down. They had gone through my head so quickly that I couldn't remember them all: God as Beholder (of Life), All Powerful, All Knowing, All Wisdom, Omnipresent, Omnipotent, Omniscient, Juice of the Spirit, and Practitioner of Health. I wondered if these represented the triune God. I latched onto the title of God as the Great Beholder of Life and have used it frequently, including at the next church prayer I was asked to pray. When I looked up the word "behold" in the concordance the next day it seemed to be a command in most of the instances it occurred in the Bible.

God is so completely interesting! Before your spiritual life can become routine, He douses it with flavor. Now I have different ways of seeing and referring to Him, the Holy Spirit, and Jesus Christ. That makes all the difference.

Jacqueline V. R. Anderson

Nature's Benefits

You care for the land and water it; you enrich it abundantly.
The streams of God are filled with water to provide
the people with grain, for so you have ordained it. Ps. 65:9, NIV.

And the leaves of the tree are for the healing of the nations. Rev. 22:2, NIV.

NATURE TESTIFIES OF GOD. The whole idea of spending time in nature is welcome to most, if not all, of us. Recently I went with some friends to the YS Falls in Jamaica. This scenic beauty, nestled in nature, reveals many wonders of God's creation. The environment is very conducive to meditation and reflection.

There are many performers in nature that make up Mother Nature's cast. The tall, towering trees offer paternal protection to the growth beneath, much like the one our heavenly Father provides for us. The supple leaves of the green plants testify to the soft and tender care God gives each one of us. The fresh, unpolluted air permeates our lungs with oxygen, reminding us of the breath of life God gives us. In addition, beautiful sunlight and the healing touch of the water on our skin reminds us of the living water that Christ offers. Complementing these is healthy laughter, smiling faces, friendly chatter of friends and family, all expressing nature's benefits.

A visit to nature can aid in invigorating the mind and refreshing the thought processes, adding new perspective to life, and rejuvenating the body. It can elevate the mood and relieve unwanted stress and tension. The soothing effect is therapeutic and mirrors God's love for us.

While on earth Jesus took time out to visit nature and enjoy a respite. This provided Him the opportunity to pray and meditate as He sought to do the will of His Father. In these times it would do us good to set time apart to get intimate with nature and enjoy the lasting benefits available. My friends and I did, and we concurred before leaving that we would make it a frequent trip.

There are so many psalms that speak of God's blessings through nature. Psalm 66:5 invites us to "come and see what God has done, how awesome his works in man's behalf" (NIV). Friends, decide today to spend quality time in nature, reaping nature's benefits—designed by God, packaged for you.

Althea Y. Boxx

I Stood Alone

And Moses said unto the people, Fear ye not, stand still, and see the salvation of the Lord, which he will shew to you to day: for the Egyptians whom ye have seen to day, ye shall see them again no more for ever. Ex. 14:13.

I STOOD ALONE, recently widowed and emotionally fragile despite being surrounded by loving friends. My late husband and I had lived in the retirement village for 18 years, and it was now time for the unit to be refurbished and painted. All this work necessitated the unit being left empty. I had chosen the carpet and vinyl floor coverings, and a date was set for the commencement of the project. The task of shifting my furniture, packing my personal effects, and moving them into the garage seemed to overwhelm me. To add even more stress, I also had decided that I would do a spring cleaning and discard all the unwanted accumulation that had collected over the years. I so missed the support of my husband and felt incapable of making important decisions to even begin what lay ahead.

A promise box had been given to me, and my name had been inserted into each text. I took out a promise and unrolled the slip of paper and read: "Don't be afraid, Joy, just stand still and watch the Lord rescue you today. . . . The Lord himself will fight for you. Just stay calm!" (Ex. 14:13, NLT). What a wonderful promise!

I decided not to worry and just look to the Lord for guidance to solve my problems. Immediately He began using my friends, and they were blessed as well as I. In next to no time I had a place to stay, a garage for my car, another garage for my excess belongings, help to pack up my possessions, cardboard boxes for packing (and later to unpack), help to dispose of unwanted goods, and help to replace some aged and crumbling furniture. I didn't have to ask for help; when people saw my need they were moved to offer assistance. The Lord, without a doubt, honored my faith and rescued me that day.

The Lord is not slack concerning His promises, and what looked to me to be insurmountable was easily surmounted. He had leveled out my path without any assistance from me. What a wonderful God we serve! I invite you to accept His promises. Put your name into them and find out what God can show you today.

Joy Dustow

Be Still

Be still and know that I am God. Ps. 46:10.

I HAVE LEARNED IN life that being impatient doesn't help. I can be very impatient at times, especially when standing in long queues, waiting for my turn. Today I'm thinking of the many things I could have accomplished while practicing patience. Psalm 46:10 has helped to bring a change into my life: I have learned that patience can be the answer to some trials that come my way.

Several years ago my house was broken into. This was the worst experience of my life. I had already gone to bed and was sleeping when I saw my lights come on. Confused, many questions went through my mind. *Did I not lock my doors?* Suddenly I heard a noise in my spare room. Trembling with fear, I got up to see what was happening. Two males were ransacking the room. Another one was in the passage, watching me, and later held me hostage.

The bottom part of my kitchen door was on the floor, so now I knew how they had entered. My cell phone was taken, so I couldn't call the police. My rooms were ransacked. I asked them what they wanted. "Money" was the reply. I prayed as never before for strength from the Lord.

By God's grace I was never harmed. After they left I looked at my bedroom. My bed was turned upside down, and the place totally ransacked. I was heartbroken. But my landline phone was in perfect condition, so I phoned the police. They took 30 minutes to arrive. I phoned a friend and told her of the incident, and she phoned the head deacon of our church, who arrived with another brother before the police even arrived. I felt relieved.

One day I saw someone in the neighborhood with a padlock exactly like the new one I had bought. A few days later he was phoning on a cell phone that looked like mine, and wearing leather gloves like mine. He could have been one of the burglars. My mind went back to the day of the incident when I heard him say, "I am going to kill you." I prayed to God for patience and not to lose my temper and confront him, as he was my next-door-neighbor's son.

Now, I know there are times and trials when I must just be still and wait on the Lord. God has shown me that He can do it all. You may be going through a trial, my friend; I say to you, be still and know that He is God, and wait patiently.

Ethel Doris Msuseni

When God Saves

But we ought always to thank God for you . . . because from the beginning
God chose you to be saved. 2 Thess. 2:13, NIV.

BEFORE ME WAS the doctor. I could hear him talking but understood nothing.
With an eerie look he pronounced the death sentence on my husband. My hopes
and dreams were shattered. Immediately I began to reason with God. "No, God," I
said. "Where is Your promise? Didn't You say that if we honor our parents we will
live long upon the land that You've given us? We love You, and all we've ever done
is serve You. I know You are mighty to save." But deep within me I thought, *Can
God save my husband's life even after the doctor gave no thread of hope?*

After much reasoning with both God and myself, I visited two other doctors for
their opinions, hoping for at least one that was different. But there was no hope at
all. Two to three months of life was all the hope they gave.

After we broke the news to Edel that he had stomach cancer, to my surprise he
said that he still believed God could do a miracle to save his life. Every day we
prayed for the Lord to preserve Edel's life. Day after day we looked for signs to indicate that the doctors were all wrong. After his first chemotherapy we saw some
improvement. Edel would reassure me of his faith that God would heal him completely.

My sweetheart, with a determined look on his face, said to me, "Prasy, please
pray with me that God will do His will. I have never given up on God. I know that
He has saved me, and I am ready. I want you and the girls to meet me in heaven."

You can imagine how I was completely devastated and torn between agreeing
with him and still believing that he could make it. Two days later, on a Friday
evening after he regained consciousness, I held his hand and prayed with him and
asked him to trust his life to God's hands. I stepped outside to wrestle with God in
prayer. Then, even while I prayed for a miracle, God in His infinite mercy decided
to save him for eternity and save him from his suffering.

It took me several years to realize what Edel meant, that God had saved him,
knowing that he was going to die. I pray that even in the face of death we will believe that God has chosen to save us forever. Eternity is what matters most.

Prasedes Gillett

The Water of Life

Whoever drinks the water I give him will never thirst. John 4:14, NIV.

TODAY, MARCH 22, is celebrated as the Day of Water where I live. Essential to the maintenance of life on this planet, the possible shortage of this precious liquid has been a concern and a reason to study water's availability. Of all the water available on earth, 97.6 percent is concentrated in the oceans, so fresh water makes up only 2.4 percent. Do you think 2.4 percent is little? Then listen to this. Of this 2.4 percent, only 0.31 percent is not concentrated at the poles as ice. Which means that of all the water on the surface of the earth, less than 0.02 percent is available in rivers and lakes as fresh water, ready for world consumption. Brazilians are a privileged people because out of this total, a good part is in the Amazon.

When it comes to our bodies, we are 70 percent water. Besides serving for hygiene and corporal hydration, water also prevents several diseases. Somebody has said that "we have to drink three glasses of water a day if we want to survive, eight if we want to be healthy, and 10 if we want to be rejuvenated." We can live without food for some time, but without water we would quickly die.

In the Bible water illustrates very well something essential to our lives: Jesus. As water brings cures and health to the body, Jesus is the cure for discouragement, for the lack of hope, for the problem of sin. Once Jesus told the woman of Samaria, "If you knew the gift of God and who it is that asks you for a drink, you would have asked him and he would have given you living water" (John 4:10, NIV). Jesus does not have a limited quantity of His grace to offer us. He is the source of our hope and salvation that wells up to eternal life (John 4:14). The way water is vital for our existence, Christ, the living water, is essential for our journey on this earth. Without Him we begin to die as we distance ourselves from His love and instruction, and we finally die when we lose the eternal life that He offers to each and every one of us. It matters that daily we look for this divine spring, words of light and life that nurture our minds and hearts and transform us into fountains of hope and light that can be shared with others.

Tell Jesus each day: "Give me, Lord, this living and wholesome water which is Your Word." Only this water can wash sin from us and guide us to the New Jerusalem.

Patrícia C. de Almeida Santos

God's Strength Is Made Perfect in Our Weakness

And he said unto me, My grace is sufficient for thee: for my strength is made perfect in weakness. 2 Cor. 12:9.

IT HAD BEEN a grueling contest, and I and my clients, who had put so much trust in me, had lost an important round. I sat in my car outside the courthouse and offered a silent prayer for the Holy Spirit's guidance as I randomly opened my Bible. My eye fell on the words "And he said unto me, My grace is sufficient for thee: for my strength is made perfect in weakness."

Then Your strength must be great, I thought, *for I have never felt so weak!* Just the day before I had received notice that my motion for summary judgment had been denied. Now dread filled me as thoughts of the gloating opposing counsel flooded my mind. *He will be even more obnoxious than usual. What am I going to do now? This will result in a protracted trial that will be a hardship for my clients, both financially and emotionally.* This I had hoped to avoid.

Reluctantly I slowly made my way to the courtroom, where the case was set for a status conference. Neither party nor other counsel had arrived. Taking a seat on a bench, I closed my eyes and prayed, "I trust You, Lord. I don't know how You are going to do it, but I trust You."

Opposing counsel and our clients arrived. A clerk directed us to come confer with the judge. *Here it comes,* I thought. *Counsel is going to slam me for losing, and the judge is going to try to push for a settlement less advantageous than my clients deserve.* How I dreaded this.

The judge greeted us and began. "I have reviewed this matter, and you two should be able to work out a settlement that will satisfy everyone. A little give-and-take is all you need." Not one word about the denied summary judgment motion. Not a word!

The judge left the room, and opposing counsel spoke. "I'm tired of this case. I could use the money a trial would generate, but my client isn't reasonable. I want to get this case over with as soon as possible." He then proposed a moderate settlement figure.

I silently thanked God, and the negotiation continued. The proposal was accepted by our clients, and an agreement for judgment was reached and executed. It was over!

God's strength was made perfect in my weakness! He had it all worked out before I even arrived at court. And He loved doing it! Just as earthly parents love it when their children turn to them and trust their counsel, so God loves it when we trust Him to keep His promises.

Jayne Strickland Colby

The Orange Tree
Is Bearing Fruit

Your thoughts—how rare, how beautiful! God, I'll never comprehend them! I
couldn't even begin to count them—any more than I could count the sand of
the sea. Oh, let me rise in the morning and live always with you!
Ps. 139:17, 18, Message.

*HOW PRECIOUS IT IS, Lord, to realize that You are thinking about me constantly. I
can't even count how many times a day Your thoughts turn toward me, and when I
waken in the morning You are still thinking about me.*

We completed a sumptuous Sabbath meal and headed for our favorite spot—
the garden. My garden, or any garden, is a cherished place to be. My friend Pat was
excited. "The orange tree is bearing its first fruits. Yesterday," she said, "I counted
four tiny oranges."

I ventured out to examine the tree for myself. Actually, I counted a few more.
Six, then nine, then 12. The more I observed, the more I counted.

In disbelief, Pat and her husband came to see what I was so excited about.
Indeed, right before their very eyes the tiny oranges displayed themselves with pride.

Later that evening I reminisced on the day's events and the lessons that I had
learned. When we stop to examine and count our blessings, we become aware of
how much more blessed we are than we even think. This reminds me of the beautiful chorus, "Count your blessings, name them one by one;/Count your blessings,
see what God hath done;/Count your blessings, name them one by one; . . . /And it
will surprise you what the Lord hath done."

We are sometimes so absorbed in what appears to be obvious that we fail to see
the many ways that God blesses us each day.

As I reflect I ask, *When was the last time I stopped to count my blessings instead
of brooding over what I don't have? When was the last time I went to bed really hungry, walked without shoes, or could not quench my thirst because there was no water to
drink? When was the last time God forgot to supply my every need?* I know I have been
blessed.

Just pause at the beginning or the end of the day to count your blessings. Are
you surprised to see how many more blessings you have than you thought? Yes! I
am shouting with you: "Lord, thank You for my many blessings!" Even the orange
tree is bearing fruit!

Gloria Gregory

Offering

No one is to appear before me empty-handed. Ex. 34:20, NIV.

ONE SABBATH MORNING, as is customary, just before the offering was taken up in church the elder on duty stood up to say a few words regarding this part of the liturgy. What he said surprised me, and actually it made me laugh a bit because it sounded like a scolding to a naughty kid. He said we shouldn't come to church without our offering—it was careless, and bringing it should be a habit. Besides, he added, it was highly uncomfortable for the deacons to pass the plate to a person who did not bring anything; they didn't know what to do, whether to smile comprehendingly, ignore, or look away from that situation. He then proceeded to state a hypothetical statistic: if we all brought the minimum amount (10 cents in this case), what would it add up to? The more I thought about what he said, the more ashamed I became of my poor, random offerings.

Our verse for today is found in the context of sacrifices and offerings in the Old Testament, with animals and food being the currency of the day. God not only expected sacrifices; He demanded the very best!

But why does God make such a request, and does this text refer only to offerings at church? That is only once a week. Hopefully we approach God more often than that. Why does God need our "sacrifices," our very best products? God is the giver of everything; why does He want them back?

Not long ago my family was invited to dinner at someone's house. Our hosts had two boys who had heaps and heaps of toys. My little son's eyes twinkled as he thought about what was in store for the evening. As is common among little ones, soon they were fighting over the same toy, my son holding on tightly to something. I thought, *How silly, not wanting to share something that is not even his!*

Suddenly it dawned on me—we are just like that with God. How dare we, who are so abundantly blessed by Him, approach Him empty-handed? I invite you to think about what you are going to give back to God when you approach His presence. Will it be only money once a week, or are you willing to offer Him your time, your favorite toy, your child, your profession?

Cintia García Block

Listening and Doing

Who are those who fear the Lord? He will show them the path they should choose. Ps. 25:12, NLT.

IT WAS 7:00 one Thursday evening when I finally returned to the office to tidy my desk and collect my things before going home. After I had been in the office for about 10 minutes, the secretary and her little daughter came in. She arranged a few things on her desk, then wished me a good night as they left for home.

After spending a few more minutes in the office, I locked the door and walked toward my car. As I went, I thought about the two of them. The sun had already set and it was dark, and although I lived in the opposite direction I decided that if I saw them as I drove toward the gate of the campus I would offer to take them home.

No sooner had I driven off than I saw them walking toward the gate. After inviting them into the car, I took them to their home. When I stopped at their gate, the secretary said, "I must tell you something."

"What is it?" I asked.

She explained, "When I left the office, I had gone to the restroom to pray. I asked God to send us a ride home. You see, this morning I had forgotten to take the money for our taxi fare. If you had not given us a ride, we would have had to walk home in the dark."

I could hardly believe my ears. I said, "You mean that God used me to answer your prayer for a ride home?" She assured me that He did.

Right there I thanked God for using me that evening to answer the prayer of His child.

This incident has led me to think of the many times that perhaps God put a thought in my mind so that I could offer assistance to one of His children and I have dismissed it. My reason might have been that I would be inconvenienced, or it was not important, or it was not my business anyway.

As I think about the experience I humbly pray, "Dear Lord, give me ears to hear the cry of Your children, a heart that is sensitive to the needs of those around me, and the willingness to always perform the tasks that You want me to do."

Carol Joy Fider

This Thing of Clay

And there was war in heaven: Michael and his angels fought against the dragon; and the dragon fought and his angels, and prevailed not; neither was their place found any more in heaven. Rev. 12:7, 8.

"I SINNED; and straightway, posthaste, Satan flew before the presence of the most high God and made a railing accusation there: 'This thing of clay has sinned.'" I don't recall the remaining words or the author of this poem that I learned and recited as a child. I do recall that it told the story of how Satan argued for my punishment and Jesus pleaded for mercy, and in the end His blood was sufficient to pay for my sin. I was set free to sin no more.

I recently had occasion to remember that poem. I had sinned. Satan immediately started a war dance to demand justice. Satan laughed loudly and snarled at me for thinking that I could be God's dedicated and committed witness. He demanded my death, my removal from spiritual fellowship, the end of my ministry. He believed that he had effectively silenced my voice.

Spiritual and financial burdens threatened to overwhelm me. I fasted and prayed to hear God's direction and for relief from overwhelming burdens that threatened to destroy my family. I expected a miracle and a victorious ending. Instead, my burdens became heavier, and I was crushed under a load of guilt, shame, and defeat. Satan mocked at my pain and laughed at my confidence in God to deliver me. A panorama of every wrong deed, every poor decision, every failure that I had ever experienced, passed before my mind's eye in slow, agonizing procession.

I was ready to accept defeat. Then I remembered my own words of witness to others, and I knew that no matter what the outcome, I could not concede the war, even if for the moment I must concede the battle. Perhaps I am just a thing of clay without inherent worth, but Jesus died for this piece of clay, and I could not be so ungrateful as to let Him die in vain. So I may need to lick my wounds for now. I may even need to rest for a while before carrying on the work that I know God gave me. But let this thing be known today and every day: God is God; and regardless of any circumstances, I will continue to praise Him and carry out His commission.

If you feel defeated today, don't give up the fight. Get up and get back in the fight. We serve under an unconquered general. Michael will stand up for His people; our victory is assured.

Beverly P. Gordon

The Musician

Train children in the right way, and when old, they will not stray.
Prov. 22:6, NRSV.

MY MOTHER-IN-LAW, June, is a musician. She has been a choir member, a choir director, and a church organist. She has taught voice, piano, and organ. Many of her stories and plans revolve around music. She tells me proudly that she was the first voice major to graduate from Union College. She speaks glowingly of singing Christmas carols for Ingathering. She sorts through her sheet music, choosing pieces to teach our daughter-in-law. At age 91 she invited 30 people to her home for a recital. She learned new solo pieces, accompanied the concert mistress of the local symphony orchestra, and talked to her guests about visiting the homes of great composers. At age 92 she finalized the plans for the musical program for her memorial service. She is hale and hearty but wants to ensure that her friends and family are blessed by a beautiful religious concert at the close of her life. A few weeks ago she even gathered the musicians to practice, under her tutelage, so they will produce flawless music when the day arrives.

June can look at a piece of music and know what it's supposed to sound like. I don't have this ability. I don't believe that it's something innate; I simply have not taken the time to develop this talent. June, on the other hand, applies herself. She not only endeavors to play the notes correctly but she also counts, working her way intently through a piece of music, making sure that each note is held for exactly the right length of time. The result? Notes that perfectly reflect the marks on the page. Even when she plays well-known hymns, her lips move, silently counting "One, two, three, and four."

When my husband, her son, shows her a picture of her childhood house, she looks at it intently and then breaks into a smile. "In this house," she says, "Mama taught 60 piano students each week." Yes, her mother was also a musician, directing a 90-voice community choir for patriotic events, teaching students, and instilling in them the important concept of counting. In fact, one family story features June at age 2 beating a spoon on the wooden tray of her high chair as she admonishes one of her mother's students, "One, two, free, Tresha. One, two, free!"

I don't know what happened to Tresha, but June, well trained by her mother, continues to count, and continues to share her love of music with others.

Denise Dick Herr

Talk to Him, Mom. He'll Hear You

The woman said, "I know that Messiah" (called Christ) "is coming. When he comes, he will explain everything to us." John 4:25, NIV.

BROKEN WOMAN. God has no place for me. Is this how the unnamed woman at the well felt before her exchange with the Lord?

I wanted my 5-year-old daughter to know Him, but I felt my poor choices made it impossible to walk closely to God. I couldn't express His wonderful love for us. Like the woman at the well, I was looking in the wrong places.

As it says in Isaiah 11:6, "A little child will lead them" (NIV). My daughter would learn about Jesus at Vacation Bible School! I took her to the church, having no intention of "getting involved" or "being converted." I was a single parent, and I was broke, trapped in a miserable living situation 30 miles from the nearest town.

My daughter returned, heart open and mind full of new knowledge. The story was familiar (Noah and the ark), but the way she joyfully explained the lesson moved me. How many rainbows had I stared at, depressed, forgetting God's promise?

We were invited to Sabbath school. I would be in an adult class, and my daughter would be in a "kindergarten" group. That first Sabbath I intended to sit in the parking lot during my daughter's class. A gentle older woman read me clearly—we sat together for a wonderful lesson.

I am forgiven? I have no reason to worry if I allow Him to take my burdens? This was not the God I had been hearing about for 32 years! Six months later I was baptized. A year ago, on a Sabbath, my now-9-year-old girl was baptized. We are works in progress.

My walk has been especially clumsy. The more I allow Him to mold me, not stubbornly pursuing my will, the more solid I become. I am now married, and this man has accepted my child as his own. She thrives in the fourth grade at the Christian school.

I have had a few of my hardest struggles these past four years. What an absolute blessing to know I don't have to face my problems alone. I don't have to worry and dwell in depression. When I catch myself in that darkness, my daughter can bring me back. "Talk to Him, Mom. He'll hear you."

Jennifer Burkes

Higher Plain

We know that in all things God works for the good of those who love him, who have been called according to his purpose. Rom. 8:28, NIV.

WE NORMALLY IDENTIFY ourselves with at least one or two heroes in the Bible. People need someone to look up to. My favorite one has always been Joseph, the great vice president-dreamer. But if I had to be true to myself I would have to admit that my past life has been more like that of the prophet Jonah. It's quite undeniable how the Lord actually works things out for the good of those who are called according to His purpose.

I was 14, newly baptized, and drawn to Christ. So I chose then to drop my interest and training in dancing, which had been my greatest interest since childhood. I solemnly pledged to devote my life to hastening my Savior's return. Unfortunately, over the days and years, I have often put aside this ideal and have gone through deception and hard times emotionally, morally, or spiritually.

I can remember waking up one day and realizing that I was at a crossroads, and I didn't know what to do or where to go. It seemed to me that there was no way out.

Then one day I was scheduled to translate during a seminar on reaching out to Muslims, held by the women's ministry department. Reluctantly, but encouraged and supported by my mothers who believed in me, I made it through. (I have two mothers—complementary to each other.) I secretly dreamed of becoming like one of those trainers. I recall one of them, while praying with me, asking God to help me understand that He needed me in His field. That was all she said before we went on stage. Immediately my mind was troubled as my earlier pledge caught me. I heard the Lord's call, but my heart was still deceitful and doubting His higher plan for me. My spiritual mother urged me to enroll in religious studies and to see where the Lord wanted to lead me. It took me three whole months to decide, three months of struggling with my own thoughts and desires, three months in the desert with my Lord!

Today I proudly say that my life is now complete, and I'm walking on a higher plain with God. Every day I'm eager to see the miracles He'll make in my life, and I assure you He is doing it already. What have you been called for? I urge you to spend time at His feet to find His ways for you—there is happiness in walking on a higher plain.

Sylvana Ramhit

Unscrambled Eggs

If we confess our sins, he is faithful and just to forgive us our sins,
and to cleanse us from all unrighteousness. 1 John 1:9.

Wherefore I say unto you, All manner of sin and blasphemy
shall be forgiven unto men. Matt. 12:31.

BEFORE MY CHILDREN were born, I was second mom to several of my nieces—OK, favorite auntie. They came up to our farm. They would sleep over, and I taught them a bit about cooking and sewing. They kept my attitude more positive. Doctors had said that I would be unable to have children because of a car accident years earlier, so I enjoyed all my sisters' kids.

Once we were going to make white cakes so that each one could take a frosted layer home with white frosting, like wedding cakes, and decorate them. In her excitement Rhonnie cracked both eggs directly into the bowl and added the butter and sugar in to cream them. Billie Jean yelled, "It is supposed to be a white cake—no yolks!" Before tears could start, I assured both that the cake would be all right; it would just have a creamy white color. Once done, you cannot unscramble eggs. We enjoyed the cakes—they tasted wonderful.

Like those eggs, we cannot "unscramble" our sins. We cannot take them back. And God knows us better than anyone. We know we cannot hide our sins from Him. We can ask for forgiveness, and as praying Christians we can be assured God will forgive us. But as humans, even when we ask for someone to forgive us we can't always know whether or not the way we may have hurt them will permanently damage our relationship.

Forgiving ourselves is the hardest thing to do, but reminding God daily of sins He has thrown into the deepest seas seems redundant. It lacks the conviction of accepting His love and sacrifice. When we approach others to forgive us, we want them to see that we are repentant, that we want their forgiveness.

Most people want to forgive, but if their pain is deep they may not want to have anything to do with you for a while—or maybe never. That's when you have to move on and ask God to somehow let those folks know that we mean it and pray for them to heal. He is the only one who can unscramble our messes. In today's texts He promises to do that.

Sally j. Aken-Linke

Egret's Landing

*Even the stork in the heavens knows its times; and the turtledove,
swallow, and crane observe the time of their coming;
but my people do not know the ordinances of the Lord. Jer. 8:7, NRSV.*

I DON'T KNOW what it is about April, but the stately white birds do. Every April morning, as I sit crunching my cereal in the breakfast nook, I know I'll see at least one egret standing in silent expectation on a limb of the pine tree beyond our window. Sometimes it is not alone. My mother and I once counted 22 of them standing among the spindly pine needles, looking out on the water below.

While surfing the Internet, I found the answer for the birds' choice of site. They come to feed on the tiny fish, crayfish, frogs, and insects they can see in the shallow water beneath their perch. Reading between the lines of Jeremiah's words in today's text, I saw the simple answer to my query regarding April: "Even the stork in the heavens knows its times." The birds know when to come, and where to stand. They know because God created them with instincts to lead them, to tell them the times.

Then I wondered what it was about the particular place they choose to land? True, it looks out on acres of rich green lawn and a shallow pond on whose banks they sometimes stalk, but why did they choose these scraggly pine trees for their landing?

That question continued to baffle me until two major hurricanes tore through our area last year. The winds bent the trees into angular shapes, twisting a few, smashing some, and tearing others apart. But what happened to the pine trees in our backyard? Absolutely nothing! As they examined the damage to our neighbors' yards, the insurance adjustors commented that our trees were too well-rooted to be destroyed.

I bowed my head in awesome wonder. I had finally made the spiritual connection. God has made us wiser than the birds, imbuing us with more than mere instincts. He's given us the Ten Commandments to guide us and the power of choice to decide where we will stand.

Now, every morning when I see a stately egret standing in quiet anticipation on a nearby branch, I pause to consider where *I* stand and what *I'm* doing with God's protective Ten Commandments.

Glenda-mae Greene

Holding On to God's Hand

But I am always with you; you have held my hand. Ps. 73:23, NCV.

EVER SINCE I can remember I've been afraid of crossing roads, especially when the traffic is bad. Even now I would gladly accept a helping hand when crossing a road. One evening my husband and I went grocery shopping and parked our car across the road from the store. On returning to the car, my husband walked ahead of me with the grocery bags and, of course, expected me to follow behind him. However, I became separated from him because of the traffic. Just when I was about to cross the road, an auto rickshaw passed by me at full speed, so close that it could have taken all my toes with it. I was terrified. My legs became jelly, and my heart raced wildly. When I finally got to the car, my husband asked, "What took you so long?" I said something about the auto, but he wasn't really listening, as he was more interested in moving on. I didn't see the need to tell him any more.

Since that incident I've thought much about my fear of crossing roads. I've asked myself, *Why am I so fearful? Why can't I be like the cows who lay in the middle of the road, peacefully chewing their cuds? They don't seem to be afraid—no driver would think of hitting them. They'd drive around them out of respect. What do the cows have that I don't? Would I be as brave if I possessed two horns?*

In the presence of fear, one can't relax. I knew I needed something better than horns. I needed to trust God and not be afraid unnecessarily. (Of course a certain amount of fear is good so we will be careful.) I'm forever grateful to God for all His protection throughout my life. I have never been hit by anything—at least not since I've been an adult. When I was 3 years old, I went out on the road by myself and walked right down the middle of it. A cyclist hit me and then fell on top of me. It was a gentle fall—he had slowed down considerably, so I was not hurt. Two women on the road picked me up and told me to go home. Perhaps that was the beginning of my fear. But I thank God for always following me, watching over me, and holding me with His hand. I never want to let His hand go. He takes me through the storms of life safely. With Him by my side I need never be fearful again.

Even if I walk across a wide road, I will not be afraid (see Ps. 23:4, NCV).

Birol Charlotte Christo

God's Words

I will be with thy mouth, and teach thee what thou shalt say. Ex. 4:12.

WE HAD JUST bid goodbye to overnight guests that chilly, rainy day and were thinking of what we might do between the time they left and a 2:30 appointment I had. I decided to take a short nap, and my husband thought it would be nice for us to have lunch at our local hospital cafeteria where the most delicious vegetarian food is always available. That sounded good to me as well, so as soon as I woke up we took off for the hospital.

We had nearly finished eating when a woman, who appeared to be about our age, came over and sat at a table near us. She had only some grapes, milk, and a couple of cookies, and my husband proceeded to tease her a little about whether or not she could eat all of that. He then went to take care of our dishes and trays.

I sensed the woman was a little troubled, so I struck up a conversation with her, and she told me she was waiting for her son, who was in the emergency room. He had been there earlier, and they had almost admitted him, but he didn't have a local doctor. She shared that some years ago his wife had committed suicide, and he had struggled ever since. She and her husband helped raise his children, but now they were grown and on their own. She also shared some of her own medical problems, as well as the fact that her husband had had open heart surgery. She was obviously lonely and anxious.

I decided to introduce myself, and she, in turn, gave me her name and told me she lived in another city some miles from the hospital. About that time my husband returned, and I felt impressed to have prayer with her before we left. I asked if I might pray for her son, and her eyes filled with tears, and she said, "Oh, yes!" We bowed our heads right there in the cafeteria, and I know God gave me the words to pray for her and her family.

How blessed we felt as we left. Not only were our stomachs full of good food, but our hearts were filled with joy that God brought us together with someone who needed a blessing, and He used us to be that blessing at that very time. How often does God give us the opportunity to share His love if we'll just take time to notice?

Anna May Radke Waters

Who Was This Man?

Looking for the blessed hope and glorious appearing of our great God and Savior Jesus Christ. Titus 2:13, NKJV.

FOR NEARLY 2,000 YEARS people have pondered the question Who was Jesus, anyway? Was He just a prophet among many prophets as some religions believe? Some of them consider Him a great teacher but certainly not "divine." The Jews had Him, and then denied Him. Jesus is even found in other large world religions, but sometimes He is barely recognizable. We Christians know who He was, is, and will be. Granted, there's a lot about Him that we don't understand, such as the 100 percent man and 100 percent God, or about the Trinity. But isn't that where faith comes in? And do we study so we really know who He was?

A very good teacher once said, "Faith is taking God at His word." What a wonderful way to put it. His Word is the Bible. Faith is believing in what the Bible says. We need to know what this Book says. We need to read it, to study it, so we will know what we know and be able to share His love with those around us. We need to be able to recognize when something is not scriptural and to call it what it is.

In 1 Timothy 2:5 Jesus is called "the Man Christ Jesus." He is also called "Son of Man" approximately 80 times in the Gospels. But so often He spoke in terms that emphasized His humanity and hid His deity.

The phrase "hypostatic union" refers to Christ being 100 percent man and 100 percent God. He came as a perfect man so as to experience all the trials and tribulations we experience, to empathize with us and all that we go through. As perfect God He was able to die on the cross for our sins, for the sins of the world.

But He was human. He had a human mother and a human appearance. He was Jewish, so it is doubtful He had those piercing blue eyes so often depicted in the movies. And He grew in the way of normal human development. But the Bible clearly says that Jesus was not only a man.

Today's verse in Titus 2:13 is one of the strongest statements in Scripture of the deity of Christ—His whole title, as it were. And that deity is right there, reachable by us: Elohim, the great I AM—just by bowing our head and saying, "Father."

M. J. Corrales

The Day I Wanted to Be With Jesus

My soul is overwhelmed with sorrow to the point of death.
Stay here and keep watch with me. Matt. 26:38, NIV.

WE SAY THAT Jesus is our friend; is that really so? Yes, of course He is our friend, because He is always ready to listen and to support us! Sometimes our friends, family, or spouses don't give us the support we might need when we need it and in the manner we might need or want. However, we can always be sure that our Lord will be there for us, giving us the necessary and looked-for comfort and support.

But are we Jesus' true friend? Not if we think of the definition of true friendship. Real friendship happens when both sides take turns in helping, listening, and supporting one another. It has to be a two-way street.

So let's ask ourselves: How often have we thought about supporting Jesus? One day a pastor preaching in our church asked: "If you were to choose one day to have been with Jesus during His life, which day would you choose?"

I thought about that and chose the night He went to Gethsemane to pray. He "began to be sorrowful and troubled" (Matt. 26:37, NIV). He knew His time was coming. So He said to His disciples: "My soul is overwhelmed with sorrow to the point of death. Stay here and keep watch with me." And yet the disciples slept.

That is a moment when I would have wanted to be there for Him, as a friend. I would like to have shown my love for Him by staying awake, praying, keeping watch. Because Jesus said He wanted support, wanted someone to be there with Him in His sorrow!

What was He asking? "Just be here, so that I don't feel so lonely." He was saying, "I know there is nothing you can do for Me. You don't have the power to change My destiny; you can't advise Me what to do or how to behave. All I need is for you to show your love for Me by being here and keeping watch." Jesus was asking them just to be His friends. That would have been the role of a friend—to have been there for Him. Oh, what a privilege!

Let's pray that when someone needs our love and support we will be there for them as Jesus is always there for us. It will be our way of showing that we are Jesus' true friends.

Joelcira F. Cavedon Mÿller

If I Be Lifted Up

And I, if I be lifted up from the earth, will draw all men unto me. John 12:32.

WHILE STILL IN Galilee, Jesus told His disciples that He "must go unto Jerusalem, and suffer many things of the elders and chief priests and scribes, and be killed, and be raised again the third day" (Matt. 16:21). He knew all too well that death by crucifixion was the most excruciating and shameful punishment anyone could experience, yet He "steadfastly set his face to go to Jerusalem" (Luke 9:51), knowing that crucifixion awaited Him there. Why would anyone choose to deliberately walk into the jaws of death? That Christ knowingly chose to suffer such shame and agony is beyond all human comprehension—until we ponder the words of today's featured text.

Today's verse is the marvelous promise of Christ. The word "men" was not a part of the original text but was inserted by translators; it detracts from the true significance of the promise. When "men" is omitted, this promise is magnified greatly to include God's entire universe—all creation, not just men.

Why is this so important? While Lucifer was in heaven he deceived a third part of the angels by defaming the character of God. Again, when Lucifer was thrown out of heaven, he came to earth and deceived Adam and Eve. Even among the loyal inhabitants of God's universe there might have been lingering doubts concerning the true character of both Christ and Satan. But when Christ was "lifted up" between heaven and earth, crucified at the instigation of Satan, the entire universe watched the scenes surrounding that cross and discerned the real character of each contender. The entire universe noted the malice of Satan in contrast to the selfless character of their Creator. All comprehended the love and justice of God and forever were drawn to Him, not by fear but by love.

But Christ's promise extends its meaning far beyond the cross at Calvary. This promise has a twofold meaning. It is just as meaningful today as it was when Christ uttered it more than 2,000 years ago. Today Christ extends the challenge and privilege to all who claim His name—if we "lift Him up" by the demonstration of His character in our lives He will, through us, draw others to Himself. Will you accept this challenge, this privilege?

H. Elizabeth Sweeney-Cabey

He Listens

If I had cherished sin in my heart, the Lord would not have listened; but God has surely listened and heard my voice in prayer. Ps. 66:18, 19, NIV.

WE LIVE IN a loud and noisy world, filled with all kinds of sounds and distractions. Add to that the internal emotional barriers born out of our past experiences and traumas, and listening becomes one of the biggest challenges in communication. Many just don't listen (or listen selectively), and come to conclusions that are way off the mark. Perhaps you've heard a child say, "Mom, listen to me; look at me!" Children are pretty sensitive to the fact that adults may be so busy with their own thoughts that they only appear to be listening.

Israel was reprimanded by God again and again for not listening to Him, and every time they chose not to listen they missed out on blessings. All through the Old Testament, God is seeking His nonlistening people, appealing to them to listen to Him and turn from their evil ways. He always hovered near, His ears tuned to their cries. He did all He could to connect with His people. He showed His presence in a cloud by day and a pillar of fire by night. He sent them prophets. He tried so hard to get their attention, using thunder, storms, earthquakes, miracles, signs and wonders—yet they turned a blind eye and a deaf ear.

When Jesus came to earth, the Son of God in person, He continued to appeal to His chosen people, but to little avail. Yet He heard the cries of the sick, the palsied, those who were hurting, the mothers and the children, and ministered to them Himself.

When finally He hung on the cross, the Son of God was still listening. The prayer of the penitent thief provided Jesus with "one gleam of comfort" (*The Desire of Ages*, p. 749). The thief had heard Jesus speaking before, but Ellen White reveals that he was misled by the priests and rulers and turned away from Jesus. As he refused to accept what Jesus said, his downward path accelerated until he was arrested as a criminal. Now, as he hung on the cross, the Holy Spirit made one last appeal to the thief. His previous experiences with Jesus came flooding back to his mind, and he yielded in surrender.

Yes, God listens—every word in every prayer, every intent behind every word, every feeling—and He understands. If you will be still, if you will take the time to stop and to drop your busyness, you can hear His voice. He is there for you—always.

Sally Lam-Phoon

Here We Go Again

*Be anxious for nothing, but in everything by prayer and supplication,
with thanksgiving, let your request be made known to God; and the
peace of God, which surpasses all understanding, will guard your hearts
and minds through Christ Jesus. Phil. 4:6, 7, NKJV.*

ON A BEAUTIFUL Texas day I was attending the North American-wide women's congress, enjoying my time with my sisters. But while walking through the hall that day I felt a sharp pain in my lower leg that got only worse as the conference progressed. When I got home, I visited my orthopedic doctor, who did an X-ray.

"I'm sorry, Mrs. Small, we are going to have to redo your knee replacement surgery."

I couldn't believe it! My replacement had been done only two years before. I sat numb in the chair, recalling the pain and agony of the first surgery. All I could think was "Please, Lord; not again."

At home I cried on my husband's shoulder and told him I couldn't do that surgery again. The first one hadn't gone well, and I knew that this time would be the same. However, it had to be done if I was going to be able to walk. So one month later I was back in the hospital—but something was different. While waiting for this surgery, I spent much time in prayer and praise. I told God if this was what had to be done, I could do it only if He gave me peace and strength.

And He did.

One of the things I've learned to do is to claim a Bible promise each day. There are some that are dear to my heart, but the promise in Philippians 4:6 and 7, today's text, is one of the dearest. I claimed that promise every day before my surgery, and on the day of surgery I had no anxious thoughts. I knew that this time it would be better—and it was. God gave me a peace and strength that took me through that trial. His Word is true.

Claiming God's promises as we face each day is a vital part of our Christian walk. Not only do we receive assurance from the Word of God, but we also experience the truth of God's Word in our lives. This experience gives us a story to tell, a testimony to the praise of God.

My prayer today is that each of my sisters who reads these words will have the confidence to claim God's promises and to know that He will uphold them through their trials.

Heather-Dawn Small

A Sharp Sword

For the word of God is living and active. Sharper than any double-edged sword . . . it judges the thoughts and attitudes of the heart. Heb. 4:12, NIV.

SPRING IS MY favorite time of year. The new leaves come out on trees that have been bare all winter. Flowers begin showing their bright colors everywhere. As the weather becomes warmer, it's time to plant our vegetable garden. We know it will take time for the new little plants to grow before we can start enjoying the fruits of our labor, but it's worth the wait.

There's one big problem with making our garden. Before we can plant, we have to clear out the sprouting weeds. Some come out of the ground easily, but others, even though they are small, have roots that go way down in the ground. Many years ago my mother-in-law gave me a handy little tool with two sharp edges for digging out weeds. Often my husband comments on the piles of weeds I've dug out with this little tool.

As I'm working in the garden I think of how I need to get rid of the "weeds" in my life, which are so like the weeds in my garden. It's important that I get them out, roots and all, or I know they'll come back again, bigger than ever. Just as I use my handy little tool to dig the weeds out of the soil, I must use the Word of God not only to judge the thoughts and attitudes of my heart, but to put good thoughts into my mind.

I feel so happy when I finish clearing the weeds from an area of ground, because it looks so much better, and it's ready to plant the good things. However, that doesn't mean the job of weed pulling is finished for the rest of the season. Before long new little weeds, sometimes of a different kind, come up, so it's a never-ending task.

In my life I need to always be vigilant in getting rid of trashy thoughts and actions. The best way I've found to do that is with the double-edged sword of reading God's Word and praying daily. When I get busy and let other activities crowd out daily Bible reading and prayer, it isn't long before I find my mind becoming cluttered with unhappy thoughts.

My prayer today is that each one of you will join me in using the Word of God and prayer to keep the weeds out of our hearts' gardens.

Betty J. Adams

Our Guardian Angels

For he shall give his angels charge over thee, to keep thee in all thy ways. They shall bear thee up in their hands. Ps. 91:11, 12.

THIS CAR'S GOING to hit me! I knew it, and there was nothing I could do but pray. My husband, our 2-month-old baby, and I had been with friends for an evening, and we were now driving home. Like all new mothers, I was totally protective of my baby; totally in awe of the tiny son God had given me.

Tony was fast asleep in his carry cot on the back seat, but he awoke when we stopped so that my husband could pick up his car. I put our precious son on the front seat and started to drive the few miles home. (These were the days before mandatory seat belts, children's seats, or special baby seats. The majority of cars had what was known as bench seats in the front that could accommodate three adults.)

Minutes later I was on one of Auckland's biggest, busiest roundabouts, when out of the corner of my eye I saw a car coming at us. Without even looking for a gap in the traffic, the driver sped straight into the roundabout. I remember my car bouncing up in the air a little with the initial bang. I steered around and into the next exit road, screaming, "My baby, my baby!" He was no longer on the seat beside me. Then I looked down, and there on the floor of the car was Tony—not crying, and not a mark on him.

Other cars stopped, my husband arrived, and people came from nowhere. The police and an ambulance were called. My husband followed the ambulance to the hospital. "You—and especially your baby—need to be thoroughly checked" was the advice we were given. We were fine; our guardian angels were indeed watching over us.

The other car was a complete wreck. The car had been stolen, and the driver had been wanted by the police for three months. He had no driver's license and was very drunk.

Our front passenger's door had to be replaced. It had been pushed in so hard that it formed a V across the bench seat, the very seat where I had been sitting not that long before.

Psalm 91:11 was the promise I claimed not only that night but all through my life. God does indeed have angels to keep us in all our ways.

Leonie Donald

God's Idol

Though the Lord be high, yet hath he respect unto the lowly. Ps. 138:6.

CANADIAN IDOL. American Idol. Britain's Got Talent. Young people dream of being the number one singing idol of their country. They dress to the nines (to their way of thinking), sport the latest hairstyles, and do moves to impress the judges and sway the audience. It takes courage, confidence, and determination to face the panel of judges.

When Susan Boyle strutted confidently to midstage in London on April 11, 2009, the judges and audience were not wowed by her appearance. The media described her as "frumpish" and "dowdy," while many TV viewers found her plainness refreshing. Her fitted beige dress matched her shoes. Her hair maybe lacked some style, but her engaging smile and twinkling eyes overshadowed her double chins.

"What is your dream?" one of the judges asked.

"I want to be a professional singer like Elaine Paige."

Some raised their eyebrows, rolled their eyes, smirked, and even laughed out loud. "How old are you?" was another question. She was 47. In spite of the gasps and snickers, Boyle set her feet in a defensive stance, placed her left hand on her hip, and said, "That's only one side of me!"

She hadn't sung one phrase before the audience, and judges recognized they had misjudged the talent of this woman by her physical appearance and age. The changed demeanor of the listeners and beaming faces of the judges were heartwarming to watch as they gave her a standing ovation. Although Susan Boyle didn't become the number one idol, she captivated millions of music lovers around the world. In the words of Amanda Holden, may this "biggest wake-up call ever" be a lesson to all of us who tend to "judge the book by its cover."

I will never be a Canadian Idol (or one from any other country), but that isn't my goal. I would much rather be "God's Idol," "the apple of His eye" (Deut. 32:10), and that is an achievement each one of us can claim without being intimidated. God may be high and mighty, but He sees the worth in each of us "lowly" ones. He can see the "other side" of us. Rather than aspiring to a short moment in the limelight on earth, let's sing praises daily to the supreme Judge who will esteem us throughout eternity.

Edith Fitch

The Miracle and the Baptism

Behold what manner of love the Father has bestowed on us, that we should be called children of God! Therefore the world does not know us, because it did not know Him. 1 John 3:1, NKJV.

WHEN THE WORD came from the doctor that I was pregnant, I simply couldn't believe it. Being a stubborn redhead, I went to the store to buy a couple more pregnancy tests. All tested positive. Wilson, my husband, and I had been trying off and on for eight years to have another child. I had accepted the fact that I was a sinner and this was my deserved punishment—even though I knew better than that. God, our wonderful Savior, had other plans for me. A heart's desire would come true: forgiveness. My Lord would show me nine months later.

I remember that night so well: Micah, my oldest son, was telling me about a dream he had had. We were laughing and cutting up; then it happened—my water broke, and the adventure began. However, Malachi was not as ready to come as we thought. For 50 hours we waited. While I pushed my dad sang "Henry the Eighth I Am," even though Malachi decided to make his appearance on the ninth. When he did come, however, he just didn't emerge slowly; he shot out like a football sailing though the air. Dr. Huff almost missed him.

I thank God that He was by my side through it all. I remember repeating the Lord's Prayer through my tears because I was able to see Malachi and his "cone head" for only a few minutes before the nurses took him off to be washed.

Wilson came in to tell me he was going home to freshen up. I was dozing but aware that the nurse caught Wilson by the arm. "Sir, you better not leave—something is wrong with your son; he probably won't make it through the night." They didn't know I had heard. I was too tired to respond other than send up a short prayer, giving Malachi to my Lord that night. I remember the peace that passes all understanding filling me.

The next day when the doctors came in and found Malachi and me asleep together in the hospital bed, they commented, "What a beautiful sight." I just smiled and agreed.

Now, 12 years later, on April 12 we watch Jonathan Malachi as he gives himself to the Lord. Our God is so faithful to us, His children. Let us pledge to rededicate our lives to our Lord and Savior as He faithfully acts as our advocate in heaven, giving us our heart's desires.

Tammy Barnes-Taylor

God's Wash and Wear

Create in me a clean heart, O God; and renew a right spirit within me.
Ps. 51:10.

"HOW CAN A family of five possibly generate such an enormous amount of laundry?" my husband asked rhetorically for perhaps the thousandth time. "It just doesn't seem possible."

We do laundry at least twice a week, and still it comes in large loads of seemingly endless socks and shirts, towels and washcloths, sheets and pillowcases, undergarments and outer garments. I've been tempted to ignore it occasionally, but I know it will only accumulate into a bigger and bigger pile.

You would think that with the invention of improved cleaning devices, such as automatic washing machines, our lives would be much easier. My grandmother used to do laundry once a week for six people on a hand-fed roller washing machine—and before that, in a washtub with a scrub board. But I believe the advancement of technology has also made us careless in our habits, making it easy to throw something in the laundry with little thought that perhaps it could be used again before washing.

I'm really glad for the invention of wash and wear. When I was young, there was the drudgery of ironing everything you washed before it could be worn or placed back on the bed. I was an avid reader, and my mother would catch me trying to read while I was supposed to be ironing! These days we can throw a garment in the washer, then the dryer, and take it out, put it on, and wear it.

God has an enormous capacity for laundry. He can clean our hearts in an instant, renewing and revitalizing our lives and making us like brand new. He has a stain remover that beats anything you'll find in any store. Unfortunately, our hearts don't usually stay clean for long. Jealousy, envy, pride, and other emotions "stain" our hearts in their peculiar way. I'm sure God gets tired of doing "laundry" again and again as much as I do, but He cheerfully answers every request from His human children. He cleanses our hearts and makes them new whenever we ask.

I would like to have the Lord do my "laundry" today and wash my heart white as snow. Do you also have dirty laundry that you'd like to have Him take care of for you?

Fauna Rankin Dean

Casting Your Bread

Cast your bread upon the waters, for you will find it after many days.
Eccl. 11:1, ESV.

KEEPING FIT MEANT a brisk walk through the neighborhood for my widowed mother. The benefits of this daily activity not only helped her physically, but acquainted her with the neighbors in her low-income neighborhood. Her friendly, kind, happy attitude and pleasant smile helped to make at least one family receptive to the religious books and pamphlets she left at neighbors' doors during her walks.

The Wayman family hadn't been attending any church. The father, a religious man (the mother was not), loved reading about various denominations. The details in the brochure Mother left him regarding an upcoming evangelistic series piqued his interest.

After attending a couple meetings, Mr. Wayman became very interested. His interest captivated the attention of his two daughters, Vinita, 15, and Lurlene, 9. Mother saw to it that their transportation needs were always met. When the call for baptism came, all three were baptized. They joined the social life of the church, and the members made them feel very welcome.

What makes this story special is that from humble beginnings in a low-income neighborhood and the simple act of passing out religious and spiritual information by a widowed mother, a witness continues to live on in a unique way.

Dad Wayman and daughter Lurlene stayed home, enjoying the community of the local church, while Vinita went off to a Christian boarding high school, and then on to college. An extra bonus for Vinita's education was studying abroad for a year. In addition, she gained an awesome Christian husband and now has two wonderful boys.

For the past 26 years Vinita has made an outstanding contribution to Christian education through her exceptional talents. She says, "I feel blessed with the abundant life given me, which would not have been possible if it hadn't been for your mother's willingness to connect with her neighbors. I can't wait to see her in heaven and admire the stars in her crown, and give her another hug."

Bonnie Hunt

A Brush With the Law

Cast all your anxiety on him because he cares for you. 1 Peter 5:7, NIV.

IT'S TIME FOR a confession—and maybe a few smiles. I know, you're wondering what my sin was. Well, maybe not a sin; but for sure I tried to be deceitful.

Wednesday is my crazy-busy day. I teach all day at school, with a two-hour break in the middle. First mistake: my clock was off in my classroom, so I messed up my break. When I found that I was an hour early for the afternoon lessons, I decided to slip over to Hobby Lobby (their fabric is so cute).

As I drove down 48th Street, my cell phone rang. As I talked to my daughter, I eased around the corner on Van Dorn—without signaling—and came, literally, eye to eye with a motorcycle police officer. He whipped that bike around faster than greased lightning and pulled me over. I met his request to find my driver's license, registration, and insurance card with a nervous smile. He assured me he would be right back, then went back to his bike.

Here's where the deceit comes in. I reached up and eased the seat belt around me and buckled it tight. The officer hadn't mentioned that I wasn't wearing it, and I assumed he didn't notice. When he came back, he told me that talking on a cell phone was impairing my driving in a safe manner, and I agreed. He gave me a warning (and I was thankful I had clicked in that seat belt).

When I got to Hobby Lobby, I had to go to the bathroom and rushed into a stall—discovering too late there was no toilet paper. Praise the Lord, there was a woman "next door." I told her about my ticket, and now no toilet paper. She had a good laugh and handed me what I needed.

When I got back to my car, I decided to read the ticket, and right there, in black and white, my police officer had circled "No seat belt," along with failing to signal when turning. So there you have it. It would have been better if I hadn't tried to deceive my friend the cop. He was merciful to me even when I was trying to help myself.

Does this remind you of anything? The truth is, when I try to take control, my heavenly Father has already been merciful and has taken care of everything. Why is this lesson so hard to remember?

Nancy Buxton

God's Rainbow Promises

By which have been given to us exceedingly great and precious promises,
that through these you may be partakers of the divine nature.
2 Peter 1:4, NKJV.

THE SKY WAS dark and foreboding as I drew near my home in the city. The clouds looked as though they would open up and drench the earth with their tears. I didn't want this darkness. I was returning from a difficult mission, and I wanted only sunshine. Though my relatives told me it was none of my business, I'd had to speak the truth to a family member who was looking for love in all the wrong places. But the Lord says that we are each other's keeper, and his life was in peril. God holds His servants accountable, and I had come too far by faith to disobey His will.

I was exhausted from the long drive back from Ohio and just wanted to get home. However, I first had to stop at the store and pick up something for dinner. Grabbing my umbrella, I dashed between downpours until I was safely inside the grocery store.

A half hour later I emerged to find that the dark clouds had disappeared, replaced by blue skies and bright sunshine. I hurriedly walked to my car and proceeded to drive home without thought or care. As I waited at a traffic light, there it was: a beautiful multihued rainbow that seemed to cover the entire city. From one spectrum to another it bowed in reverence to its Creator. Then, looking closer, I saw something I'd never experienced before—a second rainbow was tenderly cradled beneath the first. My heart was humbled, and I rejoiced at the wondrous sight. The Lord had given me a double portion of His promises!

How often we hurriedly go through life, forgetting the promises of God. How often we become consumed with the mundane things of this world, making us anxious or fearful. God's promises are real! He promises that He will be there for us during those difficult times. He promises that He will bless us, protect us, and give us His peace. He promises that if we remain faithful we will inherit His kingdom. He promises a better day, "Yes, a better day; after a while there will be a better day."

I want to remember God's promises and to keep my eyes on Him, don't you?

Evelyn Greenwade Boltwood

Even in Your Darkest Hour

Let the beloved of the Lord rest secure in him, for he shields him all day long, and the one the Lord loves rests between his shoulders. Deut. 33:12, NIV.

LAST WINTER WAS one of the harshest we've ever experienced in Maryland. Christmas had come and gone, and by mid-January we were again buried under four feet of snow. There was something fun about being snowbound with my husband with a pantry full of food and plenty of firewood. However, as we were soon to realize, this snow would forever change our lives.

At 7:30 the next morning our phone rang. Through tears, our daughter-in-law, Leesa, relayed the story that our son had gotten his hand caught in their snow blower while attempting to clear his driveway. She said they were heading to the local hospital, where she hoped they could save his hand. I had the terrible job of telling my husband the awful news. The two of us prayed together; "Dear God, help us!" was about all we could muster. We immediately jumped in our truck and headed for Memorial Hospital to see to our son.

After a long and treacherous journey we reached the emergency department and were told that the hand surgeon had had to be brought to the hospital by our son's best friend in his four-wheel truck or he wouldn't have made it. We quickly recognized that God was working, and through friends such as Herbie, God had already begun helping Todd to heal.

Because of the severity of his injury, it was determined that Todd would need major reconstructive hand surgery and would be transported to the Hand Center in Baltimore, Maryland. Again the long journey was made through the hazardous travel conditions. In Baltimore we were informed that it had been a tough day for hands. Nine other people were ahead of Todd for surgery on their hands because of snow blower injuries.

It has been four months since the accident and, thankfully, Todd is doing very well. He credits the Lord and his friends and family for their support and investment in his recovery. We saw miracles large and small throughout this experience. Even though we would never want to go through this experience again, we realized that friends truly are the family you chose on this earth. We are also thankful to be part of the family of God, a God who never departs from you, even in your darkest hour.

Rose Otis

Parable of the Blue Jay

But as many as received him, to them gave he power to become the sons of God, even to them that believe on his name. John 1:12.

MY DOG, MAJOR, and I were entering the backyard one afternoon when I spied a blue jay on the ground near the birdbath. Major saw it, too, and bolted after it. The blue jay tried to become airborne, but the best it could do was to hobble away.

"Leave it, Major!" I shouted, rushing to try to rescue the poor bird. By the time I got there, however, the blue jay had managed to reach the shelter of the prickly juniper bushes and had become inaccessible to me.

There are at least four stray cats who like to roam that section of our yard, and I fretted over the fact that while the bird thought it had reached safety by hopping under the shelter of the junipers, it actually had made itself more vulnerable. It would be only a matter of time before the prowling cats discovered it and made a meal of it.

The next day I found three blue jay feathers in front of the flowerbed nearest the birdbath. (I didn't want to look too closely *under* the bushes.) Those feathers inspired this little ditty: "I'm sorry, Mister Blue Jay; I would've saved you if I could/You didn't know that my desire was only for your good/ In fear you ran away from me—in your wounded, weakened state/In fear you turned away from life— and ended up on some cat's plate./I'm sorry, Mister Blue Jay; I would've saved you if I could/You didn't know that my desire was only for your good."

In our parallel universe I thought about how God, our loving heavenly Father, longs to rescue us, heal our wounds, and set us free to fly again, soaring on wings of the Spirit, as we are released into all we were meant to be. Jesus wants to help us fly!

Instead, in our lost state, we are like the crippled bird—our fears causing us to run from God. Even though we are wounded, we think we have to take care of ourselves. Instead of running to the Healer, we hobble away, unable to see that His desire is only for our good. The Bible tells us that Satan is like a roaring lion, prowling about seeking whom he may devour. Just as the cats posed a danger to the poor, pitiful blue jay, Satan seeks to devour you and me. Jesus says, "I'm sorry; oh, so sorry—I would've saved you if I could."

Sherrie Anderson Bryant

At the Senior Citizens' Home

Before they call I will answer; while they are still speaking I will hear.
Isa. 65:24, NIV.

MY FRIEND M is not a Christian yet, but we've been friends for 30 years. Her mother, who's in poor health, had a stroke several months ago that sent her to the hospital. Although she had a narrow escape from death, she was paralyzed on one side. It was impossible for M to take care of her mother because of medical problems of her own, and the special nursing home for the elderly was full with more than 100 people on a waiting list. Somehow, through the efforts of a welfare officer, M's mother was hospitalized in a senior citizens' hospital.

But that was a terrible solution. The nursing staff didn't respond to the call button for help. The patients' diapers were changed only at fixed times, so the clients were left wet every night. Many were in pain but didn't receive medication or rehabilitation. Under such circumstances, M's mother was wishing to die as quickly as possible.

M couldn't stand to see her mother suffer, so she asked, "Please pray to God, whom you believe in, so that Mom can escape from her suffering."

"I will pray that your mother can be transferred to a good hospital where she can live peacefully," I answered.

"It's unreasonable! So many old people are waiting to enter into the good homes," M protested.

Nevertheless, I began to pray earnestly. After three weeks I gave her a phone call. "An incredible thing has happened!" she reported excitedly. "Mom can be admitted to a special nursing home for the elderly!" In spite of 74 names on the waiting list, her mother's turn had come. The welfare officer was astonished at this news and questioned her: "Do you mean as many as 74 elderly persons died in these two weeks? Did you have any pull at the home?"

"This is a miracle from God, isn't it?" I said to her.

The truth then burst upon M. "That's it! You've been offering prayers on behalf of Mom. I get it! Jesus kindly listened to your prayers and gave us the best."

The real answer to prayer was that not only did M's mother receive good nursing, but M is very thankful and continues with Bible studies.

Shizuko Ikemasu

Be Prepared

But of that day and that hour knoweth no man, no, not the angels which are in heaven, neither the Son, but the Father. Take ye heed, watch and pray: for ye know not when the time is. For the Son of man is as a man taking a far journey, who left his house, and gave authority to his servants, and to every man his work, and commanded the porter to watch. Watch ye therefore: for ye know not when the master of the house cometh, at even, or at midnight, or at the cockcrowing, or in the morning: lest coming suddenly he find you sleeping. And what I say unto you I say unto all, Watch. Mark 13:32-37.

IT WAS JUST about 2:15 in the morning and still very dark when I heard the dogs begin to bark in my neighborhood. This alarmed my husband, who went to investigate. He didn't see anything. At 2:18 howling began, and our house started to shake, a shaking that lasted for an entire minute and a half.

This earthquake, measuring 7.1 on the Richter scale, is said to have been the strongest experienced in Belize. I say the strongest because Belize is not prone to earthquakes.

My husband sat up in bed, worrying about where the epicenter of the earthquake was. He specifically worried about the salvation of those who slept through the night, unaware of the massive calamity befalling them. For some, death came in a split second. Were they prepared to die? My husband wondered how many of us still living are prepared to face our own moment of reckoning as well.

Are you prepared to die? Where will you spend eternity? What lifestyle changes have you embraced? Is your heart right with God? Have you made peace with anyone lately?

Because of the uncertainty of life, the Master in His wisdom admonished the disciples by saying, "Take ye heed, watch and pray: for ye know not when the time is . . . lest coming suddenly he find you sleeping." We especially need to be sober and vigilant because "the end of all things is at hand" (1 Peter 4:7). Therefore we must watch and be in prayer. Now is the time to prepare our hearts to meet Jesus. Our lives must be ready—we don't want to be among those who are caught sleeping. From the parable of the 10 virgins we learn that our oil lamps must be filled ahead of time, because at any time Jesus, the bridegroom, may appear (see Matt. 25).

Velda M. Jesse

A Weed Is a Weed

When the wheat sprouted and formed heads, then the weeds also appeared.
Matt. 13:26, NIV.

AFTER AN EARLY-MORNING exercise session I come home and immediately water my plants. Sometimes I water plants that are not part of my collection but have been placed at my door by the landlord. If those plants don't receive water for even one day, they develop a lot of dry branches. So then I do for them what I do for my own plants: water them and begin to pull the surrounding weeds. But that isn't easy. It's much harder to pull the weeds out, and there seem to be a lot of them hiding beneath the plant itself. No matter how much you water a weed, caring for it as you would a plant, even fertilizing it, a weed is still a weed.

We have many bad habits in life. We nurture them—some of them grow with us; others are hidden beneath the so-called good things that we do—but we never recognize them as bad habits because we take care of them so well.

The mention of weeds in the Bible never has a positive connotation. The reference usually deals with places of ruin (see Prov. 24:31; Zeph. 2:9); or they were planted by the enemy while the man slept (see Matt. 13:24, 25).

If you read further in the parable of the sower, you will recognize that the owner did not want the servants to pluck out the weeds for fear of uprooting that which was also good; however, that was only until the harvest. Satan, the enemy of our souls, daily sows weeds in our heart garden. Sometimes we don't recognize them because they were planted while we were asleep. Other times we don't see the need to pluck them because they are so beautiful. They blossom and bear pretty flowers (at least we think so for a while).

Today I submit that according to Matthew 13:30 we must "first collect the weeds and tie them in bundles to be burned" (NIV). Why? Because we are living in harvesting time! Among the things we can learn from pulling weeds is that you can always get good counsel, but there are lessons you have to learn on your own. And no matter how many flowers the weed may bear, it is still a weed and needs to be plucked out. Finally, the more deeply rooted the weed gets, the harder it is to pluck, and divine intervention is needed. Today we need to ask God to prune and water us so that we may be a plant that will blossom and bloom weed-free.

Nadine Joseph

Personalized Passage

The Lord is my shepherd; I shall not want. Ps. 23:1.

AS I CLOSED the book I decided to take the challenge offered by the writer to take a favorite verse of Scripture and personalize it. "The Lord was speaking to you right then in your situation," the author had admonished. I chose Psalm 23, and what I needed that day—that very moment—was for the Lord to be my very own personal motivational coach. So I wrote:

"The Lord is my motivational coach; I shall not lack confidence.

"He maketh me to lie down when I need rest; He leads me beside the quiet waters of reflective time to rebuild my strength.

"He restores my battered self-esteem.

"He guides me in paths that are right for me—though I may not understand—for His name's glory.

"Even though I go through situations that are emotionally dark, barren lowlands, You will give me the inner courage necessary to proceed without fear of the situation or of evildoers.

"You empower me, Lord, through intermittent use of Your rod and Your staff—that comforts me.

"You prepare a banquet of encouragement for me to envision the completed goal, even in the midst of naysayers, the jealous, the spirit assassins, the discouragers.

"You anoint my head with the balm of Your peace for my conflicted mind; my emotional cup overflows with gratitude for Your love and grace.

"Surely Your goodness and mercy will continue to pursue me all the days of my life, reminding me that my goal is to dwell in Your house—forever."

Why not take the challenge and personalize a passage today? God wrote all of Scripture to speak to you personally. We can appreciate that more when we personalize the text to our own situation.

When I personalize, I hear God speaking to me through the verses, reaching to the depths of my present need, providing the answer even to my unspoken questions, and providing direction when I don't even realize that I've lost my way.

Maxine Williams Allen

My Dream

It will happen in a moment, in the blink of an eye, when the last trumpet is blown. For when the trumpet sounds, those who have died will be raised to live forever. 1 Cor. 15:52, NLT.

MOST PEOPLE WILL admit to dreaming at some point in their lives. I find most of my dreams are the variety that I would compare to defragmenting a computer disk, sort of rearranging bits of data stored in my brain. Rarely do I remember these dreams, and if I do, they are rather disjointed at best. Recently, however, I had a dream that seemed so real, and I remembered it so clearly, that I truly believe it came as an assurance from God.

In the dream my husband and I were traveling in our car on a two-lane road. Suddenly a car appeared from the other direction, headed straight for us. At the instant of impact everything went white, then dark. There was no thought about what was happening to my husband or the family I was leaving with my death. Just as quickly, everything was light again, and I was greeting Jesus with "Good morning, Lord!" End of dream.

Normally after a dream of a traumatic nature I awaken with a racing heart, but not this time. We were preparing for a long road trip, and at first I felt that the dream came from anticipation of that journey. But I didn't feel any fear or apprehension about taking the trip. It was as if the Lord was giving me the assurance that death is but for a moment, and not something to fear.

In an earlier dream I had felt myself falling. There is a belief that when dreaming about falling, if you hit the bottom you are dead—in real life. I guess I will never know about that, because I didn't hit bottom. Instead, I looked up, trusting in God's goodness, and simply prayed, "I am in Your hands." There was instantly a peace and a feeling of calm, as if His hands were under me, lifting me up.

No matter where I am or what the circumstances may be, I, you—each of us—can depend on and trust in our God. We each have been through many trials in life and in our walk with God, but He has never failed us, although we haven't always been nearly as faithful to Him. He has promised to always be with us, to never forsake us. "The Lord is my strength and shield. I trust him with all my heart. He helps me, and my heart is filled with joy. I burst out in songs of thanksgiving" (Ps. 28:7, NLT). What a precious promise and comforting assurance that is!

Barbara Lankford

Temporary Tattoos

I, even I, am he that blotteth out thy transgressions for mine own sake, and will not remember thy sins. Isa. 43:25.

ONE DAY, out shopping with my two daughters, we came across a vending machine that gives a temporary tattoo for a quarter or two. One was a cartoon dog, and the other a cat. With some persuasion on their part, I consented to their pleading to get a tattoo. They are harmless and temporary, I thought. It will be fun. My thinking of fun with my girls even went so far as my getting one for myself.

When we got home, we placed all the items we had shopped for in their place, the girls all the while telling me to hurry: "We want to put on the tattoos." When I had finished, we proceeded to the bathroom sink to properly place the temporary tattoos on our arms. Oh, we were having fun! Innocent fun!

The next day I decided we needed to remove the tattoos; at least I wanted to remove mine. I jumped into the shower, not thinking about the fact that the night before, when I gave the girls a bath, the tattoos hadn't come off. But then we weren't trying to take them off. I put soap onto the washcloth and proceeded to rub my tattoo. It wasn't coming off easily! In fact, I was really scrubbing my arm, but the tattoo was still there. It wasn't until the spot of flesh where the temporary tattoo was had turned red and raw to the touch that it started to come off. *Oh, no*, I thought. *This isn't going to come off—at least not so easily. What am I going to do?*

Isn't that just like sin? I thought, right there in the shower. We get into things so easily, without a care in the world. Or we think, *Oh, it is just fun—no problem. I can handle it.* And then we find out, sometimes too late, that it isn't that easy. We try to eradicate the problem ourselves, and end up hurting even more. But I am so glad we have King Jesus: He has already taken care of it. Jesus has spilled His blood that we may be spotless. Jesus is there waiting to hear our cry, "Help me!" with a willing surrender to Him. Letting go of our cherished sins is painful, just as trying to get rid of that tattoo was. We have the assurance that our sins are not forever, and He that is faithful will not remember that it was even there.

Erika Loudermill-Webb

Little Gifts Given

Lead me in thy truth, and teach me: for thou art the
God of my salvation; on thee do I wait all the day. Ps. 25:5.

HAVE YOU STOPPED lately to let God show you the wonderful gifts He has for you? In the morning there is the sunshine to brighten the day or the rain to help us stop and sit in the cozy corner of our favorite room and make time for a good book. Then there are the birds: amazing, singing, and seeming so cheery, to help us through the day. Another day there is the snow. Oh, the wonder! And when was the last time you got up to see the sunrise—or even noticed the sunset? God likes to give us gifts; we just need to be taught how to see them.

God is trying to help me see the gifts, even though my children are leaving home and starting out on their own. One daughter wants to make her own way in life, and I want her to stay home. But God has a gift for me—showing me that I have done a good work in them, and I need to rest in Him, to know that the gift is a young woman who is going to be a blessing to others. Both girls that God gave us are working toward the place that God has for them. The gift for me is to wait and watch Him work His good pleasure. God is there.

My husband has been a gift to me for 28 years of blessings. In turn, my gift is to love, by showing him each day that he is a gift.

In addition, there are my friends. Without them the world would be a lonely place. I give thanks for all my wonderful girlfriends who love and pray for me each day.

There are so many ways for me to love and pray for others. Because of my husband's military career, I move a lot and need to have a way to show my friendship. So I send a virtual hug; I call someone, send an e-mail or a card. God gives me gifts of love. I want to pass them on, although I can never match His generosity.

Another gift I can give is to look only for the good in people. I can try to be kind, to bake cookies for someone, or buy a gift for a baby whom I have noticed at church. "Because of your father's God, who helps you, because of the Almighty, who blesses you with blessings of the heavens above, blessings of the deep that lies below, blessings of the breast and womb" (Gen. 49:25, NIV). There are so many possibilities if I only look around.

Susen Mattison Mole´

Armed With Courage

But now I urge you to keep up your courage, because not
one of you will be lost; only the ship will be destroyed. Acts 27:22, NIV.

I ALWAYS HEAR people compare life to a ship tossed about on the sea. However, when I think of my own personal experience I know that there are days when there is calm and comfort. You stand tall and strong because of the apparent connection with God, and His love illuminates and brightens your heart and your days. But there are also days when the storms of life rage with troubles, and you feel as though you're drowning in despair and sorrow, and there seems to be no light of hope at all. As a matter of fact, you seem to be totally disconnected and lost.

As a follower of Christ, at some point you know that you must rely solely on God for strength and guidance. However, when many things occur in a short period of time, and tears flood your eyes, the Christian walk may seem hopeless, and you begin to ask questions. This was my experience anyway.

The worst thing that could ever happen to me was the death of my husband, my best friend and companion. With two young children, I couldn't understand why he had to die. A few weeks after his death, with a torn and bleeding heart and a serious illness, I had to undergo surgery. I thought that maybe this was God's way of putting me to sleep for good, too—the prayer of a coward. But when I woke up from the surgery, I realized that God must have a better answer than the one I thought about and hoped for. With the passing of time and the many challenges that come to a single mother trying to further her education, I realized that deep within me was the desire to fight the good fight. And so I surrendered my will to God and asked Him to take me through my trials.

I recall one morning going down on my knees and dialoguing with my God. I asked Him to give me the courage to face my trials, and to fight my battles on life's sea. Since that day I have never regretted asking God for courage. I now realize that to be victorious one's knowledge of God is not enough—we need to experience His mighty power in our life as well.

Today I am more stable after going through such tragedy, but I now know by experience that the God we serve not only allows trials to come our way but equips us with courage to face them. Let's trust God and take courage even when the ship is tearing apart. He will save us.

Prasedes Gillett

Better Plans

"For I know the plans I have for you," declares the Lord, "plans to prosper you and not to harm you, plans to give you hope and a future." Jer. 29:11, NIV.

IN MY LAST year of college, while working on a degree in administration, I decided that I wanted to be a professor and a researcher. As soon as I finished college, I planned to work toward my master's degree. Only one institution where I lived offered a master's degree in administration. There also had been only one selection process since the course had opened, which was held while I was still finishing my undergraduate degree. Nevertheless, I called the institution and left my name for the preselection group of the next master's degree class.

The selection for the master's degree class did not take place during the year, and I questioned God. Today I imagine that God looked down with His wisdom and smiled, seeing His daughter so impatient and unbelieving.

I found no other alternatives for a master's degree. I wanted to leave this problem with God, but I couldn't. My friends suggested that I needed to put my plan in God's hands. Giving it to God meant saying, "Lord, I want to get a master's degree. Do You want that for me?"

It took awhile for me to offer that prayer, but I grew tired of struggling alone. When I finally gave my plans to God, peace came. I decided to study English, as this was something that I also wanted to do, and this subject would help me in my master's degree program.

One day while surfing the Internet I found a master's degree program at the Federal University. Enrollment was open for the degree in psychology, so I called the university about enrollment since my undergraduate degree was not in psychology. To my surprise, I was eligible to enroll.

After obtaining the necessary information, I registered. I studied for the entrance examination, and I passed the English test and the test for the specific subject area. After the interview I was accepted and also received a scholarship so I could work full-time on my degree!

Later I discovered that the master's degree in the other school where I had wanted to study was facing accreditation difficulties with the Ministry of Education. If I had taken my degree there, time and money would have been wasted. Instead, I had an officially recognized school—and the scholarship! God gave me much more than I had hoped for.

Iani Dias Lauer-Leite

In His Presence Is Fullness of Joy

Thou wilt shew me the path of life: in thy presence is fulness of joy; at thy right hand there are pleasures for evermore. Ps. 16:11.

IT WAS MY BIRTHDAY! A friend and her family invited me on a picnic lunch after church. How exciting to find out it was a surprise picnic party. The community madrigal singers, dressed in period costume and who just happened to be at the gardens at the same time, sang "Happy Birthday" to me.

After the picnic everyone went their separate ways, and I made my way to the coast. The day was stunning, with clear skies and the freshness of spring all around. It was the kind of day that makes one burst forth in song to our Creator. What a blessing it was to be alive to enjoy this day!

Once I got to the beach I slowly hiked to my favorite spot, soaking in the sunshine and drinking the fresh air. God had given me such a special day. My thoughts continued to turn in praise to Him for His goodness. I spread out my beach blanket and pulled out my Bible. The text for today's thought came to mind, but in much clearer context now, especially the part that reads "in His presence is fullness of joy." My heart was so full of joy I thought I was going to literally burst.

As I sat contemplating my Creator and Savior and the joy He gives, I leaned back on the blanket and turned to face Him. From somewhere deep inside the question came, *Lord, what is on Your heart today?*

Without a moment's hesitation the answer was given: "The salvation of souls." My heart now did burst forth, and I began to talk with Him—I was so excited to hear Him speak. I rambled on for several minutes, telling Him of the joy He had given me.

Looking back, I wonder if He would have said more had I continued to listen, or had He given His answer full and complete? He needed no other words to share the deepest desire of His heart; He had lived His purpose and goal. He has given His life to pursue the desire of His heart. When God fills us with joy, don't we want to share that? As I start a new year of life, does my heart's desire echo that of my Savior?

Kimberly Goodge

The Metamorphosis of a Monarch Butterfly

But we all, with unveiled face, beholding as in a mirror
the glory of the Lord, are being transformed into the same image
from glory to glory, just as by the Spirit of the Lord. 2 Cor. 3:18, NKJV.

HAVE YOU EVER been to a butterfly house? In such a house these lovely, delicate creatures gently fly around you. Sometimes they will alight on your hand, shoulder, or head. You hold your breath, hoping you won't disturb them so that they fly away. There are so many sizes, colors, and designs of butterflies, but my favorite is the Monarch butterfly.

A number of years ago, when my students and I took a walk in the fields behind the school, we came upon a breathtaking sight: a milkweed bush was completely covered with orange-and-black Monarch butterflies. Within minutes they rose as a group from the bush and took to the air. It was one of those God moments!

I had another unique butterfly experience while in Michigan for the summer. A friend gave my daughter a plastic box outfitted with fresh milkweed leaves and a cocoon hanging from the top of the box. We didn't see a second caterpillar she said was there. Her instructions were very clear and included the dates each cocoon would "hatch."

We checked our cocoon daily. Were we surprised one morning when we discovered a rather large black-and-yellow caterpillar devouring the milkweed leaves! Our instructions told us this caterpillar would shortly cocoon. The next day it had attached itself to the lid of the water container in a J shape. Within minutes it pulled itself into green material coming from within its body, which formed the second cocoon. What a rare privilege to witness this!

What an experience to watch these beautiful butterflies struggle from their cocoons! After two to three hours of flexing and drying their wings, we set the box out on the sunny deck. Each one lingered a while longer, fanning their wings in the sunshine, before they flew away.

As monarchs go through this metamorphosis, so we go through a similar metamorphosis in our Christian life. If we give God permission and make Him our choice, we also will be changed through His grace and power from an ugly life of sin into a beautiful, God-directed Christian life. We, unlike the butterfly, can make this choice. God has given us free will.

Patricia Mulraney Kovalski

Our Father Knows Our Needs!

O Lord, you are my God; I will exalt you and praise your name,
for in perfect faithfulness you have done marvelous things,
things planned long ago. Isa. 25:1, NIV.

I ALMOST ALWAYS wear glasses. However, as soon as I get home I remove them and place them in their designated place. If I'm visiting, I don't usually remove them unless I'm going to sleep or to eat or drink something hot.

One morning I was ready for work when I realized that one of my lenses was missing. I searched everywhere in vain. I struggled without glasses as I kept searching. On the third day, I had an eye examination and bought a new pair. I received my new glasses within a week, and they worked quite well, but it still puzzled me about the mysterious disappearance of that lens.

Then one night five months later, I went to visit my aunt. On the way home, in the pocket of the jacket I wore, I found the missing lens. I was excited as I started assembling my now-old glasses. Then I decided to finish later, since I didn't need the glasses right then. I thought about the fact that I hadn't needed new glasses five months earlier, but with the found lens I now had two pairs.

I was so caught up in the excitement of finding the lens that I didn't realize that my new glasses weren't with me. So the next morning as I was leaving for work, I routinely reached for them, but they weren't there. I began my search, but concluded that I must have left them at my aunt's when I had tea with her. There wasn't enough time for me to get them and make it to work in good time. Thankfully, I reached for my old pair and went off to work. I then fitted and cleaned them, and they were still very effective. I later rang my aunt, and sure enough, my glasses were at her house.

I was truly amazed at the wonder of it all, the way in which the Lord revealed the missing lens just in time, even before I knew I needed it. It is very clear that even in very simple ways we can be assured that Jesus cares for us always. Our Father knows our needs and supplies them. "Before they call I will answer; while they are still speaking I will hear" (Isa. 65:24, NIV).

Donette James

Good and Evil

The fear of the Lord is the beginning of wisdom; all who follow his precepts have good understanding. Ps. 111:10, NIV.

WHEN THAT SERPENT, the devil, told Eve that she would "be like God, knowing good and evil" (Gen. 3:4, NIV), I'm certain she had no idea what that meant—but she soon found out. Imagine the first animal death, the first fight with Adam, the death of her favorite flower. And then one son, her precious firstborn, killed his brother, Abel. She lost two sons that day. But there must have been good things happening, too—sweet babies born, joyful family gatherings, fun animal antics, and gorgeous sunrises and sunsets. There was still a lot that was good.

It seems that good and evil are always mixed up. My mother died two days after our daughter's birthday. Does one mourn or celebrate? Good and evil; our world is all mixed up. There is enough good that most days we enjoy our lives; life on this earth is not all that bad. But then someone close to us—or even we ourselves—gets cancer, or is maimed in an accident, or a loved one betrays trust, and we don't want to live here on this old earth anymore. Hour after hour, day after day, our televisions portray horrifying famines, earthquakes, floods, fires, crimes, war, and death. We don't want to know any more of evil! We want heaven where there will be no more heartache, "no more death or mourning or crying or pain, for the old order of things has passed away" (Rev. 21:4, NIV). Evil and good will no longer be mixed up.

Today's text tells us that "the fear of the Lord is the beginning of wisdom; all who follow his precepts have good understanding." What does that mean? How do we get that wisdom? I believe it means to keep God's laws—that is, to know good. One of the things I have always appreciated about God's rules is that they always make sense; they are for our good and happiness. They aren't arbitrary rules someone just made up. When we follow them, we are healthier and happier; our families are stronger and our communities are safer.

The fact that Eve couldn't imagine evil gave her no excuse. Neither do we have an excuse; God's plan has always been for us to know good. But ever since that day in the garden, Eve's sisters have known a lot of evil. Oh, how I wish that each and every one of them knew Jesus and His plan for their lives. And that is my wish for you today, too.

Ardis Dick Stenbakken

God Is faithful

Taste and see that the Lord is good. Ps. 34:8.

IT WAS MY LAST class at college, and I was preparing for a group presentation at a seminar when I received the news that the presentation would be on a Friday evening. I was worried about having a failing grade and having to take the final exam on Sabbath, but I didn't despair. I simply prayed silently, asking God to give me strength for that moment.

After the prayer I informed the teacher and my group that I couldn't help present the seminar. The group didn't like it, and we discussed it a little, but I stayed by my decision. The teacher asked me to think a little more and told me to give her the answer at the next class, for I would lose my grade in two subjects, and this should be thought over calmly.

After a week the teacher called me in and asked if I still kept to my decision. I confirmed it with a nod. She tried to convince me to change, telling me that it wasn't good at the end of a course to have final exams in two subjects, but I was resolute in my decision. Then she took a deep breath and said that I would have to take a final exam in only one subject, because she had changed the date of the presentations. I thanked God very much, but I was still waiting for something more. When I thanked the teacher for her support and understanding, she asked me to call the group, and I did. Then she said that she respected her students' religious beliefs, and for this reason I should participate in preparing the seminar, and I would receive the same grade that the group would receive. Now I was satisfied and so amazed to see how God solves His children's problems.

As I got up and thanked my teacher again, she simply said, "Who am I to deviate a Lord's servant from His ways? Do your job and stay at peace."

At the end of the presentations I was informed that my group got a good grade for the seminar presentation, and I was even happier.

When we stand by our convictions we can know that our God is faithful and fair with us. We need to remember that. God opened the way for me when I really had no hope that there would be a change.

Taste and see—God is faithful!

Carmem Virgínia

The Door Is Always Open

Blessed is he whose transgressions are forgiven, whose sins are covered.
Ps. 32:1, NIV.

I HAVE A CAT named Dermie that is part Japanese bobtail, which is supposed to be a very intelligent breed of cat. It is also characteristic of the breed that once it picks up a bad habit, it holds onto it. Take Dermie, for instance, who's an indoor cat, and indoor cats are known to have much longer life spans and better health than outdoor cats. We love her and want her to be safe, healthy, and with us for a long time. But she loves the smell of the outdoors and loves chasing the birds that live out there. So every chance she gets, she tries to open the louver windows—and she's very good at it too! Patient and determined, she keeps pulling on a louver with her claws until she gets it open or I shoo her away. Once she gets a louver open, she squeezes her furry little body through the space until she's stuck between the screen and the window. At this point the louvers usually slam shut behind her. Then all she has to do is push out the screen and jump down to freedom. Her obsession with breaking out has gotten so bad that we've closed off those parts of the house that have windows that lend themselves to her great escapes. But she keeps trying.

Dermie always comes home after she runs away. Sometimes she just breaks out and then realizes she forgot to eat first, and she wants back in the house. But I wish she'd just stay inside where I don't have to worry about her being hit by a car or attacked by another animal, or any number of other bad things.

They say people and their pets can end up looking alike. I think in this case Dermie and I are acting alike. No, I don't crawl out the window so I can run around outside and roll in the dirt, but I do stray from my Father's will and try to do things my way. Again and again. I'm always sorry and want back within His will, but somehow I find old habits hard to break. Sometimes I'm like the Old Testament's Sarah, thinking my timing is better than God's, or that He needs my help. Sometimes I just get busy and forget to ask God what is best. Sometimes I let my wants become the focus of my thinking.

No matter why I find myself outside of God's plan, His door is always open, waiting for my return. I'm so grateful that my Father is patient and forgiving. Aren't you?

Julie Bocock-Bliss

Trust in God

Remember the Sabbath day by keeping it holy. Ex. 20:8, NIV.

I FOUND HIM at the church I was regularly attending during my studies at the University of Puerto Rico. I had seen him at the dorm, but I didn't know that he was a fellow Christian. That Sabbath I approached him and introduced myself. He immediately admitted that he had also seen me but didn't know that we had a common religion.

Juan had been baptized a year before in Mayaguez, where he'd come in contact with Jesus and His love through the exemplary life of his landlady, who was a devoted Christian. He had come from Peru to finish his master's degree and Ph.D. in physics, and he was transferred to the University of Puerto Rico in Rio Piedras, where I was attending.

We started having our Sabbath vespers together. With the inquisitive and intellectual mind of a physicist, our discussions about God, the Bible, the Sabbath, creation versus evolution, sin, heaven, etc., were profound. He was still very new in the faith and was avid to learn everything about the Bible and his new religion, and was also having his own daily devotions. On Sabbath afternoons we went with a group of church members to housing projects to give Bible studies and get contacts. Our friendship was growing, as was our personal relationship with God.

The semester was about to finish, and Juan was preparing to take the entrance exam to be admitted into the Ph.D. program. The exam was to be the following Monday, and he hadn't finished covering all the material he needed to, so he contemplated studying all Sabbath. I told him that this was the perfect opportunity to test the Lord and see how good He is. He decided to do that. On Sabbath morning, when we were leaving for church, we saw all the physics students at the study hall, getting ready to study for the exam. I looked at Juan and simply said, "Trust in God."

He studied the rest of the weekend and took the exam on Monday. One week later he received the results. He got the highest grade of his class and was immediately accepted into the program! With joy in our hearts we just bowed our heads and gave thanks to our dear God.

We serve a living and powerful God who is just waiting for an opportunity to show His immeasurable love to His children. Just trust in God!

Hannelore Gomez

Ministering Angels

Are not all angels ministering spirits sent to serve those who will inherit salvation? Heb. 1:14, NIV.

IT WAS MAY 5, around 8:00 p.m. We were just ready to have a little snack when I felt compelled to ask God in my prayer for the angels' protection for our daughter, who was on her way to pick up a girl who would be attending an evangelistic conference with Kalyna. At the exact moment when I was praying for our daughter, she was parking her car in front of the doctor's office where the girl worked. Suddenly a middle-sized man approached the car and demanded that our daughter leave the car and keep quiet—it was a robbery.

Immediately Kalyna got out of the car, pleading, "Please let me get my Bible." The other robber was getting into the driver's seat. Quickly Kalyna opened the back door of the car, grabbing her Bible and her coat. She also tried to get her purse with her documents and other important items, but was not allowed to. She was in the middle of trying to close the door, when the robbers drove away, leaving the door still open.

We, of course, didn't know what was happening. Then our telephone rang. It was our daughter, calling to inform us that she'd been robbed, that the car had been stolen, but that she was OK. We immediately thanked God, for the ruffians hadn't touched her. I was overwhelmed, and told her that at the very moment of the assault, I was praying for her because I had the feeling that the enemy could be trying to interfere. You see, the girl who was going to the conference with Kalyna was a spirit worshipper, with her belief very firmly rooted. It is very clear that the devil planned this robbery to discourage the girl. But thanks be to God, she now wishes to be baptized soon.

The car was found in good condition the second day after the assault, and all the documents were still in the car (only some objects of lesser value were missing). We were convinced that God's hand and His angels protected our daughter, who was trying to help this girl who wished to "inherit salvation."

Let's praise the Lord with all our hearts, thankful for His love and protection to our lives.

I believe in the angels' ministry. I'm sure you do too.

Marília Macieira Kettle

The Chocolate Milk Fiasco

For the Lord seeth not as man seeth; for man looketh on the outward appearance, but the Lord looketh on the heart. 1 Sam. 16:7.

WHEN MY LITTLE sister Cassandra was 6, she would have warm chocolate soymilk every night just before bed. If Cassandra got in bed without her milk, she would get up, get a cup, take out the milk, and ask someone to pour it for her. Then she would take her milk and go to bed. This happened every night without fail. However, one particular Friday night was different.

As usual, Cassandra took out her cup and milk. Then she called, "Lillian, I have everything out. Can you please come and make my chocolate milk tonight?"

"Sure, Cassandra. Give me a minute." When I reached the kitchen, Cassandra was waiting. She had placed everything on the counter, including a few "smash-mallows" (marshmallows). I smiled and picked up the chocolate milk and started to pour it out. But the milk wouldn't come out! I was surprised! The container looked like milk and felt as if it had milk in it. I thought the milk might be frozen, so I shook it and squeezed the container just in case. Still, when I tried to pour the milk, it wouldn't come out. Finally, I decided to smell the milk. I couldn't believe that something that tastes so good could smell so bad! I held it at arm's length and quickly started walking toward the garbage when my dad stopped me. "Where are you going with the milk?"

"To the garbage can—it smells terrible!" Dad took the container and smelled it. He stated that it smelled fine. (In fairness, Dad doesn't drink soymilk, so he really wouldn't know what good soymilk smells like.) Fortunately, Mom entered the kitchen and, overhearing our conversation, took the milk, smelled it, and tried to pour it out. It was thick, smelly, and slimy!

Before God comes into our hearts, we are thick, smelly, and slimy, just like the milk. The worst part is that we can't see it. We think that we're perfectly fine. We look as good on the outside as that milk container. But when God looks inside, we are slimy too! Once we accept God into our lives, we see how we used to be and realize how bad we were. I accepted God into my life when I was 10; and now that I'm 12, I love God more every day. I pray that when God looks at me He sees more than just a nice container. I hope He sees a young girl trying to live her life for Him. I hope that you will accept Him into your life too.

Lillian Marquez de Smith

What's in a Name?

A good name is rather to be chosen than great riches, and loving favour rather than silver and gold. Prov. 22:1.

IT IS INTERESTING when the initials of a person's name spell a word. Or perhaps you might wonder what your parents were thinking when they named you. I was never very concerned about my initials until the end of my eighth-grade year and got a graduation gift that the thought processes began churning.

There it was, a beautiful new set of blue-and-white Samsonite luggage, with the initials "RIB" inscribed on each case—a present from my dad. Then it hit me that I was stuck with "RIB" as my initials.

The luggage was put to good use that same year when I was sent to a boarding high school where the Bible was part of the curriculum. Bible study was a new concept in my life, and my receptive mind was opened to the many Bible stories. Reading them was a thrilling and exciting adventure. We studied the Old Testament during my freshman year. One story in particular caught my eye: God took a rib from Adam's side and created Eve. My initials were in that story! My unrenowned initials were now taking on a different significance, and I no longer would need to be ashamed or embarrassed by those gaudy letters on my luggage. I feel certain that no one really cared about my secret mortification about my initials spelling the word "rib." In fact, they probably never even noticed. As I look back, the torment was an invention of my imagination.

After I married, my initials spelled another word: "RIM." I had outgrown the discomfort of my initials spelling "rib" and was ready to accept "rim." As I read more and more passages from the Bible, I wondered what could be the connotation of my new initials.

The definition of rim, or border, is "the dividing line or territory between two countries." Aren't we pilgrims here and on the border, or rim, between earth and heaven? We're watching and waiting for that time when Jesus will come to lift us up from the rim of this old earth. He will take us across the border and through the gates of heaven. What a glorious event that will be for all who love and obey the Lord! An eternity will be enjoyed with our Creator.

Retha McCarty

Count It All Joy

How much more shall your Father which is in heaven give good things to them that ask him? Matt. 7:11.

AT THE END of the school term I was driving alone on the highway, listening to LeeAnn Womack belt out "I Hope You Dance" (wonderful tune, by the way) and thought, *Why shouldn't I make the choice to enjoy the experience of being my own chauffeur and count it a blessing?* You see, driving is not my first choice; sitting in the passenger seat and enjoying the scenery is. So whenever I have to drive, I'm not turning cartwheels of joy. But on this Friday as I left work, I had no choice. My husband had traveled overseas to participate in a cycling event, and I was on my own. So I continued in this manner of praise as I went about my errands. After collecting my groceries, mail, dinner, and other items, I headed back to the vehicle to begin my journey home. I turned the key in the ignition, but there was no familiar purring sound. I thought that maybe I needed to get comfortable because my position didn't allow me to start the engine properly. Once again, key to ignition, but no sound.

My immediate thought was *Father, I was having such a great day; what did I do wrong that this should happen to me?* My next thought was *I need to call my husband.*

"Sit tight; I'll call Billo," he promised. And he did.

A few minutes later the mechanic arrived, surveyed the situation, started the vehicle, and announced that the starter had to be changed. *Of course it will,* I thought, *but certainly not today.* I watched closely what he did, just in case I should get another surprise. Under way once more, I stopped to buy bread at the bakery. On my return, the vehicle once again didn't start. Confidently, I figured out how to open the hood, looked inside, and did exactly as Billo had done. You can imagine my joy when that engine sang its familiar tune. "Thank You, Jesus!" I whispered, and with the biggest smile ever on my face I drove home, called my husband, and proudly related my first experience as a mechanic. I felt liberated.

That evening I added one more blessing to my list: God's protection and care. If you are concerned about something today, let it go. Give it to God. See every challenge as an opportunity for praise because God is in control, and He will take care of you. He always does. I know.

Brenda D. (Hardy) Ottley

Before I Called

Before they call, I will answer; and while they are still speaking, I will hear.
Isa. 65:24, NKJV.

MY HUSBAND AND I planned our first trip to Ranchi, Bihar, in India. Two weeks before the journey, he took another assignment, which meant I had to travel alone. I was apprehensive. The train would take about two days, and I had to change trains in Chennai around midnight. Several what ifs raced through my mind. Furthermore, it had been only four months since my surgery.

I boarded the train on schedule. The train reached Chennai a half hour late. Fortunately, I found a kindhearted middle-aged porter to carry my baggage. The walk from one end of the railway station to where I had to catch the next train seemed never-ending. When we reached the platform, we found that the train was 45 minutes late.

Promising to be back when the train came, the porter left. What ifs popped up again. But true to his word, the porter settled me comfortably on the train. *Who has gotten my husband's berth?* I wondered. *Will it be a woman to whom I can talk?* Soon I heard a young woman speaking my language. She settled opposite me in the place my husband would have been. I offered a silent prayer of gratitude to God and conversed with the woman.

Priya was going to Ranchi, my destination. She knew the Adventist hospital where I was going and a few of my acquaintances. When I told her that it was my first visit, she assured me of her assistance and calmed my fears.

Around 9:00 in the morning of the third day, my new friend announced unexpectedly that she would get off at the station before Ranchi to save time. Though I was disappointed, I assured her that I would be fine. *Lord,* I prayed, *I need help to carry my baggage. You know my condition.* Priya alighted from the train, giving me a big hug.

I was left alone with a young man. Surprisingly, the man who had not spoken a word all those hours of traveling together said, "Aunty, do not worry. I will help you with your baggage." *How did he know I would need help with my baggage?*

Yes, God fulfilled His promise that day. Before I called He had arranged for Priya to have my husband's berth. While I was still speaking He impressed the young man to help me with my baggage. What a mighty God we serve!

Hepzibah Kore

God's First Gift of the Day

Every good gift and every perfect gift is from above, and cometh down from the Father of lights, with whom is no variableness, neither shadow of turning. James 1:17.

IT IS 4:30 A.M. I'm fully awake, feeling refreshed. As I turn on the light, God's gift is waiting for me—the many-faceted blessing and challenge of a new day.

I haven't always appreciated this present as I do today, but life teaches many lessons, and one of them is that real joy comes from counting your blessings.

First, I am alive. During this past night thousands have lost their lives, some peacefully, others under tragic circumstances. However, God has given me another day, full of opportunities to rejoice in the happiness that comes from making a small difference for good in the lives of others. What a privilege!

I am not in pain. There were seemingly endless months when sleep was minimal, and I lived from one painkiller to the next, counting the slowly passing minutes. God forbid that I should ever take good health for granted again. *Thank You for a pain-free start to this day, Lord.*

God loves me. How precious is our early-morning visit together! I listen to the sound advice of His Word, and we chat unhurriedly over all the joys and problems of the present. Together we remember the needs of many whom He loves. Lingering worries lose their hold, and I am ready to face any challenge the day may bring.

Through my open window I breathe in clean, fresh air and listen to the sleepy twittering of God's little creatures, praising Him in song. It will soon be time for my walk, but not yet. God's morning visit is too precious to be cut short. Of course we'll continue our conversation at intervals during the day, but now we are uninterrupted by ringing phones, looming deadlines, or emergencies to be dealt with. It is unquestionably the best time of the day.

And one more thing, Lord. Thank You that today I can still see to read your Word. What a blessing that is! God knows my optical problem, and every day that I can read my Bible is a bonus. Maybe the day will come when even large print will be illegible, but I will take one day at a time, for each day's gift is perfectly tailored to the needs and challenges of that day. Tomorrow can be safely trusted to God.

Revel Papaioannou

Flowers—A Little Glimpse of Heaven

The grass withers, the flower fades, but the word of our God stands forever.
Isa. 40:8, NASB.

I LOVE THE fact that God has given us the privilege of being creative. For me, creativity comes in various shapes and forms, and I'm always learning something new.

I decided that if I have to work in a cement box (a store) I had better choose the best job in the store. God opened the door for me to use my creativity in working with flowers.

There are many things that I like about my job, but two in particular give me moments of joy on a daily basis. When I go into the cooler, I fill up my grocery cart with flowers so that I can refill my flower display. There can be as many as 20 to 50 bouquets when I come out of the cooler, and the reactions I get are wonderful. This full cart of beautiful flowers often takes people's breath away. I love, love, love to see the reactions on their faces!

They probably don't realize that I work there; they are in awe of such beauty (no, not me—the flowers). Some people ask, "Are you really buying that many flowers?" Others ask, "Are these for me?" Still others simply say, "Wow." I feel at that moment it is a privilege and an honor to see such joy when they see what God has created. They are appreciating a little glimpse of heaven.

My second-favorite moment is when I hear a little child coming to my flower display with their mommy, and all I hear from around the corner is "Fwowers, fwowers, fwowers!" Children have much to teach us. I realize that we all need to slow down long enough to take time to smell the roses and seize the moment.

I have to take a lot of pictures for the photography class I'm taking. I usually do this homework out in nature, where there are so many things to admire. Truly God has given us so many beautiful things that offer little glimpses of heaven. It will be wonderful to be there, to look at all the wonders He has created especially for us.

Long ago the author John Keats wrote, "A thing of beauty is a joy forever." God is so generous to give us so much beauty.

Try asking God to show you something beautiful that you can share with someone every day. And take note of every glimpse of heaven that God shows you!

Gay Mentes

Wait and See!

Even though I walk through the valley of the shadow of death, I will fear no evil, for you are with me. Ps. 23:4, NIV.

THAT MORNING OF Mother's Day, as I rushed my family to get ready to leave for church, I thought about the joy of celebrating a day dedicated to me. The previous months had been hectic as I was recovering from powerful chemotherapy treatment for cancer. Thank God the cancer was in remission, and I was able to enjoy every day with my 13-month-old son. But the experience had left me emotionally drained, and with many mixed feelings.

While driving on one of the main avenues on our way to church, we saw a small kitten trying to cross the street. It looked scared and confused, so I told my husband to stop the car, and I got out to help the kitten, which promptly ran under our car. We were stuck in the middle of the road on a Sunday morning, fearing that if we moved the car we could kill the kitten. A couple stopped to ask what was going on, and we told them. The man got out of his car to help us. Then another driver stopped to help, and a woman in a truck pulled off behind our car.

The kitten hid itself in the wheel of our car, and my husband had to maneuver so one of the people helping could get the cat. The man asked for gloves to be able to put his hand thru the rim. As quick as could be, one of the drivers handed a pair of thick, winter gloves. With that he was able to get the kitten out of the wheel. The animal was so agitated that it bit the man twice and scratched him with its claws.

One of the people announced that she was on her way to the veterinary clinic with her dogs and offered to take the kitten. We needed a box to put the anxious animal in, and there was one in the rescuer's car! God provided all the people and tools needed to save the small cat.

All the people involved exchanged phone numbers to keep up-to-date with the kitten's progress and left the scene amazed. What a lesson we had learned! I think that the kitten's behavior is similar to the human instinct to be aggressive and defensive when we are scared and uncomfortable. Even if there are people trying to help us, sometimes we focus on our own pain. The lesson for me that morning was to learn to relax, be quiet, and wait; there will be a helping hand willing to rescue us from any uncomfortable situation we are experiencing.

Leslie R. Quiroz

For Love of Mother

Her children rise up and bless her. Prov. 31:28, NASB.

"MOTHER." In every language it means love. The very name invokes happy feelings of nurturing, caring, protecting, guiding, mentoring—and the list goes on. As we grow older we reflect on our childhood and the relationships we share with our mothers. It's a special blessing for those of us who can claim a happy mother-daughter relationship. After all, it's from that special relationship that we learn how to be good mothers, wives, and sisters.

My mother, Adlin (Sissy, as she is affectionately called by her siblings), is slowly slipping into the unknown world of dementia. I recently struggled to remember the words from one of my favorite poems that she taught me as a young girl. She called it "Blessing the Children." I found it in the book *The Best Loved Poems of the American People*, under the title "Christ and the Little Ones." Excitedly I recited it for Mom. To my dismay, she had no recollection of this, her favorite poem. It was even more frightening to hear her say she had no recollection of me living in the same city as she, even though she used to walk from her home to mine.

Mother was always misplacing things, so the diagnosis of dementia took me by surprise. I presumed her increased forgetfulness was part of the aging process. The fact that Mom will one day not be able to recognize me as her daughter is a thought too difficult to bear. The best I can do is to hold on to the love of Mother through the lessons she taught me in giving, sharing, caring, and being the very best I can be with what blessings God has bestowed upon me.

Some of the precious lessons I learned from my mother include the love of poetry. Mother had very little formal education, but at an early age she taught me many poems she knew from memory, and I remember many of them to this day. She taught me always to make room for one more guest at the dinner table, even though we were a large family and had little to spare. She taught me that no one in need should ever be turned away. And in a home where both parents didn't practice the same religious beliefs, she always gathered us for family worship.

There are many women in our lives who have given us a blessed legacy. And we, in turn, can be a blessing to others around us. The legacy I have inherited from my mother's love will bear fruit for eternity.

Avis Mae Rodney

Not Ready

Now I am coming to you for the third time, and I will not be a burden to you.
I don't want what you have—I want you. 2 Cor. 12:14, NLT.

WHEN MY ELDEST son moved away from home to attend Avondale College, I was both proud of him and heartbroken that I wouldn't be able to see him every day. We could chat on the phone, we could e-mail each other, and we could visit, but I could not have his company. I yearned to be with him, and longed to embrace him. I imagined him busy with assignments, catching up with friends, and working.

I grieved deeply, and I just had to visit him. I booked a ticket to the railway station closest to the college. I told him a week in advance that the train would arrive at 6:00 in the evening. I reminded him a few days later. The day I left I reminded him again, then phoned him a third time as I sat in the train, ready for departure. Later I told him that the train was running on time, and that I expected to arrive at 6:00. He said he was looking forward to seeing me, but asked that I phone him when the train got closer. At 5:30 I phoned him and told him of my excitement—it would be only 30 minutes till I saw him. He asked that I phone him again when the train was closer still. I phoned again when there were just 15 minutes to go. I got the same response: "Phone me when you are closer." He didn't understand that this *was* that call! I phoned again at 10 minutes and at 5:55. When I arrived at the station after the long trip, I expected him to be standing there with arms wide open, ready with my long-awaited Mother's Day hug he owed me. He wasn't there, and it was getting dark. It was a terrible feeling knowing I had made such an effort, and he wasn't ready.

The agony in my heart drew my attention to my relationship with our heavenly Parent and Elder Brother. He longs to be with us; He looks forward to spending time with us. He is making an enormous effort to come and take us to live with Him. He has reminded us that He is coming soon, and He has told us what to look for, how to tell the spiritual time. Imagine how devastated Jesus must be each day when we don't take the time to meet Him in personal devotions, and how devastated He would be if He arrived and found that we were not ready.

Bridgid Kilgour

First Responder

But I will restore you to health and heal your wounds, declares the Lord.
Jer. 30:17, NIV.

AS SAFETY DIRECTOR of my company I am responsible for facilitating instruction on all types of safety issues, from hazardous materials to emergency response. This training cannot be taken lightly, as it can make the difference between life and death in many circumstances. Our policy is that working safely is the responsibility of everyone. It shows respect for ourselves, our coworkers, and the company. We bring in experts in these fields to present topnotch training and ideas that have been tried and have worked in emergency situations.

One of our most recent classes was in first aid and CPR (cardiopulmonary resuscitation). The class combined watching a lifesaving drama on video, classroom training, and demonstrations on the resuscitation dummy. The instructors repeatedly stressed the need for immediate response. A patient who isn't breathing can become brain damaged, or die within minutes, and heavy loss of blood can also cause death. Many lives have been saved by these lifesaving techniques—and there are many heroes to thank.

As I contemplated this I pictured Jesus as our first responder. He saw our deplorable condition caused by sin. The plan of saving us was created by experts in the field—God the Father and Jesus, His Son. When Adam and Eve sinned, it was a desperate situation in which all humankind would be eternally lost if there was no intervention. He saw us dying without any hope of survival and came to us to give us life. As He responded to the emergency call and came to earth as a human being, He offered us His breath of life, pouring His Word into our beings. Transfusing His blood into ours by His death on the cross, He saved our lives. He restores our vital functions so that we may live with Him forever in His kingdom.

My son wears a T-shirt that says, "My life was saved by a blood donor." Yes, indeed; we can be thankful for Jesus' perfect response to our dire situation. We would have no hope without Him. He not only donated a pint to our cause—He sacrificed every single drop of His blood to cover the darkness of sin in this world. He does this every day for us. His blood is infused into our lives to give us renewed vitality, supernatural power—there's power in the blood—and sustaining life. He's our hero. He's our Savior. He's our first responder—the only one we need!

Karen Phillips

I Couldn't Stop the Car!

For he shall give his angels charge over thee, to keep thee in all thy ways.
Ps. 91:11.

OUR AIRPLANE HAD just touched down, and not wanting to allow another minute to pass, I clicked on my cell phone and called my parents. Dad answered. "We're so glad you're back," he said, then added, "And when you come by, your mother has something interesting to tell you."

After dropping our suitcases off at our house, we drove the short distance to their home. Immediately I noticed that only one of their two cars was parked in the driveway. After a brief conversation about our vacation, I asked, "Mom, what happened to your car?"

My 77-year-old mother sighed, then began relating a story that sent a tingle down my spine. "Your dad and I were on our way to church, and as I started to apply the brakes for a red light, I had none. I couldn't stop the car!"

My eyes grew big as she continued. "I worked in vain, certain that I was going to crash into the car ahead," she said. "But then suddenly something miraculous happened."

I waited, silently thanking God that they were OK.

"The car eased to a stop within inches of the car in front of it."

"Angels." The word dropped freely from my lips. "Angels stopped the car."

We all agreed. God in His mercy saw what was happening and dispatched an angel to come to the aid of my parents.

Later I again reflected on this situation and how good God really is. We put our trust in so many "things." We assume that an alarm clock will wake us each morning, an airplane will maintain its altitude and not fall, and that water flowing from a tap will be safe to drink. But these are only things. It is our Father who taps us on the shoulder each morning. It is God who keeps the worlds from colliding in space. It is God who sends angels to protect us. We don't see angels, but we know that God has put them in charge of us. It's often angels whom God dispatches to save us in distressing situations.

Trusting God in all things is critical to our well-being. He won't leave us when we put our trust in Him. And more important, He never fails. I'm so glad that He sent an angel to stop my parents' car; I'm looking forward to saying thanks, in person, to this special heavenly being!

Yvonne Curry Smallwood

When the Spirit Moves You, Listen!

*When thou art in tribulation, and all these things are come upon thee,
even in the latter days, if thou turn to the Lord thy God,
and shalt be obedient unto his voice; (For the Lord thy God is a merciful
God;) he will not forsake thee, neither destroy thee, nor forget the
covenant of thy fathers which he sware unto them. Deut. 4:30, 31.*

THE MISSION TRIP TO KAZAKHSTAN wasn't at all what I'd expected. But then, what mission trip is? They're full of surprises, joys, disappointments, trials, temptations, and surely a roller coaster of emotions. Altogether Kazakhstan seemed too much for me to handle. So I initially said no when I was asked to return. I closed my ears to God and fought Him for two weeks. But what if God wanted me to go back? "OK, Lord," I prayed, "Thy will be done." Three weeks later we were off to Kazakhstan.

We had a ritual to help us de-stress, consisting of sipping green tea, nibbling on oatmeal cookies, and sharing about the events of the day. One Sunday our ritual turned into a vital lesson. We were only 10 minutes or so into our ritual when I felt the strong urge to move. I couldn't explain it. *Why should I move? We always sit here.* Yet the feeling wouldn't go away. "Honey, we have to move into the living room," I told my husband.

"Why?" he asked. The computer engineer does nothing without an explanation. But I had none. I knew only that we had to move, and I told him so. He agreed.

We moved our cookies and tea into the living room. About 15 minutes later we heard an extremely loud crash. With a cup of tea in hand and crumbles of cookies in our mouths and around our lips, we sat there in silence and stared at each other. Frozen. Finally we moved to the kitchen door and gaped in amazement. The cabinet that had been mounted to the wall, full of plates, glasses, and food items, had crashed to the floor, but not before it collided with the kitchen table, where we had been seated only minutes before.

That day our cleanup session doubled as a praise session. We thanked God for His everlasting mercy and very real presence in our lives.

God is willing to lead, protect, and save. Are we willing to obey? If we will only listen, He will gently and lovingly lead.

LaToya V. Zavala

The Holy Spirit
Is Awesomely Fair

Howbeit when he, the Spirit of truth,
is come, he will guide you into all truth. John 16:13.

IN OUR SABBATH Bible study class the teacher mentioned that the teacher of his high school Bible class had drawn a chart illustrating the Christian walk: God at the top, us at the bottom. Throughout our Christian experience, as we worked real hard (with God's help), we gradually climbed closer and closer toward God. Many of us could picture the drawing. He said he later realized that that was not a true picture of grace. God does it all. We allow it to happen in our individual lives, but we don't accomplish it by working hard. He said that although his teacher taught it incorrectly, he didn't feel upset with the teacher. He realized we are all growing in our understanding of God and His grace.

A class member asked what brought him to a new understanding. As the class went on with their discussion, I listened, but I also sensed the Holy Spirit telling me, "I am the One who helps you understand the truth about God's grace." I pictured the Holy Spirit using nature, kind relationships, or whatever He needed to speak the truth to people who can't read or don't have any other way to learn about Him.

I thrilled to realize the Holy Spirit is awesomely fair. He uses whatever is necessary for each one of us. For those who have it available, He uses the Scriptures, but He isn't limited to that, even with us. He knows how to speak to the highly educated person. He knows how to approach those with scientific minds. He is creative in how He teaches the less educated.

I sensed Him hovering over the class where I sat, working with each person there to lead them to a deeper understanding of the truth about God.

I felt so grateful for this Gift that Jesus gave us. Only Jesus knew how much we needed the Holy Spirit when He promised Him to us.

As the class dispersed I continued to ponder this wonderful truth. I know that trying to share truth by myself won't have the same impact as it does when the Holy Spirit teaches us; it is then that our hearts "burn within us" (Luke 24:32).

For some reason the Holy Spirit knew that I needed a broader understanding of His work just then, so He spoke that truth to my heart.

Lana Fletcher

Be Faithful to the End!

Let us not become weary in doing good, for at the proper time
we will reap a harvest if we do not give up. Gal. 6:9, NIV.

SHE WAS A special woman, a woman who persevered and served the Lord untiringly. Though she's now gone, the memory of her vigilance and zeal in serving the Lord still lingers. She passed away in her sleep in 2008 at the age of 88. This woman was my mother,

P. C. Yeong was a petite, kind, and spiritual woman. For years she went door to door, selling religious books and magazines, noted for her dedication and unwavering faith in the Lord.

In her younger days she'd been active in leading out each Sabbath afternoon in a Vacation Bible School at the house where we grew up. She would send four of her six older children out to invite children from the neighborhood to the story hour. John, a Chinese teenage lad, along with his two younger brothers, came without fail to the children's story hour. (They may have been attracted by the goodies served at the end of the story hour.) Eventually, through the prompting of the Holy Spirit, the three brothers were baptized.

Hearing of my mother's death, John, who is now retired from his personal business enterprise in Vancouver, Canada, confessed, "It is because of your mother that I am a Christian today, and for what I have become. I will always remember every Sabbath at 2:00 at your house, and the hymns 'Give Me the Bible' and 'What a Friend We Have in Jesus' that I learned to sing. This made a great impact on my young life. Thinking about this brings back the fondest memories of my childhood. It was the best time of my life. Florence, my wife, and I are so blessed now. Our two young adult children have decided to work for the Lord and believe earnestly that Jesus is coming soon."

Even though it sometimes takes a long time, it is wonderful to know that the seeds of truth have multiplied from one generation to another.

Indeed, Mother's faithfulness to the Lord made a tremendous impact on me, as well. What I am today I owe to my mother. Friends, do not be weary of the good work that you do. Though it may be difficult at times, don't give up! Jesus is coming soon! Let us all be faithful. Only when His Word is carried to all corners of the world will He come again.

Ivy Ng

He Will Provide All Your Needs

For You, O Lord, will bless the righteous; with favor
You will surround him as with a shield. Ps. 5:12, NKJV.

AFTER MY RECOVERY from a serious illness, my husband and I decided to move to the Virgin Islands, where he got a job at the hospital in St. Croix. We were so excited to live on a beautiful, warm, tropical island. We bought five acres of land on a nice hill facing the ocean, and we planned to build the house of our dreams. We started the building and worked so hard. We really wanted to finish the house so we could move in. But in the midst of the construction we realized that all the materials and labor costs were three times more expensive than expected. Soon we had to stop the work because of the lack of money. We were so desperate and eager to move to our new home.

One Friday we needed $3,500 to pay the workers. Where were we going to get this money? I talked to my husband on the phone. He said he had a check for only a small amount, not even close to $1,000; nevertheless, I went to pick up the check. He also gave me some addresses of people who owed him money, but they weren't large amounts either. I went to pick up all the checks, but since I just knew we weren't going to get all the $3,500 we needed, I didn't even look at them. But I prayed all the way anyway.

When I got to the bank to cash the checks, I again asked the Lord to help me. I got to the cashier and asked her to cash all the checks for me. And to my great surprise, she handed me $4,000. I couldn't believe it! Isn't the Lord amazing?

I thanked God all the way back to the property. I knew it was God who had made this miracle for us. And I praise Him for that! In fact, I've seen His holy hand all through my life. No matter what situation you are going through, God is on your side to help you until the situation is resolved. The only thing you have to do is trust in Him with all your heart, and He will give you the petitions of your heart. I think David says it so well: "O taste and see that the Lord is good; happy are those who take refuge in him. O fear the Lord, you his holy ones, for those who fear him have no want" (Ps. 34:8, 9, NRSV).

Heidi R. Snow

Big Trouble

God is our refuge and strength, a very present help in trouble. Ps. 46:1.

TWO-YEAR-OLD Joanna found the door to her grandpa's study open and walked in to explore. A moment later she walked out with a calculator in her hand. "Phone!" she said. Joanna loves anything with buttons to push or knobs to turn, and she loves to talk on the telephone. To her, the calculator with its little window and all the numbers must have looked like a cell phone.

She punched some of the buttons, then held it to her ear. "Hello! Grandma!"

"Hello, Joanna. I love you," I answered, pretending to hold a phone to my ear.

"No! Joanna, no," her mother said. "That belongs to Grandpa. Give it to me, please."

"Phone! Mine!" Joanna said, and ran down the hall away from her mother.

After several more exchanges, her mother warned, "You're in big trouble now, Joanna!"

Joanna ran down the hall, giggling. "Big trouble! I'm in big trouble!"

We all laughed. She was just too cute. She loves being center stage. She wasn't sure what trouble meant, but she kept out of her mother's reach. Finally Sally got the wooden spoon and held it up and began to count, "One, two . . ."

There was no doubt in Joanna's mind now what trouble meant. She frowned and looked at her mother. She could see her mom meant business, so she ran to Grandma for safety.

"Big trouble," she said.

"OK; I'll take the 'phone.' Then no more trouble," I said, holding her close. Joanna surrendered the calculator, then ran down the hall to her toy box to find something to play with.

When Joanna was in trouble, she ran to Grandma. She figured the spoon would not reach her in Grandma's arms, and she was right. But Grandma didn't say she could still play with the calculator. Instead, Grandma took away her temptation, and there was no more big trouble.

How often have we been like Joanna in our handling of temptation? We want so much to do whatever it is our heart is set on, until we find that we're in for big trouble. In the face of the consequences we turn to God for help. He is always there, ready to deliver us.

The next time I find myself getting into big trouble I pray that I might run quickly to the safety of Him who is my "refuge and strength" and "a very present help in trouble."

Dorothy Eaton Watts

Lesson Learned

In all your ways acknowledge Him, and He shall direct your paths.
Prov. 3:6, NKJV.

MY DAUGHTER WAS excited about her first job (other than babysitting). This was her first real job, complete with an identification badge and payroll checks. She had received her "offer of employment" letter, confirming the position and compensation. The letter indicated more details would follow. Shortly thereafter she received another letter announcing her orientation date. The letter also indicated that attendance was mandatory, that it was a paid orientation and not attending would result in the offer of employment being withdrawn. The date was on a Saturday, the day we observe as the Sabbath.

As we discussed it, she expressed her anxiety that her job was possibly in jeopardy, and she really wanted "a good summer job." I explained that there was no summer job so good that she needed to compromise her Sabbath observance. Since she was a minor, I said that I'd call the office and explain the situation, and if they could accommodate an alternate orientation date, so be it. If they couldn't, that would be all right as well. I explained to her that there were other jobs for which she could apply, and that she was working, not out of necessity, but because she wanted to earn her own money. She was clear that she wouldn't be able to take the job if the change could not be made. I explained how it was important to be consistent about this with her employers.

I understood my daughter's excitement and appreciated her work ethic, but knew this was an important "test" for her. The way she handled this would influence her future employment decisions on this issue.

She agreed that I could call the management office. In the meantime I prayed that God would make His will clear, and that He would show my daughter how to stand for what she believed in and to trust Him, regardless of the outcome. I knew this would be an important lesson for her. When I called the human resources department, they were more than willing to reschedule her orientation to another day. We breathed a sigh of relief. She was glad to be able to continue with her summer job plans, and I was glad that she received affirmation that if you put God first He will clear the way.

Kimberly N. Sutton

Making the Team

For where two or three are gathered together in my name, there am I in the midst of them. Matt. 18:20.

MANY OF US can remember how teams were chosen for games when we were children. The team captains were chosen first. Then the rest of us stood around like slaves on an auction block, waiting while the captains picked the kids who they thought would help their team win. Of course the best were chosen first.

That's when everyone "got religion." Each one prayed that they wouldn't get chosen last.

But eventually, for better or worse, everyone got to be on a team. But how would you feel if you never made the team?

I thought about that while reading the first chapter in the book of Acts. Judas, the betrayer of Jesus, had recently committed suicide. The disciples gathered together to pick a replacement. There were two candidates: Joseph, called Barsabbas, and a man named Matthias. After earnest prayer they drew lots, and the lot fell on Matthias, who was officially added to the team as one of the 12.

I wonder what went through the mind of Barsabbas when he didn't "make the team." Did he feel hurt or angry? Was he relieved? Did he take the news as God's providence, or did he say, "If you guys don't think I'm good enough, then I'm out of here"? I'd like to think he stuck around, but I guess we'll never know this side of heaven.

We often have hopes and dreams that are never quite realized. But in God's eyes we are all important. The good news is that He wants all of us to be on His team.

The Lord has given each of us talents to use to benefit others. We don't need to invent a cure for the common cold or find a practical use for clothes dryer lint. But that's OK. Every gift God gives us is important, regardless of its size. Both small and large acts of kindness can change a life, but there are more opportunities to do the small ones.

So let's not lose sight of the fact that whatever we do for the Lord is never wasted.

There's a special blessing just in being on God's team. And I can't think of a better place to be—now and throughout eternity.

Marcia Mollenkopf

Be Anxious for Nothing

The Lord . . . cares for those who trust in him. Nahum 1:7, NIV.

"HELP! Everything won't fit in my carry-on!" moaned Melissa.

"It will contain what you *need*," I replied, adding, "We leave in 10 minutes."

Melissa rolled her large, expressive eyes and disappeared down the hall. I went to print boarding passes, and horrors! "Visa Now Needed" spread across the screen. *How had I missed that?*

By the time two electronic visas had been purchased and verified, Melissa's carry-on was packed, albeit bulging from every seam. We headed for the airport— it would be nip and tuck. "You are vibrating with tension," Melissa observed, glancing at white knuckles that gripped the steering wheel. "God wants you to present this seminar, so we'll get there."

"Thanks," I responded, a touch of irritation creeping into my voice. Under her breath Melissa murmured, "Just giving you some of your own medicine." (Ouch.)

She was right. I was a tad anxious. OK, I was really anxious. Taking a deep breath, I looked at the setting sun, changed my thoughts from negative to positive, and sent a prayer winging upward. Halfway to the airport the sky suddenly darkened as rolling waves of thick fog rippled in from the sea. "We're fortunate the fog is 10 feet off the ground," I commented.

"Oh, we are *most* fortunate!" exclaimed Melissa, laughing delightedly. "Now our plane will definitely be delayed." It was. Two hours delayed. Throughout the airport conversation buzzed about the unusually thick and unseasonal fog. *H'mmm.*

We boarded with a few minutes to spare and buckled up for takeoff. Melissa slipped her hand into mine and squeezed. "I'm not really anxious," she twittered in her big-girl voice. "I just need a bit of reassurance [how she loved long words], seeing as this is my first flight and all." I smiled to myself.

As the powerful jet-engine thrust plastered us against the seat, I reflected, *How easy it is to slip into old patterns of behavior during moments of stress. How helpful— OK, how irritating, as well—to get your own words back. How reassuring to know we can change our thoughts and get on track.* I squeezed Melissa's hand, and we were airborne. "Be anxious for nothing" (Phil. 4:6, NKJV).

Arlene Taylor

God's Strength and Protection

The Lord is my strength and my shield;
my heart trusts in him, and I am helped. Ps. 28:7, NIV.

I WAS RAISED around horses. My mother bought me a Shetland pony, named Honeydew. She was a beautiful chestnut paint mare. I had many good rides on her while I had her, but after a few years I grew too tall for Honeydew. So my mom decided to sell the mare and get a new horse. When I was in first grade we went to look at a friend's horses that were for sale. My aunt bought a Standard bred mare named Country, and my mom bought me a beautiful chestnut pony that was half Welsh and half Arabian, named Ginger. I fell in love with her the minute I saw her! She was very loving and well trained.

When I was around 7 years old, I was playing out in the pasture, following my pony, Ginger, around, acting like her foal. I'd been playing for a while when she decided she wanted to go by the gate. She started jogging and went around the corner of our barn with me behind her—I had to run to catch up. As I rounded the barn I caught my aunt's horse, Country, by surprise, and she kicked out with her hind leg, striking me in the stomach area by my ribs. I dropped to the ground, unable to breathe. I crawled to the gate and tried to get my mother's attention, trying to yell to her. At first she thought I was fooling around, but in a few minutes she realized I wasn't joking and came over. She saw me on the ground, hurt, and ran to get Uncle Garry.

He picked me up and carried me to the house. He laid me on the couch, and my grandmother looked me over and found that I hadn't broken my ribs or any bones. When I finally got my breathing back to normal, they asked me what had happened, and I told them. I had learned my lesson. I would never again run up behind a horse, catching it by surprise. I always start talking to them when I approach any horse.

God was definitely there for me that day. He had wrapped His strong arms around me and protected me. I realized God is always there for me—and for all of us. All we need to do is place our trust in Him and talk to Him. Here's a promise of His protection for you for today: "The Lord will keep you from all harm—he will watch over your life; the Lord will watch over your coming and going both now and forevermore" (Ps. 121:7, 8, NIV).

Ashley Anne Nelson

The Sweet Sound of "Grace"

For it is by grace you have been saved, through faith—and this not from yourselves, it is the gift of God. Eph. 2:8, NIV.

AS I WRITE this the calendar reads May 26, 2009. Today I celebrate my seventy-eighth birthday. However, publication of this devotional is not for a couple years. I'm in reasonably good health, and hopeful that I'll still be around then. If I'm not, I know that the words I write can remain. If there's only one thing that I can leave as a writer, should I not see more years, it is to ask you to think on the word and the meaning of "grace."

Grace. Such a lovely word! It almost has a tune to it. Is that why John Newton, the writer of the hymn "Amazing Grace" wrote the words "how sweet the sound"? Indeed, the very sound of the word "grace" is comforting. There are words that possess a built-in beauty, and grace is one of these words. Many women are named Grace. I had a friend whose name was Carolyn Grace. She preferred both names in addressing her. "I favor the sound of 'Grace' because it sounds like a sweet song," she said.

In the Christian vocabulary our Father God's forgiving character becomes profound through the understanding of this word "grace." It is an awesome act of God for Him to pronounce grace upon us, because by nature we are born sinners, undeserving of grace.

Recently I heard a story told by a Holocaust survivor, a heart-wrenching tale of how her family suffered through horrific atrocities during World War II. Though she was a very young child, she recalls a tragic place where corpses were heaped up like cordwood. The family was liberated by the Soviets, and though her father died soon afterward, he died a free man, not a prisoner. His free-man status made all the difference to the little family. They considered it God's graciousness.

Her story caused me to ponder God's grace anew. Grace is the only escape for a prisoner of sin. Fortunately, we don't have to wait for an army to rescue us; we can simply accept God's grace. That act of ours brings joy to the heart of Jesus because He is the one who made it possible. Yes, Jesus is our liberator. Thus, the act of grace is truly an amazing, sweet song ringing forth from heaven.

Betty Kossick

You Are a Channel of Blessing

Bless, and curse not. Rom. 12:14.

SELFISHNESS IS A sentiment that prevents us from receiving great blessings from God. One of the greatest blessings He wants for us is that we in turn be a blessing to others. But the selfish person looks only to their own desires. They decide what they desire, and then don't think about others; nothing good flows from them, because God doesn't have a place in their life. There's no place for God's will to be done in them.

When our first parents sinned, selfishness took over and, as result, Adam and Eve realized they were naked. Selfishness made them focus on themselves—and it still does. They also blamed others while defending themselves. "The serpent fooled me," the woman claimed. And Adam passed the blame to Eve: "The woman you gave me . . ."

We can see the result of Adam's and Eve's actions today. Instead of blessings, there were curses for the entire planet. The human tendency today is to defend and serve ourselves, accusing and oppressing others, and as a consequence, many are deprived of receiving blessings that they could receive only through another person—love, affection, understanding, empathy, or simply having someone listen for a minute.

What is the antidote for this great selfishness? Look around you; stop and observe those who may be in need; stop looking at yourself for a moment. Right away you will notice that there is more than one person who needs something that you abundantly possess.

Next, stop defending yourself. When we indulge in "self," we become insensitive toward others, and we blame others easily for situations for which we are the only one responsible. This is done so as not to hurt our "self." Instead, if we are wise with ourselves, we would even scold the "self" in us, which on occasion needs to be done.

Someone has written, "The greatest blessing a person could receive is that of being a blessing to others. The kingdom of God will not have men and women who in their lifetime had the habit of not sharing their happiness. In the perfect universe the only interest of the intelligent beings will be to make others happy."

As an heir of blessings you are called to be a channel through whom heavenly riches can flow for others. May this be a reality in your life.

Gisselle Lavandier de Vásquez

Flying Behind the Line

He gives strength to the weary and increases the power of the weak.
Isa. 40:29, NIV.

IT'S BEEN SO dry lately that I get out early to pull a few weeds and start the water. One morning I was enjoying the coolness when I suddenly became aware of a far-off calling high above me. I scanned the sky in the direction of the voices. Suddenly I saw the long jagged line of migrating geese, their beating wings glittering silver in the morning light. I knew they had hundreds of miles to go before they reached their destination in the nesting ground of the North. I felt so completely small as those beautiful creatures journeyed on with full confidence in their Creator.

In the several V's passing overhead, the leadership passed from one bird to another so that each follower could rest in a pocket of less resistance behind another bird. Some distance behind the line two or three birds flew, keeping pace with the group, but alone in the sky. I wondered if they were weak and unable to keep up, or if they had just gotten a late start.

I knew that in the evening, after flying all day, the flock would float down to shimmering waters for food and rest. Then in the first light of dawn, renewed by the respite, they would continue on toward home. On they would go, closing ranks if one bird fell, taking turns leading and drafting, resting when they must. They were absolutely unstoppable. They were going home.

The kingdom of God is like wild geese migrating to nesting grounds. Everyone must fly individually. We must communicate as we go, oblivious to the distractions above and below. We must keep flying, intent on the destination. The shadows of those obviously flying in the opposite direction should not tempt us.

And yes, the Christian life is sometimes like geese flying behind the line! We find ourselves with a group, all eternity bound, but somehow struggling alone. Circumstances push us back until we perceive ourselves out there without anyplace to draft. Many things can happen; we lose a mate, we go bankrupt, our children take a wrong path, we battle with some cherished sin, our health deteriorates, we find ourselves traumatized. We are flying behind the line.

What can we say to those who feel separated? Don't ever give up! Remember that with God's help you can keep up the pace even if you are alone. Tomorrow, by God's grace, you will rise to be part of the line—unstoppable—almost home!

Beth Wells Carlson

An Extra Room and Kitchen Counter Space, Lord

Delight thyself also in the Lord; and he shall give thee the desires of thine heart. Ps. 37:4.

WHEN YOU ARE married to a pastor, moving becomes a science. You learn how to pack so that your dishes don't break, how to mark your boxes properly so that when you arrive at your destination your dishes don't end up in the bedroom. After being in the capital city of our archipelago for 17 years, however, I thought our moving days were over. But God has an interesting way of taking us out of our comfort zone so that we can learn to depend on Him.

After the sudden death of an administrator on another island, my husband was asked to pastor the city church in that area, and after much prayer we decided to accept. Our first priority was to find a house. My husband and I flew to the island on two different occasions to search for a house, but with no success. Our biggest concern was finding space to put my husband's books. He's an avid reader and over the years had accumulated quite a library. So my prayer to the Lord was simple: "Lord, we don't need anything big or fancy. But I would like a kitchen with a lot of counter space, and an extra room big enough for my husband's books."

We looked at some beautiful homes, but none fit our purpose. The following week we made one last house-hunting trip. I prayed again, reminding the Lord that we were moving at His command, so He needed to provide a house for us. After two days we headed to the airport, disappointed and frustrated.

On the way our driver stopped for gas. He returned with a newspaper, and my husband glanced at the real estate ads. One particular ad caught his fancy, and I dialed the number listed. When a very pleasant-sounding woman answered the phone, I explained the purpose of the call. She offered to meet us at the address.

As we toured the house I could hardly conceal my excitement. The master bedroom was huge, and there was a family room. But more important, there was a good-sized kitchen with lots of counter space—and a spare room that could hold all my husband's books!

God is so wonderful to us. He promised to give us the desires of our hearts, and now I know that it sometimes means giving us a kitchen with lots of counter space and a room that can be turned into a study.

Lynn C. Smith

Pray Without Ceasing

For his God doth instruct him to discretion, and doth teach him. Isa. 28:26.

EIGHT MONTHS HAD passed, and I hadn't yet received final payment for the project. It had been a difficult consultancy, entailing working with a large team, overcoming numerous obstacles, and a redefinition of goals. In fact, the 12 months originally estimated stretched into two years, with ups and downs at every corner, not the least of which was the rewording and rewriting of the final report.

After all this effort and a two-month delay, I was informed that additional changes were required before acceptance, and, of course, payment for the work done. I was unhappy, and decided that no more changes would be made. Too much time had already been invested, and to my knowledge, the report was well done. It reflected the activities developed, presented clear-cut, well-defined recommendations and the program to be implemented for the desired outcomes, all of which were laid out in the format designed by the contracting agency for this purpose. I pushed the matter from my mind.

After several months the problem resurfaced, and I wondered what to do to get payment. Finally, about 3:00 one morning it dawned on me to ask the Lord for guidance in handling the situation, after which I went back to sleep. When I awoke, it came to me to write the head office. While I was thinking about composing the letter, a better idea struck me: telephone the in-house project director about the problem. He was surprised that payment had been so delayed and was well aware of the work done, having actually participated in various project-related meetings. In addition, he had received and approved copies of all the interim reports, including the final one! He assured me that he would take care of the matter immediately.

It makes me wonder. Had I approached the Lord sooner, would He have illuminated my mind with the problem-solving thought then, thereby sparing me much concern, worry, and delay in the cancellation of the debt? It is important for us to pray first rather than last when situations arise that we can't handle on our own. In fact, we should pray at all times!

Marion V. Clarke Martin

Faith, Demonstrated

And it shall come to pass, that before they call, I will answer; and while they are yet speaking, I will hear. Isa. 65:24.

A FEW YEARS ago God gave me a demonstration of faith to show me how useless it is for me to worry. My youngest son, Rod, had just finished high school and was in need of a job. The start of college was still a couple months away; however, the part-time job he had at a nearby fast-food restaurant helped but wasn't enough.

I mentioned Rod's plight to a close friend. She had a suggestion. Her employer needed a nightshift person to operate their copier, preferably a high school graduate with basic computer knowledge, one who was also planning to go to college. The position seemed perfect. Rod was a natural with computers, and he'd always been a night owl. He made the call.

I prayed that Rod would get the job, but that's where my test of faith began. Rod was told that the man would call him back in a couple days. I was fine on day one; by the second day I found myself getting anxious every time the phone rang. That day came and went. I started bugging Rod to make a follow-up contact.

Rod has much more faith than I do. He takes life as God presents it to him, always calm and confident. I knew he wasn't the least bit worried about getting the job, but he obediently made another call. He again was told that the man was out of the office and would call him back. "Don't worry, Mom. I know I already have the job," he assured me.

"How can you be so sure?" I demanded.

"I just know."

Then it struck me. "I just know." That's faith! Just knowing. It's that inner peace that comes from trusting in God and accepting His control. It's knowing that God has already answered our prayers before we pray them, and that He's doing everything for our good. We don't have to wonder and fret and worry, because He's already taken care of it.

I stared at my child for a moment, reflecting again on what he had said: "I just know." Once again, God had given me a lesson, and I began to understand. Rod was hired the next day.

Marcia R. Pope

Even Greater Blessings

Be of good courage, and he shall strengthen your heart. Ps. 31:24.

WE HAD HAD a difficult two months. I'd been ill, and my husband, Ted, had suffered three broken ribs after falling down our open stairway—all 14 steps. I had called an ambulance at 3:00 a.m. The doctor shook his head in disbelief and said, "You could have broken your neck or killed yourself. You were very lucky." We knew better. It was not luck!

Now it was time to get ready to go to our 10-day camp meeting, a yearly treat because we need the spiritual refreshment. Could we do it? We prayed for a way. Our granddaughter Andrea and her husband, Mac, offered to take our car a day ahead of time. They packed and loaded the car, then drove the 100 miles, unloaded, and set up our room. We arrived on the day camp started and oh, how good it was to be there! God had taken everything into His hands.

On the third day my breathing became more difficult, and I went to the emergency room, where it was discovered that I had pneumonia. Then Ted fell down at our daughter's house and broke two more ribs. Now what? Here we were at camp meeting, both of us very disabled. How disheartening! We both went to bed to stay. Some seminars and sermons were broadcasted on the local radio station, so we could at least enjoy some of the camp meeting.

An added blessing was the many friends who stopped by our room to visit and pray with us. Friday afternoon I had to revisit the clinic. As we were going to our car a group of students asked to pray with us. Then they helped us find our car (we forgot we had moved it), running all over campus looking for it until they found it. What an inspiration those young people were!

On the last weekend Shawn Boonstra, from the *It Is Written* TV program, was to speak. Of course we would miss out. The last Saturday night I was especially blue because we couldn't go to the final meeting. Then 20 minutes before meeting time someone knocked at our door—and there stood Shawn Boonstra! He had come to our room to visit and pray with us. A friend had explained our situation to him, and it lifted our hearts beyond measure that he came to be with us.

On Sunday friends offered to pack our car for the trip home. We had been so ill and disappointed that we had missed so much, but God had sent us many even greater blessings.

Darlene Ytredal Burgeson

Today, if You Hear His Voice

So, as the Holy Spirit says: "Today, if you hear his voice, do not harden your hearts as you did in the rebellion, during the time of testing in the desert, where your fathers tested and tried me and for forty years saw what I did." Heb. 3:7-9, NIV.

I DROPPED OFF the out-of-town youth at the train station in Arnhem. The Netherlands was a new country to me, and I spoke only a few words of the language, but I was learning fast. After waving goodbye to the young people I turned to go home.

My eyes caught sight of a young woman standing on the platform as the international train to Germany pulled out. She was sobbing uncontrollably, and I thought she might jump in front of the next train that would come by. Something told me to step up to her and put my arms around her and ask if she was all right. Why was she so sad?

Instead I turned away and walked toward my car and drove home. Why hadn't I comforted her? The Savior's words rang in my head: "What you have done unto the least of these my brethren, you have done unto me." I nearly turned back, but I told myself that I didn't speak the language; it would be embarrassing.

However, I learned a valuable lesson and promised myself that if I ever again felt impressed to take action, either in word or deed, I wouldn't let pride come in between. Whatever the cost, next time I would respond.

Years later my husband and I drove past a woman sitting at the curb, obviously crying. By the time we had realized it, we were much farther down the road, but as one person we agreed we needed to go back. We pulled up at the curbside, and I got out. She stood up as I approached her. Gently I put my arms around her and asked her if she was all right. She told me that her aunt had just passed away, and everyone was in the house. She couldn't take it any longer. I told her that I had just lost my father, but that God knows all of us and loves us. She returned my hug as I asked her if she was going to be all right. She assured me, "Yes, I will be all right now."

Oh, that God will teach us to walk with our eyes open and our antennae out so that we don't pass people by. We are God's tools for reaching out to people in our sick, sad, and wicked world.

Sinikka Dixon

Rejoice in the Lord

Rejoice in the Lord alway: and again I say, Rejoice. Phil. 4:4.

IT WAS THE summer I graduated from high school in California. It had been a good year, my senior year. My mom and dad stayed until after graduation, then they were moving back to Michigan. I was alone in California except for my sister. She'd been living in Glendale, but was going to a nursing school in Paradise Valley, near San Diego, and said I could live in her apartment in Glendale and get a job to pay the rent.

She had paid the first month already, so it was just a matter of my getting a job now to pay the bills. I had been young for my grade, graduating as a 17-year-old. I went out each day hunting for a job; however, it became more and more apparent that I was going to have a rough time because nobody wanted to give a job to someone not yet 18, even though I had graduated from high school. It would be October before I would turn 18, and I wondered what I was to do about this problem in the meantime. There was only one thing to do: leave it in the Lord's hands.

I really prayed for a job and for God to look out for me. One Sunday I noticed a help-wanted ad in the newspaper. It was a cookie company that needed nine people, and to please come at 10:00 Monday morning. When I arrived, I discovered that I was one of 35 applying for the positions. A man lined us up in a straight line and walked up and down, looking us over. Then he chose nine of us—and I was chosen! They put us to work that day. We didn't even fill out an application until several days later. When we did, they never caught that I wasn't 18 yet. You can be sure that I worked there until well past my birthday! I was praising the Lord for this opportunity and for answered prayer.

It's wonderful how God takes care of every aspect of our lives. He knows what we need even before we ask. Talk about a wonderful Friend! I don't understand how people survive without a connection with God. I'm glad I learned about the Lord, and I asked Him to direct every aspect of my being early in my life. Long ago it was written, "In all thy ways acknowledge him, and he shall direct thy paths" (Prov. 3:6). When we do that, there will be much for which to rejoice! I invite you to ask Him into your life today and every day.

Anne Elaine Nelson

God's Watchful Eye

Fear thou not; for I am with thee: be not dismayed; for I am thy God:
I will strengthen thee; yea, I will help thee; yea, I will uphold thee
with the right hand of my righteousness. Isa. 41:10.

I WAS STANDING at the kitchen sink one morning, looking out the window and becoming immersed in the scene of God's handiwork, enjoying nature in all its splendor when it happened!

My eyes were transfixed on an event unfolding inside the gazebo located on the deck of my house. There was a bird flying around in circles, frantically trying to find its way out. As I watched, the bird repeatedly returned to the corner where it had probably entered, then mustered up all its strength, set its wings into flight, and soared—only to be rebuffed by the enclosed screen.

Sensing the bird's fear and rapidly diminishing hope for escape, and its increasing helplessness, I sprang into action. I went out onto the deck and opened wide the door to the gazebo, knowing that the bird would sense the incoming breeze and follow the current to freedom. But it didn't happen. Eventually, it seemed to understand that the way it got in was not the way out. That's when the path to freedom became a reality. The bird altered its direction, set its wings into flight, and with all of its might soared through the open door.

How like us! Often (in fact, probably every day) we make our plans for the day and set about accomplishing them, meeting the many deadlines set by ourselves or others when—it happens. We find ourselves in a difficult situation, but with a strong sense of confidence we try to resolve the problem, relieve the distress, and move on. We keep doing the same thing again and again, trying to find a solution. But as we discover that our plans A, B, or C are not successful, we begin to worry, to become anxious, and to fear.

We forget that our heavenly Father has been watching us all along: He saw us when we got ourselves into the situation and had already prepared a way to escape. We forget that "God is our refuge and strength, a very present help in trouble" (Ps. 46:1), that God has already made a way to escape and is eagerly waiting for us to cry out to Him for help. How blessed we are that God tenderly watches over us, because He loves us, cares for us, and wants nothing but the best for us.

Cynthia Best-Goring

Forever Friends

A [woman] that hath friends must shew [herself] friendly: and there is a friend that sticketh closer than a [sister]. Prov. 18:24.

THIS IS HOW the letter was written:

"Dear Mattie, just a note to let you know I'm thinking about you. I've missed you so much since you moved away—nothing is the same around here. It was always so much fun to come to your house; you always stopped your quilting and sewing to show us around. The kids loved the kittens, and Buster was always ready for a game of tug-of-war with an old sock. I'm remembering all the times you made Mama feel at home if we needed to be away overnight. That was more Christlike than we deserved or could ever repay. Thank you so much for the lovely flower arrangements you sent for her funeral service. Everyone said they looked like they were just picked from your yard.

"How is Hannah? You are the best babysitter in the world—she must be on cloud nine, being the only child right now. You're the only one I know with such patience and love for the little ones. I've often thought that I could see Jesus in you—you seem to be so close to Him that it reflects in your actions! We will treasure your friendship in our family forever.

"Hope to see you soon, Carol."

But time went by. I was busy and didn't get around to mailing the letter. When I thought about it at all, I'd tell myself I had plenty of time. Mattie wasn't going anywhere. So I didn't mail it, and she never knew.

So this is the letter I did send:

"Please accept our sincere sympathy in the loss of your loved one. Mattie's love and friendship will be treasured by our family for all our days. May you find comfort in the hope of the second coming of Jesus when we will be reunited forever. May God bless."

I suppose—I hope—I learned several lessons from this incident, but mostly I'm ashamed that I didn't put forth a little more effort to show my friend that I loved her. It's just too easy to let time go by, to let things become more important than people, and not to reach out to friends and family and let them know they are loved. Today could make a difference.

Carol Wiggins Gigante

O You of Little Faith

O thou of little faith, wherefore didst thou doubt? Matt. 14:31.

IT HAS BEEN six years since my daughter Jeanine's legs started shutting down from a neurological condition that began when she was 18. One night I dreamed that she called me from her hospital bed and told me she would like to go for a walk with me. I said, "Honey, you can't move your legs, and your arms are too weak to hold you up." But she insisted, "I want to go for a walk, Mom. Let's walk to the river the way we used to do!" As she was saying this, a special strength came over her, and she sat up in bed. I was surprised! I sat there, afraid that if I helped her both of us would fall on the floor and be hurt, but she was determined that she was going to walk, no matter what. She sat up again, then stood, and began walking to the living room. I saw her legs walking slowly, then get stronger and more coordinated. I began jumping and shouting that it was a miracle and couldn't wait to call friends and family who have been praying for her to let them know about this great event. But as we returned home from the walk, my mind grew apprehensive, and I felt my faith fading. As I cherished negative thoughts her body grew weak, and I became afraid that she wouldn't be able to make it back to her hospital bed again. How sad and disappointed I felt

As I watched my daughter walking in my dream I was reminded how feeble is our human faith. Peter was shocked when he was invited to walk on the water, and as he looked away from the Savior his faith faded, and down he went. But Jesus still loved Peter and reminded him that he couldn't depend on himself, because even faith is a gift from God. It's important for us to remember that when we belong to Jesus Christ we aren't our own; we are bought with a price. God paid a ransom to save Jeanine, a ransom not of mere gold or silver. He paid for you and for me with the priceless lifeblood of Christ, the sinless, spotless Lamb of God.

Do you remember the story of the father who brought his son to be healed by the disciples but they were unable to heal him? "Jesus said unto him, If thou canst believe, all things are possible to him that believeth" (Mark 9:23). The father cried out, "I believe. Help thou mine unbelief" (verse 24). Despite conditions of bodily weakness, it inspires faith to know that Jeanine is a child born to the family of God, and that His love will one day make her whole.

Betty Cummings

Welcome Home

Blessed are they that do his commandments, that they may have right to the tree of life, and may enter in through the gates into the city. Rev. 22:14.

OUR FAMILY VACATION took us to a beautiful hotel overlooking a lake, and how quickly room 8205 became our home! To get there we turned left at the pool and walked past about 10 rooms to reach our home for four days. The view from the balcony soon became our view, the skyline ours. The chugging of the boats, the splashing of the jet skis, and the mournful cry of a ship's horn soon failed to startle us. Those were our sounds. By the end of the first day I knew the quirks of the shower nozzle and could humor it to enjoy the most satisfying shower.

However, I reminded myself that this lovely place was not our home. We lived hundreds of miles away, where there are beds to be made, garbage to be put out on Thursdays, and bills to pay. This gorgeous hotel was *not* our home.

But neither is the home on which we pay a mortgage our real home. We must remember, as the old spiritual says: "This world is not my home/I'm just a-passing through." No matter how the mint greens of spring and the yellows of autumn amaze us, this is not our home. No matter how comfortable the inner-coil mattress and how spacious the designer kitchen, this world is simply not our home. Yet how soon we all become accustomed to it all—the child abductions, the drive-by shootings, abuse, and the teen violence. We must keep reminding ourselves that all of this is just temporary.

I trust that, like me, you have become restless with the status quo. I hope you remember that it is all just for a while—that new car in the driveway, the widescreen plasma television, the broken families, and the tears for children who have gone astray. One day we will leave all these behind for a place where there will be no more weeping, no more tears.

Get ready to say goodbye at a moment's notice, for soon we'll be checking out of room 8205, the one we call this world, and moving to our eternal home, to "a city which hath foundations, whose builder and maker is God" (Heb. 11:10). I can't wait to see my Savior's face as we walk the streets of gold and hear Him whisper, "*This* is what I have been preparing for you. Welcome home forever."

Annette Walwyn Michael

See the Cross? Jesus Died for Me

Jesus was given to die for our sins, and he was raised
from the dead to make us right with God. Rom. 4:25, NCV.

While we were God's enemies, he made friends with us through
the death of his Son. Surely, now that we are his friends,
he will save us through his Son's life. Rom. 5:10, NCV.

IT WAS GRADUATION weekend in Walla Walla, Washington. Early Friday morning four of us flew to Portland, Oregon, where we were picked up by Stan's Mary Lou and her husband. Their son was graduating that weekend, and four of us were going: Stan, Jamie, and his 2½-year-old daughter, Isadora ("Izzy," for short), and me. Izzy's mother was unable to make the trip.

Since our flight arrived around 1:30 p.m. and our daughter and niece's flight from Europe was expected that evening, we had plenty of time for sightseeing and touring the Portland area.

Our two vehicles were the first at a red light intersection. As we were waiting for the light to turn, I noticed a church at the top of the bluff we were facing. Its steeple was in the shape of a cross, which was slightly obscured from the front seat by the height of the bluff that went straight up. Izzy, sitting in her car seat in the back, had a clear bird's-eye view of the church with the steeple cross.

As we rounded the corner of the busy intersection, we heard a small voice from the back seat say, "See the cross? Jesus died for me."

"Did Izzy say what I thought I heard her say?" asked Mary Lou as she steered the car.

"Yes, she did," the rest of us answered in unison.

Jamie explained that a week before, during evening worship, he and Izzy had looked at one of her Bible story books. When they came to the picture of Jesus on the cross, Jamie explained that it was Jesus on the cross, and that He had died for your sins and mine. Jesus didn't sin, but He loved us so much that He had died for Izzy's sins and Mommy's and Daddy's sins. He wasn't sure how much of the plan of salvation Izzy could grasp or understand at her age.

We marveled and were humbled by the clear, innocent statement Izzy made. We were reminded of Jesus' gentle rebuke to His disciples in Matthew 19:14, when He said, "Let the little children come to Me, and do not forbid them; for of such is the kingdom of heaven" (NKJV).

Anna (Ivie) Swingle

Lord, Have Mercy

The whole head is sick, and the whole heart faints. From the sole of the foot even to the head, there is no soundness in it. Isa. 1:5, 6, NKJV.

THE BOOK OF Isaiah is one of my favorites in the Bible. Isaiah was called the "Prince of Prophets" because of the depth and importance of his message. He began his ministry as a young man, and died a martyr's death as an old man. There's no doubt he was a servant of God. When I decided to reread the book of Isaiah, today's text grabbed at the core of my existence. I couldn't proceed any further into my reading. All I could say was "Lord, have mercy!"

I was compelled to scrutinize myself. Am I truly a servant of God? Do I glorify Him in all that I do, or do I glorify myself? Do I attempt righteousness by works? Do I really trust God in every aspect of my life? Do I just exist on this earth while awaiting heaven's door, or am I fully in this world? It's no problem for me to say, "Praise the Lord," "Thank You, Jesus," "Hallelujah!" and "God is good!" But have I gotten so accustomed to those catchphrases that I have forgotten the true significance of praise through service? Whose life have I touched? What young person or acquaintance have I brought to the knowledge of God? I know that I'm not an Isaiah, but I acknowledge that I am God's servant in His chosen capacity.

At a youth leadership convention we held our elections. The current president became disturbed when she was not voted back into a position within the youth ministry. I wondered if I would have behaved as she did if I had been voted out of my current position; but I knew in my heart that the position entrusted to me was not mine. I see it as a ministry, and my responsibility is to groom someone to take over in my stead while fulfilling the requirements of the ministry. I want to exude the humility of Christ when my turn comes to relinquish a position. How can I glorify God if I'm upset over a title? Isn't humility the truth of being a servant of God? If Isaiah was a young man, then who are we, as the older generation, to hold on to positions that the younger generation can adequately fulfill?

I may not die a martyr's death, but I pray that my death will not be in vain. I pray that the Lord will mold and guide every aspect of my life. No righteousness by works. I want my service to be for His glory and to conduct myself accordingly. Don't you?

Evelyn Greenwade Boltwood

The Eagles' Dance

They shall mount up with wings as eagles. Isa. 40:31.

SOMETIMES GOD SENDS a messenger to tell me of His love. In fact, throughout the day He sends little messages just to tell me He's thinking about me.

He knows what I like. He knows things of nature especially delight me, and so He has given me a little spot on this Planet Earth that is especially rich in pleasant things of nature. Last year He gave me a pair of robins that built a nest in the yew tree just outside my front door—at eyelevel, no less! The father warbled his favorite songs from the nearby chestnut tree. Again and again I was delighted by each little improvement to their home, and each little blue egg brought great delight. Four naked little robins cried for food. Four full-grown robins, with yellow still obvious at the edge of their beaks, flew away one day, and I waved goodbye from the wooden fence at the edge of the horse pasture. I wondered, *Would God send them back this year?*

Last week God surprised me with a new delight. About six feet over the top of the barn that's characteristically connected to the old New England farmhouse, appeared a huge brown bird with a magnificent wingspread. I blinked in astonishment when I saw its white head and white tail! My dog noticed the golden talons and sharply curved beak and looked at me as if to say, "Should we duck for cover?" It flew low, as if on a scenic tour of the area. It cocked its white head, not 15 feet above me. Its eye met mine, and we smiled together as it moved away.

Today God gave me another delight. The bald eagle brought its mate. No; not for the scenic tour, but for the dance. Not far overhead the two began to circle. The circle of one joined the circle of the other in a figure eight. Together briefly, then circling away and back again, they delighted me with their dance. It was almost like watching God's version of Ice Capades in which the swirling young girl floats gracefully across the ice, making circles with her mate!

The two magnificent birds soared and swooped, then flew together, wings almost touching. They circled again, this time returning to loop over and under each other. Again they joined wings and circled. With the wind beneath their wings they glided, one over the top of the other, then with a final figure eight they soared high and out of sight. Would I see them again?

I can only hope, but I won't complain. Today I saw the eagles dance.

Elizabeth Boyd

Bow Promises

I have placed my rainbow in the clouds. It is the sign of my
covenant with you and with all the earth. Gen. 9:13, NLT.

THE SUN BEAMED through the clouds with intense heat, and there was humidity in the wind. I had to get to the city, but this weather wasn't helping. I reminded myself of my purpose in going: to get my hair done for the graduation ceremony later that day, because my very good friend, whom I really cherished, was graduating, as well as leaving. I was happy for her—she'd had a tedious four-year roller-coaster ride while at the university.

Meanwhile, my friend joined the queue that led to the administration building to make final financial arrangements and to get her gown and cap ready and fitted for the gala occasion. As her turn came and the computer was scanned for her name, it indicated that she wouldn't be able to graduate because one of the prerequisites for the course she was taking didn't show up as a pass. This meant she wouldn't be able to graduate.

Her first question was "Why didn't they indicate this earlier in my school year?" This was unfair, and something had to be done—and quickly.

Later that day she telephoned and asked me to pray for her. She told me about the situation, and I reassured her that she had no need to fear since God had helped her overcome many giants before. "Listen, people of Israel! . . . The people themselves are tall and strong; they are giants, and you have heard it said that no one can stand against them. . . . He will defeat them as you advance . . . as he promised" (Deut. 9:1-3, TEV). She proceeded with other preparations for her graduation, reminding herself that God was able to resolve any problem.

My hair done, I hurried back home through the rush-hour traffic so that I could be on time for the ceremony. I was thinking of her and constantly interceding for her in prayer. As I neared home, I glanced out the window to see a lovely rainbow! I smiled delightedly—I just knew my God had answered our prayers. When I got in the house, my mom informed me that my friend had phoned with the good news that she would be able to graduate.

"That's stale news," I grinned. "I knew that already, but thanks!" When she looked puzzled I added, pointing out the window, "You know—'I do set my bow in the clouds.'" God is never slack concerning His promises.

Susan Riley

A Labor of Love

For God so loved the world that he gave his one and only Son, that whoever believes in him shall not perish but have eternal life. John 3:16, NIV.

AS PAIN PIERCED her body she sang praises: "Jesus, keep me near the cross." The baby's head appeared as the doctor and nurse worked toward a safe delivery of the newborn. Even through her pain she continued to sing like a songbird: "There's a precious fountain." The baby's head escaped from the birth canal, but something went amiss, and the doctor used a medical instrument. As the baby was torn and twisted from the birth canal, he died. He never breathed the first breath of life. He was laid to rest upon his birth.

Now, how do you continue to worship a God who would permit this to happen? Yet she did. And my parents were blessed with more children, and at each delivery she continued to sing praises. The medical staff became accustomed to her singing. It was as if she had bargained with God for a safe delivery each time she brought a child into the world, and God heard and answered.

My mother shared this story with me when I became a young adult. It was a special testimony of her faith. She also shared that she was instrumental in starting a ministry in her community that brought many people to Christ. Several decades later she told me her thoughts about how people came to the Lord and then seemed to move on, and she questioned her labor in the ministry. I reminded her that the church building was just an incubator that gave each new convert to Christ an opportunity to grow in strength, like a bird that leaves the nest and learns to trust God in flight. She seemed to accept this explanation.

A few years ago my eldest brother moved on, too. As my family struggled with his death, my mother continued to trust God to carry her through the pain of losing another child. It was through this laboring process of grief that I learned to trust God to give me strength, too. I knew that my brother was only sleeping until the Second Coming when the dead in Christ will rise. I learned to accept that God knew what was best for my brother at that particular time in his life. Inscribed on his grave marker is John 3:16; it is a message to all who might visit his burial site, proclaiming that God gave up His Son, Jesus, out of His love for us, that we might have eternal life.

Fartema M. Fagin

God Hears and Answers

Even before a word is on my tongue, behold, O Lord, you know it altogether.
Ps. 139:4, ESV.

WHILE I WAS vacationing in Florida, something kept nagging me to check my e-mails. I got on my sister-in-law's computer and found an invitation to interview at two public schools in Maryland. Only one principal would be available—the next day!

Dear God, we have fasted and prayed. We need an answer from You. Should I accept the private school position with the low salary, or consider the public school despite my fear of Sabbath conflicts? We want to move from New York, but waiting would allow our youngest to start kindergarten at her sister's school. She could wear her sister's old uniforms. Please be with me during my interview, but above all, not my will but Thine. Amen.

My previous interviews had been for sixth-grade teaching positions. My secret preference was fourth grade, and my favorite subject was reading.

As the interview began, the principal explained that the county was advertising for a sixth-grade teacher, but that the opening was for fourth grade. She added that there would be two fourth-grade teachers: one for math and science, and the other for reading and social studies. "What I need is a teacher for reading," she said.

My résumé stated that I taught at an Adventist school in New York. She asked if I had interviewed at a certain Seventh-day Adventist school in Maryland. I said that I had inquired, but there were no openings. Then she said the unbelievable: "I am a Seventh-day Adventist."

God was leading! Eventually I was offered the job, and I accepted. She stressed that school would begin at 7:30. I explained that the school my daughters would probably attend was near our house and would start later. She asked if I considered enrollment at the school she mentioned earlier. I hadn't, because I assumed it was too far away. As God would have it, that school was on the same street as the school that had just hired me.

After the interview my husband and I drove to that school for applications. It was closed, but someone was in the office. Upon our return to New York I telephoned the girls' school for uniform information. To my amazement, they described the same uniform my older daughter wore at her school in New York.

Praise God that we can always trust Him to hear and answer our prayers!

Wanda Van Putten-Allen

The Main Line

And it shall come to pass, that before they call, I will answer; and while they are yet speaking, I will hear. Isa. 65:24.

I WAS ENJOYING a bright, sunny June day, and I had been blessed by God to be able to attend a Sabbath worship service. Upon returning home and seeing that I hadn't received any calls, I decided to relax, eat dinner, and listen to music.

Shortly after dinner my cell phone rang. It was my granddaughter; she said that earlier she had tried unsuccessfully to reach me several times, dialing my regular phone. My son had also been trying to call me and had become concerned, but instead of calling me on the cell phone, he decided to drive by.

At this point I picked up my phone and began dialing. When I discovered that there was no dial tone, I began checking the other phones in the house, thinking maybe I'd left the receiver off the hook. But I had not.

I called the telephone company on my cell phone to find out what the problem was. They informed me that the entire area had no telephone service, as workers had cut the main cable line. An apology was given, which I accepted, realizing mistakes do happen.

Sunday passed. Monday passed. There was still no phone service.

Then late Tuesday afternoon the telephone rang. All was well—the phones were in operation once again. Within a half hour, though, when I decided to call my next-door neighbor so we could share the good news, once again there was no dial tone.

Upset, I began complaining aloud to the phone company as if they were within hearing distance, saying they had better deduct this situation from my telephone bill. Then Matthew 7:1 clearly came to my mind: "Judge not, that ye be not judged. For with what judgment ye judge, ye shall be judged: and with what measure ye mete, it shall be measured to you again."

At last, on Tuesday evening the telephone rang—the phones had finally been repaired.

Won't you join with me in remembering that whenever unforeseen circumstances occur, prayer, with faith in the God who is the master operator and always on the line, really works?

Annie B. Best

Questioning

Blessed are the poor in spirit, for theirs is the kingdom of heaven. Blessed are those who mourn, for they will be comforted. Matt. 5:3, 4, NIV.

ARE THERE STORIES in the Bible you simply don't understand? Do you wonder at the meaning of such a story being placed in the holy pages of wisdom and grace? Judges 19 includes one of those stories for me—it is the story of a concubine.

She was a slave who was also her master's sexual partner. Her master, a Levite no less, offers her in his place to a mob of depraved men. She is raped, sodomized, and tortured until dawn. Her clothes hang in shreds; she is mostly naked. Her body is bruised and distorted. Her hair is matted with dirt and secretions. Dried blood and filth cling to her thighs. She shivers in the dawn as she crawls to the home she was sent from. She tries to knock, to cry for help—but there is none. The man she has served with every part of her sleeps. At daybreak he finds her clinging to the threshold—dead.

But there's more! Instead of burying her, he takes her corpse home and cuts it into 12 pieces and distributes it to the 12 tribes of Israel. Her corpse then starts a civil war, and thousands of Israelites die.

I've read this story in several translations, and my heart still screams *Why?* Where was the God who counts the hairs on my head and sees the sparrow fall? How do I balance what I believe with this story of depravity and shame? Judges 21:25 ends with one final phrase: "Everyone did as he saw fit." There's the answer to my question. Personal will and pleasure over God's will, the same explanation for the incest, rape, child abuse, and depravity we still witness. It is a reminder that we live on a sin-filled planet, and there are days that evil calls each one of us.

In my mind I see this woman dying on that stoop. I see her shame, feel her pain, and I'm overcome by her suffering. Then I see a picture of God, holy and awesome, wrapped in the iridescent colors of the rainbow with light shining from everywhere. His hand, like the caress of moonlight, reaches for this broken creature and wipes her brow. Her breath rasps in the final labor of life. God Himself draws closer and ever so quietly. Though I cannot quite hear what He says, I know He speaks my name.

Selena Blackburn

Following the Light

For it is the God who commanded light to shine out of darkness who has shone in our hearts to give the light of the knowledge of the glory of God in the face of Jesus Christ. 2 Cor. 4:6, NKJV.

SWEETY, ONE OF my two small Boston terriers, is slowly going blind because of eye ulcers received when she and her sister, Honey, fought our third dog, Sugar, a miniature dachshund-Chihuahua mix. Honey and Sugar were the best of friends but, as many friends do, they could become upset and squabble, resulting in one or more becoming hurt. Sweety always jumped in to help her sister, since they were both Bostons. Dogs aren't unlike many of us humans who also jump into trouble.

I'm an early riser so that I can begin my Bible reading and other devotionals. At one time a woman and her three children were living in my home. They were not early risers, and I didn't want to waken them, so when Sweety decided she wanted to go outside at 5:15 a.m., I took my small LED light to help her get from the living room to the doggy door in the laundry room. She faithfully followed the light, which is a help for her poor eyesight. There are floodlights in the back fenced-in yard, so she can navigate quite well once she gets through the doggy door.

We also have a light that we can follow to cure our spiritual darkness. We would be spiritually blind without it, but with it we can discern things the Lord wants us to know. Are we faithfully following the light God gives us in His Son, Jesus? When we read His Word, the Bible, we are told that Jesus is the light of the world, and He will be our light for our own personal world if we ask for it.

We're told to give glory to God in whatever we do. Often we take the glory that belongs to God when someone gives us a compliment. I teach a Bible lesson in our church, and people tell me how much they appreciate the lesson. I respond that we need to praise God, because He helps me make the lesson interesting.

In heaven we won't need light because God will be there. When I read my Bible and ask the Holy Spirit to guide me, my day seems to go more smoothly. I still have challenges, but I also receive help to meet them that I might not be given otherwise. My prayer is that we will all be faithful, follow His light, and live eternally in that light.

Loraine F. Sweetland

This Kind of Dad

But from everlasting to everlasting the Lord's love is with those who fear him, and his righteousness with their children's children. Ps. 103:17, NIV.

MY FATHER WAS gentle and meek, someone who exuded a sense of security and safety without saying a word. He was steadfast and true to his commitments and responsibilities in life.

His widowed mother raised six boys on her own. They lived very simple lives during pre-Depression times, existing on their faith in God, generosity from others, and love for each other. My dad tells a story about receiving food from a church, but all of the labels on the cans had been removed. So they just opened a can and ate whatever was in it!

As a man of very few wants, he married my mom and provided for the daily needs of our family. There was very little money, but all five of us grew up feeling loved, cared for, and protected. We attended church every week, and completed elementary education at the church's elementary school. My dad worked three jobs at times to keep food on the table, and my mom was the homemaker. My parents were faithful to the Lord in all they did, especially their tithe. They had been married for 62 years when my mom passed away.

In his quiet manner Dad endured each passing day without his lifelong partner. He was 80 percent blind and 80 percent deaf, so he couldn't read, write, or watch television, and had difficulty walking. I visited him weekly at his assisted living apartment, pulling my chair up as close as I possibly could so he could hear me. On one of my visits I asked him, "Dad, what do you do all day long, just sitting here?" He replied that he prayed and he sang, stating that I would be surprised at what the old hymns could do for a person. From then on I brought my guitar, and we'd sing those hymns together. I never left dry-eyed.

Our heavenly Father is also this kind of dad. He is steadfast and true—always being the perfect gentleman in His relationship with us. He provides us with love, protection, and a sense of security. His Son, Jesus, intercedes for us in prayer and has a love song in His heart for His followers. He is faithful in His commitments and always keeps His promises. Today, won't you sit and listen to what He has to offer you in His gentle and quiet way? Pull your chair up real close. You'd be surprised at what it can do for you!

Karen Phillips

Remote Control

The Lord is near to all who call upon Him, to all who call upon Him in truth.
Ps. 145:18, NKJV.

"NOW, WHERE DID I put that remote?" I grumbled, as my eyes swept the room, hoping to catch a glimpse of the small gray-and-white rectangle. "I always keep it right here on the table; so where could it be now?" Thinking that maybe it had fallen behind the table, I searched behind it, under it, and around it. Shivering a little, I looked around again. The room felt cold, and I decided to change the setting on the air-conditioning unit. Working in the garden always made me feel hot, and now I couldn't find that elusive remote control device to make the room more comfortable.

I attempted to smile in the midst of my frustration, for I was getting additional though unwanted exercise. *Lord, You know where that remote is; please help me to find it soon*, I prayed silently. Then I started to think: *It is such a little thing; maybe* . . . The negative thought was cut immediately and replaced with more encouraging and uplifting thoughts: *God counts even the hairs on my head.* Still not feeling too happy about my two-minute additional workout, I got a light sweater and sat down to get a few minutes of well-deserved rest. I leaned back and wiggled to get more comfy in my easy chair. *What's that? A lump under my cushion!* You guessed it—my remote control! The answer to my prayer!

Sitting more comfortably after adjusting the air-conditioning, I got to thinking how dependent we have become on remote-control devices, and how much faith we have in them. We use them to operate so many things: the air-conditioning, the garage door, the car doors, the television, the sound system, the fan. The power is at our fingertips whenever we choose to use it. We can't see the source of the power, but we just know that when we touch the button we will get action immediately.

Many of us go through difficult situations in life without tapping into the power source that is readily available to us. We worry unnecessarily and dread the what ifs. There is power in prayer! All we have to do is ask, for Jesus is interested in even the minute details of our lives, and He is in control! Sometimes we may think He is too remote and far away, but He is near, very near to all who call on Him. His awesome power is available to us anywhere all the time.

I leaned back in my chair, closed my eyes, and thanked Him. God is so good, even to me!

Ruth Esther McKinney

The Gift of Forgiveness

Let all bitterness, and wrath, and anger, and clamour, and evil speaking,
be put away from you, with all malice: and be ye kind one
to another, tenderhearted, forgiving one another, even as
God for Christ's sake hath forgiven you. Eph. 4:31, 32.

WHAT WOULD YOU feel if someone you think is on your side is the one who turns against you, disappoints you, and just breaks your heart?

Since my husband and I have no children, we decided to help our close relatives gain their education. We did this from the time they were small until they finished their studies. We faithfully supplied their financial needs. As the old saying goes, not all the fruit of the trees is good. One of them turned out to be a traitor and became my greatest enemy. She became disrespectful and ungrateful and gave me much heartache and pain through the bad things she said about me. I was so deeply hurt that I couldn't even concentrate while driving my car, which caused me to have two accidents. (Thanks be to God that they were only minor ones.) It created a hateful feeling deep inside of me. I wanted revenge. I was scared that the bitterness and anger I felt was eating me up, little by little. Then I noticed something in my behavior: the more I thought of revenge or how to get even, the more I became rude and unpleasant.

I turned to our Lord for help and asked for forgiveness. I asked that through His grace I would be able to forgive those who had wronged me. God answered my prayer and led me to His promises in today's text, as well as Romans 12:19: "Dearly beloved, avenge not yourselves, but rather give place unto wrath: for it is written, Vengeance is mine; I will repay, saith the Lord." I felt the Lord in me, and it lifted me up. I was free, free from anger and bitterness.

I poured out my heavy burden to Him because only He could understand what I was going through, because God Himself experienced all of this while He was here on earth. His own disciples denied Him, betrayed Him, and His friends became His enemies and nailed Him to the cross. I read in the book *What's So Amazing About Grace?* by Philip Yancey, that God's forgiveness is unconditional; it comes from a heart that doesn't demand anything for itself, a heart that is completely empty of self-seeking. This is divine forgiveness that I have to practice in my daily life. God forgives my debts as I forgive my debtors.

Loida Gulaja Lehmann

Even a Little Child Shall Know Him!

But when Jesus saw it, he was much displeased, and said unto them, Suffer the little children to come unto me, and forbid them not: for of such is the kingdom of God. Mark 10:14.

ON A RAINY Saturday night in Hosur, India, Sheena, my 6-year-old daughter, wanted to give her friend across the street a card she had made for her. I told her it was very wet outside and she could give the card the next day. However, Sheena insisted, "Mama, only one minute; I'll come back immediately." I reluctantly agreed, and in just a minute or so I heard her footsteps, so went to the screen door to open it for her.

As I began to open the screen, I saw something on the hinge side of the door. Thinking it was a millipede that was trying to get in, I put on the porch light. To my shock, it was a black snake. The tail portion was on the inside, but the rest of the body was outside. I yelled, "Sheena, there is a snake! Move toward the pots on the right side!" She moved away, but started to cry loudly with fright. I was afraid the snake might strike if I opened the door to let Sheena in. Then I saw the snake curl up a little, so again I shouted to Sheena to run. She ran down the porch steps, still screaming loudly. Hearing her cry, our neighbors came out and carried her away. Then a brave neighbor came and killed the snake, which turned out to be a viper.

Just that morning at church Sheena had participated in the children's program and given a talk. She ended her talk with these words: "God is good all the time. I can never stop thanking the Lord for His goodness." Before going to bed that night Sheena said, with tears in her eyes, "Mama, God saved me because I thanked Him in church!"

My older son, Sean, immediately took the Bible and read Psalm 46, and all of us prayed, thanking the Lord for His protection. I told Sean, "Son, I just cannot imagine where the snake was when Sheena went outside, because she came back in just a minute."

"Mom, if Sheena hadn't gone outside, the snake would have come to the door—and even gone away—and we wouldn't have even known about it. But the Lord showed us this snake so we would know how kind and loving He is." What a profound statement! As I write this to you, I am so touched by God's loving care that my eyes are filled with tears of joy.

God has a special love and care for little children, and He wants us to be like them!

Stella Thomas

Hi, Church

Encourage one another, especially now that the day of his return is drawing near. Heb. 10:25, NLT.

"WHERE IS YOUR handsome son?" asked the kindhearted gentleman.

"Sonny is very spiritually sensitive, so I don't bring him to memorial services," I whispered. In his own way, Sonny had previously said his goodbye.

The church family had been sad because we knew that Doug, our brother and friend, was slipping away from cancer at age 53. Sonny hugged Pastor Lew before the congregation knelt together for the Garden of Prayer time. During the prayer Sonny, age 23, shed some tears. He was following his heart without knowing why or who needed our prayers. Because of his significant developmental disabilities the concept of death means absolutely nothing to Sonny.

The following day I went to the hospital chapel to pray with Doug's family. It was Glena, Doug's lovely wife, who uplifted my spirits. She told Doug's mother and sister about Sonny's developmental disabilities, and how he greets her with "Hi, Church" every time he sees her—regardless of where they are.

Laverne, Doug's sister, and I instantly became friends and comrades when I found out that she too has an autistic son. A few days later at his uncle's memorial service, I was blessed to meet handsome 13-year-old Rusten. Every day Christians with challenged children live life "on the front lines" in a war zone, and often we are wounded and in need of healing.

At Doug's service Pastor Lew shared these thoughts: People seem to enjoy sending off ships with fanfare and excitement, but seldom is there a crowd to greet the same ships when they return home. Doug and Glena had made a living as commercial fishermen, and Doug had proudly served in the 4th Canadian Ranger Patrol (similar to the U.S. Coast Guard).

Doug also served his church family with genuine affection. One of his jobs was church greeter, and he made us feel special. God's children are vessels; every day we go out into the sea of life not knowing what will happen to us. We are so blessed to be able to come to the church harbor where we should be able to safely love one another in the spirit of friendship until Jesus comes for us all.

Glena Knopp and Deborah Sanders

The Gift of Prayer

Rejoicing in hope; patient in tribulation; continuing instant in prayer.
Rom. 12:12.

PRAYER IS THE most powerful gift that God has given us. Because it's a powerful weapon against evil and sin, you can say a prayer wherever you are. You can whisper a prayer at work; you can even whisper a prayer in a crowd of people. If you can't whisper, you can say a prayer in the stillness of your heart. Nothing can stop you; no one can stop you.

Sometimes I become overwhelmed by the pressures of life. I see no way out. But the moment I call to my God I find sweet relief. Although I sometimes don't get the answer that I want, somehow the burden feels lighter, and I can smile even in that storm because I'm able to remember that God is still in control. Romans 8:28 says, "And we know that all things work together for good to them that love God, to them who are the called according to his purpose."

It's not always easy to buy Christmas or birthday presents for our loved ones, but prayer is the most beautiful gift you can give to anyone. It is my hope that we will always remember to pray for ourselves, for our families, for our church families, our friends, and our neighbors.

Sometimes I spend days thinking about a church brother or sister for no obvious reason, and sometimes I don't think to pray for them. But when I meet them they will tell me they have been going through a rough time. Either they or their kids were not well, or they lost their jobs, or something else was not right. When I look back to the time that they were struggling and realize that it was the same time they were constantly in my mind and I did not pray for them, I deeply regret it. These experiences have taught me to try to pray for anyone whose name comes in my mind or in my dreams.

I don't know about you, my sister who's reading this, but I get so much comfort from prayer. If people tell me they are praying for me I am encouraged. It is so uplifting! Let's lift others up by sincerely praying for them and, when possible, let's tell them, encouraging them. As we pray for others there is a wonderful promise to us as well: "But God has surely listened and heard my voice in prayer. Praise be to God, who has not rejected my prayer or withheld his love from me!" (Ps. 66:19, 20, NIV). Let us carry other people's burdens in prayer.

Peggy S. Rusike

Flowers With Love

For your Maker is your husband—the Lord Almighty is his name—the Holy
One of Israel is your Redeemer; he is called the God of all the earth.
Isa. 54:5, NIV.

ONCE I READ the story of a woman who expresses divine promises with a unique
poem. She shares that her husband had died. They had been very happy, and his absence caused her great pain. One day as she was lying under a tree, she thought
about her unfortunate situation and the flowers that she would never receive again.
She felt a stab of jealousy of other women who received flowers, especially the flowers that came for no special reason other than to say "I love you."

Unable to contain her tears, she closed her eyes and felt the wind touch her face.
At that moment something extraordinary happened. The wind blew harder and
covered her with a shower of flowers. There she recognized the presence of a greater
Companion. God was with her! She saved a flower, and as she looked at it she
thought, *I am not alone; He loves me!*

Of all the arts, love is the most sacred and necessary. We can't live without be-
longing to someone, and there is a type of love that can be greatly missed: the love
of a spouse. This was especially true for someone who had little children and a life
filled with challenges to overcome, as was the case of my mother. She had to raise
her children without the presence of my father, who had passed away when we were
children.

The hurts had to be erased; her eyes had to be turned away from her own hurts.
It was necessary to seek strength in her heavenly Father. My brothers, sisters, and I
were very poor in terms of money, but we were not poor in terms of a Father. We
learned of riches from my mother through the morning prayers, and again the
prayers at night and the prayers returning thanks for our food. She filled us with the
love that comes from God. In Him she found a strength that she transmitted to her
children even through just a look.

The reason we are separated from the one that we loved—or still love—is not
important. With unexpected flowers God is telling us, "I am beside you; do not be
afraid. I will continue to take care of you."

Eunice Michiles Malty

June 24

Ignoring the Signs

For you know very well that the day of the Lord will come like a thief in the
night . . . as labor pains on a pregnant woman, and they will not escape.
1 Thess. 5:2, 3, NIV.

FOR YEARS I'VE BEEN monitoring my high blood pressure, and with medica-
tions I have kept it controlled. But the last week of May, when my pulse began slow-
ing down, it didn't occur to me that I was having a problem. That happens to
others, not to me! Wednesday my pulse was 40 beats per minute when I checked my
blood pressure and pulse. I went about my daily tasks at my volunteer job at Gospel
Outreach, feeling tired. Thursday morning my pulse was 36, but since I was just getting started with Warm Water Therapy at the YMCA I didn't want to miss my second session, so I ignored my pulse. After 45 minutes of mild exercises I was tired,
of course, but after I got home I checked my pulse again. It was 32, so I spent a quiet
evening and wondered what was going on.

Throughout the night I had other "weird" symptoms. When I got up Friday,
both my blood pressure and pulse were low—in fact, the pulse was 31. I had more
dizziness and felt so weak that I wondered how I should get to the emergency room
as I didn't feel that I should drive. That's when I called my granddaughter, a nurse
practitioner, who sent her husband to take me to the hospital emergency room.
After X-rays, an EKG, and blood tests the doctors admitted me to ICU. I was scheduled for surgery that same day, the Friday of Memorial Day weekend. The cardio
surgeon inserted a pacemaker, and I stayed overnight in a "step-down" room next
to ICU.

As I saw my pulse dropping it didn't alarm me—until Friday. In reality, my
heart was close to giving up! In our walk with Jesus we see signs that He gave us to
prepare us for His coming, the signs that tell us His coming is very near. Are we just
going along as usual, unaware that our lives might end soon? "And when these
things begin to come to pass, then look up, and lift up your heads; for your redemption draweth nigh" (Luke 21:28).

I'm happy to report that my pulse is holding steadily at 60, and I have felt my
strength renewed. I am chagrined to have had this wake-up call since I am a retired
nurse who should have recognized what was happening! Let's not make a mistake
about Jesus' coming!

Barbara Wyman

Pay Forward

Great are the works of the Lord; they are pondered by all who delight in them. Glorious and majestic are his deeds, and his righteousness endures forever. Ps. 111:2, 3, NIV.

"PAY" MEANS TO REWARD, or to settle. "Forward" means to send, or to transmit. "Pay forward," then, means transmit the reward. Today's text reminds me of my friend's experiences in the middle of difficulty while battling the ill effects of cancer.

Donna, a single mom who earned her Doctor of Education degree while raising her two children, became an expert in quantitative research and mentored doctoral students to understand this discipline. I was one of those doctoral students she mentored in the analysis and interpretation of my data. Her passion brought success to many students.

Then in 2007 she was diagnosed with aggressive uterine cancer. The repeated surgical procedures and chemotherapy affected her financial stability. That summer she drove her Toyota without air-conditioning. One day one of her students asked her to take her car to a certain car dealer's on Sunday and meet him there. Without question she brought her car in, but she was informed that there was no repair on Sunday. She lingered, waiting for her student. Soon he and his wife arrived and asked her to wait while they spoke with the dealer. She thought that they were negotiating for a rental car. A few minutes later, though, the student came out to ask her which car she would like to have.

"I have dreamed of a Prius," she said, "but I couldn't afford it. I would settle for a Toyota Corolla."

"It doesn't matter," the student said, and the negotiation went on. When the student handed Donna the keys to a Prius, she was stunned and couldn't speak. With tears flowing down her cheeks, she finally said, holding up the keys, "How could I ever repay you for this?"

The answer was to pay forward. Donna went home driving a brand-new Prius. Bothered by the two words "pay forward," she asked her son if he needed a car. When he said he could sell his car, Donna said, "That is not what it means." She didn't give her old car to her son; instead she gave it to her secretary's daughter, who needed a car. Donna fulfilled the meaning of pay forward. Her heart was filled with joy knowing that as a recipient of kindness she was able to transmit and pay forward. Wouldn't it be wonderful if each of us paid it forward?

Edna Bacate-Domingo

A Special Gift From God

But my God shall supply all your need according
to his riches in glory by Christ Jesus. Phil. 4:19.

FOR MANY YEARS I suffered from asthma. Those of you who suffer from this affliction know that there is no remedy for it. I've had many sleepless nights and have lost weight because of it. A number of times I've had to be rushed to the hospital for oxygen. At night it was often impossible for me to lie down on my back and breathe normally without lying on several pillows. Many times I slept in the spare room so as not to disturb my husband, a busy man with heavy responsibilities who needed his sleep.

On one such night I was sitting propped up with pillows in the spare bedroom, wide awake, troubled with thoughts about my illness. I was feeling lonely, too, almost sure that this sickness would take my life. But I wasn't afraid of death. Death could be a blessing in disguise, as it would end all suffering. On that lonely night the moon cast the shadow of the branches of a tree on the wall. The leaves of the tree seemed to be asleep, the night as still as the moon was bright.

Suddenly the leaves were shaken, and something flew and rested on a branch. It was an owl. Oh, I was so thrilled! This was the first time I'd seen a live, silhouetted picture of an owl sitting on a branch. I got out of bed and got a pencil to trace the owl's outline on the wall. The owl didn't move, and I got a perfect picture of it. I lay awake until it flew away. In that hour I forgot my illness and my unhealthy thoughts. I was so happy for the owl and knew that it was a special gift from God to cheer me up. I thanked God for the gift, fluffed my pillows, and slept.

Even today the beautiful picture of the owl is forever etched in my mind. God allowed me to suffer in order to experience His love. Today I am free from asthma—for 20 years I have had no attacks.

God's gifts to us aren't always tangible. It could be a rainbow in the sky, a lone rose on a bush, a compliment from someone that made your day. God keeps giving us gifts all the time. "Moreover, when God gives any [woman] wealth and possessions, and enables [her] to enjoy them, . . . this is a gift of God" (Eccl. 5:19, NIV). May God help us to recognize all the gifts that He gives to us.

Birol Charlotte Christo

The Truck Nobody Likes

I am small and despised. Ps. 119:141.

HAVE YOU EVER found yourself driving behind a garbage truck? It's not a very pleasant place to be. The truck moves slowly, and that acrid odor it gives off is disgusting!

I found myself behind a garbage truck one day, and I was annoyed. Nonetheless, I began to observe those hard workers. They ran to the sidewalk and bent down to pick up the bins containing everything the homeowners didn't want. Judging from their movements, I realized that some loads were heavier than I thought. Balancing that load of unwanted trash, they ran up to the truck and threw in the contents. Sometimes a bit of disgusting liquid would splash back onto them. Then they ran back to the sidewalk to set down the empty bin before running to the next bin, thus repeating the whole process once again.

Bending down, picking up, carrying, emptying, bending down again, always moving quickly, always accompanied by that disgusting smell. Rain or sun, icy cold or suffocating heat, there they were. I was filled with admiration. How many pounds of garbage disappeared? How many miles did they run next to the truck? How many muscles were used simply getting rid of waste? And all for an activity that isn't considered a profession but that is carried out with much responsibility and great care.

Do you ever stop to thank the person who picks up your garbage? Do you ever tell them how much you appreciate what they do? Do you at least smile at him or her, or do you look at them with contempt or indifference because they handle garbage all day? Do you take the time to observe their weatherbeaten skin, their hands damaged by cuts and rough spots?

There is no such thing as an unworthy task; nevertheless probably none of us would be proud to say "My husband/boyfriend/son or daughter is a garbage collector." I invite you to think about these workers who perhaps feel small and despised. Maybe their knees hurt from so much running, or their back aches from bending down so often. Maybe they have a problem that is heavier than any load they might have to carry that day. Show them your appreciation, just as Christ would. A sincere thank-you could change their day—or their life.

We may consider someone's occupation small, but it is not so in the eyes of the Father.

Susana Schulz

The Comfort Zone

So, my son, throw yourself into this work for Christ. Pass on what you
heard from me—the whole congregation saying Amen!—to reliable leaders
who are competent to teach others. When the going gets rough,
take it on the chin with the rest of us, the way Jesus did. A soldier on
duty doesn't get caught up in making deals at the marketplace.
He concentrates on carrying out orders. An athlete who refuses to play by
the rules will never get anywhere. It's the diligent farmer who gets the
produce. Think it over. God will make it all plain. 2 Tim. 2:2-7, Message.

WE ARE CREATURES of habit—even in the church setting. At my church many
members have their designated seats, chosen by themselves. The Franklin family
may enjoy sitting on the end of aisle three, on the right. The Pride family may enjoy
sitting in the back in order to make a quick exit. Mrs. Songbird may enjoy sitting
close to the choir. Some always come early; others always arrive "just in the nick of
time" for the service. We each enjoy our "comfort zones."

I would like to share a personal "comfort zone" moment with you. I had severe
flooding in my basement a few weeks ago. The summer had brought much rain to
Maryland and the Washington, D.C., metropolitan area. On top of it all, I had no
air-conditioning.

Finally I got most of the water cleaned up, and I quickly left for choir rehearsal.
I thought it would help to uplift my spirits! Well, I was wrong. The women's group
was scheduled to sing that Sabbath. In an instant the choir director made some seat-
ing modifications. Generally the second sopranos sit behind the first sopranos. I'm
a second soprano, and I've held my usual second soprano seat for a long time. It is
my comfort zone. I also connect with the Christians around me.

We were told to wear black skirts and white tops. So I couldn't wear my bright
colors of cheer that Sabbath. After praying and reading devotional selections, I decided to comply with the requests. I had come to rehearsal to be in harmony—and
not only through song. But I did express my feelings regarding the change to the
choir director. Then at the last rehearsal the music became very healing to me. I realized that I couldn't let my preference cause a division. My work is for the kingdom. Being uncomfortable wasn't good enough as an excuse.

Even now the summer changes haven't thrilled me, but the music has! It is
God's music. God rejoices when we share His message through music and song.
Hallelujah!

Patrice Hill Taylor

Cast Your Burden on Him

Cast thy burden upon the Lord, and he shall sustain thee. Ps. 55:22.

I STOOD THERE, my heart filled with joy and pride, as the church members greeted my son and congratulated him for the powerful sermon he had just delivered. He had preached for the worship service that Sabbath morning, and the congregation was touched and blessed by the message. My eyes filled with tears when one of the women came over to me and said, "You must be proud to have him as your son."

Yes, indeed, I was proud and happy and excited. But above all, I was thankful—thankful to God for making this possible.

As I looked at my son that day I remembered the first few days after his birth when we had cried and prayed for his health while the doctors fought for his life. He hadn't been well from the moment he was born and kept falling ill again and again those first few weeks. He'd been kept in the incubator for more than a month, and yet there seemed to be no signs of improvement in his health. The doctors conducted all sorts of tests but couldn't come to the right diagnosis. They finally decided to perform surgery on his stomach to find out what was wrong, although they had no hope that it would solve the problem. I wept and prayed that God would intervene and heal him.

When I opened my Bible I came across today's verse. I prayed and made a vow with God: "Dear Lord, I am leaving my son at Your feet. If it is Your will then please touch him and heal him and help him to be a healthy child. And I promise to dedicate him to Your service."

The next day, as if by a miracle, the vomiting and stomach illness stopped. When the doctors conducted a scan they found out that everything was perfect. He was in good health and wouldn't need surgery after all. We rejoiced in God's miracle and thanked Him for His wonderful healing. My son completed his master's in theology and became a pastor. Above all that, he has become a great preacher of God in his young age.

What a wonderful God we serve! "Commit thy way unto the Lord; trust also in him; and he shall bring it to pass" (Ps. 37:5). There is nothing impossible for God! We just need to trust in His abilities and leave everything to Him.

Saramma Stephenson

Finding Peace

Fear thou not; for I am with thee: be not dismayed; for I am thy God: I will strengthen thee; yea, I will help thee; yea, I will uphold thee with the right hand of my righteousness. Isa. 41:10.

IT'S ALMOST TWO YEARS NOW since I've held a full-time job, but the Lord has been good. I continue to pay my tithe as if I still held my full-time position, and the Lord has showered me with abundant blessings.

When I lost my job, I was extremely angry. I questioned God. *Why have You allowed me to accomplish so much educationally and then allowed my enemies to rip it away from me?* I wasted my days and nights feeling sorry for myself. During the nights I would cry out to God, and during the days I would seek refuge in the television.

This went on for several months until the answer came. What was I to do? First, I would increase the time I spent with God. Next, I decided that I would stop complaining. I wouldn't question God. I would accept, through His help, whatever happened in my life. I chose a simple way of giving praise to God. I began to say, "I am blessed" to each person who asked, "How are you today?" This simple step I've taken to praise God has brought me both physical and spiritual blessings. The Lord has blessed me abundantly.

I now realize that I didn't need the type of education I had acquired in order to serve the Lord. The Lord allowed my job to be taken away from me so that I could spend more time reading His Word and praying. I can give more of my service to the church. I can give of my best to the Master. We're told in so many ways that He promises that no good thing will He withhold from those who earnestly seek and serve Him.

As I think about my experiences I have come to the conclusion that the Lord knew that I didn't need that job. For Him to save me I had to give up my job. I believe I'm now a much better person; I certainly have a closer relationship with God. He also promises that He will never leave us nor forsake us: Thank the Lord! I no longer get angry with Him nor blame Him when I go through my crucibles.

"Hide not thy face far from me; put not thy servant away in anger: thou hast been my help; leave me not, neither forsake me, O God of my salvation" (Ps. 27:9). The Lord wants us to lean on Him.

Patricia Hines

Too Small, or Too Large to Ask?

If you ask anything in My name, I will do it. John 14:14, NKJV.

WE'D HAD ONE guest after another. Now my husband had left at 6:00 a.m. to take our most recent guest to the Bangkok International Airport, as he was flying back to British Columbia, Canada. It was Sunday, and I needed to wash our huge laundry, including all the bedsheets and towels. However, I hesitated because the dark clouds were threatening rain at any moment. There was no doubt a heavy downpour was imminent. But then, whether I liked it or not, I had to do the laundry.

While washing the first batch, I began to talk with God. "Lord, You know I have no place to hang these clothes, these sheets and towels. You see that I have no dryer in this house, either. But God, I know You can hold the rains—although the parched earth needs to be watered. I leave this problem in Your hands, trusting that You will answer according to Your will."

After that prayer I began to hang the first load of wash on the lines. I noticed thankfully that a mild breeze had come up. All the time I was finishing the second batch of wash I continued talking with my heavenly Father. The dark clouds loomed across the sky, but peace swept over my soul.

Soon the sun peeped out a little bit. The black clouds were still up there, threatening to drop rain, but I held my peace and continued my constant communication with the One who controlled the situation. I began to clean the house, closely listening should the raindrops begin to fall. As soon as I finished cleaning the house, I went outside to feel if the clothes were dry enough to gather. And most of them were ready to take from the clotheslines! I hurriedly began folding them, one by one. At last all were in the basket except one pair of thick socks. As soon as I finished gathering the clothes and stepped into the kitchen a heavy downpour tumbled down. The big wash was finished, and all were dried and folded. What a relief! I continued to pray, but this time I said, "Thank You, God, for keeping Your word, Your promise, that if I ask anything in Your name, You will do it."

He who controlled the wind and rain on the Sea of Galilee still controls the elements. All we have to do is seek His will. I want to do that every day, don't you?

Ofelia A. Pangan

Black Pants

Lo, I am with you alway, even unto the end of the world. Amen. Matt. 28:20.

SOMETIMES WE FORGET how precious we are to God. He tells us in Matthew 10:29-31 and Luke 12:6-34 that God remembers the sparrows, numbers the hairs on our head, feeds the ravens even though they don't sew or reap, and clothes the lilies and the grass. How much more will He clothe us? He also promised in Matthew 28:20 and Haggai 2:4 that He will always be with us. What more can we wish for? What more do we need?

One Monday I was browsing through the clothing department looking for pants. My only pair was more than a year old, and both knees were torn and patched. I could hardly spare them long enough to launder them. One table held stretch pants in black, brown, and tan at a 50 percent discount. Just what I was looking for! I managed to dig up one tan pair in my size, but I wanted black. I reluctantly bought the tan pair, knowing that once the price is slashed no new sizes would be put out.

Tuesday was a holiday, so until Wednesday morning I kept praying that someone would return a pair of black pants. I determined to be in line on Wednesday when the store opened, just in case they had put out the last stock.

Wednesday morning I arrived 20 minutes late and went directly to the table of pants. I dug through the first stack and found nothing. Then I gasped in surprise! There on the very top of the second stack was my size. It was obvious that someone had bought them and taken the labels off, as now the new tag was handwritten.

"If then God so clothe the grass, which is to day in the field, and to morrow is cast into the oven; how much more will he clothe you, O ye of little faith?" (Luke 12:28).

As I bought those pants and came home, I was totally awed by the works of God! He cares so much about even the little things in our life. He brought the right pair of pants back—on the very day that I went looking for them. What if I had arrived at 10:00 a.m.? Would those pants have been out there, or did someone return them to the table just before I arrived?

God is so good! Take time to think of all the times that He did something special for you, and then take time to praise Him today. And after that, take time to share with someone else how good He is. They may be in need of encouragement too.

Elizabeth Versteegh Odiyar

A Word "Fitly Spoken"

Blessed be the Lord God of Israel, who sent you this day to meet me! And blessed is your advice and blessed are you. 1 Sam. 25:32, 33, NKJV.

A FOLDED NOTE was passed to me in church as I listened to the choir sing. I took the paper and put it into my handbag. My sister, sitting beside me, nudged me and whispered, "Open it; they're expecting a reply." I looked at the person who had sent the note and then at the paper. The words "You're telling the children's story" stared back at me. I grew up keeping a song in my heart—apparently that would extend to stories also. I looked across the aisle and nodded assent. Then reality dawned. They were collecting the offering, so only the prayer remained between that moment and the children's story. I had, at most, five minutes to think of a story.

I prayed silently and opened my Bible. As a woman called to speak for God, it was important that I find a story about the right word at the right time. Who would encapsulate that idea? Then it came to me: Abigail, a wise woman who communicated for God at a crucial time in two lives, hers and David's. I prayed silently as I walked to the front, sat down, and began.

"Have you ever done something good and received something bad in return?" The children nodded. "Well," I continued, "David had that problem. He had protected the herdsmen of a man called Nabal when they were out shearing sheep. Later on, David heard that Nabal was having a party, and he asked Nabal for some of the food. Nabal refused rudely, and David was so offended that he threatened to retaliate with terrible violence."

The children and I discussed what to do when faced with humiliation and rejection. Speaking to myself as well as to the children, I took my Bible and turned to 1 Samuel 25:28-31 and summarized Abigail's words of advice to David: Sometimes we meet people who will hurt us because of their bad-tempered, rude, and selfish behavior. What we must never forget is that as God's children on God's business, with a glorious future ahead, we can trust God to take care of every negative situation. When we look back over our journey we need to be able to look back without regret or guilt, free to accept God's blessings with grace, because He is delivering on His promise to us.

As the children bowed I prayed, "Lord, thank You for being the Wonderful Counselor and the Prince of Peace."

Judith Purkiss

Keep Your Eyes on the Prize

Forgetting those things which are behind and reaching forward to those things which are ahead, I press toward the goal for the prize of the upward call of God in Christ Jesus. Phil. 3:13, 14, NKJV.

OUR DAUGHTER, Ngozi, had finally overcome her fear of drowning. Sometime before, when she was 9 years old, she had experienced a scare when she dove into the swimming pool after only a few swimming lessons. Having watched people jump into the pool and swim, she thought she could do it too; but instead of swimming, she began to sink. Fortunately, someone was watching nearby and immediately came to her rescue and saved her from drowning.

So after several more lessons, she performed well in her swimming class. At last the day came to compete with her classmates. I stood nearby and looked on with all the excitement of a proud mother. She was the lead swimmer and had almost reached the end of the pool. Then, without any warning, Ngozi took a quick look backward to check the position of her competitors. In a split second one of them instantly plunged past her and came in first. I can still recall the sad and disappointed look that came over Ngozi's face. I felt bad for her! She was almost in first place, but one brief glance backward had cost her the coveted prize. She had to settle for second place.

The Bible tells the story of a nameless woman who took one look backward and lost it all—her beloved family, beautiful home, luxurious lifestyle, and her wealth. She was turned into a pillar of salt (Gen. 19:26). What an awful price to pay for looking back!

In Philippians 3:13 and 14 we read these poignant words: "Forgetting those things which are behind and reaching forward to those things which are ahead, I press toward the goal for the prize of the upward call of God in Christ Jesus."

We human beings have a tendency to look back, to recall experiences and situations that happened in our lives—some memorable and some not so memorable. Every so often some of my friends and family remind me of something I said or did more than 40 years ago that I don't even recall. Paul admonishes us to forget those things, to leave them behind and press onward and upward till we reach our ultimate prize—eternal life with Jesus! Today may God's Word encourage our hearts as we keep our eyes on the prize till we see our Savior face to face!

Shirley C. Iheanacho

How Much More?

The greedy person stirs up strife, but whoever trusts
in the Lord will be enriched. Prov. 28:25, NRSV.

THE BUSY SUNDAY morning was disturbed by a knock on the gate. Gloria
looked out to see who her guest could be. "Mi Friend," as he was affectionately
called, was a homeless man who had a few mental challenges. After exchanging
pleasantries, he asked for something cool to drink. Gloria soon returned with a jug
of refreshing lemonade and filled his container to the brim. The smile of contentment on his face was short-lived when he noticed that while his container was full,
there was still lemonade in Gloria's jug. He looked at her with a puzzled expression
as if to say, "What are we going to do with the extra?" Then a flash of enlightenment
covered his whole being as he began emptying his container on the side of the road,
making room for the remainder of Gloria's lemonade. Gloria's disbelief was soon
replaced by uncontrollable laughter, a response that is still guaranteed every time
we recall this saga.

His mental challenges made his actions acceptable; but how do you explain the
same response by those of us who claim to be clothed in our right minds? Do you
ever find yourself wanting more, even though you don't have room to receive it? I
am thinking of valuable assets such as marriage, children, church life, friends—and
even you.

So often we look across the fence and drool at what the neighbor enjoys, ultimately burning with dissatisfaction. This discontent is often grounded not so much
in what we don't have, but in how much more they seem to possess. Then like the
homeless man, we set about disposing of what we have so as to make room for what
we do not have.

Are we any smarter than "Mi Friend" when we pressure ourselves to be like
someone else who seems to epitomize success? In so doing, we often empty ourselves of our sense of worth and uniqueness with which God has blessed us.

Today, look again at your container. Preserve what you have and trust God to
send the overflow. Live a life that agrees with Job's friend when he said, "If they
obey and serve him, they will spend the rest of their days in prosperity and their
years in contentment" (Job 36:11, NIV).

Patrice Williams-Gordon

A Present of God

Sons are a heritage from the Lord, children a reward from him. Ps. 127:3, NIV.

MY DAUGHTER WAS pregnant with her first son. Between the second and third months she suffered a spontaneous abortion. We prayed to God asking that, if it were His will, she could conceive again and have her next baby perfect, healthy, and at the right moment.

One Sunday morning as my daughter was deciding what to read in the Scriptures, she opened the Bible to a page and read a verse at random, Judges 13:7: "But he said to me, 'You will conceive and give birth to a son. Now then, drink no wine or other fermented drink and do not eat anything unclean, because the boy will be a Nazirite of God from birth until the day of his death.' " She quickly underlined this wonderful passage and wrote the date, July 6, in her Bible margin.

She began to wonder if she was pregnant, or if she would get pregnant in the near future. Four months later she found out at a checkup that she was pregnant. She had a great surprise when the doctor told her that her baby's birth would be on July 6 of the next year. Then she understood the message that God had sent to her that Sunday morning. It would be exactly one year after reading that message that she would have her baby.

If the hospital allows, I want to see my grandchild's first bath. It will be exciting! When I listen to him crying for the first time, I know I will begin to cry too. It will be an unspeakable emotion, for this little boy will be the son of someone who once was my little girl. Later on, still in the baby nursery, I will have the opportunity of holding him. I am very happy to know that he will be brought into the world by the hands of a qualified obstetrician. I thank God that she is our friend and a sister in the Lord. There will also be a team of responsible professionals—nurses, a pediatrician, and an anesthetist. I know my daughter will be in good hands, for all this team is safe in the hands of the greatest doctor, our Lord Jesus.

It is the responsibility of each of us to raise children in the Lord, just as my daughter read about in Judges. As Moses instructed Israel: "Only be careful, and watch yourselves closely so that you do not forget the things your eyes have seen or let them slip from your heart as long as you live. Teach them to your children and to their children after them" (Deut. 4:9, NIV).

Ester Loreno Perin

One Strong Angel

For he will command his angels concerning you to guard you in all your ways; they will lift you up in their hands, so that you will not strike your foot against a stone. Ps. 91:11, 12, NIV.

MY HUSBAND, Norman, and I decided to take my oldest grandson, Tyler, on a bike ride on the Blue Ridge Parkway. Highway 276 is a section of road with numerous curves and breathtaking scenery. We loaded the bikes and the dog for the 20-mile trip. We made sure that shoes and helmets were strapped securely. Tyler objected to the helmet, but I insisted. Norman and Tyler were to ride their bikes, and I was to follow behind to keep an eye on them.

Everything was going well, and I could see the exhilaration on both their faces as they raced down the winding road. A few miles farther on, however, I noticed that Tyler was straying to the left, near the double yellow line, so I tooted the horn lightly to get his attention. He turned his head slightly, and suddenly, right before my eyes, his bike veered toward a rock wall. He went airborne and disappeared over the wall. I pulled off the road and yelled to my husband. We raced to the wall and peered over. There lay Tyler, faceup, in a shallow creek. Norman jumped over the wall and ran to him. Tyler's color was pale as looked up at me and said, "Grandma Rosie, I'm hurt bad." My husband, who works in the medical field, began to check him over carefully. He could move all his extremities, and he was alert. We had no cell phone signal to call 911, but we managed to get him up to the truck using an old blanket for a stretcher. I was grateful to God that he was still alive. We made our way back down the road to the hospital, and I was able to phone his parents to meet us at the emergency room.

When the ER doctor questioned Tyler about how he landed, he said, "I hit my head." We then looked at his bike helmet and discovered a huge dent in the part that covered his right temporal area. "Son, that helmet just saved your life," the doctor stated emphatically. There were a few scrapes and small lacerations and a bruised clavicle, but otherwise he was fine.

As we left the ER I said, "Tyler, the angels surely took care of you today." He quickly replied, "It took just one big strong angel, Grandma Rosie."

Frequently my mind goes back to that day the angels lifted Tyler and prevented serious injury or death. Somehow I feel that Jesus has a special plan for Tyler—and for each of us.

Rose Neff Sikora

If We Have This Love

This is how we know what love is: Jesus Christ laid down his life for us. And we ought to lay down our lives for our brothers. 1 John 3:16, NIV.

HAVE YOU EVER loved a person until you felt as if you wanted him or her to be around you all the time? When I was expecting our first daughter, Orupa, I always wanted to have my husband around. Sometimes I'd get sick when I knew that he was to travel away from home. I felt more secure when he was nearby, but since he was employed, that didn't work out well. Each time he told me he was leaving I'd feel so bad! Finally at one point he said, "You know what, honey? I love you so much, and I know you would wish I could stay with you here at home all the time. You should remember, though, that God called us to work for Him."

Whenever I heard him talking about our calling, I became speechless, because before he was ordained to the pastoral ministry I assured him that I would support him in his ministry. But now each morning, as I saw him dressing up to go to the office, I'd get uneasy. Sometimes he'd work from home just to make sure that I was OK.

I know I'm not the only one who would love to spend as much time as possible with a loved one. We all wish to have our loved ones around us; we feel more secure. We spend time to show them that we love them and appreciate their presence; we plan birthday parties and anniversaries. These loving gestures help us to maintain a marriage and relationship with those we love.

I really felt good (in fact, more secure) when my husband took some time off— or even worked from home—to stay with me, but he couldn't leave his work and stay with me for the whole time when I was expecting. So the question comes to my mind: If I can feel so secure when my fellow human being is with me, how much more safe should we feel when we know that there is a person who loves us more than our husbands, our wives, or our parents. He even went to the extent of dying for us and has promised to be with us wherever we are. And this is none other than our Friend, the only one who died for you and me, Jesus Christ. "Greater love has no one than this, that he lay down his life for his friends" (John 15:13, NIV).

I don't have to beg Him to stay with me the way I begged my husband. He is always there for me. And He is always there for you, as well.

Nakku Mbwana

He Finds Passports as Well

Ask, and it shall be given you; seek, and ye shall find; knock, and it shall be opened unto you. Matt. 7:7.

I WAS BORN on one of the Greek islands, and we now own a small house where my husband and I spend our summer holidays. I used to go to the island 10 to 15 days earlier than my husband. Last summer, a few days before we returned to Athens, my husband told me that before he came to the island he had lost my Australian passport.

He explained that he'd had to fill out some forms for the government, and that it was necessary to have my passport as a proof. When he returned home, he discovered that he didn't have my passport. He went back to the office but couldn't find it there. He called the police and the Australian embassy, asking if they would call him if someone found it.

Ten days later he came to the island, but he didn't say anything to me, hoping that someone would find the passport. In the end he had to confess what had happened because three weeks after our return to Athens we were to travel to Melbourne, Australia, for our youngest son's wedding.

I was very upset in the beginning, but finally I calmed down. My husband told me that it had been 42 days since he lost the passport. The embassy told us that we didn't have enough time to get a new passport before leaving for the wedding, and also that we had to pay a fine for losing it.

I said to my husband, "There are a lot of people who are coming to us, asking us to pray for many different things. So why don't we fast and pray, knowing that there is One who can find it." He agreed, and all that day we fasted and prayed, asking God to find my passport.

The very next morning our phone rang. It was our nephew who lives on the second floor of our house in Athens. "Uncle, did my aunt lose her passport?"

"Yes. Why?" my husband asked.

"When I came home this morning, I found her passport on the pathway," he said.

We praised the Lord, and I said to my husband, "When I get to heaven, I will ask Him, 'How did You do that?' "

Truly, we can ask, seek, and find!

Georgina Maglis

Along the Dalton Highway

Take the veil from my eyes, that I may see the marvels
that spring from thy law. Ps. 119:18, NEB.

"THERE'S AN ARCTIC loon and its babies. Hopefully winter won't come before the chicks are ready to migrate," our guide told us.

Our family had left our son's home two days earlier and driven north past Denali National Park, past Fairbanks, along the Dalton Highway, following the Alaska pipeline to Dead Horse. There we had joined a guide and two other tourists to go to the Arctic Ocean.

"What animals did you see on your way up?" we asked the others.

"Animals? We saw no animals along the road. What is there to see?"

My husband and son motioned for our new friends to look on the screens of their digital cameras. "Of course there were moose farther south and some foxes. Herds of caribou crossed the tundra and drifted on the hills. We saw no bears, but there was a wolf."

"Best of all," my daughter-in-law said, her eyes shining, "we saw a herd of musk oxen near Franklin Bluffs."

Musk oxen. They had been hunted to extinction in Alaska, but some reintroduced animals have grown into herds, and we had been blessed to see one. Stephanie, awaking from a nap, had called out, "Stop! There's something by the river." We piled out of the truck, slopped our way across the boggy muskeg, and crouched on the riverbank, looking down at 26 shaggy animals—bulls, cows, and calves. They saw us but kept browsing. One curious cow ambled closer. When she stopped to eat, we crept back to the truck, adrenaline coursing through our veins.

"You saw all that?" exclaimed Nafiz. "We saw nothing. But we're from Turkey, and we didn't know there was anything to see."

Driving south the next day, we frequently saw a small mud-covered car, driven by our Turkish friends. When both our vehicles waited for a road grader to smooth the gravel, Kerem said excitedly, "We passed your Franklin Bluffs. No musk oxen, but brown-and-white birds."

"Ptarmigan," stated Garrick. "We saw those, too. They're turning white for the winter."

Later, as we repaired a flat tire, Nafiz and Kerem passed us, pointing excitedly at the horizon. Caribou! Their eyes had been opened, and they could see.

Denise Dick Herr

The Helping Word

A word fitly spoken is like apples of gold in pictures of silver. Prov. 25:11.

IT WAS A HOT, humid summer afternoon. Though the bus was air-conditioned, the passengers were quiet, and there was none of the usual after-work banter. A look at their faces told the story: hot, tired, stressed, and not wanting to be bothered by anything or anyone.

Then it happened. At one stop a man embarked and, smiling, he said, "Good afternoon, everybody!" The passengers looked up grouchily, thinking, *What's his problem? In this city no one greets a busload of passengers. You may greet the driver or your seatmate, but you don't give a general greeting.* So no one responded. He quietly paid his fare, smiled, and this time said, "You all don't seem to be feeling too good today, so let me try again: Good afternoon, everybody!" and humming softly, he took his seat. This time it worked. Most people laughed and many responded, "Good afternoon to you, too!" The mood changed, and people even began talking to their seatmates!

Life is like that for many people. They are bothered by life's challenges—family, job, relationships, finances—and the list could go on and on. They are quiet and lost in their own thoughts, probably trying to figure out what their next step should be, stressed by economic situations. Keeping it all to themselves may seem to be the easiest and safest way to cope. But then someone comes along, someone who may be facing some of the same challenges but who has learned to cope, and then others realize things aren't so bad after all. They realize that their situation isn't hopeless but hopeful! They talk with others and may find answers to some of their problems. They may even begin to use the same formula this man used.

As I continued on my bus trip home I thought, *What a difference one man made with a positive attitude, a kind word, and a song in his heart.* This experience reminded me of a song I learned as a child: "If any little word of mine may make a dark life brighter, if any little song of mine may make a sad heart lighter, God help me speak the helping word, and sweeten it with singing, and drop it in some lonely vale, to set the echoes ringing."

Will you join me today in looking for opportunities to change situations by speaking the helping word, sweetened with singing? It may just turn someone's situation from being helpless and hopeless to hopeful.

Maureen O. Burke

July 12

Topia and Sam Learn a Lesson

Obey my voice, and I will be your God, and ye shall be my people: and walk ye in all the ways that I have commanded you, that it may be well unto you. Jer. 7:23.

MY NAME IS CASSANDRA, and I'm 5 years old. I like telling stories, and I wanted to share this story I made up:

"There was a girl named Cassandra who loved dogs. The name of her dog was Topia, and Topia's good friend was a dog named Sam. They lived in a beautiful place filled with many different plants and flowers. One of the plants was the lizard thorn, with long, sharp thorns that grew on beautiful purple flower bushes. The flowers smelled so sweet, but if you got close the lizard thorns would shoot out of the flower stem and stick you. They were very painful. Cassandra's parents told everyone to stay out of the lizard thorn garden so they could be safe.

"Knowing not everyone would listen, Cassandra's parents created special mittens and boots that protected people and animals from the thorns. One day Topia and Sam were chasing a ball near the lizard thorn garden. All of a sudden Sam knocked the ball into the middle of the lizard thorns.

"Sam decided to get the ball, but Topia told her it was a bad idea because Sam needed the special mittens. But Sam didn't listen and ran inside the garden. Topia grabbed two pairs of mittens and put them on her paws. She took her first-aid kit and ran after Sam. When Topia got near the garden, she could hear Sam crying. Topia helped Sam out of the garden, then pulled out all of the thorns. Sam cried the whole time Topia was pulling out the thorns. Topia put a big bandage on Sam's paws and helped her stand up.

"Finally Sam stopped crying and said that she would never go into the garden ever again. Topia shook her head and reminded Sam that she should listen when someone speaks. Sam thought about that and realized that if she had listened to Topia she wouldn't have been hurt and should make better choices. Topia decided that she would make better choices too."

I told my mom that God gave us a world that was perfect, and all He asked us to do was not eat from one tree. Adam and Eve loved living in the Garden of Eden, but after a while they decided not to listen to God, and this caused pain that we didn't have to have. But just as Topia was there for Sam, God is there for us. We just have to listen and do what God asks us to do.

Cassandra Marquez de Smith

Anywhere With Jesus

Why are you so afraid? Do you still have no faith? Mark 4:40, NIV.

WHEN I WAS a small girl in the 1950s, we had a "real live missionary" visit our church. She told of an experience she had recently been through in a raging surf, holding a 6-year-old native child up out of the water while their boat sank beneath them after foundering on a coral reef. The missionary had to float, supporting the child, for several hours until she and others with her were rescued. I clearly remember her having us sing "Anywhere With Jesus I Can Safely Go" when the story was finished. It made a major impression on my young mind. Ever since, I have thought of her story when we sing that song.

But it wasn't until many years later that the full impact of this song really came home to me. As a "real, live missionary" myself, my husband and I were traveling home from an outer island to our home base on a larger island. As we boarded the small and somewhat rickety Twin Otter airplane, the pilot informed us very matter-of-factly that we would have to travel through a thunderstorm to get home. He said, "I will do my best to fly around this storm, but we will probably have to go through some of it."

Naturally, we didn't feel very comfortable with that announcement. We chose to sit in the back seat of the plane, as close to the door as possible in case we needed to escape quickly.

We flew steadily for a while, and then the plane began to buck and slide through the dark clouds. I tensed and held my breath. Rain began to spatter onto my foot through the gaps around the well-used door. My stomach twisted itself into tight knots. Terror gripped me. Just when I thought I would go crazy from fear, into my mind came some calm, questioning words—almost as though Someone had spoken: "Why were you afraid when I was in the boat?" The words were a direct quote from a children's Bible story book we used to read to our kids when they were small, the story of Jesus stilling the storm on Lake Galilee.

Peace descended on my frenzied soul, and in that moment I knew for myself that indeed "Anywhere with Jesus I can safely go!" It isn't that other missionary's song anymore. Now it is mine! "Anywhere with Jesus I am not afraid./Anywhere! anywhere!/Fear I cannot know;/Anywhere with Jesus I can safely go."

Janette Kingston

Don't Be Deceived

Jesus said to them: "Watch out that no one deceives you." Mark 13:5, NIV.

EVERY SUMMER SOME of our family members enjoy getting together for spiritual and physical restoration at a church campout. This year when we heard that for financial reasons the retreat in our area wouldn't be held, one of our daughters decided we should attend a retreat in another state. So instead of driving, we would go by plane. Another daughter and our youngest granddaughter would join us, so this would also be a mini family reunion.

When we landed at our destination and went to baggage claim, most of the baggage had already been picked up by the other passengers. Our daughter quickly identified her distinctive blue duffel bag, and then we saw our dark-green suitcase with the red yarn tied to the handle.

Before long the five of us and our baggage were packed into the car for the two-hour drive from the airport to the retreat. It was quite late by the time we reached our destination, and after getting settled in our little apartment, I got ready to go to bed. It had been a long day.

What a surprise when I opened the suitcase the next morning and found only men's clothes—not the clothes I had packed before we left home. Then I looked more closely at the suitcase. It was the right color, and it had the same identifying piece of red yarn, but my name tag was missing. As I looked at the baggage claim tag, I saw another name on it. Someone else had claimed my suitcase before we got to the carousel, but I should have checked more closely before leaving the airport. When we called the airport, we found that indeed someone else was looking for their luggage, just as we were. Everything was straightened out the next day after a trip back to the airport, but so much time and stress could have been saved if only I had paid more attention to the details.

This experience taught me a lesson. It's so easy to think something sounds all right without paying attention to the details. By studying my Bible carefully every day I won't be deceived by overlooking some thought that could mean the difference between eternal life and the road to destruction. It will help me to remember what Paul wrote in 2 Timothy 3:16: "All Scripture is inspired by God and is useful to teach us what is true and to make us realize what is wrong in our lives. It corrects us when we are wrong and teaches us to do what is right" (NLT).

Betty J. Adams

The Ways

Great and marvelous are your deeds, Lord God Almighty.
Just and true are your ways, King of the ages. Rev. 15:3, NIV.

GOING TO GUARUJÁ beach on Sundays was my family's favorite outing. One Sunday the sun was shining and the shore was full of bathers as my children and I found a place to spend our afternoon. Marcio, 3 years old, and Vini, 18 months old, took their toys and stayed by my side. My husband went to buy ice cream, and I think I snoozed a little, long enough for Marcio to get away from my side. I tried to believe that he was with his father, but when Milton came back, the child was not with him.

I looked around frantically, but he was nowhere to be seen! Such a big crowd—where should I look? I lifted my eyes to heaven and cried out, "My God, where is my son? Where should I go?" Ahead was the great sea, behind me was the bustling avenue, and at either side was the shore. Immediately I felt an impulse to run to the right. I don't know how I found strength, but I ran a lot.

I went to several lifeguard stations, asking the lifeguards about my son, then continued running. In some booths there were no lifeguards. I didn't stop. Then, passing by another empty booth, I felt compelled to climb the stairs. When I got to the top, I saw a couple of foreigners offering candies and soft drinks to my son, who was in tears. When Marcio saw me, he ran to my arms, and we left the place happy and thankful to God.

I know that alone I would never have found my son. I treasure the promise: "He who dwells in the shelter of the Most High will rest in the shadow of the Almighty" (Ps. 91:1, NIV).

As I remember what happened that day I think of the difficult decisions we must make in life. We are pressed by the enemy behind us, and we ourselves are full of pride and selfishness. We have two ways to go: the way of life, or the way of death. We want to follow the way of life, but our eyes are blurred and we can't see our goal. What to do?

We need to consult our divine Father and ask, "Lord, which way should I go?" Then we must listen to His sweet voice telling us, "This is the way; walk in it" (Isa. 30:21, NIV).

Lourdes S. de Oliveira

Don't Open the Door

All things work together for good. Rom. 8:28.

In every thing give thanks.
1 Thess. 5:18.

I WAS AWAKENED from a sound sleep and began praying in my heart for the Lord's will to be done in my life. Then my husband, P.M., said, "Let's have prayer about our moving situation, our district, and the recent death of my brother, Herman. Finally, I want you to write a letter to the church headquarters concerning help with our moving to LaGrange."

We proceeded to have our devotions. Just as we were saying amen I said, "It smells like something is burning!" I jumped up and put my shoes on. P.M. pulled on his pants and ran down the hall, checking all the rooms. He came back to the bedroom and said, "I didn't see anything. Let's check again."

He ran to the kitchen, put one hand on the garage door and the other hand on the doorknob. He turned to me and said, "Don't touch the garage door! I think the fire's in there." He had heard a voice that told him not to open the garage door.

P.M. obeyed that voice. We believe it was the Holy Spirit. I obeyed P.M.'s voice when he told me not to open the garage door. As I called 9-1-1, I put on a shirt and grabbed my eyeglasses, cell phone, purse, and a bag of personal mail.

Five fire trucks came to the house. The captain kept commending us again and again, saying that we saved our lives by not opening the door to the garage. If the Holy Spirit had not awakened us for prayer, the captain was sure that the fumes could have put us to sleep forever.

Because we obeyed quickly, our lives were saved. We give thanks and praise God we obeyed the voice that said, "Don't open the door!"

Let's practice listening to and obeying our God—and those His Holy Spirit impresses. Proverbs gives us good advice on this: "Let the wise listen and add to their learning, and let the discerning get guidance." "But whoever listens to me will live in safety and be at ease, without fear of harm" (Prov. 1:5, 33, NIV).

Today we personally give thanks for the way God "worked" the house fire for our good. God gave us a new house in our new district.

Helen Lennear Florence

Chances and Miracles

Then you shall call, and the Lord will answer; you shall cry,
and He will say, "Here I am." Isa. 58:9, NKJV.

IT WAS JULY 17, 2005, when I suddenly felt my stomach aching. I didn't mind it, thinking it was just an ordinary gas pain. The pain was bearable—until we got home. Lying on the bed to find comfort and ease, I suddenly vomited, the retching, dry heaving kind. The pain was now severe, unbearable, and steady. My husband rushed me to the hospital, where nurses injected me with some pain reliever. I was relieved, but only for a short while. I tossed on the bed till morning, robbed of sleep. The pain in my stomach was so excruciating that I avoided anybody's touch. My doctor referred me to a gastroenterologist, who ordered a nasogastric tube (NGT). White and green liquids flowed out from the tube to a small container that had to be emptied every time it got full. Two doctors observed my condition. After three days they referred me to a surgeon, who ordered blood samples, X-rays, and various laboratory tests. They noticed my stomach bulging, but once again test results were negative.

On the seventh day the surgeon did some manual tests on my stomach. Using the stethoscope, he could barely hear the sound of my intestines. He ordered one last test, a CT scan. He found out I was having ileus, the inability of the intestines to pass contents because of a physical obstruction or muscular inadequacy. We had no choice but for me to submit to an operation.

One week after the pain started I was ushered into the operating room. My family gathered around me to plead for God's intervention. Personally, I was ready for death. Should I die, I had confessed my sins, asked God's forgiveness, and committed myself to Him.

Inside the operating room, before the anesthesia took effect, I remembered my 8-year-old boy, so sweet, young, and innocent. What would happen to him if I should die? Who would take care of him? Who would soothe the pain of bruises and hurts? I prayed, *Lord, have mercy; spare my life. My son needs me to care for him.* I pleaded that God would give me a second chance to live. When I woke up, my surgeon told me I had had an intestinal adhesion.

What do we do when we face serious illness, or even death? What a comfort to know that sins are forgiven, and that we can rest fully in His love. He will always do what is best.

Fe C. Magpusao

7:05 p.m.

But of that day and hour no one knows, neither the angels in heaven, nor the Son, but only the Father. Take heed, watch and pray; for you do not know when the time is. Mark 13:32, 33, NKJV.

TWICE A MONTH patients involved in a gastric bypass process get together to support one another. They have learned so much from each other that they truly look forward to the meetings. Their excitement brings them to the gatherings anywhere from 30 to 90 minutes early on the special evenings. Prior to undergoing the surgery they must lose 10 percent of their weight and attend at least two support group meetings.

The patients are kept in the waiting room of the clinic until 7:00 p.m. when the doors are opened and the large group streams in. For one or two hours they attentively learn from each other, show off their scars, talk about the process, and swap recipes.

During one week's meeting I heard a very angry, unfamiliar voice at the front desk. I went out to see if I could be of assistance. The young woman standing there was frustrated as she told her story. She had come to the clinic to "sign the sheet" so that credit could be received for attending the meeting. Her surgery was scheduled for the following month. She had walked in at 7:05 p.m., just five minutes late, and sat alone until 7:45 p.m. Frustrated, she finally approached the front desk to inquire about the meeting. Angrily she asked, "Why didn't someone come out to call me in? Did you start the group early? No one was here when I got here!" Further, she wanted to know if she would, or could, receive credit for waiting in the waiting room. On questioning, we determined that she had been fully aware of the date and time for the meeting; nevertheless, she was "just a little late." One year had been given to every pre-op patient to attend two meetings, but she had chosen to wait until one month prior to the surgery to do so—and then she was late. Unfortunately for her, these decisions would cost her the coveted "spot" on the surgical schedule.

We know that Jesus is coming and what the signs will be. We know that we must make our decision now as we are not promised tomorrow. If we are truly excited about spending eternity with our Savior we will be ready before He comes, and we will eagerly await His return.

But will we be ready? Being one minute late will be too late.

Sharon Michael

Be Still

A furious squall came up, and the waves broke over the boat, so that it was nearly swamped. Jesus was in the stern, sleeping on a cushion. The disciples woke him and said to him, "Teacher, don't you care if we drown?"
Mark 4:37, 38, NIV.

I HAD FLOWN many thousands of miles in the past 10 years, but this was the most violent storm I had ever encountered. Leaving the country of Moldova on a beautiful sunny day, I was on my way from Kishinev to Washington, D.C., when suddenly the airplane began to buck like a wild mustang with its first rider. It felt as though no one was in control, and the lightning was constant. For nearly 15 minutes we seemed to be surrounded by a violent wind that never ceased. I had good reason to believe that the plane would soon plummet to the earth.

The disciples had shouted to the Lord, "Save us; we're sinking!" In the same manner I began to pray. As the small plane bounced and swayed, I held tightly to the armrest. I felt fear, but as I prayed I had the assurance that God was in control, no matter what happened.

I thought more about the boat ride taken by the disciples and our Lord. Everything was fine until the storm hit; then all the disciples grew fearful and distraught. Jesus was asleep in the back of the boat. He was calm because He was in control. It was the disciples—and me—who let our fear get the best of us!

Almost immediately the turbulence stopped, and we continued on to our destination.

One of the blessings to come from this experience was learning that when we face a storm in our lives we have to remember three things. First, we cannot control the storms; we have to pray and let God care for us. Second, storms do not last forever. Jesus will not allow you to be overcome. You are safe in His loving protection. Sometimes He will calm the storm; sometimes He will calm your heart. Either way, He wants you to know peace in the midst of your difficulties. "Be strong, fear not!" Third, you aren't alone. There is no storm we face that Jesus hasn't already weathered. And He promises to accompany us through everything we experience

When we are caught in the storms of life, it's easy to think that God has lost control and that we're at the mercy of the winds of fate. In reality God is sovereign. He controls the boat. As we spend time getting to know Him and experience His love, we learn to trust Him no matter how large the waves and no matter how scary the storm.

Raquel Queiroz da Costa Arrais

Of Roots and Returns

But our citizenship is in heaven. And we eagerly await a Savior from there, the Lord Jesus Christ. Phil. 3:20, NIV.

I WAS HOMELESS by the age of 3 when my family became refugees because Communists had taken over my homeland of Estonia. The KGB targeted my father, who was the church president for that area and considered to be a leader of the people. Therefore our lives were imperiled. We fled, just the four of us in my family, leaving behind our homeland, extended family and friends, my father's work for the church, and all that was familiar and treasured. Consequently, my earliest memories involve a loss and recovery. I lost the treasure of having relatives and felt like a blown-away leaf from a family tree. I knew firsthand the reality of threat to life and experienced terrors represented by sounds and images—bombings, sirens, flight, fire, screams, the destruction of what humankind had built and the destruction of what God had made. My losses were represented by enormity—country, family, identity—as well as by minutiae: basic essentials of life, the few toys I possessed, the few friends I could make in our wanderings.

Then we arrived in what, for us, was the "promised land." We found refuge in America, and our wanderings were over. Eventually, however, the unexpected happened. The Soviet Union fell apart, and I could return to my homeland. I could rediscover my identity, my people, my relatives, my language, my beautiful country. This unplanned gift, so to speak, brought a richness to my life I had never expected.

More important, I learned more fully the lessons of loss and recovery, of roots and returns, and I could apply these more readily to our experience as Christians who are looking toward our return to a homeland that God has promised us. By sin we were cut off from our originally intended roots. But God isn't happy with the "refugee" experiences we must endure and therefore has a better place for us; things we haven't dreamed of are waiting for us.

Just as it was my choice to return to my roots, we can look ahead to a return to our heavenly homeland. I am grateful for my United States citizenship, so significant when my own country was destroyed, but my life was enriched and became whole when I could reclaim the citizenship of my roots. In the same way we can look forward to our citizenship in heaven, which we will receive when our Lord returns and takes us home.

Lilya Wagner

Big Barrel Prayers

Before they call I will answer; while they are still speaking I will hear.
Isa. 65:24, NIV.

MY 14-YEAR-OLD SON, Spencer, was having a particularly difficult county recreational baseball season. The majority of his teammates played baseball for their middle school during the school year, but Spencer hadn't tried out, so he opted to play county recreation baseball instead of school ball.

Each baseball game produced worse results. Though he was fielding well, it became painfully obvious that he couldn't hit the ball with the "big barrel" bats that his teammates were using. His father and I begged him to use his bat from the prior season, but he argued that he couldn't use it since he would be ridiculed by his teammates. I enlisted my mother, a prayer warrior. She prayed tirelessly that he would hit the ball and salvage his self-esteem. We weren't asking that he would singlehandedly win the game, but that he would be able to finish the season with some measure of dignity and self-confidence.

Then I read the women's devotional reading of June 29, 2009, written by Jacqueline Hope Hoshing-Clarke, "An Encounter With God at the Clothesline." In it the author struggled with the idea of praying for something seemingly selfish, such as asking God to have the sun shine in order to dry her clothes. I had often felt ashamed for praying before Spencer stepped up to the plate, thinking that there are so many tragic situations, and I felt guilty for merely wanting my son's self-esteem to be bolstered. Then I read that devotional reading with reference to the hymn "O for a Faith That Will Not Shrink." It occurred to me that God is very concerned with what concerns me, and my son's self-esteem was a huge concern for me, so I prayed and sang that song.

I called my mom, who also reads the women's devotionals. She prayed, and we called on other prayer warriors to pray. That night (yes, the night of June 29) Spencer hit the ball with all his might, got on base, and eventually scored a run.

The next day I wrote at the top of June 30's devotional page, "Last ball game! O for a faith that will not shrink." Mom and her prayer warriors prayed more, and that night Spencer hit two singles and a double, and brought in five runners. God cares about even the smallest, seemingly insignificant, cares of His children. Aren't we blessed to have a Father like that?

Melissa (Missy) Daughety McClung

Algae and Sin

Wash away all my iniquity and cleanse me from my sin. Ps. 51:2, NIV.

SEVERAL YEARS AGO my husband and I bought a home with a swimming pool. Even though we didn't swim, I often enjoyed the beauty of the crystal-blue water.

Last year, for the first time, we began having algae problems. The beautiful blue water turned a nasty green. We got it under control during the winter, but with the dawn of summer and hot weather we once again began battling algae. How quickly blue water can turn green. And within three days we couldn't even see to the bottom. I also noticed that after three days of looking at green water, it didn't look so bad. Climbing roses on the back fence reflected pink in the green pool and at times almost looked pretty and "normal" to me.

We dumped gallons of chemicals into our green pool to "shock" it back to its crystal-blue color. It would approach normal and then slide right back to murky green again. Our pool was very sick. After weeks of trying to handle it ourselves, we gave up and turned it over to a professional pool service. I was amazed to see how quickly professionals could turn a sick pool around. Their chemicals and 24 hours did it. Now, in order to keep our pool clear, we must have pool service.

There was plenty of time to reflect on our pool dilemma while dealing with the algae problem. The algae seemed very much like sin to me. When first we indulge in sin it doesn't appear so bad. But after repeated indulgence that sin appears "normal," since we no longer see the hideousness of it as Jesus does. Just as my pool began to look normal in its murky, filthy state, so does repeated sin begin to appear normal to us within a short period of time. The only way to get rid of the sin or algae in our lives is to turn it over to a professional pool service—in this case, Jesus, who shed His blood on Calvary to cleanse us.

If you have any sin or algae in your life, you can try to clean it up yourself by spending money, putting on a happy face and tons of makeup, purchasing new clothes or a beautiful home, or by driving a fancy car—all vain attempts to hide the real problem. But there's One who sees what no one else can see. He'll remove any trace of algae from your life if you ask. Why not do that right now?

Nancy Van Pelt

Practice What You Preach

And they that were ready went in . . . and the door was shut. Matt. 25:10.

THE WOMEN'S MINISTRIES department of our church area announced a convention to be conducted for our territory. It was to be a one-day affair, dubbed "grandiferous" because the organizers had lofty expectations and projected the participation of 7,000, or more, women.

Week by week I announced the "grandiferous" convention and encouraged—yes, urged—the members of my church to prepare to attend. The response at first was not very enthusiastic, but as the scheduled date drew closer and the "grandiferous" aspects were clearly emphasized, the list of registrants expanded surprisingly, and even included a "few good men." Most of the women agreed to travel by bus, for which the church had made the necessary arrangements.

We planned to leave the church at 6:30 a.m. Because the occasion was a one-day affair, punctuality was a major consideration. I seized every opportunity not only to urge the members to participate but also to warn them to be on time or the bus would leave without them.

At 6:30 on the morning we planned to leave, almost 100 percent of those who had signed up to travel on the bus were comfortably seated and ready to go. The one person missing was the individual who had "preached" so vigorously, demanding that the 6:30 schedule be observed.

At 6:30 I was suddenly disturbed by the telephone, and I could distinctly hear two voices anxiously, urgently demanding, "Where are you?" "Are not you going with us on the bus?" "Have you changed your mind?"

I had not changed my mind; I was still going on the bus; but, like the foolish virgins, I had fallen asleep. Now between elation and despair, I pleaded, "Please wait for me!" It took only a few minutes to get to the bus, but I was too embarrassed to make a decent apology. I had preached punctuality, and I was gravely accountable.

I needed a whole day to decide what I could say to the driver and the others on the bus. On the return trip I humbly requested forgiveness and expressed my appreciation for the infinite compassion so readily exemplified by all. This experience made me think of the information in 1 Corinthians 9:27: "I keep under my body, and bring it into subjection: lest . . . when I have preached to others, I myself should be a castaway."

Quilvie G. Mills

Early Flight

A friend loves at all times. Prov. 17:17, NIV.

IT WAS ALMOST 10:00, and I should have been in bed. Instead I was at the sewing machine, finishing a project for one of the grandchildren I would be seeing the next day. I had chosen to fly on the 6:30 a.m. flight because it was the least expensive. But it meant getting up very early so that I could be at the airport by 5:00 a.m. Ordinarily my husband would have taken me; but he had come down with the flu and wouldn't be able to. I suggested that I cancel my trip, but he wouldn't hear of it. He was sure that in a day or so he would be fine. I planned to call a taxi that night and make the necessary arrangements, but I hadn't done it as yet.

Just then the phone rang. "Do you need a ride? I'll pick you up." It was my friend. I didn't want to bother her because she lived across the city and it would take 20 minutes to get to our place. She had done this for me another time when my husband was out of town and I had an early flight. Reluctantly, I agreed.

Others have also benefitted from my friend's unusually big heart. When her ex-husband had to move, she helped with packing. She drives another woman to medical appointments. Every Sabbath she goes out of her way to pick up a woman and take her to church. She has even shared her home with a single mom and her three children. "I wish I had a friend like that," my sister has said to me.

My friend loves unconditionally. This past year a single mother from church gave birth to adorable twin girls. My friend was the first to suggest that we have a baby shower for these babies. A critical comment was made by someone who disapproved of the entire process of in vitro fertilization. "We'll have a shower, and those who want to can come" was my friend's response. She was certainly manifesting a Christian attitude.

As I reflect on the way my friend is always there for me, I feel very blessed. In fact, she not only is my friend, I have adopted her as my sister. Truly she is a friend who loves at all times. "Dear friends, let us love one another, for love comes from God. Everyone who loves has been born of God and knows God. Whoever does not love does not know God, because God is love" (1 John 4:7, 8, NIV).

Vera Wiebe

The Day the Rain Came

Why are you so downcast, O my soul? Why so disturbed within me?
Put your hope in God, for I will yet praise him, my Savior and my God.
Ps. 42:5, 6, NIV.

OUR CHILDREN WANTED to save our daughter-in-law's parental home in Bulgaria by a complete renovation of the building. They could then go there for vacations and preserve for their children a contact with the family's home country. So they planned a working holiday for the summer of 2008. When they left I jokingly said, "I hope you will miss us grandparents!"

Their relatives, who also live in the village, were so occupied with their farming work that they had little time to help, so our son and daughter-in-law, always accompanied by their small children, set out to buy building materials. They had made detailed plans while still in Germany. After a few days new windows had been installed in the whole house. It was very hot, 104°F (40°C), so they took off the roofing of the house, as the whole roof construction had to be renewed. Village men had offered to help with this job, but they didn't turn up. Then clouds came up, and several times it looked as if the gates of heaven would be opened shortly. We were kept informed of the emergency situation by text messages on our cell phone: "Please pray with us that the Lord will hold back the rain—we have no covering for the roof."

By e-mail I at once contacted 50 prayer warriors, and we all pleaded for God to intervene. "Ask and it will be given to you" (Matt. 7:7, NIV)! We reminded God of His promises and were ready to wait for His help. I asked the Lord to give us an awesome experience, particularly for my dear daughter-in-law, who had been a believer only a little while. They had been able to procure a thin plastic sheet to cover the most important parts of the gaping hole for the night.

God held the rains back, and the next morning the workers arrived. Since the weather stayed good, they worked quickly and fixed the roof. When the job was completed, the roof was beautifully covered. Five minutes after the last worker got down from the roof a downpour, lasting more than an hour, began! Our children were awestruck by this wonderful experience.

Yes, the Lord worked a miracle, and a few minutes later we, at a distance of 1,350 miles (2,200 kilometers) in Germany, were thankful to be able to take part in it via text message. We too praised the Lord for His love and mercy. God is so good!

Ingrid Bomke

By Beholding
We Become Changed

(And we beheld his glory, the glory as of the only begotten of the Father,) full of grace and truth. John 1:14.

I'M NOT A graceful person, a discovery I made as an adult when I took a class in which we exercised to music. The first couple of classes were easy enough, but soon I began to lag noticeably behind the rest of the class. I bought a CD of the music and took it home to practice in front of a mirror. That's when I made the shocking discovery that even when I succeeded in doing the motions correctly I looked like a total klutz. As much as I practiced in front of the mirror, I never learned to do the exercises gracefully.

Years later I bought an exercise DVD, but even then I had trouble making my hands and feet do the complicated motions together. Finally I learned not to look at myself but to concentrate instead on watching the teacher on the video. Amazingly, as I watched the teacher the subconscious part of my brain took over, and soon I was able to do the exercises properly. As long as I focused totally on the teacher I did well, but if I started to think about what my hands and feet were doing I became my old klutzy self.

It's a lot like that with God's grace in our spiritual lives. We can know the right things to do, and we can even do the right things; but if God's grace isn't present in our lives, even when we try to do the right things they can come out wrong. Just knowing the truth isn't enough. When God's grace is not living in us daily, even when we're right we can hurt people and turn them off—not just to us but to religion and to the gospel.

The way to become a grace-filled Christian is to concentrate on the One who *is* grace—Jesus. We need to spend regular, quality time beholding Him, reflecting on the One who took time to have a life-changing conversation with a woman who had had five husbands. The One who had dinner with a dishonest tax collector. The One who was humble enough to wash the feet of the very one who would betray Him.

When we concentrate on Jesus instead of on ourselves a funny thing happens. Slowly, imperceptibly, we begin to change. His will becomes our will; His thoughts become our thoughts; His ways become our ways. We become grace-filled, loving, and lovable Christians.

Carla Baker

My First Day in Heaven

Fear none of those things which thou shalt suffer: . . . be thou faithful unto death, and I will give thee a crown of life. Rev. 2:10.

SOMETIMES WHEN LIFE'S burdens threaten to discourage me on my Christian walk, I just take a few minutes to be still and simply imagine my first day in heaven. I think it will go something like this:

I'm here! I'm actually here—*in heaven!* The natural beauty everywhere calls me to examine it with wonder and awe. Shining angels surround me and point out my loved ones and friends with whom they want me to reunite. Yet I have only one desire in my heart. That's what keeps it pounding with excitement. That's what causes tears of joy to flow like rivers from my eyes. I want to meet Jesus!

Surrounded by a retinue of angelic beings, He approaches the jubilant multitude around me. Though He is still in the distance, I can already hear His melodious voice, and I gaze upon His unspeakable beauty, a beauty more comely than I had ever dreamed!

I imagine Him approaching beneath an overarching rainbow whose myriad colors fall upon the people, bowing as He passes among them. His attending angels hand Him bejeweled crowns that He places upon the bowed heads about Him. Then, as if overcome by waves of ecstasy, cries of "Hosanna!" rise from the mighty throng and fill the skies with praise, adoration, and thanksgiving.

I tremble at His awesome closeness, and I fear I will fall to the ground. How can I stand before my mighty, loving, and holy God? Slipping to my knees, I feel a gentle touch on my shoulder. An angel's wing? No! The hand of my Savior, the hand that has led and sustained me during life's tests, temptations, and trials. I dare to raise my tear-stained face and find my sweet Lord smiling into my eyes. Awestruck, I can't talk. But that doesn't matter. He has heard the hallelujahs in my heart.

He wipes away my tears with gentle hands, the same hands that were nailed to the cross for me. With those same hands He takes my crown from an attending angel and places it on my head. I join in a shout of victory as thousands of voices once again erupt around me.

My Lord, what a morning! And to think that this is just the beginning!

Janet Hatcher

Tale of Two Hawks

For we are not contending against flesh and blood, but . . . against the spiritual hosts of wickedness in the heavenly places. . . . To that end keep alert with all perseverance, making supplication for all the saints.
Eph. 6:12-18, RSV.

I WAS RIDING up the Alaskan Highway in Canada during a vacation. Suddenly my eyes caught sight of a soaring bald eagle, a fairly common site in the Yukon. What was uncommon was the fact that a red-tailed hawk was in hot pursuit. It was disturbed, angry, and determined. Its legs dropped straight down, talons extended as far as possible, to attack the back of the bald eagle right beneath it.

On a previous Sabbath, as we walked along a high bluff not far from the highway, we could look down on a red-tail sitting on its nest in the top of a spruce tree. That was the red-tail's problem. The eagle is known to grab hawks' eggs and chicks to provide food for itself and its young. No wonder the hawk was so ferocious in its attack on the eagle.

In retrospect, I pondered whether I had the same unwavering resolve to rid myself of Satan's temptations—those critical, self-centered thoughts, those "darling" sins that I am tempted to rationalize away. Seeing that hawk's ferocity in protecting its young made me all the more determined to protect the most precious aspect of my life—my close relationship to Jesus.

Back home on my daily walk, I was surprised one morning to hear an amazing commotion in the sky behind me. I whirled around to see four very angry crows chasing a red-tailed hawk. Their loud, guttural caws began attracting more crows. Before long there were a large number of fellow attackers, and the red-tailed intruder beat a hot retreat.

This time the hawk was the enemy. It was exciting for me to watch how quickly the crow community gathered together to rid themselves of this menace. I've often seen my church come to my aid in prayer and assistance when my archenemy has attacked me. Many times I've watched prayer warriors in my church help turn the tide for those suffering under Satan's attacks.

In the traumatic days ahead let's never give up our vigilance in relying on the mighty right hand of our Deliverer to defeat our enemy and take us through to the end.

Donna Lee Sharp

Jesus' Love

"I tell you," he replied, "if they keep quiet, the stones will cry out."
Luke 19:40, NIV.

LAST WEEK I stopped at Paboo's little market on Main Street. Only she and her 5-year-old daughter, Naree, were there. Naree was drawing on paper at the counter as I chatted with her Laotian-born mother. Paboo asked about my recent treatments for cancer, then she asked Naree to pray for me. The three of us held hands. Naree was a little shy, so I prayed first. Then Paboo, in her very broken English, prayed such a sweet prayer while Naree repeated all her words. It was very touching to hear them ask God to keep me safe and give me a long and healthy life.

The Holy Spirit impressed me to sing with Naree. I asked her if she knew the song "Jesus Loves Me." She shook her head, and I sang a verse for her. Naree loved it, and Paboo asked me to write the words so they could learn it together. Then we sang it together several times. I also wrote *Jesus* in bold letters on her paper. Thinking they might enjoy other Sabbath school songs, I taught them "With Jesus in the Family, Happy, Happy Home." They were delighted. I left the shop promising to bring a DVD with music about Jesus so they would be able to learn and remember these wonderful tunes.

On Monday I went back to deliver on my promise. Paboo was in her shop alone. Naree wasn't there, but her mother was so excited to see me. She could hardly wait to open her desk drawer and show me copies of the music sheet that I had written. Naree is only 5 years old, but she knows how to run their copy machine and had made copies for all the children in all the shops next to theirs. All the shopkeepers are raising their children in their shops, just as Paboo has been doing since Naree's birth. (No paid nannies here!)

Now Naree is teaching them all to sing "Jesus Loves Me." She asks each customer if they would like to know that song, then copies a sheet for them. Some were already Christians, so they sang the words with Naree, reinforcing her memory. Isn't that great? She has taught me a most valuable lesson about planting the smallest of seeds.

Today I am reminded of a verse of Scripture that tells me that Jesus said if we keep quiet the rocks themselves will cry out. I don't want the stones to cry out in my place!

Claudia Parks

Wake Up! Pray!

The end of all things is near. Therefore be clear minded and self-controlled so that you can pray. 1 Peter 4:7, NIV.

Stay wide-awake in prayer. 1 Peter 4:7, Message.

"Wake up! Pray for Mark!" The voice jolted me out of my dozing. Was it an audible voice, or was it in my head? I didn't know, but I was now wide awake. I'd seen a fleeting vision of my teenage son Mark, with his characteristic cheeky grin, running across a panoramic screen, looking straight at me and waving. At the same time I also saw vivid images of him from babyhood through to his teens. *They say that when you're drowning you see your whole life flashing before you,* I thought. And here I was seeing my son's life flash before me. Mark was in danger! Immediately I obeyed the voice I had heard. I pleaded and agonized with God for my son. How long this went on I cannot recall. But at last I felt an overwhelming peace. I sensed that God had answered my prayer and that my son was safe.

A few days later, when Mark returned from summer camp on the North Wales coast, I learned what had happened at the precise moment the voice had told me to pray.

Mark and a group of teenage friends had gone to a place where the cliff dropped steeply to a small inlet of sea. The water was very deep there, and the kids enjoyed jumping off the cliff into the waves below. "Tomb-stoning," they call it—a thrilling but extremely dangerous activity. Mark is a competent swimmer but not an experienced diver. Nevertheless, he took his turn. He hurt his back as he hit the water, then struggled frantically to resurface and catch his breath. But my prayer was answered. He made it back safely onto dry land.

I know that God saved my son's life that day and on other occasions for a purpose. That purpose was for him to help save other people's lives, the job he now does as a humanitarian worker providing aid for those living on the edge.

We are living in dangerous times! We need to wake up and pray as never before for ourselves and our young people, because the enemy is looking for those vulnerable ones he can catch and drown in the sea of indifference to God's call, in the waves of cheap thrills. None of us is immune to his attacks.

Antonia Castellino

Lost and Found

Rejoice with me; for I have found my sheep which was lost. Luke 15:6.

YOU MIGHT SAY I'm a loser. I lose (or misplace) car keys, house keys, post office box keys, letters, addresses. Well, you get the picture. There have even been a couple times I thought I had lost (or misplaced!) one of my children.

When Teddy was a very small boy he was prone to wander off if I turned my back, but he was never really lost. His brother, Tim, once briefly disappeared from view at a small shopping area, but he was just at the other end of the sidewalk. It would be much more dangerous for a child to do that today, but it was not safe even then.

Then there was a time when Tim was lost in church. He was about 4 years old, and I had safely deposited him in his kindergarten Sabbath school while Teddy went to his own department and I went to the adult division. My husband, Ted, was visiting another church that weekend.

When I went back after class to get the children for the church service, Tim was nowhere to be seen. The very old church had about 80 rooms, I'd been told, and although I had never counted them, I believe it was true. Some were almost like cubbyholes, spread out over different levels, and in trying to track down one very small boy, I realized that there were many nooks and crannies that an adventurous kid like Tim would delight in exploring. Upstairs and down, in and out, with no results; I was beginning to get quite frantic. Finally, in desperation, I peeked into the sanctuary. There he was, sitting quietly on the front pew, completely unaware of my agitation. He wasn't lost in church after all.

Unfortunately, it is possible to be lost in church, as well as being lost outside church. Having one's name on the church roster isn't enough. Attending church faithfully isn't enough. Taking part in all the activities isn't enough. Returning tithe and giving generous offerings isn't enough. Important as these things are, nothing we do can earn salvation; it must come through a relationship with our Lord and Savior, Jesus, the spotless Son of God. "For God so loved the world, that he gave his only begotten Son, that whosoever believeth in him should not perish, but have everlasting life" (John 3:16).

I want to be found in church. Don't you?

Mary Jane Graves

Precious Stones

I will make a [woman] more precious than fine gold. Isa. 13:12.

MY HUSBAND AND I had gone to an IMAX to watch a 40-minute film of men and women climbing Mount Everest. We had a 15-minute wait, so we decided to browse the gift shop in the Museum of Natural History, which was in the same building. As we entered, my attention was drawn to a collection of precious stones displayed behind a thick glass pane. Because I couldn't afford the stone that I wanted, I kept looking around the shop until I came upon a small case of shiny little stones. I purchased one of them.

On the back of the case, it read: "Rough gemstone material, when tumbled in drums with grit and polish for weeks at a time, becomes very slick and shiny. Any stone that is valued for its beauty is considered a gemstone." The little box contained various types of stones.

As I read the label I thought about how God regards us as precious. Even though we are "in the rough," we are invaluable to Him nonetheless. I thought, *Just as those small stones had been tossed in grit and polish, we, too, go through a process that will help fit us for the kingdom.* I likened the grit to our trials and challenges, our temptations and struggles, our sickness and tribulation, which we all face in this life.

We're all on our journey, and we experience trials that don't feel good but often prove beneficial to us. Sometimes God chastises us because He loves us and sees great value in us that we often don't see in ourselves or others, so He lets us tumble in the drum seemingly forever because the process is meant to clean and shine us up. While tumbling in the grit of trials and circumstances (sometimes of our own making), I see the polish as God's loving grace and mercy. It acts as a buffer between us and those trials so that when we emerge we are often shinier and smoother and more fit for His use—even before we reach heaven. We are more precious in His sight than the jewels that will decorate the gates and streets of heaven. Oh, how precious He must regard us to be!

As we recall the sacrifice Jesus made for us, let's daily recommit and surrender our lives to Him so that one day we will not be mere stones in the rough but living, precious gems for eternity.

Gloria Stella Felder

Little Things

And my God will meet all your needs according
to his glorious riches in Christ Jesus. Phil. 4:19, NIV.

RECENTLY I WENT on a mission trip to the Philippines with some students, our pastor, and one of my colleagues. We flew out of Seoul, Korea, to Manila with no problems whatsoever. We stayed in Manila the first night because of an early flight the next morning to Davao, another island in the Philippines.

As it was the rainy season, it was wise to take an umbrella along. My coworker brought his large university umbrella and had no problems taking it on the plane from Seoul or retrieving it at the airport in Manila. However, when we went through customs the next morning as we were to fly to Davao, Jonathan's umbrella was confiscated. He was told he should have checked it in as baggage to go below with the luggage.

He was understandably a little upset, but I found myself very upset and disappointed that he wasn't told this when checking in earlier. Finally Jonathan told me not to worry; it was OK. But it would have been nice to have a souvenir since he wasn't returning to the university where we both taught. We finally reached the Davao airport, and soon everyone had claimed their luggage except me. Again Jonathan came to the rescue, checking all our bags and baggage claim tickets, but my luggage was nowhere to be found. We located agents who called the Manila airport, who confirmed that my bag was still in Manila. Now Jonathan and I had a laugh because I was so furious about his umbrella, and now here I was in a city with no luggage—and therefore no clothing.

Here I'd been worried about a little thing such as an umbrella when I had no knowledge that I would be without something a lot bigger—my luggage with everything in it that I needed for my stay in the Philippines.

Little things matter to God, but we shouldn't waste time worrying or fretting about things over which we have no control. We're told in Luke 12:6: "Are not five sparrows sold for two pennies? Yet not one of them is forgotten by God" (NIV).

I shouldn't have worried, because the Bible tells us not to worry about big things or little things—our God will supply all our needs.

Bessie Russell Haynes

Learning to Ride a Bike

They that trust in the Lord shall be as mount Zion, which cannot be removed, but abideth for ever. Ps. 125:1.

I GREW UP IN Fremont, California, with my younger sister, Leah. We were each other's best friends. One afternoon I got it in my head that I was going to help her learn to ride her bike. She got on, and I ran behind her, holding the back of the seat for her as our dad had done for me. She knew I had her back secure, and after I gave her some helpful advice, she took off. But after a minute or two I stopped to catch my breath. When I looked up, my little sister was off on her blue bike with no problems.

I'm an adult now with two little girls of my own. When my oldest was around 7 or 8, I decided I was going to teach her to ride her bike. But it wasn't as easy as when I taught my sister. India was not getting it at all. Instead of keeping her head forward and her feet on the pedals, she'd look back at me nervously, checking to see if I was still there, holding the back of the seat. Her feet would hit the ground at any hint of unsteadiness, such as the bike wobbling left or right; all the while giving me instructions what to do and not to do. I became so frustrated and tired of telling her to keep looking forward and to keep her feet on the pedals to keep in motion—and to just *trust* me! As you may have already guessed, we didn't make it too far.

And just like in a flash, as I was questioning and trying to figure out why India wouldn't trust me, the voice in my head asked, *Is this how the Lord feels when He keeps telling you to trust Him, and you keep stopping and looking back, instructing Him what to do and how to do things?* Right then and there I stopped and knew God was telling me to trust Him. I needed to treat my children as God treats me, with love, patience, and understanding.

Oh, how we need to pray that the Lord will continue to hold us, that our trust goes beyond ourselves, and that we rely on Him. I might paraphrase Isaiah 30:21 this way: Whether you turn to the right or to the left, your ears will hear a voice behind you, saying, "This is the way; ride your bike in it this way." God has hold of us; let's keep our eyes looking forward and keep moving!

Erika Loudermill-Webb

Only a Little Finger

Delight yourself in the Lord and he will give you the desires of your heart.
Ps. 37:4, NIV.

IT HAD STARTED OUT a day like any other day. The children had gone outside to play. Patti, my 2-year-old, was happily making mud pies, and the two boys were playing with their little trucks. I had gone into the house to prepare lunch when I heard the scream.

Patti's folding chair had collapsed, pinching her little finger. I removed her from the trap and saw that her finger was severed except for a flap of skin. There seemed to be a lot of blood.

I pushed the two pieces of finger together and wrapped it with a cold cloth, telephoned my mother to take me to the hospital, and prepared to head to the emergency room. Mother dropped me at the emergency door, then took my two little boys home with her.

The doctor on call took a look at the situation and gave me two options. I could have him cut off the skin holding the end of the finger and graft skin from Patti's hip over the stub, or I could have him try to reattach the finger. He warned that there wasn't much hope that the finger would reattach. I asked him to try. Then I headed for the little chapel.

Until that day I had been a nominal Christian. I went to church, read my Bible once in a while, and remembered to pray when time allowed. On this day I sat down to calm myself. The front of my maternity smock was blood-soaked. I suddenly started to shake. I picked up a Bible from the table and opened it to the Psalms. As I read the familiar words I began to calm down.

In that quiet place I pleaded with God to save Patti's finger. Then a peace came over me. For the first time I began to realize the mighty power of God. Yes, He could heal my child if He chose. I took Him at His word. To seal my covenant with God I promised that if He would heal her finger I would become His child in both thought and practice.

The surgery was over, and Patti had been admitted to the children's ward. I telephoned my mother to give her the news and then had my husband paged at work. He arrived, took one look at me, and decided that he had better get me home.

From that day forward God became my closest friend and solace, no matter what happened. I never felt alone again. Truly He is concerned with the tiniest problems. When Patti's bandages came off, the scar was a constant reminder of my pledge.

Patricia Cove

A Place Called Takarakka

The Lord has done many wonderful things! Everyone who is pleased with God's marvelous deeds will keep them in mind. Ps. 111:2, CEV.

AFTER SPENDING A number of months traveling around Queensland, Australia, my husband, Keith, and I met with relatives who joined us for a visit into a very rugged and beautiful place called Carnarvon Gorge. We camped in a park called Takarakka, and set up among the tall gums near the creek. We were fortunate to see the home of platypuses. Kangaroos grazed around our van, and each morning dawned to the laugh of kookaburra and chattering apostle birds. I celebrated my sixtieth birthday there. What a special memory and wonderful gift to have nature surround us at such a time!

We were all keen to explore the walking tracks in this area. Some were short, less than four miles (six kilometers), and easy to negotiate, but the main gorge presented quite a challenge, requiring a full day to walk more than 15 miles (25 kilometers). Fern and moss formed mystical gardens in pools among unique rock formations hidden far into a side gorge. For those who are fit, there is a steep climb up the cliff to the lookout for breathtaking views across the canyon and beyond.

Far below, the walking trail meanders through the bush land with its tall gum trees, palm, cycad, and yellow wattlebirds that delight the eye at every turn. The track crosses the creek 22 times over rock and stepping-stones. On either side of the gorge the majestic sandstone cliffs tower to the blue sky, giving a wonderful reminder of the greatness of our Creator.

While many have the opportunity to visit places of scenic wonder, there are some who never have this experience. However, the greatness and power of our mighty God is not limited to the traveler; there is a blessing for all, every day, wherever you may be.

The same sun that rises over Australia rises over every country in this world, and the moon and stars shine upon us all. Truly we can say "How Great Thou Art."

This mighty Creator of all things is also the loving Savior of us all. He says, "Though the mountains be shaken and the hills be removed, yet my unfailing love for you will not be shaken nor my covenant of peace be removed" (Isa. 54:10, NIV). Each of us can experience God's Takarakka, because the aboriginal meaning of this word is "place of peace and tranquillity."

Lyn Welk-Sandy

I Saw Jesus

And calling to him a child, he put him in the midst of them and said, "Truly, I say to you, unless you turn and become like children, you will never enter the kingdom of heaven. Whoever humbles himself like this child is the greatest in the kingdom of heaven." Matt. 18:2-4, ESV.

HAVE YOU EVER seen Jesus? I have. And I will never forget it.

It was a summer job to earn a little money for college, and I was thrilled to work at a day-care center. Eight hours a day with a dozen 4-year-olds added up to countless crafts, puppet shows, shoe-tying, and outdoor fun. One boy stood out from the rest amid all this activity.

I learned that Alan arrived first at 6:00 a.m. and left last at 6:00 p.m., only to join his single mom's night school's child care until 9:00 p.m. He was the quietest of the bunch, and usually played alone. It seemed he always wore the same clothes and was often the target of unkindness from his peers. But there was something special about Alan. He stole my heart.

With persistence, encouragement, and a little joke here and there, I worked hard at building a friendship with Alan. I believe he fully chose to trust my friendship one morning after I spent a long time combing his hair and complimenting him on his talents. I can't imagine now what we must have talked about day in and day out, but soon Alan smiled more, and he began to walk taller. Alan and I were buds. Most important, he ran and played with his friends more.

One day as I sat at the lunch table with my excited youngsters, I waited for my vegetarian plate to arrive from the cafeteria. The children were busy devouring their franks and beans. Alan sat nearest me. His hand held a forkful of hot food. Just as the fork was inches from his mouth Alan suddenly froze. Putting his fork down, he asked, "Teacher, where's your food?"

I gave a simple answer, "I don't have any lunch now." I should have explained further. Alan just sat there and watched his friends slurp up their favorite meal. He suddenly stood, picked up his little plate, stepped to my side and said, "Here, Teacher, you can have my food." And with that he gently set the plate before me.

Now I was the one who froze, overwhelmed. After catching my breath, I told Alan that my food was coming, but he chose not to eat until it arrived. How can one small boy, who had so little, give so much love—unconditionally, joyfully? And my life has never been the same. I want to allow Jesus' love to fill me so I can share as Alan did. So others can see Jesus too.

Jodie Bell Aakko

A Place

Let not your heart be troubled: ye believe in God, believe also in me. In my Father's house are many mansions: if it were not so, I would have told you. I go to prepare a place for you. And if I go and prepare a place for you, I will come again, and receive you unto myself; that where I am, there ye may be also. And whither I go ye know, and the way ye know. John 14:1-4.

WHEN A 6-YEAR-OLD smiles and you see the missing front tooth, what comes to mind? The tooth fairy or money tucked under the pillow? Maybe you simply see a space that will soon be filled with a larger, stronger tooth.

I see a *place*. A place that is prepared for one specific tooth. Not just any tooth will do—only the one that was designed to fill that one specific place.

Jesus promised that He was going to prepare a place for us. Right now, as we go about our daily activities, Jesus is preparing each one of us a place. A place in heaven that can be filled only by the one for whom it was designed. A place that will remain empty if you choose not to accept the gift of salvation that Jesus offers.

Unlike modern dentistry, which can fill in the empty gaps with false teeth for those who have lost their second set, Jesus doesn't fill in the empty places with false children—for Him nothing but the original will do.

Think for a moment: what do you want your place in heaven to hold? It's your choice. Many of us get busy and either forget to make a choice or forget to follow it through. When Jesus called His disciples He didn't have a long discussion with them about what He expected or what they would do at His side. He said, "Follow me." There was no debate and no discussion; they had to make a choice. And they did. Their choice was to follow. Many came and went from following Him in the three and a half years of His ministry. Each one had a choice to make daily: to continue following Him, or to leave Him; to believe, or not to believe.

We too must make that same choice. It is that choice that determines how we live each day: if we are going to believe, or not believe; if we are going to accept His saving grace, or not. And that will establish our place in heaven when Jesus comes as He promised to do. Make a point of renewing your choice every day, just to keep it fresh.

Juli Blood

More Than a Destination

And thine ears shall hear a word behind thee, saying,
This is the way, walk ye in it. Isa. 30:21.

MY FRIEND AND I had waited several hours at the airport for our plane to take us to Miami. Then we heard an announcement for boarding. We hurried to the plane and took our seats. In a short while another passenger came to my seat and showed me her seat number. It was the same seat as mine. *Two of us have the same seat assignment!* At least that's what I thought.

Then to my utter horror I realized that although both of our boarding passes had "Miami" written on them, there was a difference. My flight number was different! I was on the wrong plane! I was heading for the right destination but on the wrong aircraft, as was my traveling companion.

The flight attendant was willing to let us stay on the plane, but we had checked luggage. Therefore, we needed to transfer to the plane that carried our baggage. We made a speedy and embarrassed exit from the plane in an attempt to escape the stares of the other passengers. I blamed myself mercilessly for not listening carefully to the boarding announcement and for not checking my boarding pass. *How could I have been so stupid?* In less than 10 minutes I was seated comfortably on the right plane, bound for Miami. There was no doubt about it this time. I had checked and double-checked my boarding pass multiple times to reassure myself.

This happens to so many of us Christians. We think we're going to heaven, but we get on the wrong plane. We listen to the wrong announcement, the wrong voices of selfishness, unkindness, prejudice, and conceit. Then we ride on the plane of pride, secret sins, lack of Bible study, careless prayer lives, and unforgiving spirits. Sometimes our friends are also on the wrong route; yet in our complacency we continue. We say we are planning to get to heaven, but our lives say something else.

Then there is the baggage. We hold on to our past sins, our sad memories, our hurts, pain, and regrets. It's time to get on the right plane. We're bound for heaven, aren't we? Today we have another chance! We're preparing for more than a simple destination—we are going to heaven! The journey is important, too. Let's listen to the right Voice: "And thine ears shall hear a word behind thee, saying, This is the way, walk ye in it."

Gloria Lindsey Trotman

Though I Pass Through the Valley

Fear not, for I am with you. Isa. 41:10, NKJV.

I WAS TRAVELING from Atlanta to Johannesburg via Amsterdam when the captain of the plane announced that there was a patient on the plane who needed to be taken to the hospital as soon as possible. The nearest hospital was Rome. So we watched the tiny plane on the little TV map making a U-turn to Rome.

I wasn't sure whether this was real or just a hoax. When we landed in Rome, we were told to stay seated for security reasons. Then two men disembarked from the plane because they also weren't feeling well, they said. This made me even more doubtful. The question that was ringing in my mind was *Why did the two men leave the plane also?*

After refueling, the plane took off for Johannesburg once more. As we were approaching North Africa, I could see from the map that the plane was diverting to West Africa. To make matters worse, there was no word from the captain. It was all quiet. I became very worried, thinking that we'd been hijacked, and began jumping to conclusions. First, the plane went back to Rome, then the two other passengers got off the plane, and now the plane was heading for West Africa without any explanation. Every passenger was worried, and many, including me, began to pray. I was anxious and didn't know what would happen next.

After traveling for about an hour, the captain made an announcement that there had been a diversion because of turbulence, and now that we were out of danger we could proceed on our journey using the normal route. The journey from West Africa to Johannesburg was still turbulent, but we arrived at our destination, although five hours late.

This reminds me of my faith journey. There are times when I am faced with uncertainties that make me question God's wisdom and His plans and decisions in my life. Turbulences in my days have made me panic, and His dealings in solving my problems have not seemed to be logical, and yet He says, "Trust in the Lord with all your heart, and lean not on your own understanding" (Prov. 3:5, NKJV). That prevents our jumping to wrong conclusions.

I ask the Lord to help me know and believe that He will always be with me, even though I may pass through the valley of the shadow of death. I want Him in control of my life.

Caroline Chola

I Am

So do not fear, for I am with you; do not be dismayed,
for I am your God. I will strengthen you and help you;
I will uphold you with my righteous right hand. Isa. 41:10, NIV.

WHEN I FINISHED high school, my parents told me that I wouldn't be able to study at the Peruvian Union University, and they registered me in a preuniversity academy. During this time I prayed ardently to the Lord so that His will would prevail. He knew that I didn't want to study in a state university. Our Father in heaven didn't delay in His answer, and acted through my sibling's father-in-law. They told me that I could study in my desired Peruvian Union University, a Christian institution.

After my sixth semester in that university, however, a series of economic difficulties began to appear. My benefactor had to make payments to a rehabilitation center for drug addicts, where my brother was receiving treatment. During the time he spent in the clinic I saw people gossiping to our relatives, and I prayed to the Lord for my brother's recovery. Then my mother found out that she had cancer, and this aggravated the financial and emotional situation even more. However, the Lord who enabled me to study in a Christian school worked powerfully in my life through various ones of His children, and He supplied my needs.

During all these years God has showed me His love and mercy. He has been by my side in the most difficult moments and has supported me with His right hand. Each experience, including the negative ones, has been an opportunity to demonstrate our God's greatness, for the Lord blesses His children who fully trust in Him and enjoy serving Him. He renews our strength and prepares us to fulfill the purpose for which we were created.

We serve a great God, the God who is always present, always able, the I Am. He told Moses, "I am who I am. . . . I AM has sent me to you" (Ex. 3:14, NIV). He will always be there to help us, no matter what the circumstances may look like.

Dear sister, remember that "the Sovereign Lord comes with power, and his arm rules for him. See, his reward is with him, and his recompense accompanies him" (Isa. 40:10, NIV). So we can live each day fully, not allowing negative situations to oppress us because we can count on I Am, and He will never abandon us.

Melissa Harumi Acosta Mau

August 11

The Love of God

Behold, what manner of love the Father hath bestowed upon us, that we should be called the sons of God. 1 John 3:1.

GOD HAS CREATED in His human children a deep need to love and be loved, and those who have such relationships experience a joy that is hard to adequately express.

But even for those who have no living loved ones to meet this love need, every day can be just as replete with joy as we experience God's parental affection to us, His human children. We can feel the heartbeat of His love in His Word, the story of all He has done and continues to do for us, and the magnitude of His sacrifice, that we might have eternal happiness. However, even outside His Word, His love is so evident.

Take color, for instance. How easily our Creator could have made our world in tones of black, but He didn't. Why? Because He wanted us to have a deeper, richer experience of the beauty of His love as it is expressed in radiant color. Then there are shapes, more numerous even than the many hues of color. The variety is endless. Not even two leaves are exactly the same or two sparkling snowflakes alike in every detail.

Consider sound. It ranges from the softest whisper of a summer breeze to the reverberating thunder of the mighty Niagara Falls; from the blood-chilling howl of a wolf to the sleepy twittering of small birds at dusk. And let's not forget the variety of sounds we humans can't hear but others in God's creation can.

Variety is the key to the ways God shows His love—variety of form, sound, texture, taste, and so much more. Only thus can He adequately express the richness of His creative love as He seeks to satisfy the needs of His children to the fullest. Then, as we grow to know Him better, we have a greater appreciation for all His creation, including His earthly children of every shape and color. Even with different races and belief systems, they are all His children.

May we never make the mistake of criticizing someone because he or she is different from us in some way, and may the celebration of the infinite variety in our fellow human beings be a living expression of the outworking of divine love as it flows from the heart of our Creator, who is love.

Revel Papaioannou

232

Angelical Touch and Care

For he will command his angels concerning you to
guard you in all your ways. Ps. 91:11, NIV.

ALL MY LIFE I have appreciated the care that the angels have for us. Not only have I appreciated it—I have received their care as well. Now I want to tell you three stories that bring me goose bumps.

When I was little, I liked to ride a trolley. One day I noticed that in my father's woodworking area there was a machine that worked with a rail and moved when someone pushed it. I didn't think twice and invited my sister, Ellen, to play with me. I set up the trolley, and Ellen began to push it with all her strength. However, she didn't know that there was no barrier to keep the trolley, weighing more than 60 pounds (about 28 kilograms), from running off the end. The worst happened: the cart ran off the rail and fell over on top of me. Even though Ellen was only 4 years old, she lifted that cart off me. I believe that Ellen's guardian angel lifted the cart with her, and my guardian angel served as a shield. Otherwise, I could have become quadriplegic. When Ellen was asked about how she had done it, she said, "Actually the cart felt very light when I lifted it."

The second story is about my older brother, Andrew. He was working on a full-moon evening, building a lumber mill for my father. At one point he was under a board that weighed more than a half ton. Disaster was about to happen, because the board had come unfastened. My brother suddenly noticed that a figure crossed over the moon. Then, quick as a wink, with an incredible burst of speed, he jumped to the other side, barely knowing what he had done. He's sure that his angel pulled him to another place, far from the spot where the board fell.

It was the evening of my first day of school in my eighth-grade year when the third story happened. Before going to bed, I asked God to wake me up at 5:00 in the morning to study His Word. I was afraid I wouldn't wake up because during vacation I had gotten up later. Exactly at 5:00 a.m. I felt two light touches on my right arm. All day long I remembered those touches, and I'm sure it was my angel who touched me.

I'm so thankful to God because He sends His angels to protect us.

Mayla Magaieski Graeps

Darkness to Light

You are my lamp, O Lord; the Lord turns my darkness into light.
2 Sam. 22:29, NIV.

WHEN I VISITED my cousin in Boston for two weeks in August 2008, the Olympic Games were going on in Beijing. As I was watching the events on TV, the power went off in the middle of a race. Luckily, it was noon, so the house wasn't in total darkness. My cousin's wife, Maureen, seemed confident that the blackout was the result of construction work nearby and thought that the lights would be on soon. We waited for hours and nothing happened, so when my cousin came home we went out for the evening. When we returned, the house was still in darkness. William retrieved a couple of flashlights, and we all retired for the night.

Morning came, and the power was still off. I'd forget that there was no power and try to turn on the light or try to heat up food in the microwave. Thankfully, we had a gas stove, matches, and good old pots. At least we were able to eat.

Maureen called the city, who suggested some troubleshooting tips. They confirmed that the power was not turned off at their end, so the problem had to be at the house. It was very frustrating not having power for several days and not knowing the source of the problem. William had checked the power box on our floor the day before, and everything was fine.

After talking with the city, William ventured into the basement to check the circuit down there. A few minutes later we had power. In fact, we had had power all along and didn't know it, as we hadn't done what was needed to access it.

That situation made me think of life without Jesus—darkness! Some people are walking around in darkness, going about their daily business without tapping into the source of light. They wake up without acknowledging the One who breathed the breath of life into them. Some hurry off to work without so much as a "Good morning, heavenly Father." Some lead empty lives, seeking but never finding as they are in spiritual darkness. The adversary, the devil, is doing all that is in his power to keep them disconnected from God, the Light of the world and true source of life. Satan is like a roaring lion, seeking whom he can devour.

Are you groping in spiritual darkness? Let Jesus light your path today!

Sharon (Brown) Long

The Fearful *Vestibular*

Look on me and answer, O Lord my God. Ps. 13:3, NIV.

I'VE BEEN MARRIED for 24 years to my doctor husband. Sometime before our marriage my future mother-in-law had a conversation with me and asked, "Is this what you want? You know that my son is a doctor, and his patients will always be in first place." My blood ran cold; I had goose bumps, but I had prayed, asking God to show me the right person, so soon after that we got married. My mother-in-law has now passed away, but things happened exactly as she said. I've learned to accept this fact, although sometimes, especially after the children grew up, I felt a little lonely.

We had two children who also decided to study medicine. Everybody knows that this career is very fulfilling and offers good salaries. However, in order to enroll in a college, especially public ones, the candidate needs years of preparation. Private colleges are very expensive. My children began to prepare and took years studying. When the result of the vestibular* was divulged, we didn't find their names on the list. Some relatives and friends comforted us, but others mocked them and us as well. As I am a worried mother, I always comforted them and said, "Victory is right. Let's trust."

This torment made me meditate on our heavenly Father. How many times we are desperate and forget that we have a very kind Father, ready to help and comfort us. I am only a simple mother, sinful and lacking of God's mercies. However, I knew how to comfort my children in the vestibular battle. I have learned a truth that applies to all of us. Thus, if today you woke up sad and low-spirited, know that we have a powerful God who loves and comforts us. He is always concerned about us and our needs and dreams. Today my older son is in his first year of medicine, and my younger son is expecting the next tests to be his victory.

Be strong and trust. The same way He comforted me in moments of loneliness and heard our prayer regarding our sons' studies, He also will completely take care of you today. You only need to allow it.

Elizabeth Grécia Coutimho

---

*The vestibular is a competitive examination system used by Brazilian universities to select their students. The term derives from the word *vestíbulo*, which means "entrance hall" in Portuguese.

Heat, Mosquitoes, and Weeds

But blessed is the man who trusts in the Lord, whose confidence is in him. He will be like a tree planted by the water that sends out its roots by the stream. Jer. 17:7, 8, NIV.

HEAT, MOSQUITOES, and weeds are closely associated for me, because it's when the weather is hot that mosquitoes are at their liveliest and weeds are most prolific in their growth. I don't particularly enjoy being out in the heat and certainly don't like the mosquitoes. As a result there are weeds growing where there shouldn't be any, and the thought of going out to eradicate them isn't pleasant. Add to this the fact that gardening isn't high on my list of things to do. It makes me embarrassed to look at my flower garden and see weeds amid the blooms.

Given all these thoughts, I also have to admire the fact that flowers are not particularly put off by the weeds. They burst forth in bloom at their assigned times. The colors are vibrant and alive, and I find joy in seeing the beauty of the flowers.

Heat, mosquitoes, and weeds are similar to the little things that hinder our vision when we look for the beauty in people. The small irritants are allowed to bite through our thin skins and make us uncomfortable. Habits we don't appreciate become like weeds in our minds. When we see undesirable character traits in people we are often tempted to think that their beauty is diminished. Instead of appreciating each person for their worth, we negate who they are.

As I view my flower garden I choose not to dwell upon the ugliness of the weeds and uncultivated areas. Instead I can find much to enjoy between the weeds. That's the way it is with our friends, family, and neighbors, too. There's so much to like about each person. Building walls to close off the weeds is easy to do. Keeping our thoughts focused on the good and beautiful allows us to enjoy being with those we care about. This same thought pattern helps us find the good in people about whom we haven't been concerned or we haven't held in high esteem.

When we're tempted to complain and be discontented, it is well for all of us to look for something good to think about. Just a change of attitude does much to make our days brighter. In spite of the heat, mosquitoes, and weeds in our life, we can find unspeakable joy.

I will choose to cultivate positive attitudes and look beyond the weeds, heat, and mosquitoes. I will ask the Lord to guide my thoughts and direct them in a positive channel.

Evelyn Glass

A Look of Love

The eyes of the Lord are upon the righteous,
and his ears are open unto their cry. Ps. 34:15.

KLAVIERSTUCKE, OPUS 118, Intermezzo A Major, by Johannes Brahms, was the title of the piece I was required to play for a college recital. If I sat at a piano today, even with the score in front of me, I'm sure I couldn't make my fingers recall the piece. I tried to hum a little of it the other day, but most of it is gone from memory. Back then, in the early 1980s, I had practiced it for hours, day in and day out, until the notes were floating out of my ears. Mr. Brahms' music had become my friend. I was sure every note was perfect, every dynamic and tempo was in order. My interpretation of the piece was great. This would be my star performance.

But as I sat that day at the keyboard, I suddenly realized that all that relentless rehearsing had left me terribly fatigued. I couldn't concentrate. A few folks in the audience were whispering; I was distracted. I was only moments into the piece when I had to stop. *What is supposed to come next?* I couldn't recall another note. I anxiously glanced at my instructor. With raised eyebrows, her expression was quizzical. Her look said it all. She was expecting me to proceed, but I could not.

If I just had the score! I thought frantically, my heart pounding. But it wasn't there; recital pieces had to be performed from memory. Fear had taken control, and the beautiful Brahms piece had abruptly vanished from my mind, a dangled fragment of what should have been a beautiful performance hung in the air. Had there been a hole in the floor I would have gratefully dissolved into it. I glanced at my instructor as I left the room. I remember the look of disappointment in her eyes.

I left school that day in tears. I felt like such a failure, so disappointed in myself. At home in my solitude I picked up my Bible, not knowing what to read but hoping to find some comfort somewhere in its pages. Was Jesus disappointed with me too?

We've all had moments of failure in life. But it's during those times that God is very near to us, when His promises are most precious and meaningful to us. Those times of apparent failure can help us grow spiritually if we let them. Even when we feel we've done our worst, there will never be a look of disappointment in His face—just a look of love.

Marcia R. Pope

God's Plans for Us

For I know the thoughts that I think toward you, saith the Lord, thoughts of peace, and not of evil, to give you an expected end. Jer. 29:11.

I'M FAMILIAR WITH many of the promises that are in the Bible for me; however, being familiar with the promises and actually experiencing them are different things. After a larger hospital bought out our hospital, planning to close it forever, God gave me the opportunity to see the fulfillment of the text that says that "before they call, I will answer" (see Isa. 65:24).

I was one of the few workers they retained to work at the new facility. My anxiety level was high the weekend before starting my new job. I wondered how I would be accepted by my coworkers. As a registered nurse working in the operating room, I'd be part of a team consisting of a surgeon, surgical assistant, nurse, and technician. All must work closely together. My prayer that weekend, even on my way to work, was for God to help me find a Christian coworker.

On Monday, my first day, I arrived much earlier than most of my coworkers. Someone showed me the schedule with my room assignment for the day. I continued to pray silently as I familiarized myself with the new surroundings—my new locker, the nurses' lounge, the flow of patients into and out of surgery, and much more. Then I changed into my scrubs and entered my assigned surgery suite. I took the opportunity to discover the layout of the room and know where things were stored.

Minutes seemed like hours as I waited for the rest of my team to arrive. I was still praying. Then 20 minutes before the first procedure start time, a cheerful nurse with a kind smile walked in and introduced herself as my preceptor for the day. What she said next amazed me: "I have been looking forward to working with you! I am a Christian, and I heard from others, including my favorite surgeon, that you're a Christian too." When she told me that the schedule had been made one week in advance, the Holy Spirit reminded me that before we ask, God will answer, and that I should be anxious for nothing. "It was obviously God who arranged for us to be scheduled together!" I smiled, and felt like a weight was lifted from my shoulders.

Priscilla Charles

Help in Tough Times

I lift up my eyes to the hills—where does my help come from? My help comes from the Lord, the Maker of heaven and earth. Ps. 121:1, 2, NIV.

IT WAS A glorious day in the beautiful Rocky Mountains. The sun was shining through the pine trees, and the miniature waterfalls in the crystal-clear stream gave soothing sounds, complementing the bird songs and chattering squirrels.

Our family had enjoyed a picnic and then a hike to Ouzel Falls, one of my favorite places. As we packed up to go home and I got into the car, I noticed I had carried many small black ants in on my shoes. They were scurrying about, crawling up my legs and on the car floorboard. I tried to brush them off me and out of the car, but as we traveled home there were more crawling around. Then I noticed one ant carrying a small particle of sand as if it were beginning to build a house for all the ants in the car.

This may sound silly, but watching that ant doing something about its difficult situation and making the best of it by giving hope, help, and encouragement to the other displaced ants was a sight to behold. Although I was at peace that day being with those I loved so much and in God's beautiful nature, there have been many other times that life wasn't as peaceful, and I thought of that ant. I believe God allowed that nature object lesson that day to give me encouragement and lead me to Him, seeking His help with trials.

This object lesson may seem small and insignificant, but we have so much more than that tiny ant—we have our Lord to give us help from on high. He is always there if only we turn to Him. He gives us encouragement, discernment, and wisdom to persevere through any trial.

I think of Esther in the Bible who was displaced from her childhood home. How frightened she must have been to be snatched away from her loved ones, taken to an unfamiliar place, and forced into a role she hadn't asked for or desired. She didn't know what plan God had for her, yet she relied on Him. God put her there for "such a time as this."

"For I know the plans I have for you," declares the Lord, "plans to prosper you and not to harm you, plans to give you hope and a future" (Jer. 29:11, NIV). This promise has meant so much to me during times of trials and hardships in my life.

Ginger Bell

I Not Sick!

If we claim to be without sin, we deceive ourselves and the truth is not in us.
1 John 1:8, NIV.

IT'S 5:00 P.M. when I receive the call from the nursery to pick up my 3-year-old son right away because he is throwing up.

Sick? My son can't be sick. He made it through the whole day, and now he's sick?

It's 5:50. I get home and take my son from my husband, who has picked him up and brought him home. *Wow, he really is sick. He threw up again,* I think in amazement.

It's 6:15, and our son finally goes to sleep.

Then at 10:30 my husband and I go to sleep. But not for long. At 10:45 my son wakes up from sleep. When I go to tend to him, I ask, "How are you feeling?"

"Fine."

"Are you sick?"

"No." By now he's awake. He asks for juice. When I tell him that he can't drink juice because he's sick, he replies, "I not sick!" Then he throws up again. Of course this pattern repeats itself. He's unable to keep anything down.

How many of you can relate to this experience? Yes, all of us. At one time or another we've all been sick. Sometimes we're so sick that we don't even realize how sick we are. Isn't that just like us sinners? We know that we're sinners but don't realize that we're sick with sin. We know that we're sinners but don't realize just how sick we are! Some people convince themselves that they're fine. They don't need a doctor. They think that they can handle it themselves. Maybe we try to do that, too. We take natural remedies. We don't take anything at all. We have only liquids. We take this pill and that pill. We will eat this; we won't eat that. In the end we find out that none of these remedies work. We wait for days instead of going to the doctor right away. Why? Because we are trying to heal ourselves on our own. Wouldn't it better to get a real diagnosis? Wouldn't it be better to be reassured by the doctor who knows you?

Friends, Jesus is our doctor. He knows our family history. He is the only one who can heal us. He is the only one with the cure. Don't wait until it's too late. He has the right remedy.

Dana M. Bean

Such Little Faith

She said within herself, If I may but touch his garment, I shall be whole.
Matt. 9:21.

JESUS SAID THAT if we have faith as small as the mustard seed we can command the mountains to shift positions, and nothing would be impossible for us. (See Matt. 17:20.)

Such was the faith of the woman who suffered with the issue of blood for 12 years. She had been spreading offensive odors into the air for years. She was frail, anemic, tired and weak to the bone; in rags and in penury because nobody dared employ her; and she had spent all her money on doctors. Husband, friends, and neighbors must have deserted her. Her children may have even felt embarrassed to introduce her as their mother.

One day her little mustard seed of faith got to work. A small voice in her heart propelled her from her hiding place to where she used to peep at Jesus. *Today,* she decided, *this odor will be gone! After today, no more rags, no more flies swarming after me. No; no more!* I imagine she managed to put on a fairly clean dress so that she would be presentable, and then she did what looked so foolish to so many.

Prior to this Jesus had seen whom He would heal. He touched, spoke to, or mixed clay to heal the blind, the dead, the lame, the paralytic. In fact, He was on His way to wake the ruler's daughter, so the bleeding woman was not part of His agenda that day. Therefore this woman couldn't have come face-to-face with Jesus. She moved from behind quietly because she knew people would not see her that way; she sneaked into the crowd, determined. *I must touch the hem only. I dare not touch His body. I must do it before the crowd starts to shout "Unclean! Unclean!" I don't want to put the miraculous healer to the trouble of seven days of cleansing. Just let me touch the seam of the garment!*

And it worked instantly; the little mustard faith healed her. The same can be yours. Don't be overwhelmed with your troubles. Tell Jesus; He listens with total attention every time, everywhere, and in the most inconvenient circumstances you may think of. Press on. Touch His hem in faith, and you shall be delivered.

Oh, that God would plant in me this little—but great—mustard seed of faith. I want to use it to touch some burdened heart today!

Dorcas Modupe Falade

Peace:
The True Prosperity of God

Peace I leave with you, my peace I give unto you: not as the world giveth, give I unto you. Let not your heart be troubled, neither let it be afraid. John 14:27.

These things I have spoken unto you, that in me ye might have peace. In the world ye shall have tribulation: but be of good cheer; I have overcome the world. John 16:33.

IN JULY I began to feel cramps in my stomach, and by December I faced two major surgeries. In August I went to the doctor, but it seemed that it was only the changing body of a 46-year-old. Within two weeks, however, I was confined to my home with sickness for three days.

In September I began to feel an urging in my spirit to seek God with fervency. As I began my study I opened my Bible to John 14:27. From there I went to John 16:33. I spent the next two weeks doing practically nothing but studying the peace of God. How I desired to have it! During the next three months I was admitted to the hospital five times. Each time I faced the possibility of surgery. In November, on my third trip to the hospital, a CT scan of my abdomen showed there was a blockage in my system. Then an unrelated problem was found—a 5.5-centimeter tumor on my left kidney. My response to this news was a paraphrase of Hebrews 12:12, 13: Let us lift up our hands and strengthen our feeble knees, and let's go.

My health was going downhill fast, and my food was no longer digesting properly. I lost 12 pounds in two weeks, and it was determined that surgery should happen on both my kidney and my gastrointestinal system. On the scheduled day of the gastrointestinal surgery the surgeon saw something new and determined that my stomach muscle was the problem and could be treated with medication. After five months of escalating sickness, my healing began. Then two days before the scheduled kidney surgery the surgeon determined that there was a complication, and he needed to send me to the University of Michigan Hospital for further analysis.

When I saw the doctor there, the first thing he told me was that he deals with kidney tumors every day and there was a 90 percent chance that it was cancerous. However, a biopsy determined it to be benign with no surgery necessary.

Throughout all this my peace was intact, and my faith and trust in God elevated greatly.

Chrisele Green

The Short Plane Ride

"Because he loves me," says the Lord, "I will rescue him; I will protect him, for he acknowledges my name. He will call upon me, and I will answer him; I will be with him in trouble, and I will deliver him and honor him." Ps. 91:14, 15, NIV.

WHEN I ARRIVED at the Baltimore-Washington International Airport in Maryland for my flight back to Greenville, South Carolina, it was a hot summer day. I'd had an enjoyable weekend visiting my daughter, who was getting ready for her sophomore year at college, and attending an alumni convention in New Jersey. It was fun seeing old friends and classmates from the Philippines. We were inspired by a message encouraging us to serve Christ for eternity.

Now I was ready and eager to go home. Delta Flight 684 to Atlanta, scheduled to leave at 1:30 p.m., was delayed because of mechanical problems. We finally boarded the plane about 2:15 and settled into our seats. I must have been really tired, because I don't remember the plane taking off.

The next thing I knew, people were screaming in the rear of the plane. I smelled smoke and heard people demanding that the plane turn around and go back to the airport. The gentleman seated next to me tightened his seat belt, so I did the same. I closed my eyes and prayed that God would put His loving arms around this plane and help it land safely. I couldn't see what was going on outside, but I could definitely smell the odor of burning rubber. I could also sense the wheels of the plane shaking and making strange noises as the plane turned back toward the airport. I turned to my heavenly Father to calm the passengers who were panicky, and to help the pilot bring the plane down safely and avoid a crash landing.

Emergency personnel met the plane as we stopped on the tarmac and checked the problem out before we were allowed to taxi back to the terminal. The flight was ultimately canceled, and we were asked to deplane and rebook our flights. I'm grateful to the pilots who landed the plane safely that day. But as much as I enjoy flying, I went home by Amtrak the next day.

I thank and praise the Lord for preserving my life. I have renewed my commitment to Him and have a new respect for life. Really, shouldn't we do that every day anyway?

Rhona Grace Magpayo

More Than Outward Beauty

For the Lord does not see as man sees; for man looks at the outward appearance, but the Lord looks at the heart. 1 Sam. 16:7, NKJV.

SHE WAS OBVIOUSLY poor, this short, plump, elderly woman stuffed into clothes that would have been rejected by any self-respecting thrift store. The large oval cameo she wore at her throat completed her outfit. On her feet were tan, scuffed slippers topped by white anklets. Yet here she was in a beauty salon, ready to pay for a permanent that she likely could ill afford. I appreciated the fact that she was willing to do this for herself, for her self-respect if nothing else. When the beautician had completed her work and the woman stood at the door waiting for her ride, her white hair did indeed look beautiful.

As I thought about her it occurred to me that our heavenly Father has given each of us a desire for beauty, for acceptance, a yearning to belong, an eagerness to please. He loves beauty, and we admire the beautiful, whether in people, nature, art, music, or architecture—wherever it is found. Many of us have never attained true physical beauty, but we like to feel that we are doing our best with what we've been given.

How reassuring and comforting to know that even though outward beauty is so much admired and sought after, inner beauty is to be valued above rubies (see Prov. 31:10). Attaining beauty of character is something that cannot be bought at any price. It is found only as we spend time in Bible reading, in meditation and prayer, and in contemplating God's marvelous handiwork in nature. From the tiniest budding leaf to the magnificent display of swirling galaxies in the heavens, we see His creative power and are led to bow before Him in awe and wonder.

I hope that the little woman I saw in the beauty salon is seeking that beauty of character that is of infinite value, the character that can be comfortable in Christ's robe of righteousness that is so freely given to those who seek it with all their hearts. I also hope that each of us, day by day, will be pressing forward "toward the mark for the prize of the high calling of God in Christ Jesus" (Phil. 3:14). Nothing could be more important than being able to look up with rejoicing when the sky is ablaze with the splendor of Christ and innumerable shining angels, and know that our place is secure in Him.

Lila Morgan

A Beloved Songster

Oh that men would praise the Lord for his goodness, and for his wonderful works to the children of men! Ps. 107:8.

WE WERE DELIGHTED to find many varieties of birds among the trees on the campus of the boarding school where we worked in India. One of these birds was the magpie-robin that delighted us with its songs. It became our beloved bird, singing along with our tape recorder whenever my husband had it on. It also sang along with my melodica whenever I played. Salim Ali, the author of the *Book of Indian Birds,* reports that this bird is a very good mimic of other birds' calls. This bird just loves to sing—not just its own song, but likes to learn new songs, too.

On a visit to Thailand we were delighted to hear the magpie-robin there, also. I went to the terrace of our son's place to look for this bird and spotted it on top of a tall antenna, where it was singing lustily. It's during breeding season when its sweet song is most conspicuous. While mama bird is faithfully sitting on the eggs, father bird is there to cheer her. And when the babies are hatched he shares the domestic chores.

As I looked over that Thai town from the terrace, it looked like a concrete jungle. Yet this bird sings even when there is nothing green to be seen. While there we visited many tourist spots and beautiful resorts with beautiful landscaping. We saw lovely forests and waterfalls. I wondered why this bird didn't move to these beautiful areas. I concluded that the magpie-robin has learned to be content wherever it is.

If the magpie-robin brings so much joy to others by its songs, then why couldn't I, who was created as a crowning act by my Creator? Perhaps this world would be a better place if God's children sang more than they complain. My favorite author has written: "If the saints wept through discouragement, or were in danger, the angels that ever attended them would fly quickly upward to carry the tidings, and the angels in the city would cease to sing. . . . But if the saints fixed their eyes upon the prize before them and glorified God by praising Him, then the angels would bear the glad tidings to the city, and the angels in the city would touch their golden harps and sing with a loud voice, 'Alleluia!' and the heavenly arches would ring with their lovely songs" (*Early Writings,* p. 39).

Isn't this the best reason we should sing praises to the Lord?

Birdie Poddar

Blessings Like Rain!

But seek first his kingdom and his righteousness, and all these things will be given to you as well. Matt. 6:33, NIV.

IT WAS THE most difficult decision for me to make at age 17! Just out of high school and newly baptized, I had to decide to be loyal to God's command or forfeit my chance to be admitted into the government teacher's training college. The letter that I opened up distinctly marked the date of the interview as a Sabbath. "Oh, no, Lord!" I cried.

I'm sure God will understand if I go this once, I rationalized to myself. *I can't afford to lose this once-in-a-lifetime opportunity. Only those with good results will get an interview. Surely God knows that! It's about my life career!*

I wrestled with this issue for days, and I prayed and prayed. Finally I decided to talk with my pastor about this. He comforted me and assured me with Jeremiah 29:11—God had plans for me. Before I left, he looked me in the eye and said, "Linda, seek first God's kingdom, and all these things of life will be given to you. Just remain faithful and let God work in your life."

It was difficult for a teenager, who was only a spiritual baby. I prayed and prayed for God to strengthen my faith in Him and to give me the courage to be loyal in keeping His Sabbath.

Finally, on the fifth day, I felt a peace come over me once I had decided to follow God's command. *So if I can't make it to the teacher's college, so what? God will give me bigger things.*

Of course, I didn't go for the interview. I never got admitted into the prestigious government college, though two of my friends did. So what was God going to give me then? You may not believe it, but when God's blessings come, they come pouring down hard!

One month later my pastor informed me of a scholarship to study at our local Christian college. I enrolled, completed my associate degree in two years, and met a wonderful Christian young man who became my life partner for 42 years. Together we went for studies overseas in the United States, where the training prepared us for leadership in the church. Yes, never could I imagine that God's blessings and leading would give me the opportunity to serve the world church at our headquarters someday.

So seek God first!

Linda Mei Lin Koh

God's Loving Care and Healings

Dear friend, I pray that you may enjoy good health and that all may go well with you, even as your soul is getting along well. 3 John 2, NIV.

IN THE EARLY SPRING, when the chilly winds still blew and the daffodils had come and gone, I caught a nasty cold with a sore throat and headache—this in addition to my battle with lymphoma cancer and painful arthritis. So I was miserable, to say the least. The next day my oncologist put me on antibiotics for a week and delayed my cancer treatments for a week. Wanting to get well from cancer quickly, I obeyed, but was disappointed by the delay. Day after day I prayed for God's healing.

As I faced this debilitating illness I had more time to study my Bible and pray. I found promises of His faithfulness to me in God's Word that I remembered as I waited for treatment. Some were in the Psalms, and some in Lamentations 3:22, 23. And I sang the hymns of comfort—"Under His Wings" and "I Need Thee Every Hour."

When my cold was gone and my cancer treatments resumed, I kept faith in the promises of healing. Three months later my treatments were completed, and I was sent for a set of scans to prove the results. There was good news—the cancer was almost gone! My doctor gave me two months off and ordered another set of scans. All these months I had been on a vegan diet, taking all sorts of advised supplements, and praying a lot for healing. I even asked my church media programs for prayer on my behalf.

When the next set of scans was taken on August 24 and I saw my oncologist on August 27, the doctor told me the reports showed that I was clear of the cancer! I rejoiced in God's healing power. Of course the doctor believes it was the chemotherapy treatments that healed me, and I'm sure it was an important part, but I believe that God's healing power took place in answer to my prayers and the prayers of others. I believe that God works with our human efforts when we cooperate with His health laws as written in His Word and as has been revealed to His saints on earth. I'm sure you do too. I praise God for His healing power every day as I continue to follow these rules.

How do we thank God for His tender loving care and healing? Let us praise His name!

Bessie Siemens

A Mother's Heart

For I am persuaded, that neither death, nor life, nor angels, nor principalities, nor powers, nor things present, nor things to come, nor height, nor depth, nor any other creature, shall be able to separate us from the love of God, which is in Christ Jesus our Lord. Rom. 8:38, 39.

I'VE KNOWN AND admired my friend, often identified as the notetaker, for many years. Recently she shared more of her challenge with me. She said I could share with you.

She says, "There was a sad look in my friend Carol's face as she took me aside, explaining that the friendly letters I'd been receiving and answering were not from a man but a woman, actually one of my college classmates. I was bewildered and confused till it dawned on me that this was no ordinary prank. I felt ashamed that I hadn't realized what was going on; and I felt an irritating anger begin to grow deep inside.

"The years passed; I graduated from college and married, and one day God laid a baby girl in our arms. I dressed my little girl in bonnets and frilly dresses and dreamed of the day she would float down the aisle with her prince charming. But as the years passed my husband and I both sensed that our sweet tomboy was unique.

"Then one day after work my teenage daughter asked to join me as I walked the dogs. As our conversation unfolded she told me she had a girlfriend she loved very much. I tried to put up a brave front and be the good mother, but inside a dream was crumbling. Back home in the living room, through tears and hugs, we continued talking into the night. It was a sweet time of communion with my girl.

"My beloved husband and I struggled with our emotions and our faith, but we knew God had placed our girl in our arms years before, and He loved her. We vowed that we would embrace her no matter what. But when she announced she and her longtime friend were planning a wedding, I became very anxious to know how to cope publicly as the mother of the bride who would be the groom. Then our friend, Chaplain Tom, said simply, 'Just be her mom!' What a novel idea! But he was right, and that's just what I did. I realized that I wasn't the only mother struggling with a gay child, and that instead of feeling robbed of a dream I was actually blessed to know and love her as Jesus would, the one who also carries a mother's heart."

Ardis Dick Stenbakken

Sometimes You Just Gotta Laugh

A merry heart does good, like medicine. Prov. 17:22, NKJV.

IT HAD BEEN a dismal week—no, a dismal month, and more. Not that anything really awful was going on. No illness. No money problems, other than never having a cent left over for extras. Simply the usual bits of life—working, cooking, cleaning, washing . . . and there was never, ever enough time.

So when Noelle had a fever that morning and didn't feel like going to church, I was glad to stay home and let the others go without us. I was too tired to go anyway. Or maybe I was more weary than tired. At any rate, I was happy to forgo pantyhose for my comfortable old robe. For a few hours it would be just me and our 10-year-old daughter. We'd have a quiet, relaxing morning.

First there was orange juice and cereal; then we decided to play Bible charades. I sat comfortably on the floor, resting against the wall, and let Noelle go first.

She stood before me in jeans and T-shirt, her pale-gold hair in thick braids. Hands at her sides, she jumped straight up, then came down. Up. Down. Up. Down. *What is she doing?* A smile lit her eyes. "Mommy, guess!" she commanded, but my mind was blank. She did it again. A smile filling her face, she raised herself on her tiptoes, then went down. Up. Down. Up. Down. For variation, a little jump up, then back down.

"Old or New Testament?" I asked.

Up . . . down . . . up . . . down. "Old."

This went on for a few minutes, with brief stops for Noelle to giggle and for me to laugh. I had no idea what she was doing, what Bible scene she was reenacting. "Give me a hint," I begged.

"It has to do with Daniel," she said. Up. Down. Up. Down.

"I give up!" I said at last.

"Are you sure?"

"Yes, I'm sure."

"I'm one of the teeth in the lion's mouth that couldn't eat Daniel!"

I started giggling, then laughing. Soon I was doubled over with laughter as I pulled my little girl down on my lap. We sat there together, laughing until our sides hurt. Laughing until I felt neither tired nor weary nor depressed. Laughing until my heart sang!

Sometimes, what you need most of all—is to laugh.

Penny Estes Wheeler

Live Long for My Sake!

Therefore he is able to save completely those who come to God through him, because he always lives to intercede for them. Heb. 7:25, NIV.

WHEN I FIRST met my mother-in-law she was still a very strong, determined woman. As I look back, it seemed as though she was living in the wrong generation. Instead of the generation in which women were still wearing kimonos and being submissive to their husbands, she had broken through and gone out to be a career woman. She was determined to change the ways of her family by moving from the old thatched-roof house where the Ishii family had lived for centuries to a new wooden-style, modern home. She set her mind to help her children have a life.

Every year the children got together to plant the rice fields, harvest them, and to pound the rice as we were having and raising children. Now we no longer work the fields—we all have jobs. What remains? The heart of this dear woman who keeps the family together here in Japan.

One day about 30 years ago, as she was watching our children, a tragic accident occurred. Our little 18-month-old wandered off toward the train tracks and was killed. I had gone back to teaching after having our third son, and as I drove into the driveway after work I had a dreadful feeling. A neighbor came to me and said, "Be of strong heart!" I could hear my mother-in-law sobbing and calling, "Peter! Peter! Peter." I did not know what to do but to hold her. I had never seen this tough woman cry and sob like a crazy woman. When I found out Peter had died, my heart broke. This began many years of my own healing and being patient with and for her. It takes a lifetime sometimes to work through what is destroyed in just a split second.

Just recently we were having a talk, and all of a sudden she shared something with me that she hadn't expressed to anyone before. After Peter died, she was very depressed. Only God knows what might have happened to her. "But," she told me, "I was asleep, and in a dream I seemed to hear Peter whisper in my ear in his sweet childlike voice, 'Grandma, live the years that I cannot live. Live long, Grandma, live!'" That gave her a brave heart to want to love, to live for, and to fight for her children. That is a mother's heart.

We have a Savior who is telling us to live. He could live only 33 years, but He tells us to live, live for eternity with Him. He tells us, "I have given the sacrifice. Live! And be with Me."

Rebecca Ishii

Rags, the Cat

The Lord your God is with you, he is mighty to save.
He will take great delight in you, he will quiet you with his love,
he will rejoice over you with singing. Zeph. 3:17, NIV.

THE SUMMER OF 2009 we moved into a lovely house on 11 acres nestled in the rolling hills of the Tennessee highlands. The day we signed the papers and got the house keys we went directly to our new house. As we drove up and parked in the driveway, a kitten crawled out through the crawl space vent and scampered off. We didn't see it again until the beginning of December.

It came back a large cat with long gray hair and a white chest and paws. It looked a bit bedraggled and we felt sorry for it, so we put some of our dog's food and a bowl of water on the porch for it. It continued coming around every day but wouldn't let us near it. When we opened the door, it would jump off the porch, so we'd put the food on the porch and go inside the house. Then it would come back and eat. This continued all week long, so when we did the grocery shopping on Friday we bought a bag of cat food and named her Rags. Someone told me to handle the dry cat food before putting it down for her so she would get my scent.

After several weeks Rags allowed me to stay on the porch, several feet away, while she ate, all the while keeping an eye on me. If I made the slightest move she would bolt off the porch. As I spoke softly to her, she'd watch me. Slowly, day by day, I moved the chair closer and closer to her food and water bowls. Weeks went by as we continued to try to get close to Rags. Then one day we noticed that she looked fat. Were we feeding her too much, or was she going to be a mother?

I was so excited the day she finally let me pet her! Now Rags allows me to pet her even when she's not eating. Of course it is still on her terms, but I feel that we have finally convinced her that we mean her no harm. Rags had her babies last night somewhere in the woods. She came this morning to eat then went back to her brood.

We get excited when a wild animal allows us to befriend it. Just imagine how God rejoices when one of His "wild" children surrenders to His love and accepts His gentle touch! I can't wait to see Him face-to-face and bow at His feet in reverent awe!

Celia Mejia Cruz

God Will Take Care of You

For he orders his angels to protect you wherever you go. Ps. 91:11, TLB.

MY FIRST DAY of work was exciting! All my life I had dreamed of being in a classroom as a teacher. But now I had more than that—I was principal of an elementary school, grades 1 through 6, with 93 students and three teachers, two grades for each one. My grades were fifth and sixth. I had so many dreams in my head. I just wanted to please God and do my very best—that was my goal.

The mission office team offered me a little apartment located in the same building as the mission, facing the main road and an old rock road up a hill. On the right side of the road were the mission office and the church. Behind the church were the school classrooms and a backyard where the students could play.

That night, as always, I prepared for all my classes, studied the subjects I had to teach the next day, read my Bible, prayed, and got ready for bed at 9:00. I checked my front door and went to sleep. About an hour and a half later I suddenly woke up to a loud knocking on my front door. Half asleep, I got up, turned on the light, and opened the door. That was my first big mistake. A young man handed me a piece of paper so I could see the address he was looking for. Everything was so dark outside and quiet. I saw the man place his shoe in the doorway so I couldn't close the door. Now I was fully awake—and very afraid. *What is going to happen to me?* I thought. Then I remembered my mom always saying, "There are two eyes from heaven watching over you always." I know for sure those two eyes were watching over me because suddenly I heard footsteps coming up the road and up the few stairs to my front door. That "angel of the Lord" stepped beside me and in a firm, deep voice said to the young man, "What are you doing here, knocking on doors this late at night?"

The young man, in a twinkle of an eye, fled as fast as he could. There was another man waiting for him down the stairs, hidden by the tall wall. They both ran until they disappeared. Who knows what their plan was? But my heavenly Father, who was watching over me, sent Mr. Ignacio, a brother in my church, to protect me.

"For the angel of the Lord guards and rescues all who reverence him" (Ps. 34:7, TLB).

Emma Lutz

The Leaning Tower of Pisa

The Lord is my rock, and my fortress, and my deliverer, my God, my rock, in whom I take refuge, my shield, and the horn of my salvation, my stronghold.
Ps. 18:2, RSV.

IN PISA'S CATHEDRAL Square stands a bell tower called the Leaning Tower of Pisa. It started to sink shortly after construction began, causing it to lean increasingly over the years. The tower has some parallels to my life.

I see an increasing tilt in my spiritual experience over the years that corresponds to times I sank with the vicissitudes of life and leaned more on the Lord. I was baptized in 1959, but I think at that time (and for years afterward) I leaned on my grandmother more than I leaned on the Lord. My grandmother would rise before daybreak, kneel by her bed, and audibly talk to the Lord. She prayed for the country, the government, friends and family whom she called by name. I remember being thrilled each time I heard my name. Her prayers on my behalf were so comprehensive they made mine seem redundant. She made me feel safe and blessed. When she went to sleep in Jesus while I was in medical school, I was devastated. I didn't think then that I could survive without her intercessory prayers, and surely I would never be successful in my final examinations, as she had prayed me through every examination that I had sat for to that date. That's when I really started to lean—but this time on the Lord.

Over the years I've had what seems to be more than my fair share of disappointments and challenges related to my job, family, health, retirement, and events that I file under miscellaneous. I've experienced sorrow as I watched close friends suffer and die. With each event I have tilted more, as I leaned more on the Lord, who not only has been my greatest source of support but also has blessed me with great friends who provide earthly support.

My angle of tilt continues to increase, and I'm now close to horizontal. This has placed me in a wonderful position to look more upward, and I am amazed by the big picture of my life—a fulfilled life, totally ordered by God. I've seen disappointments turn out for my good. Most of my goals now have been achieved. All my need, and some of my wants, have been supplied. I enjoy better health than many, and I now see each past trial as a learning experience that tilted me one degree closer to the Lord. I feel blessed and totally protected in His arms.

Cecelia Grant

Miracle of Miracles

His angel guards those who honor the Lord and rescues them from danger.
Ps. 34:7, TEV.

IN SEPTEMBER I went on my long-anticipated vacation. I had plans to rest, sew, do serious housecleaning, and visit my sick sister. Early in my leave all my plans were thrown off. My father fell ill, and I had to deal with it. Then even stranger things began to happen.

I dreamed that Norman and I were traveling, but somehow I found myself on an adjacent road. When a train passed, a boulder fell onto the road. Afterward there was an earthquake, and after the quake I didn't see the car or my husband. Frightened, I shouted, "Norman! Norman!" He seemed to get up out of a ditch and waved to assure me that he was all right. I awoke so frightened that I lay there pondering the dream. It was scary, and I decided not to tell my husband.

The next day, however, I was able to gather enough strength to go visit my sister. After leaving her home we reached the intersection with the Spanish Town Bypass. We had barely turned onto the bypass when we heard an explosion. The windshield shattered. This time I managed to cry, "Jesus!" I thought my nightmare was coming true.

My husband stopped on the soft shoulder to examine the windshield more closely. After consulting two brothers at a nearby church, he decided he could make it home. Fortunately, he could see at eye level. The ride home was slower than usual, but we prayed that we would arrive before it got too dark. Truly God answered our prayers.

We had the windshield replaced; however, it was disconcerting to discover, validated by two persons including my mechanic, that the explosion was quite likely the result of a gunshot. A car backfiring could not cause the windshield to shatter. A bullet must have glanced off the glass, even though we weren't necessarily the intended target.

Has your windshield of faith been shattered by the trials and struggles of life? Then stop on the soft shoulder of grace and consult your road map, the Bible. In it you will find all the directions you'll ever need. Now drive slowly home in the light of His eternal glory to your eternal destination: heaven. Our heavenly Father will welcome you. He will reveal myriads of miracles He has performed to save our souls from the gunshots of the archdeceiver, Satan.

May you experience a miracle today!

Bula Rose Haughton Thompson

The Work of a Lifetime

I press on toward the goal to win the prize for which God has called me heavenward in Christ Jesus. Phil. 3:14, NIV.

EVERY FALL MY family takes a trip to the Black Hills area in South Dakota. And every year one of our stops is to visit Crazy Horse, the enormous sculpture taking shape out of a mountain near Custer.

The Black Hills area has always been sacred to the Native Americans. In the early twentieth century as nearby Mount Rushmore was being carved, several Indian chiefs approached Korchaks Ziolkowski, a Polish sculptor, and asked him to carve a statue of Crazy Horse, one of their Indian heroes.

A site was selected, and the work began. It was slow and laborious, but over the years the sculpture took shape. Ziolkowski married, had 10 children, and continued working day by day. He died in 1982, but his wife and children continue his work. Day by day, blast by blast, a legacy of which the Native American people can be proud is taking shape.

While on a tour we were told that the work on the front (it is being carved from a granite mountain and will be presented in the round) will take another 39 years, and then another 20 years will be spent completing the back side!

As I walked around the site I wondered what would induce a man to work most of his lifetime on a project, and then near the end of his life know it could not be completed by him. He had to be extremely dedicated to train and encourage his children to carry on the work after his death. As we visit each year it's not always easy to tell that much change has taken place, but I'm sure that someone who has not seen the sculpture for several years could notice a difference.

God is also carrying out the work of a lifetime in my life. No dynamite is required, but there is much carving out of undesirable elements and reshaping of my character. I've been given the gift of justification, the work of a moment, by Jesus Christ, and now it's as if I've never sinned. However, sanctification is the slow process of preparing me for the heavenly delights above. This process will take the rest of my lifetime to complete, but it's definitely worth the time and trouble He's taking to change me into a person He wants to take back home with Him.

Fauna Rankin Dean

September 4

A Woman of Prayer

I will contend with those who contend with you, and I will save your children. Isa. 49:25, ESV.

THE YEAR 1974 was a joyous time in our lives. Out of a family of eight, seven of us were buried in the watery grave of baptism on a memorable Sunday night. We all gathered at the Shiloh church for this great event.

Obviously it's been almost 40 years since we made our commitment to God. Unfortunately, through the years some have left their true love. Our mother, Christophine, however, has always been a prayer warrior.

She is the one we ask to intercede on our behalf for the success of an exam, protection while traveling inland or abroad, for our marriages, the birth of a newborn, or for the success of a business venture. We siblings have come to realize that our mother has developed a powerful connection with the King of kings. We often heard her praying audibly or saw her silently praying to God on her knees. We can only imagine the intensity of her communication with her Maker. Many times she was crying and sweating profusely. I always wondered what conversation my mom was having with God.

After her routine prayer time, which was usually at noon, she'd rise from her knees with a radiant smile on her face. By that smile we knew that she had been energized with the great power supply source.

When I was a student in college I always felt assured that at noontime my mother was praying for me and my siblings, and that made me feel secure. Through the years Mom has experienced many challenges with her health and with the passing of our father. There is, however, one thing that has never left our dear mom, and that is her constant relationship with her Lord and Savior.

My mom talks about seeing her Lord face-to-face someday. Her experiences remind me of the importance of developing a personal relationship with Christ Jesus. As often as my mother would pray on behalf of her children, families, and friends, each of us needs to know Him for ourselves. She would often say, "Have you accepted Jesus as your Lord and personal Savior? Why not do it right now? He is waiting with outstretched arms. He wants to have a dwelling place in your heart. This day give Him your all."

Naomi J. Penn

Golden Morning

And the street of the city was pure gold. Rev. 21:21.

"O, WE SEE the gleams of the golden morning piercing through this night of gloom! O, we see the gleams of the golden morning that will burst the tomb."

The words of this lovely hymn come to mind as I watch the sunrise a short distance from home. Karaka Point, high land jutting into the deep Queen Charlotte Sound, from which I watch, offers a great vantage point. Early morning, as the sun comes up, everything looks golden—the hills, the sea, and the sky.

The bush-covered hills, most of which are several hundred feet high, plunge straight down into the sea, which is very, very deep at that point. Everything is golden. The dark of night vanishes as the sun makes its appearance. Some mornings a few fluffy lines of clouds drift out toward the open ocean, clouds low, so I see both hills below and hilltops above the clouds.

The coast road on which I walk back home is narrow and twisting but sealed. Fortunately little traffic uses it, and wildlife abounds.

Birds sing their early-morning chorus—tuis with their conspicuous white throat feathers, the smaller bellbirds with the loveliest of dawn songs consisting of belllike notes, and cute quail that scurry into the undergrowth on my approach. Several rabbits run into the security of their burrows.

It is at this time of the year (spring in New Zealand) that I always spend some time on a little bridge only five minutes from home. The water in the stream that flows here is so clear and clean and, as their morning ritual goes, a paradise shelduck family comes swimming along—mother, father, and babies (this year there are six). And what protective parents they are! Continually calling to their ducklings to stay together, the family swims under the bridge and downstream. For several months these ducklings will have distinctive brown-and-white feathers—beautiful bundles of fluff. As they swim out of sight, reluctantly I leave to walk home.

What a wonderful Creator to have made all of these creatures! The gold of this particular early morning has well and truly gone; but with what joy I look forward to the golden morning when Jesus will come to take us home to His golden city.

Leonie Donald

A Mother's Kiss and a Father's Praise

But encourage one another daily, as long as it is called Today. Heb. 3:13, NIV.

ON THE DAY of my baptism I awoke with a feeling of expectancy. The service, solemn and so beautiful, made heaven seem very near. Nothing could equal the feelings of purity and wholeness that flooded my soul as I emerged from the water a new creature in Christ.

It seems as if I floated home and, with the peace and serenity of a newborn baby, drifted off to sleep on the sofa. As if in a dream I felt my mother bending over me and placing a gentle kiss on my cheek. Suddenly the best day of my life became even better! This was super-special because it's the only time I can ever recall my mother kissing me. She believed that praise engendered conceit and complacency and that compliments bred pride and vanity, none of which she wanted to instill in her children. I often felt I could never please her, but now I knew differently. I had been affirmed by the crowning act of that eventful day—my mother's kiss. I doubt she ever knew that I was conscious of her kiss and the impact it made, but it is indelibly etched in my memory.

Recently, in reminiscing on this incident, my mind flashed back to another baptism. The evangelistic meetings were well under way and the baptismal service was in progress at the riverside. Several candidates had already been baptized when a young man walked into the water and requested baptism. The preacher was obviously surprised and visibly hesitant. However, after a brief exchange of words the candidate was baptized. As He emerged from the water, His Father, observing everything from a concealed vantage point, could hold His excitement no longer, and in a thunderous voice shouted, "This is my own dear Son, and I am pleased with him" (Matt. 3:17, CEV). Can you imagine the joy in the Son's heart as the startled congregation looked around to see who was speaking?

Ultimate affirmation, that's what it was! I wonder, if affirmation meant so much to God and His Son, what must it mean to us? I know! In a small but powerful way I have experienced it. I believe with all my heart that God expects us to practice it.

There are so many texts in the Bible that speak of encouragement and affirmation. You might enjoy—and be encouraged—by spending a few minutes looking some of them up. And then encourage someone else!

Daphnie Corrodus

Jesus' Flower Message

He will swallow up death in victory; and the Lord God will wipe away tears from off all faces; and the rebuke of his people shall he take away from off all the earth: for the Lord hath spoken it. Isa. 25:8.

MANY DAYS DURING the spring and summer of 2009 my heart was sorrowful as I mourned the loss of my brother and sister-in-law. In mid-February they and fellow passengers disappeared in the Venezuelan jungle when the mission airplane my brother, Bob Norton, piloted went down. Weeks of searching turned into months as summer lengthened toward autumn, and still nothing. My heart was often heavy with grief and lack of answers. I couldn't understand how any good could come from such a tragic loss. The indigenous people served by the airplane now had no one to come for their sick and wounded. My tears were for their loss as well as my own.

One morning as I watered the ivy we grow in our greenhouses I noticed my special azalea plant still had blooms. As I gazed at the red flowers I recalled that the first flowers had appeared in February, and it had been blooming ever since. Usually my bush blooms two, or possibly three, times a year, but never continually. Jesus whispered, "These blossoms are from Me. They are to remind you of life. In this season when you mourn, these blooms are My gift to you."

It is September now, and my bush continues setting buds. The lovely blooms are a constant reminder to me of the eternal life I will share with my dear ones who love Jesus. Although what happened to the airplane and passengers remains a mystery, I have the assurance of being reunited with Bob and Neiba when Jesus returns.

In this sinful world tragedies occur. Death rips loved ones from us. Sorrow is our lot. We have more questions than answers. There is silence and darkness. But friend, I can testify that in the midst of suffering and pain, God is there. During my difficult experience I have clung to His promise, "I will never leave you nor forsake you" (Joshua 1:5, NIV). I have cried out to my heavenly Father, and He has whispered messages of love and comfort to my aching heart.

Today I pulled off the dried, dead blooms from my azalea bush and marveled at the tiny buds still forming on its twigs. Jesus' message is clear: "I am the resurrection and the life. He who believes in me will live, even though he dies" (John 11:25, NIV).

Barbara Ann Kay

A Change of Plans

"For I know the plans I have for you," declares the Lord, "plans to prosper you . . . plans to give you hope and a future." Jer. 29:11, NIV.

MY MOTHER WAS a special education teacher in New York. She was a phenomenal teacher, and her students grew and excelled. As much as I enjoyed spending time in her classroom, I wanted a 9:00-to-5:00 job. So I became an audiologist and found it challenging and rewarding.

When we moved to Florida, that state determined that I needed to take a few courses, amounting to two years and a doctorate in audiology, before I would qualify for state licensure. I asked God to open the door for me to find an alternative form of employment. Before I knew it, I was a professionally certified teacher in the state of Florida. I became a varying education exceptional education teacher—I had become a special education teacher! After my mother stopped laughing she told me that God knew what He was doing.

Every morning I pray for my students, asking God to help me be exactly what each student needs that day. I utilize a color system for behavior: green is great, yellow not so great, and red means we need to have a conversation with a parent. One day one of my students had a difficult time. After numerous warnings he was told to change his color to red. When it was time to go home he turned to me and said, "Have a good evening, Mrs. Marquez." Without hesitation I replied, "You too, sweetheart!"

He looked astonished and asked, "How could you still call me sweetheart after how poorly I behaved?"

I said, "I don't approve of the behavior, but I still love you."

He walked out the door shaking his head. Apparently this really had an effect on him as he went home and told his mother, "Can you believe she said that after how terrible I was?" His mother sent me a note of thanks to say how much she appreciated my being nice to him and not quitting on him despite his behavior.

I wondered how many times he had gone home and said his teacher wasn't exactly patient or nice to him. How many times over the course of his education had he ever received grace? How many times does God extend grace to me? Doesn't He reply again and again, "I love you, My child"? Just so, let me offer forgiveness and kindness to those around me.

Tamara Marquez de Smith

God Is With You

I can do all things through Christ which strengtheneth me. Phil. 4:13.

I WAS 15 and had just been baptized, giving my heart to the Lord. I thought I'd really like to attend a Christian high school in Glendale, where we lived. I also thought that the kids in that school would be walking around with halos on their heads. Was I in for a shock!

I asked my dad if he'd pay for me to attend the school. He said, flat out, "No!" He felt that public school was good enough.

"If I get a job and pay for the tuition myself, can I go?" I asked.

"You can do with your money whatever you please," he agreed.

I began looking for a job and found an ad in the paper for a babysitter. When I applied for the job I found out that the mother had just had a baby girl, now 6 weeks old. The mother, who had fallen and broken her back, had three other girls, ages 2, 3, and 5 years old. The father was a construction worker out in the San Fernando Valley and needed someone to come early Monday morning so he could go to the hospital and visit his wife before going to his job, where he stayed all week. On Friday afternoon he came back to visit his wife, and then on home for the weekend. So I would have a full-time job.

Even though I was only 15, I had lots of babysitting experience, so he hired me. I stayed from 8:00 Monday morning until 5:00 Friday afternoon, then went home for the weekend. It was a challenge with three little girls and a 6-week-old baby, but I managed just fine.

I don't think my father thought I'd work all summer and get enough money for school. But the family paid me well, and at the end of summer, on Labor Day, the mother was able to come home from the hospital. I had enough money for tuition for my junior year at Glendale Academy. I was thrilled!

God was so good to provide a job so I could earn the money. I even was able to buy myself a watch. It was a blessing to attend a Christian school with Christian teachers and to be able to take part in social things that were planned around the Sabbath. I give God all the glory for His great help! He will strengthen us to meet our needs—God knows what you need even before you do. Praise God!

Anne Elaine Nelson

Fairy Tale Book

Order my steps in thy word: and let not any iniquity have dominion over me.
Ps. 119:133.

I SCANNED THROUGH the enormous book with a considerable lack of interest when I first received it years ago. It was a collection of 365 fairy tales—a present from my stepmother—and it became a bedtime routine for my little half sister to say, "Read me a story from the big book."

However, fairy tales didn't begin to measure up to the books that my Christian aunt sent at Christmastime. Books from my aunt, compared to the fairy tale book, were as diverse as black and white. Her gifts sowed the seed to shape my life for the future, although at the time I couldn't see beyond the fairy tales. Her books were a good influence and, later in life, I was able to fully appreciate her talent for sharing character-building books.

Books have always been persuasive at different stages of my life, beginning with *More Dick and Jane Stories,* my first reader in a country school. Those stories were believable and taught by repetition of words. I graduated to the next course, *Elson-Gray Basic Readers,* book one, which had great stories for beginners. My favorite story from that book was "The Little Red Hen." The hen did all the work while the other animals refused to help. Talking animals weren't believable, but I gleaned a moral lesson. Later, in elementary school while browsing in the school library, I discovered a series of pioneer stories by Laura Ingalls Wilder. My interest was intensified by true stories about the early settlers of our country, which offered new and exciting opportunities for reading material.

Eventually the Bible developed into my source of inspiration after I was sent to a Christian boarding school and became involved with their curriculum. I'm thankful that God directs in our lives, guiding us in the path of righteousness regardless of whatever avenue it requires. It alarms me to think that my entire life could have been molded by fairy tales and fiction books of no eternal value. A quote from James Russell Lowell states, "Books are the bees which carry the quickening pollen from one to another mind."

Thankfully, all of those fairy tales have been erased from my memory and are now being replaced with 365 devotionals from books for women, written by women. Of course, the main book that gives me (and you) power for living the Christian life is the Holy Bible.

Retha McCarty

When God Says No

"For I know the plans I have for you," declares the Lord, "plans to prosper you and not to harm you, plans to give you hope and a future." Jer. 29:11, NIV.

MY TWO YOUNGER DAUGHTERS and I returned to Brazil after spending a season in Florida to study English. My eldest daughter had decided to spend four more months studying there. Then after those four months I'd have to go back, settle the rental of the apartment that was still in my name, sell the car she was using, and bring her back.

The situation wasn't very good, for there was a great difference between the Brazilian currency and the U.S. dollar. However, I had some airline miles I could use for travel. In slow seasons the airlines offered specials in which only half the miles were needed to get a ticket. When I called the airline, I was informed that the sale hadn't been confirmed yet. As I had a month until I needed to travel, I relaxed, hoping that in a few more weeks the sale would be confirmed. I began calling weekly, but each time was told that the sale hadn't been confirmed and might not happen that year.

Persistent as I am, I didn't give up, and on my knees I begged in prayer, "Lord, You are the God of gold and silver, owner of all the airlines. You know that I need to go to Florida and that I can't afford a ticket at this moment. You also know that I have miles and could use them to obtain the ticket without paying anything more. Help me solve this problem, Lord. May Your will be done!"

And I kept praying this way for many days. I called the airline for the last time only to hear that the sale would not happen. Disappointed, I looked for other airlines with reasonable prices, and I finally found a ticket for a price that fit my budget.

If I had gotten the ticket with my miles I would have stopped over in New York at 8:00 a.m. on September 11, 2001. But God is so good that He didn't let me travel that route. I probably would have been stuck there for days without contact with my family during the terrible tragedy of September 11.

God says no when He knows what is better for us. Dear sister, if you cried out to the Lord and He answered no, maybe you can't understand why, but remember that God always wants the best for His children. We must trust.

Ivani Viana Sampaio Maximino

When Praises Go Up, Blessings Come Down

Make a joyful noise unto God, all ye lands: Sing forth the honour of his name: make his praise glorious. Ps. 66:1, 2.

THE PAST FEW YEARS have been very difficult for my family. We've had to face many trials, but I've learned that when complex, unexpected situations catch us off guard, we can turn to the One who sees it all, knows everything, and understands all. I have nurtured an intimate relationship with God through meditation on His Word and communication with my Savior. I have also discovered how to praise Him through tribulation.

I would like to say to all who are going through the valley of the shadow of death, "Do not become discouraged! And do not allow yourselves to sink into depression." Too many of God's children are trapped in this cycle. Many of them are brought to the hospital where I work.

I encourage you to experiment with praise. Praise God through the difficulties, through anxiety, pain, and suffering. Do not limit yourself to a superficial form of worship. Sing His praises! Read psalms and verses that exalt the name of the Lord. Keep reading words of encouragement and comfort, words that have the power to renew your mind in God. Take time to fast, and praise and worship God. When praises go up, blessings come down!

My children, my husband, and I have shared precious moments in worship together. We have been encouraged, and our bond with God and with each other has been strengthened. Never cease to praise His name! God is pleased when we feel at perfect peace because of His name. He is pleased when we put our trust in Him and rely upon Him to take control of all aspects of our lives.

Through praise we thank God for what He has done for us and for the wonderful things He will do for us. I've discovered that I must not focus on the difficulties but keep my eyes on the Master's promises. In Psalm 40:1, 2, David puts his trust in the Lord. He sings: "I waited patiently for the Lord; he turned to me and heard my cry. He lifted me out of the slimy pit, out of the mud and mire; he set my feet on a rock and gave me a firm place to stand" (NIV).

I believe God heard his cry and delivered him. God put on his lips a new song. So let us sing a song of thanksgiving and praise to our Deliverer. Let us put our hope in Him; trust and patiently wait on the Lord. Praise Him, for He will surely deliver us!

Flora F. Beloni

Train Up a Child

Train up a child in the way he should go: and when he is old, he will not depart from it. Prov. 22:6.

WE WERE BROUGHT up with strict Christian principles to worship and obey God. Going to church is what we were taught, and we obeyed. My youngest brother, Curt, was all too happy to join in these practices. From an early age he'd proudly hold his Bible and hymnal and walk to church every Sabbath. However, when he was still very little, something happened that almost caused all of his desire to worship God and attend church to change.

One Sabbath he returned home from church visibly upset. He rushed ahead of all eight of us, stormed into the bedroom, tossed his Bible and hymnal down, and announced, "I am not going back to church!" We were all shocked. As far as we knew there was nothing untoward that had happened that should have upset him. "Mommy, do you know that the people were cursing in church today?"

He had our attention now!

"When they were reading the Bible, they were cursing," he went on. "They were cursing when they were singing," he added. "Even the pastor was up there preaching and cursing. I am not going back!" Mom knew he meant it.

By this time we could barely contain our laughter because we began to understand his problem. Mom, who had been absent from church that day, asked us about the hymn and scripture that had been used. The hymn was "Blessed Assurance," we told her, and the Scripture text was Matthew 5, the Beatitudes.

Our mother was suddenly embarrassed, remembering that whenever she was angry she shouted such things as "This blessed child," or "Give me the blessed thing." This had led my brother to believe "blessed" to be a swearword.

Mom knew she had to have a serious conversation with Curt to reverse his early apostasy. And thereafter she was very careful about the "angry" words she used on us, realizing that what she was inadvertently teaching was the wrong lesson.

How careful are you with your words? Do you know who is listening? The Bible says, "A word fitly spoken is like apples of gold in pictures of silver" (Prov. 25:11).

Brenda D. (Hardy) Ottley

The Protected Receipt

Hear me, O Judah, and ye inhabitants of Jerusalem; Believe in the Lord your God, so shall ye be established; believe his prophets, so shall ye prosper.
2 Chron. 20:20.

THERE ARE PROBABLY few things that are more frustrating than to leave the house to go to work and discover that the car won't start—especially if there's no one nearby to help. Recently this happened to me. I knew that I had a battery charger that not only charges batteries but jump-starts them. So I hurriedly got it out, plugged it in, and got the car going. *Ha! It was the battery,* I congratulated myself.

I took my husband's lunch to him at work and got in the car to leave. The car wouldn't start again. So I called my husband and asked him if I could take his truck to my work because time was of the essence. "Wait a minute!" he said. "I'll be out to help."

When he came out, he said that he'd taken a couple hours off work to help his "stranded wife," so I was grateful. He dropped me off at my job, then left to buy a battery.

An hour and a half later he was back, stating that he'd bought a battery—for more than $80. This was a bit frustrating, as we'd been trying to hold on to some extra money for bills, and especially some college expenses. But we had to have a car to travel to work, so this was indeed a necessity.

As he pulled out the old battery we noticed that there was a little pocket on the side where the receipt had been put. On the top of the battery it said, "Three-year warranty, money-back guarantee," but we had little hope that the battery would fall into that three-year time span. After all, Murphy's Law generally prevents this kind of luck from happening. He checked out the date on the well-worn receipt: "Oct. 6, 06." This was the middle of September 2009.

Could it truly happen? We had almost a whole month to spare!

He rushed the battery back to the store, and the full $80 was refunded, making us grateful children of God, sorry for our disbelief and our negative thoughts.

Truly God does care for His erring children. How many gifts of His love do we need to believe that His love for us is genuine and perfect?

Charlotte Robinson

A Book That Keeps on Being Read

It is more blessed to give than to receive. Acts 20:35.

THIS WAS THE down season for my little store; not much business for a party planner this time of year. Besides, most parties are on Saturday anyway. So I decided I must consider other business opportunities. For now I'd just work part-time until business picked back up.

As I sat at my dressing table getting ready for work, I turned on the television. A television evangelist was in the middle of a sermon on giving, and how to be a blessing to others. As I listened, I asked God to help me be a giver and to guide me to someone in need. I turned off the television and hurried out—I was going to be late for work! I called my job to let them know I was running late.

Just as I headed for the front door a thought popped into my mind: take a couple of the women's devotional books and drop them in the book exchange box at work. I began to look through them to make sure I hadn't left anything in them and that my husband hadn't inscribed any love notes on the flyleaf, then gathered them up, plus a copy of *Steps to Christ.*

Once I arrived at work I placed the books in the book exchange box. Every day I checked to see if anyone had taken any books, but they seemed to all be there in the same position I had placed them. One day I decided to bring my new devotional to work with me so I could have something to read on my lunch break. I put the book on the table in the lounge room.

At lunch break a few women asked if that was my book. When I said it was, they wanted to know where they could buy it. I told them I'd be happy to order it for them, but that there were more books over in the book exchange box. But they weren't interested—they wanted *my* book. Maybe they'd already begun reading that one.

One of the women was so adamant about getting the book that I let her have my brand-new copy. The very next day she rushed over to thank me once again for her book and to tell me that her daughter had begun reading it also and that she was enjoying the book too.

It felt good to be able to give from the heart. I thank God for any opportunity to give.

Avis Floyd Jackson

September 16

Leave It There

Come unto me, all ye that labour and are heavy laden, and I will give you rest. Matt. 11:28.

THE STORY IS told of an old man who was traveling by foot on a long journey. On his head he carried a heavy case of his belongings. A motorist who was passing by felt sorry for him and stopped to give the old man a lift in the back of his open truck. They had traveled for a half hour when the motorist noticed that the old man was still carrying his case on his head.

I liken this man to myself. Many times, when I'm passing through the storms of life, I ask God for help, but I don't leave the burden with Him; I still carry it myself while I try to find other ways of solving the problem.

When I was growing up, my father worked a long way from home, coming home only every other weekend. Before he arrived Mother would make a list of chores for him to do around the yard. Then instead of letting Father do the work by himself, she'd tell him exactly how he was supposed to carry out each and every task, forgetting she had waited almost two weeks for him to do those jobs she couldn't do herself. This used to annoy my father.

Recently my daughter had to send some important original documents out. For some reason I became very concerned that the documents would be lost. I prayed about it, but I still fretted over the whole thing. One night God said to me in a dream, "Why are you still worried about these documents after you have asked Me to protect them?"

God wants us to stand aside while He fights the battles for us. This requires total surrender to Him. It's not easy to be at peace when we are in a storm, but let's remember Matthew 6:25-27: "Take no thought for your life, what ye shall eat, or what ye shall drink; nor yet for your body, what ye shall put on. Is not the life more than meat, and the body than raiment? Behold the fowls of the air: for they sow not, neither do they reap, nor gather into barns; yet your heavenly Father feedeth them. Are ye not much better than they?"

It's also good to remember Psalm 57:1: "Be merciful to me, O God, be merciful to me! For my soul trusts in You; and in the shadow of Your wings I will make my refuge, until these calamities have passed by" (NKJV).

Peggy S. Rusike

The Lesson Beneath the Surface

And we know that all things work together for good to them that love God, to them who are the called according to his purpose. Rom. 8:28.

THERE WAS A time when I lived off the fumes of this verse. I was so upset. I entertained the notion that in real time the consequences of life's infractions are dichotomous: some people are more equal than others. And as I was thinking about this kernel of truth a police officer gave me a ticket for a minor traffic violation.

At one time I traveled daily to Belize City from the Cayo district with my two small children. One night I cruised to a halt at the Belmopan checkpoint. One of the officers asked to see my driver's license and inspected the particulars of my vehicle. He had noticed that my brake lights weren't functioning and brought this to my attention as he handed me a ticket.

Simultaneously, a fellow police officer drove by in a vehicle without any lights and got a free pass from this officer. For a moment I just sat there in utter disbelief! How could a police officer drive on this road without any lights and thus endanger my life? Why did they turn a blind eye to him? And why was I slapped with a $25 penalty for a minor infraction?

The events of that night continued to circle through my mind, and had I not dug deep enough I wouldn't have uncovered the true blessing of God's purposeful plan for me. I realized that I had put my life and the lives of my two small children in danger. The traffic ticket was God's gentle notice for me to go and get my brake lights fixed, because stopping on the road without indication of doing so could have also negatively impacted the lives of those traveling behind me.

As the apostle wrote to the Romans in today's text, things did work out. The Lord warned me in time that my failure to attend to such a small, seemingly insignificant yet vital part of my daily travel possibly could result in my family's death. Therefore, He gently reminded me, "Great peace have they which love thy law: and nothing shall offend them" (Ps. 119:165).

I got my brake light checked out and fixed, and the peace and confidence I had were the fruits of abiding by the law of the Lord and also recognizing that God's providence is always guiding me, watching over me with tender and loving care.

Velda M. Jesse

Healed

Is anyone among you sick? Let him call for the elders of the church, and let them pray over him, anointing him with oil in the name of the Lord. And the prayer of faith will save the sick, and the Lord will raise him up.
James 5:14, 15, NKJV.

ONE SEPTEMBER DAY I was notified that my third son, who was in junior high, had collapsed from an intracerebral hemorrhage. Of course I rushed to the hospital. I believed that God would keep my son alive, and I eagerly prayed during the 1½-hour drive.

When I saw Mamoru on the stretcher, he looked entirely different than he had just that morning. His head was shaved for an operation. According to the doctor, he needed to be operated on because he had a seven-centimeter area of bleeding.

A small circle was cut in the right temple, between the frontal lobe and the temporal lobe. The blood was evacuated and the area irrigated, and finally the spot of the bleeding was found. We waited and prayed during the more-than-two-hour operation.

Even though it was late at night, at least 10 church members came over to the hospital, and they kept on praying during the operation. The local mission circulated a prayer request to all the churches in Japan and every church in Okinawa. The junior high school students offered prayers with tears. We experienced the power of prayers by brothers and sisters in the Lord, as the operation was successful.

"Since an intracerebral hemorrhage in a 15-year-old boy is uncommon, I thought it was possibly an inherent deformity," the doctor explained. "But I found no deformity or trouble in the blood vessel. In another 24 hours another scan will be taken, and if there is no abnormality, we will bring him out of sedation."

When Mamoru began rehabilitation he couldn't walk at all. They said, "He won't be able to walk for two years after such a serious bleeding. In fact, we've never seen anyone who could survive such a large bleed."

Thanks to the many prayers, in a week Mamoru miraculously walked, and in two months he returned to school. I believe that it was only by the grace of God. Our extremity is truly God's opportunity.

Naoko Watanabe

God's Plan

I know what I'm doing. I have it all planned out—plans to take care of you, not abandon you, plans to give you the future you hope for. Jer. 29:11, Message.

I WAS THE eighth of nine siblings, and the youngest daughter. Our father passed away when I was a 4-year-old, and our youngest brother was adopted by our aunt when he was only 3 months old. Poor Mother—how she could raise all of us?

Our father left us almost nothing for a living. We were lucky he had a sister in America who took over his responsibilities. Our dear aunt Mathilde, with her kind heart, extended her help to us. Her family assisted as well, and we will be thankful for the rest of our lives.

She sent me to school until college. In my second year as a nursing student my aunt's brother was rushed to the hospital and later died. I had to quit school because my aunt had to pay all the hospital bills and for the funeral.

I didn't know what to do next. Before I left our province and went to Manila for adventure, I dreamed about the second coming of Jesus and about some beautiful scenery: I could see green grass, beautiful hills, and snow-capped mountains.

In Romans 8:28 we read, "All things work together for good to them that love God." It is clear to me now that God is in control of my life. I went to Manila, and it was there I accepted Jesus as my personal Savior. My older sister, who had worked as a sales representative for religious and health books and magazines, introduced me to the publishing director. I joined this exciting work for 10 years. This transformed me from a very shy and timid person into a woman God can use. I moved to Germany to continue this work, got married, and live there still.

It was while traveling to Garmish in Bavaria that I saw for the first time the green land I had seen in my dreams. We were on our way to a yearly religious retreat when I told my husband to stop at the side of the road. I pointed out to him that this was exactly what I saw in my dream almost 20 years before.

When I think about where I came from and where I am now, I can only say that truly God has a plan for me. It is amazing that the God of the universe cares about, and leads, each of us. He promises in Psalm 84:11: "For the Lord God is a sun and shield; the Lord bestows favor and honor. No good thing does he withhold from those who walk uprightly" (ESV).

Loida Gulaja Lehmann

The Christian School

Take heed to yourself, and diligently keep yourself, lest you forget the things your eyes have seen, and lest they depart from your heart. . . . And teach them to your children and your grandchildren. Deut. 4:9, NKJV.

WE LIVED IN a large new house with a beautiful garden in front and a big backyard full of trees. Our children were small and loved to play outdoors. There were shade trees, where a hammock hung; fruit trees; and lots of space where our little dog, Timi, could run with the children. There were many songbirds and hummingbirds (which were my favorite). But there was one concern: should we settle down here, or should we move close to a Christian school?

After much thought and research on education, we decided to move near a school and began looking for a house. However, our budget was too limited for a house with much land in the school neighborhood. We finally found an unfinished house near the school, but it had such a small yard that we couldn't take Timi. And there were no trees or birds—only walls separated us from the neighboring houses. The children played quietly inside, rather sadly I thought. There was nothing to see outdoors except a small geranium that bravely showed its pink flowers amid the sand and brick of the construction site.

Was it really God's will that we live here? We had understood as much, but the place depressed me. In my heart I felt guilty because I had insisted that we move. Was I wrong?

One day I went to the front door where the geranium grew. There the children couldn't see me cry. Through my tears I prayed, "Lord, how did we move here, wishing to do Your will, and yet we feel so sad? I don't even see one bird!" Suddenly, there in the corner where the little geranium grew, a hummingbird was flying to each small flower. This was God's answer! It may have seemed ugly to me, but it was the right place. He could send us birds here also, and I could plant more flowers to attract them.

When the construction was finished, I planted a flowering bush in the small, grassy backyard. Every day a little hummingbird came; it became like a pet. The children named it Little Jacob, after the patriarch who had to leave his home to fulfill God's purpose. My faith was strengthened, and the children loved their Christian school. Even now, this experience remains in our family as an example of God's leading.

Leni Uría de Zamorano

Eyes of Understanding

The eyes of your understanding being enlightened; that ye may know what is the hope of his calling, and what the riches of the glory of his inheritance in the saints, and what is the exceeding greatness of his power to us-ward who believe, according to the working of his mighty power. Eph. 1:18, 19.

THAT SEPTEMBER 21 I followed my usual early Monday morning schedule. The half-hour ride went quite smoothly, considering Miami's traffic at any time of the day or night.

I parked my car and proceeded to the passenger side to retrieve a book bag, my packed vegetarian lunch, and two gifts for coworkers. To do this I needed to arch my back, bend forward, and lower the upper half of my body. As I turned the upper half of my body—something I do on a regular basis—*wow!* Misjudgment! I hit my head—hard! I rubbed my neck and shoulder, but couldn't lessen the pain.

I struggled to walk the two minutes to my office. The pain was now a 10 on a pain scale of 1 to 10, with 10 being the worst. I grimaced, holding my neck as I prepared for my 8:00 lecture. My day was filled with tests, seeing students, faculty meeting, college meeting, preparation for final examinations, study group. And pain, pain, pain. When I got home, I tried a home remedy.

Tuesday morning I was back at work and very busy. The excruciating pain continued, until I knew I had to find medical care. Praise God, I found a chiropractor close to home who was able to see me immediately. He examined me carefully, but nothing remarkable was found. The X-ray results, however, dumbfounded me. The vertebrae in the neck were in an S shape—quite abnormal. Diagnosis: a pinched nerve, scoliosis of the neck, and developing arthritis. After more appointments, treatments, and tests, it was determined that my problem could be corrected only with six months of various therapies.

What an amazing God! This was His way of sending me to get help for an area of my body that had bothered me on and off, but the cause wasn't suspected, and I had put it off. His eyes of understanding revealed a physical problem.

My prayer is that He will reveal to each of us our spiritual problems and lead us to His overcoming, healing grace.

Pauline A. Dwyer-Kerr

Strengthen These Hands

But the Lord stood by me and strengthened me. 2 Tim. 4:17, ESV.

I WAS TO ATTEND a Christian women's convention at which one of the activities would be to provide homeless women with a "day spa." When the convention was only a few weeks away, my friend Joanne asked if I could be one of her helpers when we visited the homeless shelter. She had arranged for a few qualified women to assist her in giving neck and shoulder massages, but now, for reasons that were unavoidable, they would not be able to attend.

I knew I was in trouble, because massage is not a gift that I've been able to use with any success; however, I knew that Joanne needed help and that God could make up for my shortcomings. So on spa day Joanne gave me a crash course on the techniques of massage.

Many prayers had been offered for this God-in-shoes-ministry project. We boarded the bus and headed for the location. When we arrived we found more than 100 women standing in lines to take advantage of this special opportunity. Some had been there since 4:00 a.m. to be sure they could participate.

In our assigned room we began giving facials and the massages. As the first woman sat down in front of me I offered a silent prayer that these women could feel God's love for them through my hands, that each woman would be able to relax, and that my hands would have the strength to be able to do this for the hours that we'd be there.

God didn't disappoint! Knowing my problem, Joanne was barely able to suppress a chuckle as one of the women, as she savored the massage, asked me if I was a masseuse. Several times Joanne whispered, "You're putting these women to sleep!" A prayer of faith had been answered. It was amazing to see what God was doing through my hands. I was grateful and thankful, whether it was temporary or permanent, for God to use my hands in this way.

Ephesians 3:14-19 says, "For this reason I bow my knees before the Father, . . . that according to the riches of his glory he may grant you to be strengthened with power through his Spirit in your inner being, so that Christ may dwell in your hearts through faith—that you, . . . may have strength to comprehend with all the saints what is the breadth and length and height and depth, and to know the love of Christ that surpasses knowledge" (ESV).

This is my prayer for you this day as well.

Rita Kay Stevens

The Power of Prayer

Don't worry about anything; instead, pray about everything. Tell God what you need, and thank him for all he has done. Then you will experience God's peace, which exceeds anything we can understand. His peace will guard your hearts and minds as you live in Christ Jesus. Phil. 4:6, 7, NLT.

I GREW UP IN a Christian home in which both parents contributed largely to our knowledge of Jesus. But it was our mother who taught us what kind of strength comes from having a relationship with God.

My brother Arnaud received that same training. When I left home to go away to school, it left a big void in Arnaud's life. We were close and shared our every sorrow and joy. Technology wasn't as advanced back then, so it wasn't easy to communicate regularly. As the months went by the letters from Arnaud became fewer, and after a while they completely stopped. I wondered why, but I had to wait three years to find out.

Left alone, Arnaud had found comfort in his non-Christian friends. Satan had seized that loneliness and used it to his advantage. Arnaud spent all his time in bad company, doing all kinds of immoral things. Nonetheless, he was always at church on Sabbath morning. Once church was over, though, he was back to his normal ways. This went on for more than two years.

Mom suspected what was happening, and one day she found out the truth. She was upset, but beyond her anger was sadness. How could this have happened? That child became the focus of all her prayers and that of her prayer partners.

Then one day the prayer group decided to go on a spiritual retreat. Arnaud didn't want to go, but Mother forced him to. He thought that somehow he'd be able to leave unnoticed and go party. He tried, but every situation kept him indoors. He found himself spending the whole evening singing and praying with the others.

When he got home after the retreat, he fell on his knees and said, "Lord, I don't know how to stop all my vices, but please help me. In Jesus' name, amen!" God answered that prayer.

Arnaud is now in Mauritius, where he is serving as the chaplain in our Christian secondary school. God is using his experience to touch the lives of young people. I believe that his life is a true testimony of the power that resides in prayer. Each of us can have that power!

Natacha Moorooven

Fall Time. Get Ready!

Preach the Word; be prepared in season and out of season; correct, rebuke and encourage—with great patience and careful instruction. For the time will come when men will not put up with sound doctrine. Instead, to suit their own desires, they will gather around them a great number of teachers to say what their itching ears want to hear. They will turn their ears away from the truth and turn aside to myths. But you, keep your head in all situations, endure hardship, do the work of an evangelist, discharge all the duties of your ministry. 2 Tim. 4:2-5, NIV.

WHILE ON VACATION in Washington, D.C., at the beginning of autumn, I traveled with my violin so I could practice daily, as I had decided to master it. I sat by an open window, enjoying the fresh air. The temperature, about 60° F (16° C), was very cool for me, as I am used to Caribbean weather. While playing at this window for a while, I noticed a squirrel, a very active one, scurrying all around, looking for things. Up the tree it ran, then down again. I was so fascinated by it that I decided to do some research on this interesting little animal.

I found out that during the short months of spring, summer, and fall, squirrels collect as much food as they can and bury it in safe hiding places, called caches, hidden throughout their territory. Throughout the winter they periodically visit these places for sustenance. Some squirrels maintain up to 1,000 caches! God has created these animals to know when and how to prepare. Fall reminds the squirrels of what is coming, so they make preparation, get ready, and remember what is ahead. The squirrel's body goes through changes in order to help it cope with the colder weather. Warm coats of fur appear as though by magic.

In this world of turmoil and uncertainty, when all humanity is living in anxiety, we, as God's children, have a call to fulfill. Get ready! While surrounded by enemies, battered by economic challenges, violence, corruption, and demoralization, the Word of God is calling us to prepare, to be ready. Like the squirrel, we too are aware of the times ahead of us. There is indeed some preparation that needs to take place in our lives, and now is the perfect time to do it.

Think of what kind of spiritual food you have to store, and during your heart searching find out what preparation you have to make now. Get ready. Our Lord is coming. Be ready, in and out of season!

Shelly-Ann Patricia Zabala

My Baby Is Alive

Verily I say unto you, Inasmuch as ye have done it unto one of the least of these my brethren, ye have done it unto me. Matt. 25:40.

THE NEW LINOLEUM was laid in the food area, and even the sink had been installed. All was in readiness for the planned open house. Edith, the leader, had worked hard and made the place into a busy concern for feeding many people in this recession time in the Boston area. We wanted the church members to know about what we were doing and to become involved, too. We would share with them the blessings we received from our many projects.

One day I said to her that we needed to announce the open house in church and promote it. Edith replied that it had been in the church bulletins, but I was remembering back to the days I was president of the home and school committee and what I'd learned from the pastors I had worked with. They had told me it was important to tell the people again and again about activities we had planned. So I told Edith, "I will get up and announce it from the pulpit in church."

So I was up front again at church. I said, "Did you know that our community service receives bread from several of the supermarkets, enough to feed 700 people a week? And did you know that our hospital and Kentucky Fried Chicken restaurant are helping in this Yankee Harvest program, and that we feed a meal to 50 to 100 people three nights a week?" I also told them about the baby whose medicine we paid for, and how the mother had written us a note and said, "Because of you, my baby is alive!" There was much to be thankful for and rejoice over!

Now today is open house day. Edith and her workers have been busy, and all is in order. Even cookies and punch are provided. I go early and am eagerly welcomed by all. They know I, too, am a vital part of this organization, even as I do my treasurer's work at home. And then I see our church members coming, and I am so happy. It shows support for those of us who work such long hours, and we want them to be of help too. It is our community service, that is, *all* of us. When Jesus comes, He will ask, "When did you clothe Me or feed Me?" (see Matt. 25).

Here is the opportunity to care for Jesus by caring for His children in such need. Join us in giving blessings and receiving blessings.

Dessa Weisz Hardin

But What About Little?

Cast all your anxiety on him because he cares for you. 1 Peter 5:7, NIV.

Be anxious for nothing, but in everything by prayer and supplication, with thanksgiving, let your requests be known to God. Phil. 4:6, NKJV.

ON A ROUTINE VISIT to the vet I got very bad news about the health of my beloved little dog, Tai. After giving a diagnosis of congestive heart failure, the doctor indicated that I had only a very short time left with him, and that I should enjoy the couple of months we might have.

After a day or so of sobbing and worry, I asked the Lord to extend his life because he brought me so much joy. I also asked the Lord to please let me know for sure when, and if, it was time to euthanize, for I didn't want Tai to suffer. It was hard to tell when he was in real distress versus when it might pass. I didn't want to have to second-guess my decision.

Because I live alone, the thought of having to deal with his illness or death in the middle of the night frightened me. So again I gave the whole thing to God, asking Him to work it all out.

Early one Sunday morning 15 months later I could see Tai was in distress and wasn't quite himself. I called the vet, although I believed they would be closed on Sundays. But I was informed that they were indeed open from 9:00 to 10:00 a.m.— only one hour—that very day.

We arrived at the doctor's office at 9:05. About 10 minutes after our arrival, Tai went into respiratory arrest. With the doctor's assistance, he passed away peacefully in my arms. The only thing I could think of as the tears rolled down my cheeks were the words of a hymn by Fanny J. Crosby: "For I know what-e'er befalls me, Jesus doeth all things well."

My prayers had been answered in the most beautiful way. Even in the pain of loss I could see how my heavenly Father gave me not only the time I'd asked for, but He'd put everyone in place at the perfect time so that there would be no suffering, and I wouldn't be alone. My heart was filled with gratitude that my cares and worries were God's cares as well.

Many times we remember to take only our big problems to God. Remember, He cares about the "little" things in your life as well. Today, cast all of your cares on Him and let Him take care—of you.

Stephanie A. Grant

Thank You, Holy Spirit

For it is not you who will be speaking—it will be the Spirit of your Father speaking through you. Matt. 10:20, NLT.

THE CHURCH BOARD had just voted me in as youth counselor, and it was the first day of group counseling at our church. The kids seemed a lot less interested than were their parents or the educational director, whose dream this was.

About 15 teenagers dragged themselves into the room. Some were noticeably tired. Three girls fell asleep before the program even began. Two young men told me politely that they didn't need counseling; they were present because they had to be. I had my work cut out for me! Smiling at the reluctant group, I began. "Don't think of this as mandated counseling," I advised. "These are life strategy sessions; Psychology 101, more or less." Some perked up.

While the cards were being passed around I told the teens the story a friend had e-mailed me just that morning. It was the tale of a young woman's final assignment for her last class before graduation. All she had to do was smile at three strangers and document one encounter. She chose to report on a particularly edgy experience in which she did more than smile at two smelly, homeless men—she gave them food. Just as I was ending the story I was prompted, somehow, to make a change. "And she failed," I told the group, bringing the expected conclusion to a startling halt. My entire audience sprang to attention. "That's not fair!" "How could that happen?" And the heated questions and more staid observations flowed. Even when I told them the real ending, the discussion continued. They were connecting.

I could only whisper, "Thank You, Holy Spirit." The next morning I had even more reason to smile. Turning to the suggested passage for my Bible reading, I read today's text: "For it is not you who speak, but the Spirit of your Father who speaks in you" (Matt. 10:20, NKJV).

In 30 years of teaching I'd never before applied those words to an educational setting. Now I could. How many other times, I wondered, had the Spirit whispered a suggestion, and I, rushing headlong in another direction, ignored Him?

Think about the times the Holy Spirit has been able to speak through you. What varied methods has He used to bring each of us closer to God?

Incredible, right?

Glenda-mae Greene

Learning to Really Trust God

Without Me you can do nothing. John 15:5, NKJV.

MY HUSBAND AND I had the joy of rearing two lovely daughters. They were both bright, beautiful, and talented. They could both play the piano, and one also played the flute. The younger daughter played the accordion and, later, also played the organ.

Our older daughter was a very happy youngster, which is apparent in pictures we took of her as she grew. She married the handsome young man from across the street and was very happy. She became a dental hygienist, which proved to be a great choice for her as she was also artistic, and a three-day-a-week job was greatly to her liking. We adopted her when she was 2 days old, and she has been a great joy to us.

Our younger daughter was born to us, and when she was about 13 she became very depressed. We soon learned that she couldn't handle much stress. We took her to see many doctors, and she was often hospitalized. She got 95 percent better, but we couldn't seem to help her with that last five percent. Every time we had a crisis I suffered with intense nervousness. I prayed a lot, and I finally learned to pray, "Dear Lord, this child's problems are too big for me to handle. I will put them in Your hands and leave them there." Trusting God fully has given me inner peace.

She is doing quite well these days. The new medicines are better than the ones she first took. We have arranged yearly trips for her to come visit us, and we see improvement each time. Recently we had a two-week visit with her. Her plane was delayed several times, so she arrived six hours late. When she called at each change, we would cheerfully encourage her that she would get here just fine. When she finally arrived, she said it hadn't been too hard an experience. She was so eager to get here that she tried very hard to take it in her stride. In days gone by she would have emotionally fallen apart, and it would have been stressful for all of us. She was cheerful and content during her stay, and we are glad to see her better than ever. We are also grateful for a good doctor and modern medicine.

How do we trust God for the long term? How do we face problems that are bigger than we can handle? By giving our problems to God and trusting that He really does care—about us and those we love. We really can trust Him! And without Him we can do nothing!

Frieda Tanner

The Dress and the Blouse

But the very hairs of your head are all numbered. Matt. 10:30, NASB.

Keep me as the apple of the eye. Ps. 17:8, NASB.

LIKE MOST GIRLS, I like clothes. The truth is, however, sometimes I can't figure out what to wear. Believe it or not, God has literally helped me in this. I recall one Sabbath I had a program to chair. The notice came late, and as I wasn't even home I didn't have sufficient time to get things in place. I got in Friday evening, still unsettled as to what to wear. I had visualized some grab-and-go outfit. That Sabbath morning as I woke I saw a suit hanging on the wall in front of me and had a strong urge to wear it. So I did, and received many compliments. I thought to myself, *God, what an interesting being You are! You actually care about how Your children look and are groomed.*

It happened again. This time I was heading to a friend's family dinner, but I was clueless about what to wear. I got dressed—and even reached the car—but felt distinctly uncomfortable. I went back in the house, opened the wardrobe—and there hung an item of clothing. When I arrived I could only thank God. I would have been seriously uncomfortable, if not embarrassed, had I worn the first outfit. There was no other human in this experience. No one to ask, "What do you think?" or "How does this look?" But God was there! I daresay if He is interested in what I put on, can you imagine how interested He is in all the other aspects of my life? I'm amazed over the mundane, simple, yet intimate details God attends to. It means that undoubtedly He will indeed take care of the critical issues of life.

We women have many different concerns. At times we pray, but nothing seems to happen, and we wonder, Does God really care? I too have prayers, hopes, desires that are yet to be fulfilled; nevertheless, I must confess and confirm that God does intimately and deeply care. He not only knows, sees, and is aware of everything, but He literally, specifically, lovingly cares about each of His precious daughters in every single aspect of her entire existence. When the tempter crushes us and tempts us to doubt, may we remember that He who numbers the very hairs on our head does care about what we eat, where we sleep, how we cope, whom we marry—what we wear—and all our other feminine cares. May we lean on Him always.

Keisha D. Sterling

Is Anything Too Small for the Lord?

Before I finished praying. Gen. 24:45, NIV.

A FEW YEARS ago we were downsizing to move from our home into a retirement apartment. It was a struggle to know what to keep and what not to keep. Although I didn't often use my cabinet-type sewing machine, I decided to keep it. It would be useful as a small desk and still available for a few mending jobs.

After a long absence from sewing, the day finally came when it was time to do some of that anticipated mending. The top of the cabinet was opened, and the machine pulled up into place and ready for use. But it still had to be threaded and a bobbin wound.

"What you don't use you lose" proved to be very true. The instruction book had to be consulted before I could wind the bobbin. I started to sew, but the thread knotted and the needle stuck firmly in the cloth. I pulled and pushed on the wheel, but the more I tried, the more firmly it stuck. Nothing moved.

The phone rang, and a nice visit with my daughter released some of my tension as I shared my frustration. When our conversation ended I went back to the sewing machine. I pushed and pulled some more and tried with all the feeble strength I had to move that needle—but no luck. Finally, after what seemed a very long time, I audibly said, "Well, why don't you pray?" Immediately, before I had finished speaking, the wheel released and the needle moved. What a God! I sat in stunned silence, and then gave profuse thanks to such a prayer-answering Savior. Surely Isaiah 65:24 is true: "Before they call I will answer; while they are still speaking I will hear" (NIV).

As I resumed sewing, I continued praying. Each time I needed to thread the needle my simple prayer was answered, and I could see the needle's eye.

I wondered how long—if ever—I would remember to keep in a constant attitude of prayer. God cares about everything in our lives. He cares about the salvation of our children, grandchildren, and great-grandchildren, and everyone on this earth!

I learned some spiritual lessons that day: keep current by reading the instruction book; be constant in prayer; God cares about all things; and He keeps His promise and is very safe to trust.

Mary Paulson-Lauda

A Listening Heart

And thine ears shall hear a word behind thee, saying,
This is the way, walk ye in it. Isa. 30:21.

ON A COLD and windy Thursday evening I took my son to the JC Barber Shop in Toronto. While he got his hair cut, I sat in the barber shop and waited.

Haircut finished, he asked if we could eat at one of the nearby restaurants. Initially I said no because we had dinner waiting at home. But then I considered the fact that he was on his way home from school and probably really hungry, so I agreed.

As we were leaving the restaurant, our bus passed by, so we started to cross the street to the bus shelter. Then right in the middle of the crosswalk a voice told me, "Do not go into the bus shelter; go straight into the pizza store right across from the stop." But I thought—and said—that if we went into the pizza restaurant we wouldn't be able to see the next bus when it came.

"Mom, don't worry," my son said. "We can see from the window in the pizza restaurant."

Less than five minutes after waiting in the restaurant we heard a screeching sound and shattering glass. We were so frightened; we thought it was the glass front door of the restaurant. But when we looked, the glass door wasn't broken—no damage at all. My son thought maybe the pizza sign outside the restaurant had fallen down, but it was still standing.

Then we looked outside, and there it was: a small white car had hit the bus shelter, and the front end of the car was completely torn off. The bus shelter had fallen down, shattering all the glass and scattering it all over the sidewalk and into the street.

Now we were really frightened! What could have happened to us had we been in that bus shelter? I was speechless and certainly didn't know what to say. After a few minutes all that I could finally say was "Always listen to that soft voice when it speaks to you." I'm certain it was the voice of the Holy Spirit speaking to me. That voice protected my son and me from this accident.

If I had disobeyed that voice and gone into the bus shelter, only God knows what would have happened. My Christian friends, God wants us to be obedient. I am encouraging you today to listen and obey the voice of the Holy Spirit. As God says in Isaiah 28:23, "Listen and hear my voice; pay attention and hear what I say" (NIV). It really is the difference between life and death.

Annette Howell

The Power of Prayer

Commit your way to the Lord; trust in him and he will do this: Ps. 37:5, NIV.

SINCE THE DAY I got married five years ago, my female dog, Rhana, stayed with my mother. She is a very docile dog and gave my mother company. One Sunday evening sometime after my marriage, my mother walked Rhana to my house. I played a lot with her, and then they left. Without our knowing it, Rhana had eaten some rat poison we had.

My husband, Elizandro, is a tradesman, and he always comes home late. However, on that day he came home early to invite me to go to an amusement park. But as soon as he entered the house and discovered that Rhana had been there, he looked for the poison. It was gone. Desperately, we called our friend Carlão, thinking he would know what to do. He told us we should obtain some medicine to give her quickly. So Elizandro went after the medicine, but he had trouble getting it. In the meantime my mother and I were taking care of Rhana. My mother gave her a homemade mixture of things to drink that would cause her to vomit.

I was very sad and cried a lot, seeing my little dog dying in my arms. I asked God to save Rhana's life. Soon after my prayer, Elizandro came with the medicine that was to be the remedy. He spent a sleepless night medicating the dog hourly. In the morning Rhana was alive but very weak. Because of Rhana's condition, Elizandro and I went to Venda Nova do Imigrante, a neighboring city, to take Rhana to a veterinary clinic, where she stayed in seclusion for some hours as she was medicated.

Today Rhana is fine, very happy and lively. The veterinarian said the mixture that my mother had made saved her life. But I know that God listened to my prayer and instructed my mother. God loves us so much that even before I prayed, He was already taking care of everything. Most important, He sent my husband home earlier than usual.

I believe that Psalm 145:17-19 describes how our God loves and works: "The Lord is righteous in all his ways and loving toward all he has made. The Lord is near to all who call on him, to all who call on him in truth. He fulfills the desires of those who fear him; he hears their cry and saves them" (NIV)—and their dogs. I thank the Lord very much for loving me and guiding me. Trust always in the Lord; if we depend on Him, everything ends well.

Marcilene Kapich Souza

He Cares About the Small Things, Too

Consider the lilies of the field. . . . Even Solomon in all his glory was not arrayed like one of these. Matt. 6:28, 29.

"RAIN, RAIN, GO away; come again another day!" I'm sure this was the song many children sang during the rainy season of October 2007. But the weather forecast for the hurricane season didn't show any sign of clear blue skies. It rained and poured "cats and dogs," as the saying goes. The ground was so saturated that potholes appeared everywhere on not only the major roads but the secondary roads as well. Imagine driving on roads on which you can't see the potholes because they are covered with water! The risk of damaging the front end of the car was high, and we preferred not to take the risk; however, the kids had to attend school, and above all, I had to go to work. So the trip was unavoidable. Of course, all this created long delays in traffic. This was a total nightmare.

Despite all the negatives, I don't remember this time because of them. Instead I remember it because of a miracle that took place, proving to me once again that the God we serve cares about not only the big things but the small things too.

On Tuesday the rain seemed to be abating, so I went ahead and washed some clothes, hanging them on the line overnight. There were clear blue skies everywhere, but as Wednesday progressed the weather changed; dark clouds appeared everywhere, and then the rain began. Feeling a bit apprehensive about what the journey would be like with the rain, potholes, and traffic, I left work earlier than usual and headed to Portmore to pick up my kids. All the while I thought about the clothes, hoping they weren't soaking wet.

As we continued our journey home we had to pass through several communities. But as we approached these communities I noticed that the road was hardly wet—in fact, the road was dry. Totally amazed, heart racing, I drove on home as quickly as possible, shooed the kids inside, and rushed with lightning speed to get the clothes off the line. Just moments after completing the task, the rain began. A few clothes got a little wet, but the majority were dry. I was overjoyed and overwhelmed with the thought that God cares about the little things. What, indeed, do we have to be concerned about?

Thamer Cassandra Smikle

October 4

The Lord Knows Best

Cause me to hear thy loving-kindness in the morning; for in thee do I trust; cause me to know the way wherein I should walk; for I lift up my soul unto thee. Ps. 143:8.

I WAS TRAVELING alone from Los Angeles to Arizona and was really worried because Arizona was a new destination for me. Moreover, it would be almost night when I arrived there. I had reserved a taxi, but I didn't know how everything would work out. My heart was pounding. My uncle and I both prayed before I left on my journey, asking that God would take care of all the details.

When I arrived at the airport, I looked around for any familiar face. A small voice guided me toward a woman who was eating ice cream. As I sat behind her, a voice again prompted me to ask her where she was going.

"I'm here to attend some philanthropic meetings," she responded.

My heart started beating faster. "You mean the ones at the JW Marriot hotel?"

Yes, those were the ones, the same meetings I had come to attend. Both of us were so happy to find each other and became friends right there at the airport. I just thanked the Lord! We then exchanged names, and I learned her name was Jasmine.

When we arrived at the hotel, I went to the registration desk to get my room number and key. The clerk asked for the room rent for the entire meeting session: $729. I brought it out of my purse, but then she said, "You have to pay $250 more as security. It will be refunded."

"I'm sorry; I didn't receive any information about that. I have only $280 for my food and return taxi. Being a foreigner in the United States, I don't have a credit card."

What was I going to do? I had traveled so far, and now this. Just then Jasmine came forward and told the clerk, "Here is my credit card. Put my name as her security."

I was speechless! Once again I thanked the Lord for His leading. How wonderful is our God! When we surrender fully to Him, He clears the way before we even think about it. Don't you want to surrender to Him fully right now, without hesitation?

"Happy are those who make the Lord their trust" (Ps. 40:4, NRSV).

Sweetie Ritchil

A Longing for God

O God, thou art my God; early will I seek thee: my soul thirsteth for thee,
my flesh longeth for thee in a dry and thirsty land, where no water is. . . .
Because thy lovingkindness is better than life. Ps. 63:1-3.

SHE HAD BEEN my best friend, my constant companion, my little helper for 21 years, and now she was gone. It hadn't been an easy departure. She had insisted on going to a college 1,000 miles away. But we knew she'd be joining her boyfriend, a marine stationed nearby. Her father and I resisted in vain and finally had to "let her go." My heart left with her.

Now she calls for advice about her too-early marriage, about raising her first child. I am now content, but in between there was a huge struggle. I had to release her to God repeatedly, but I wanted her back. Prayer became my solace. I knew God understood my pain, because He'd had to give up His precious Son. Psalm 84:2, 3 was especially comforting: "My heart and my flesh crieth out for the living God. Yea, the sparrow hath found a house . . . where she may lay her young, even thine altars, O Lord." As I cried out to God daily, prayer time became my home, the altar for my broken heart. Little by little, God gave me peace. Gradually I learned to live again.

After a while I found that my longing for my lost daughter had turned into a longing for God, which turned into a passion for Him. I felt at one with David in Psalm 63:1-3: "O God, thou art my God; early will I seek thee: . . . my flesh longeth for thee in a dry and thirsty land, where no water is. . . . Thy lovingkindness is better than life."

Psalm 84:5-7 expresses what I have learned: "Blessed is the [woman] whose strength is in thee; in whose heart are the ways of them. Who passing through the valley of Baca make it a well. . . . They go from strength to strength, every one of them in Zion appeareth before God." We may feel as if we are in the Valley of Baca ("weeping"), but if we seek the Lord with the passion of our loss, we can turn the weeping into a "well" of abundant water, the water of life.

There is nothing better than living in the courts of the Lord. I proclaim with the psalmist, "A day in thy courts is better than a thousand. I had rather be a doorkeeper in the house of my God, than to dwell in the tents of wickedness" (Ps. 84:10).

Mary McIntosh

False Alarm

Be not deceived. Gal. 6:7.

OH, NO! I DID IT AGAIN! After putting another cup of water into the pot of pinto beans on the stove, I went to the alcove where I do my devotional reading. As I finished, I smelled something that caused me to quickly run back to the kitchen in a vain effort to rescue the beans. Rather than just throw them out, we did eat some of them for dinner, but they weren't very good. The rest went into the compost bin.

It reminded me of a time years ago when we were living in the mile-high city of Denver, Colorado. At that altitude it takes a long time to cook dried beans, so before going to work one morning I turned the burner on to give them a good start. While I was at work something seemed to nag at me—then I remembered the beans! Mile High Academy, the high school where I worked, was only a couple blocks away from home, so I had walked that morning. But thinking about the possibility of the house burning down from that forgotten bean pot, I started on foot, full speed for home.

As I rounded the corner to our street, to my horror I saw a fire truck in front of my house. I thought perhaps the neighbors had smelled smoke and called the fire department, but to my vast relief it was a false alarm. There was no fire at our house or anywhere in the neighborhood. The firemen had evidently stopped there briefly for some nonemergency reason, maybe to check a fire hydrant. Such perfect timing! The beans were burned and the kettle was scorched, but other than giving me a scare, there was no harm done.

Other false alarms could have much more serious consequences. Matthew 24:23-26 tells us that there will be false Christs and false prophets arising, "and shall shew great signs and wonders, insomuch that, if it were possible, they shall deceive the very elect." The passage goes on to say that if you are told that Christ is in the desert or the secret chambers, don't believe it and don't go to see if He is there. According to verse 27 His coming will be like the lightning that goes from east to west, and Revelation 1:7 says, "Behold, he cometh with clouds; and every eye shall see him."

"Take heed that no man deceive you" (Matt. 24:4). In other words, don't be fooled by a false alarm!

Mary Jane Graves

A Personal Tsunami

Yea, though I walk through the valley of the shadow of death, I will fear no
evil; for You are with me; Your rod and Your staff, they comfort me.
Ps. 23:4, NKJV.

MY HEART WAS at its lowest ebb. I felt lonely and devastated physically, emotionally, and spiritually as I fought the rush hour traffic to be with my husband,
Abe, my best friend, teacher, and confidant, who lay in the hospital.

I always greeted Abe with a big smile and a kiss on his forehead, whether he was
awake or asleep. I carefully hid my grief and unceasing temptation to lose faith in
God, family, friends, and health-care providers. By the grace of God Abe's frail body
was withstanding all the assault and trauma heaped upon it. Our sons, our siblings,
nephews, nieces, other relatives, and friends all over the world prayed for his recovery, but days and nights came and went, and no one heard our prayers.
However, this night as I kissed him good night so I could get some sleep at home in
our bed, my heart was cautiously peaceful. He looked restored even among tubes
and wires of all sizes running to and from his overladen body.

That night I dreamed that I was following someone down a steep, boulder-
strewn mountain. It was muddy at the bottom of the mountain, with troubled
water as wide as my eyes could see. Halfway down a wave rushed at my feet, rising
up to my waist, ready to sweep me down the rocky mountainside. I heard a voice
tell me to turn back and head up to the mountain top. I hurriedly turned to face the
mountain just as a furious wave hit my back, pushing me up the mountain to safety.

Still in my dream, I saw my husband beside me. Hugging him, I told him of my
personal tsunami which God miraculously transformed into a powerful yet tender
force that pushed me up the rugged mountain. He whispered back, "That's exactly
my dream! A lifesaving wave pushed me up the mountain."

I awoke in tears, thankful for God's love that surpasses understanding. He turns
the ocean's fury into His rod and staff to lead us to safety. I called Abe's nurse. He
informed me that my husband had had a very good night. Thank the Lord for reminding us of His love, power, and glory. We still have a long way to go. Only God
knows what the future holds, but I know Jesus is always there to transform our personal tsunamis into a lifesaving wave to take us to the top.

Rose Constantino

Stuck on You

A friend loves you all the time, and a brother helps in time of trouble.
Prov. 17:17, NCV.

DID YOU EVER notice how all our days seem to be filled with thoughts about *us*? It starts in the morning with *Do I really need to get up yet? What'll I wear? How soon do I need to eat breakfast? Do I have time for devotions and exercise before leaving the house?* Even in our morning prayer we're usually telling God our plans for the day, asking Him to bless them rather than asking Him if that is His plan for us for that day. It's all about us, stuck on us.

Has your day ever been so full that you're too busy to interact with your neighbors? I usually am—or think I am. I was reminded of this not long ago when three of my neighbors died within one month. There are only five houses in our cul-de-sac, but I didn't know these individuals had died until almost a week later. Embarrassing! I have vowed to do better.

Can I even do that on my own? No. Only as I invite God to be in charge of my day can I expect to be successful in reaching out to others and being open to their needs.

During the time I worked in retail stores, when the checkout line was long and it was time to bag the purchases, invariably that was when the plastic bags wouldn't open. I'd rub them back and forth rapidly, but they were *so* stuck together. One day it hit me—that's *so* us: stuck on ourselves. It seems as though even God has a hard time opening us up to His voice, to His Word, to loving and helping others.

I pray that the Lord will help me to be more aware of others around me and their needs. I want a servant's heart for others. There are so many things we can do to help others using our time and money, but the most important thing is to uplift each other in prayer.

A while back a pop song "Stuck on You" was popular. Let's make the "you" in the song stand for our wonderful Lord and Savior, Jesus Christ. May we always be as stuck to God as those plastic bags are stuck to each other. And may it be just as hard to separate us from Him and His love.

"Then Jesus said to his followers, 'If people want to follow me, they must give up the things they want. They must be willing even to give up their lives to follow me. Those who want to save their lives will give up true life, and those who give up their lives for me will have true life. It is worth nothing for them to have the whole world if they lose their souls" (Matt. 16:24-26, NCV).

Louise Driver

Look at the Birds

Look at the birds of the air; they do not sow or reap or store away in barns, and yet your heavenly Father feeds them. Are you not much more valuable than they? Matt. 6:26, NIV.

IT IS SPRING in Australia as I write, and there is much activity in the bird world, with nest building and raising of families. It's interesting to watch and compare parenting styles. At one end of the scale are some feathered creatures that take no parenting responsibility at all. For example, koels, although large and handsome, are disliked by both birds and people. By birds because, in true cuckoo fashion, they lay their eggs in other birds' nests and leave all the work to them. By humans because the koels' loud and penetrating calls often disturb the peacefulness of the predawn hours.

Other birds seem to be committed to parenting and try hard, but just aren't very effective. Plovers (or lapwings) lay their eggs in a slight depression in the ground in open grassy areas with no shelter at all. When the chicks have hatched, the parents screech loudly and fly at intruders, or try to act as decoys, but the infant mortality rate still seems quite high. Even Scripture acknowledges that some bird species really are "bird brains." Job 39:13-18 describes the inadequacies of the ostrich when it comes to parenting, noting that "God did not endow her with wisdom or give her a share of good sense" (verse 17, NIV).

By contrast I have enjoyed watching a pair of Australian wood ducks raising their family of seven on a small pond in the grounds of the hospital where I work. When resting, the family stays close together with father standing tall on a rock or small tree stump, keeping watch. When on the move, whether on land or water, there is a parent at each end of the line of ducklings to ensure that none of them strays. They remain constantly alert for any danger. I can almost hear mother duck instructing her children, "Now keep together, and don't dawdle while we're crossing the road!"

God cares for the birds no matter what their parenting skills; and He cares even more for us, despite our many limitations. There is something wonderfully reassuring in the psalmist's depiction of our heavenly parent as a nurturing and protective bird: "He will cover you with his feathers, and under his wings you will find refuge" (Ps. 91:4, NIV). Thank You, Lord!

Jennifer M. Baldwin

October 10

He Erased the Pain

Therefore if any man be in Christ, he is a new creature: old things are passed away; behold, all things are become new. 2 Cor. 5:17.

HAVING A FATHER who was an alcoholic was painful and often embarrassing. While today this disease is recognized as a debilitating illness and resources are available to help families cope, such tools weren't around during my early years. I grew up believing that only my family had this problem.

During my senior year in college I stopped by a dormmate's room to pick up some study materials from a class we had together. As I knocked on her door and entered, I found her sobbing as she watched the movie *The Burning Bed.* While the movie played she shared with me that her father had a drinking problem. She then began to tell me what it was like for her, living with an alcoholic. I was stunned! So I wasn't the only one!

Although my father recommitted his life to Christ during my freshman year in college, I still harbored resentment toward him for the pain he had caused me and my family. To help resolve my anger, I began attending Al-Anon meetings and made several attempts to tell my dad how much he'd hurt me as a child. Finally, in desperation, I asked God to "grant me the serenity to accept the things that I cannot change," and tried to get on with my life.

Months later, while my dad was in the hospital, he said to me, "Kid, I've done some terrible things to you, and I owe you an apology." The next evening my poppy died in his sleep.

At the funeral home, as I made my way to the front to view my father's remains, I was awestruck as I gazed down at him—my dad had the most peaceful, angelic smile I'd ever seen on anyone's face, and for the first time in my life I believe we both had finally found blessed peace and healing in Jesus.

The Bible speaks of what can happen to individuals and to families: "But now in Christ Jesus you who once were far away have been brought near through the blood of Christ. For he himself is our peace, who has made the two one and has destroyed the barrier, the dividing wall of hostility" (Eph. 2:13, 14, NIV).

I am so thankful to our heavenly Father for His healing touch, and for taking His giant eraser and removing all traces of hurt and pain from our lives. May you, too, find that peace today.

Cheryol Mitchell

Being Watchful, While We Wait

You also must be ready, because the Son of Man will come at an hour when you do not expect him. Luke 12:40, NIV.

AT 8:30 ON A cold October morning I arrived at the London Gatwick Airport after a short vacation in Florida. I had already picked up my luggage and was awaiting the train with a prebooked ticket for 10:05 a.m. This was no easy wait. Chilled and tired, I just wished I could get home quickly.

After settling myself inside the building where it was more comfortable and the approaching trains were in full view, I informed family and friends of my whereabouts. I read for a while, then decided to rest. Just in case I dozed off, I set my mobile phone alarm for 9:50. The train stop was, literally, just outside the door, so I thought there wouldn't be any need for more time.

Sure enough, I dozed off for a few moments. At the set time my alarm sounded, and I knew I had 15 minutes more to wait, so I wasn't very concerned. Five minutes later I looked out and saw a train. It wasn't the one I was waiting for, though, and I was about to get comfortable, when I thought I had better check to see if there were other trains behind the visible one. I was utterly surprised when next in line was the very one I was waiting for. Furthermore, as I hurried toward it, I realized that the driver had only stopped long enough to remove the baggage of a passenger who had boarded by mistake. He was ready to close the baggage compartment and set off on his designated route. I almost missed the train totally!

As I traveled home I thought about the morning's event. It would have been hard enough to sort out getting on another train, but then I thought of the bigger picture. How applicable this is to our Christian life and the importance of being ready and waiting at all times for Jesus' return. We know not when He shall return. Are we awake, with lamps burning bright? Are we ready for Jesus to come? Oh, what joy it will be on that great day when we will join others of God's children for the final leg of our journey.

My prayer is that we will all stay connected to Jesus, ready and waiting for that day when the "heavenly train" comes to take us home.

Donette James

October 12

Daily Commitment

Commit your way to the Lord, trust also in Him, and he shall bring it to pass.
Ps. 37:5, NKJV.

I'VE PRAYED MANY times in the past two years to become like Jesus, only to realize that the obstacles, challenges, and trials have increased. I know that I should depend upon the Lord every day to guide and direct my path. But I realize that sometimes I have called on Him only in times of great difficulty.

The Christian life is a journey, and we will experience various difficulties along the way. When a person becomes a Christian, the journey has only begun. We are then called to press on in Christ toward the great goal of becoming like Jesus.

If we don't surrender our lives daily to Christ and be committed to Him, we won't surmount our struggles, and we won't gain the victory.

My year began with numerous obstacles blocking my way. I couldn't manage the burdens; they were so overbearing and overwhelming. There were times I was in tears, and my emotions were out of control. Now I realize that God was teaching me a lesson. He wanted me to know that I should depend on Him, and that I should call on Him every morning, asking Him to direct my path and to lift my burdens.

On this Christian journey the path can become so thorny that it's impossible to trudge along it by ourselves. We need to daily commit our lives to God and depend on Him. In the Hebrew language, the native tongue of the psalmist, the word "commit" suggests the act of rolling your burden onto another. Let us roll our burdens onto Jesus. He has invited us to do just that: "Come unto me, all ye that labour and are heavy laden, and I will give you rest" (Matt. 11:28). He is waiting for us to place our trust in Him daily. Let us therefore commit ourselves to the Lord and place our trust in Him always.

A commitment to Christ requires a step of faith and an acceptance of the sacrifice He made for us. By dying on the cross Jesus has washed our sins clean with His blood. We must thank Him for the sacrifice He has made for us because we aren't worthy.

May we accept Jesus as our Lord and Savior and make our daily commitment to follow Him as we consecrate our lives for His glory and honor.

Carol J. Daniel

Miracle in Techiman

How much more will your Father in heaven give the
Holy Spirit to those who ask him! Luke 11:13, NIV.

I WAS GOING to Techiman, in Ghana, an English-speaking country, for the first time—alone. My husband and I often go together, and that way I have no problem because he's fluent in English and can help me. This time, though, more than 250 pastors' wives of my church were awaiting me to speak to them during their national spiritual retreat.

When I received the invitation to go, I was assured that there would be a translator for me. Consequently, I prepared my sermons in French, which was easier for me because I went to school in a French-speaking country, and my husband and I have worked as missionaries for the past 20 years in a French-speaking country.

I arrived in Techiman without incident. An hour before I entered the meeting hall to speak, the translator informed me that since the majority of the women could understand only the local dialect, it was preferable for me to deliver the message in English directly; it would be extremely difficult to have two translators for one presentation.

What should I do? I spoke to God in a short and urgent prayer: "Savior, do with me now what You did in the past with the disciples. You gave them the gift of languages. I urgently need to speak in English now! You know that I have never taught or preached in English before. May the Holy Spirit help me." I ended with a hymn from the French hymnal that goes like this: "Fear not, I am with you, supreme promise that strengthens my faith." So I gained new courage.

All went marvelously well. In fact, the participants asked for copies of my sermon, thinking it was written in English. Furthermore, I was invited again to Ghana in 2008 and 2010. Since then the Lord has performed the same miracle, but in an even better way for me each time I have gone there.

I understood that the eternal God responded to my prayer by permitting me to preach in a foreign language that I don't even understand that well. It was just like Acts 2:4: "All of them were filled with the Holy Spirit and began to speak in other tongues as the Spirit enabled them" (NIV). May His name be glorified!

Angèle Rachel Nlo Nlo

The Omnipotent God

Yea, though I walk through the valley of the shadow of death, I will fear no evil: for thou art with me; thy rod and thy staff they comfort me. Ps. 23:4.

OCTOBER 14 DAWNED like any other day. However, I never dreamed that it was going to be an unforgettable day. Uttering my usual prayers, I rushed to the Sanatorium railway station to catch the 7:05 to Egmore to reach my school at Vepery. Getting off the back of my husband's bike, I crossed the track to find that I was the only person at that peak hour of the day. Suddenly, something somewhere went wrong. Before I knew what had happened or why, I was thrown onto the railroad tracks. I hit the track with my nose, my feet resting on the track just behind and my body lying in between. Unable to get up and needing some help, I yelled, wriggling like a worm in agony, struggling in vain to get up. Though people glanced at my miserable plight, no helping hand was offered.

As my attempts to save my life proved futile, the thought of the electric train in two minutes flashed through my mind. Then I cried at the top of my voice, "O my God, don't leave me alone!" Instantly I felt two invisible, mighty hands lifting me up and setting me on my feet. My guardian angel had dragged me off the track just as Lot had been dragged out of Sodom and Gomorrah. I had barely gathered my wits when the 7:05 train came howling up and passed over where I had just been, leaving me untouched.

Hearing my hysterical cry my husband came running to see my bloody, battered face. My upper and lower lips had been smashed as they hit the track; skin dangled almost to my chin. My nose was completely flattened and my nasal septum twisted. There was a big black bruise on my cheek, and my four front teeth in the upper jaw had broken off.

As part of my recovery, I underwent root canals, had four ceramic teeth implanted, and two nasal surgeries. The non-Christian doctor who treated me exclaimed, "It's the hand of God who brought you back to yourself!"

Four years have now passed. As I reflect on that incident, tears fill my eyes and I praise the omnipotent Lord who preserved my life. How true are the promises of the Lord. Even though I walk through the valley of the shadow of death, I will fear no evil, for God is with me. My friends, if God doesn't remove the obstacles on our way, then He'll give strength to overcome them.

Valsa Edison

Love Your Neighbor as Yourself

He said to him, "You shall love the Lord your God with all your heart, and with all your soul, and with all your mind. This is the greatest and first commandment. And a second is like it: You shall love your neighbor as yourself." Matt. 22:37-39, NRSV.

I WOKE UP today on the wrong side of the bed—actually, the wrong side of my world. I really wanted to crawl back into bed, sleep some more, and hopefully wake up without the discoloration of my world. Who put the sunglasses on me that caused me to feel so blue and see the glass half empty? I should be greeting this crisp, sunny day with joy in my heart and eagerness in my steps. Instead, they just add feelings of guilt to my repertoire of emotions. Yup, it's going to be one of those days.

Or is it?

I am beginning to know myself, to know that these dark emotions are a reaction to something. Even though it hurts, I search my heart for the buried experience. It's like searching for a missing sock in a basket of laundry. My mind breezes through the events of yesterday, and I know what it is that's bothering me as soon as I allow myself to acknowledge it happened.

It was the experience of being insignificant.

Even as I write it, my heart bursts with the pain of remembering it—to be present but not wanted; to speak with fear of knowing that what you say will be wrong mainly because it came from your mouth; to adjust behavior in hopes of receiving validation of worth but to be denied it. We have all been there—and it hurts.

I have struggled for years trying to be the person everyone loved. I tried to do it by the things I did or said. However, what developed was a distorted view that worth was based on behavior rather than being. I know that Jesus' love for me is not based on what I do. In fact, (praise God!) it is there—in spite of what I do! However, I also realize that what my heart needs is for *me* to love me, too. Jesus said, "You shall love the Lord your God with all your heart, and with all your soul, and with all your mind. . . . You shall love your neighbor as yourself" (Matt. 22:37-39). These commands include three directions of love: love to God, love to neighbor, and love to self. Don't mask false humility with neglect to love and care for yourself. Take that walk, bubble bath, or quiet time. And remember to give yourself a hug.

Judi Penner

Backyard Dilemma

[She] must also have a good reputation with outsiders, so that [she] will not fall into disgrace and into the devil's trap. 1 Tim. 3:7, NIV.

OUR BACKYARD WAS overrun with destructive ground squirrels—whole families, whole generations of them! They dug large holes along the fences next to the forest behind us. What attracted them to our yard was the birdseed dropped from the feeders hanging from the patio cover. They had become a nuisance and a hazard, frightening away the beautiful tree squirrels that we prefer to see feeding on the peanuts we put out. So we had to figure a way to get rid of those pesky ground squirrels. We were running out of the unsalted, unshelled peanuts that we bought especially for the tree squirrels who liked to eat them.

We bought a live animal trap and set it on the ground where the birdseeds fell and added peanuts to the bait. One by one, we caught the ground squirrels and took them to a dry area across the river. Still, there were so many of them that it would take lots of trapping to get them all. We hoped to discourage enough of them that they quit coming to our backyard. But we will continue trapping them until that happens or else we eliminate the species in this neighborhood!

All that trouble reminds me of Paul's Epistles to Timothy, advising him about deacons and all church workers, to watch that they didn't fall into the devil's traps. As 2 Timothy 2:26 further says, "and that they will come to their senses and escape from the trap of the devil, who has taken them captive to do his will" (NIV).

Unless I am careful in my deportment and conversations, my actions or my countenance, my composure or a neglect of compassion where it's needed, how easy it is to fall into an unforeseen trap of the devil's making. Paul especially warns in our day's text that we need a good reputation to lead them by our example to a fellowship with the Lord and eternal salvation.

If I have worldly priorities rather than the spiritual ones, I might lead some soul innocently into a trap of the devil's making. What may be all right for me may be a stumbling block for someone else. "Therefore let us stop passing judgment on one another. Instead, make up your mind not to put any stumbling block or obstacle in your brother's way" (Rom. 14:13, NIV).

Bessie Siemens

Teach Me Thy Judgments

For my thoughts are not your thoughts, neither are
your ways my ways, saith the Lord. Isa. 55:8.

IT WAS A busy night for both my husband and me. We put the boys to bed a little earlier than usual. My focus was on the baby, while my husband was taking his turn with 4-year-old Eric. We both then settled down in different rooms to the work of marking exams and scripts.

Eric, who normally settled down for sleep with no fuss, appeared at my elbow. He explained that he wanted a cuddle. "Why not ask your father? He put you to bed," I suggested.

"Daddy's busy," he replied

"What is Daddy doing?" I asked.

"Marking papers."

"And what am I doing?"

"But you're a mommy. Mommies' laps give the best cuddles."

It was a plea impossible to resist. I put down my pen, took his hand, and headed for the room with the old bentwood rocking chair. "So Mommy's lap gives the best cuddle?" I teased.

"Oh, no!" he responded. So of course I asked whose lap does give the best cuddles.

"Granny in Barbados has the best lap, then Granny in Santa Cruz, then Auntie Linn, and then you."

I realized that I had been assessed on a standard of which I was barely aware and that I had never consciously identified, but which was nevertheless very important to my young son. Such a thought was chastening. As a mother of young children, I tried to be aware of all the things that mattered to them and thought I was succeeding at it.

My thoughts moved from my son to my heavenly Father. Could I be making the same error in assuming that I understood what He required of me and what was the basis for His judgments? The children of Israel certainly appeared to understand His promise: "I will redeem you with a stretched out arm, and with great judgments" (Ex. 6:6) until their actions proved otherwise. Am I like them in thinking "All the words that the Lord hath said I will [try to] do" (see Ex. 19:8) without realizing the full import of those words? The lesson learned that night has remained with me over the years.

Hortense Headley

The Event

Let us be glad and rejoice and give Him glory,
for the marriage of the Lamb has come. Rev. 19:7, NKJV.

I HAVE TWO friends who are dying,* and even though I am physically far away from their deathbeds I feel sad and broken. One of them is perhaps living her last minutes as I write this meditation. The other one lives under the shadow of helplessness and suffering. At times it seems that everything is somber around me. I feel like crying. This is not the world God had in mind.

Imagine you are preparing your home for an important event. You clean your house, put out flowers, draw the curtains back to let the sun in and make it cozy. You place scented candles around and even put up a welcome sign on the door and prepare your best meal. You look for music that best expresses the joy of the occasion. You dress up and do your hair, taking time for each detail. Suddenly a wave of mud, a strong wind, a cloud of smoke, a swarm of harmful insects, a revolting and intense odor fill the room. Any horrible, uncomfortable, or destructive metaphor is nowhere near the sudden and drastic change that has just taken place.

That is what has happened to this world. The perfection of Creation was destroyed. Every beautiful, pleasant, sweet, or soft thing that you and I know today is nothing compared to what God had originally made or what He is re-creating. However, when we are enveloped in the pain, sadness, and misery sin has placed in this world, we often forget about that which we have never seen, felt, or experienced. Nevertheless, we know it is for real!

Soon we will be there. Soon we will enjoy that "event" that takes place in heaven and will last for eternity. Your pain, your distress, your shame, your disappointments and failures will disappear. Do not grow weary, because the Lord keeps His promise.

My friends are dying, but I will soon see them, and they will be healthy, happy, graceful, and radiant. You and I are in a hostile and difficult world, but very soon we will take part in "The Event" that will never end and will never be destroyed again. Hallelujah! For the Lord God omnipotent reigns! Be of good courage—"The Event" is at the door.

Susana Schulz

*One of my friends died the same week I wrote this, and the other one died 15 days later.

Behind the Clouds

The Lord is a refuge for the oppressed, a stronghold in times of trouble.
Ps. 9:9, NIV.

IT WAS A COLD, misty morning. The area around the airport was covered with fog. The clouds, lying close to the ground, made it hard to see very far. The night before, the newscaster had announced a super typhoon was expected to hit the country the following day—the day of my flight to Manila.

Those of us in the waiting area were informed that our flight was delayed because of a technical problem, causing a commotion among the passengers. I tried to remain calm, but I felt despondent and affected by the weather. Nothing gave a hint of a good day. Suddenly they announced that the passengers bound for Manila were to board the plane. As the plane lifted in the air, a feeling of fear and hopelessness enveloped me. I caught a glimpse out the window of dark clouds that looked ready to pour down on us. I closed my eyes. "Lord, take us in Your hands safely."

Just then the voice of the flight attendant reminded us to check our seat belts because of possible turbulence. Then the sound of the engines changed; I could feel us climbing higher and higher. When I opened my eyes all around was bright, beautiful sunshine! White cotton-candy clouds surrounded us. My fear transformed into unspeakable joy. My spirits rose higher and higher, to the throne of God. I can truly exclaim, "The sun is shining brightly behind the clouds."

Life is like that. Sometimes our eyes are blinded by circumstances. The reality is that God allows certain things to happen. When my father died before Christmas, I was able to comfort myself that everyone has to face the same fate. We have to welcome death as we do birth; but when my grandmother followed him several days later, and death and sickness struck other family members in the next six months, I could no longer find a reason why. I felt defeated and afflicted. I wondered why God allowed all these things to happen.

Then the light behind the clouds redirected my thoughts. The sky may be gray, but behind the clouds the sun is shining. In God's plan sorrows and discouragement in life are not the same as defeat. He wants us to rise above any circumstance, no matter how difficult. In life's journey He didn't promise comfortable travel, but He offers Himself as a divine shelter so that His children will experience a safe landing. What a comfort!

Leah A. Salloman

Wrong Keynote

Wait on the Lord: be of good courage, and he shall strengthen thine heart: wait, I say, on the Lord. Ps. 27:14.

LEARNING TO PLAY the guitar is such a lovely thing to do. It gives me relaxation, and every time I play religious music it truly uplifts my spirit. I especially love playing the song "Why Have You Chosen Me?" This song refreshes my mind and gives me new strength to live life amid uncertainty.

Sometimes we make mistakes and get wrong ideas, which can lead us to question if God is still willing to listen to us. Is He still willing to forgive and to love us?

While holding my guitar I said, "The Lord will forgive me my sins if I play 'Why Have You Chosen Me?' perfectly, without making a single mistake in my keynote." But I placed my finger for the B-keynote wrong. When I tried again to get the right chords, I still failed. This made me believe that God would never forgive me.

Then my cousin sat beside me and offered to help. "You should change the placement of your finger to get the right note for B," he suggested. I finally got it right!

The signs we ask from God may not be the right signs or give us the assurance of His will. What He wants is our sincere hearts, repenting; our own hopelessness to lead us to God, surrendering our all to Him. God is always listening to an honest heart asking for His help and learning to ask for His forgiveness, because He is just and will always forgive. He will extend His helping hand in His own way to enable us to get the right keynote to play the most beautiful music He desires from us. As I look back on my experiences during my college years I am reminded that when I allowed God to lead, things went right.

Sometimes, though, we attempt to understand why God allows certain things to happen. We question His authority, and then make decisions on our own. When the result of our own actions turns out unfavorably we begin blaming Him. That's where prayer comes in. Just as my cousin helped me with my guitar fingering, God will help us get the right key if we allow Him. For when we work, we work; but when we pray, God works. He puts our finger on the right key; He forgives; He guides.

Kathy S. Zausa

Tragedy to Triumph

And they shall fight against thee; but they shall not prevail against thee; for I am with thee, saith the Lord, to deliver thee. Jer. 1:19.

THAT OCTOBER DAY in 2003 probably started out as an average day for Bethany Hamilton, but average would not be the word to describe what would happen to her. Bethany was getting ready to go surfing with a friend and was in the ocean water lying on her surfboard. As she paddled along she felt a tug on her arm. When she looked, it was gone! She had been attacked by a shark. This was the beginning of Bethany's tragedy and the event that would change her life forever.

After Bethany made it to shore and underwent medical treatment, she found she had to find her balance all over again to adjust for the missing limb. She worked hard, trying to adjust physically and mentally. Amazingly, within a few weeks of the accident she was back out surfing. How could she do that? In many of the interviews with her following the attack, she consistently gave credit to God and expressed gratefulness for His impacting her life in spite of the tragedy. Each time I think of what she went through and her response, I'm amazed all over again. Just as it says in Psalm 9:9, "The Lord also will be a refuge for the oppressed, a refuge in times of trouble" (NKJV).

When I've gone through my own difficult times, it has helped me to focus on God. He has blessed me with His presence, and I've been assured that He was with me. Many times He would also bless me with friends who helped to carry me, encourage me, or even to straighten me out. Many of these situations required me to pray for the Lord to change my attitude or the way I looked at my situation. It was a matter of changing my perspective of the situation. He can turn our tragedy into triumph. Is there something that you need to take to the Lord? Trust Him.

When God does make something tragic turn into a triumph for us it helps us to understand His awesome love and grace a bit more. We, in turn, can reach out to those who are going through their own personal tragedies and offer them the same peace that Bethany has experienced. I pray that God will be with Bethany and continue to bless her as she blesses others with her story. And we too have a story to share that can be a blessing.

Mary Wagoner-Angelin

Have Reservations, Will Travel

And if I go and prepare a place for you, I will come back and take you to be with me that you also may be where I am. John 14:3, NIV.

LAST YEAR MY daughter-in-law invited me to take a trip to Ireland with her and my grandson. While the trip wouldn't take place for several months, the deadline for making reservations and paying the fee drew near. It didn't take me long to decide to go. Ireland is a place I had wanted to visit for a long time.

I already had the necessary passport, but I needed to arrange transportation from Tampa, Florida, to O'Hare Airport in Chicago, Illinois, where our tour began. I did some research on the anticipated weather so I could pack the appropriate apparel. Then, of course, I needed to take the toiletries that met my personal needs. Most important, proper picture identification, airline tickets, and accommodation documentation must be produced. While these plans didn't capture my attention and energy every waking hour, I always kept them in the back of my mind.

In the not-too-distant future I anticipate another trip. It will be farther away than Ireland, but I won't need an airplane to get there. My Lord Himself will be the sponsor. He will be my personal escort once He raises me from the grave—or, if I'm still alive, catches me up in the air. Homeward bound, with heaven as our destination, we will fly through space together with all those who love Him. The journey to that place will be unprecedented. Having wings enabling me to fly will be a brand-new experience. Talk about space travel—this will be the ultimate!

Never mind packing a suitcase—that won't be necessary. Neither will a passport, airline tickets, or any other documentation. My character is the only requirement. Can you imagine what it will be like to associate with angels and ascend to heaven with people such as Abraham, Mary, Peter, Paul, and many others we have known only from reading about them? Most of all, Jesus will be the central attraction, the only one with nail-pierced hands and feet. He gave His all that we might be with Him in Paradise.

What a wonderful God I serve to include me in His plans for eternity! If I never leave my hometown again, this is one trip I must not miss. As my very best Friend, He assures me of this fantastic trip with its destination—heaven, my eternal home.

Marian M. Hart

Encouragement

After the reading from the Law and the Prophets, the synagogue rulers sent word to them, saying, "Brothers, if you have a message of encouragement for the people, please speak." Acts 13:15, NIV.

WE NEED TO be encouraged, to feel we are needed and wanted, in the church community, the body of Christ, and not rejected. Everyone is able to do something, whether it is putting out the front doormat, washing dishes after potluck lunches, collecting funds for the poor, sharing in Sabbath school Bible class, or reading in church when asked.

Let's be encouragers, not discouragers. Jesus did not despair, even with all the heavy load of criticism and hatred from the so-called Christian leaders of His day. Why? Because He was in constant communication with His heavenly Father, nothing could discourage Him. We should do the same.

No doubt the disciples were also discouraged, but they looked to the Lord, and He gave them encouragement. Encouragement was important even in the early church. Acts 14:21, 22 says, "They preached the good news in that city and won a large number of disciples. Then they returned to Lystra, Iconium and Antioch, strengthening the disciples and encouraging them to remain true to the faith" (NIV). Let's be encouragers to one another. The devil is the prince of this world. We have a fight, so let's be overcomers of this evil one.

As a young girl I'd go into the blacksmith's shop where my father had horses' shoes replaced by the blacksmith. The blacksmith hammered the shoes on the anvil so they would fit the horses' hooves properly. We Christians should be like steel that needs to be hammered into shape. Sometimes this process is severe and painful, but it's necessary to produce a lovable and humble Christian character to fit us for the kingdom of heaven.

Hebrews 10:24 says, "And let us consider how we may spur one another on toward love and good deeds" (NIV). If a brother or sister is in trouble, whether it's financial, health, marital, or whatever, let us encourage, be there to support and give hope, and when the Lord appears in glory may we all hear, "Well done, good and faithful servant . . . enter thou into the joy of thy Lord" (Matt. 25:23).

Joan D. L. Jaensch

Where Are the Plans?

"For I know the plans I have for you," says the Lord. "They are plans for good and not for disaster, to give you a future and a hope." Jer. 29:11, NLT.

BEING A SUBSTITUTE teacher is one of a myriad of things I've done since retiring. Substitutes in our area can go to an Internet Web site to find assignments, and that's how I get most of my subbing jobs.

When I was teaching, we were expected to leave adequate plans for a substitute. In fact, a few years before I retired we had to submit plans to the office at the beginning of the year that would be sufficient for one week in case an emergency precluded our having them available.

When I accept an assignment I always try to arrive early so that I can find the plans, read and understand them, and get the materials ready. Each classroom is different. Most teachers leave very sufficient, detailed, step-by-step plans on their desk, and the day flows easily. Behavior problems are minimized, students stay focused, and assignments get completed.

There are times, though, when the scenario is different. Sometimes it takes a little searching to find the plans. I have to look beyond what I think is the teacher's desk. Sometimes plans aren't current, and a chorus of student voices sing out, "We've already done that!" Occasionally there are no plans at all. When that happens I have to rely on other teachers, the students, or God-inspired ingenuity regarding what to do for the day. That always leads to an interesting and sometimes chaotic day, because students' antennae are always ready to pick up on things that are amiss so that they can incorporate their own plans! And their plans seldom match academic expectations.

Today's text is rendered differently in the King James Version of the Bible: "For I know the thoughts that I think toward you, saith the Lord, thoughts of peace, and not of evil, to give you an expected end." Either version is good; it has become a text of assurance because it tells me that God does have plans for me and wants what is best. When I neglect to accept His plans, my life falls short of what He wants for me. We can't make better plans than God's. We just need the wisdom to accept and follow these plans. Or as it paraphrases our text in *The Message:* "I know what I'm doing. I have it all planned out—plans to take care of you."

Sharon M. Thomas

The First Few Days

But if I do judge, my decisions are right, because I am not alone. I stand with the Father, who sent me. John 8:16, NIV.

HAVE YOU EVER made a decision—I mean a decision that changed your entire life? One that not only altered your daily routine but changed everything you've ever come to know and understand? Well, I have, and I'm here to say that it changes you. These changes shape and mold us as if we were clay in the hands of the Potter, being created into His image. Change, real change, requires a dedicated thought process. We weigh all the pros and cons, we barter, we cry, we talk to people, we feel angry, we deny, we cry some more, and then at some point we finally accept and make the decision. After that, we act. Then we come to the first few days after the decision and the hours of "Did I make the right decision?" knowing full well that it was absolutely necessary to make the decision that brings us to: the first few days—after the decision.

To illustrate, look at the biblical story of Esther. Esther didn't choose to be taken away from her uncle Mordecai and the home that she had grown to love and accept. We can also agree that she wouldn't have necessarily chosen this course for her life. However, it's what she faced and, as a result, she changed the course of history for an entire race of people. I can well imagine those first few days that led up to her decision—and the first few days after.

Another fine example of this painstaking decision-making process would be Jonah. We all know the story, right? Called by God to do a job. And then the decision process: Jonah weighed all the pros and cons and then, at some point down the line, he decided *not* to do what God had asked him to do. That's where Jonah's problems began. It was only when Jonah finally rethought his decision and came to another conclusion that everything began to fall into place.

How do we make our decisions? I don't know about you, but if anything teaches me about the process of making decisions it's the Scriptures. Time and again, and story after story, we see revealed within the Bible hundreds of amazing up-close and personal experiences of God's people. Throughout the course of biblical history we see decisions made that have altered lives forever. We have, at our fingertips, all that is needed to meet the daily challenges to all of life's problems. By following its instructions, we can avoid the "Did I make the right decision?" the first few days after.

Cathy Roberts Ward

Pray Without Ceasing

Rejoice always, pray without ceasing, in everything give thanks; for this is the will of God in Christ Jesus for you. 1 Thess. 5:16-18, NKJV.

AT THE TIME of this writing I am two weeks from having found out that I have an unhealthy breast lump. After further testing it's been determined to be malignant.

Now let me tell you, in an instant I got a greater and clearer understanding of what "pray without ceasing" means. I now have a greater sense of what "lean on Me" and "in everything give thanks" means. You see, I am a go-get-'em type of woman. Yet on this occasion I heard, "Be still and know that I am God." I heard, "Wait, I have a plan."

Let me share. You women who have experienced a mammogram machine might get a laugh (obviously, a man designed that machine). I had avoided it, but this time it was unavoidable. Actually, that process wasn't too bad. Yep, I know: in all things give thanks. It was when I went from the mammogram to the biopsy, where they take out core cells to check, that I was sweating—perspiration wall-to-wall. My blood pressure went up, although I was humming hymns out loud and tears were filling my eyes. And this was all before they even started.

Now, I was praying up a storm. In fact, I was praying up a tornado. And then it was that I heard, "Praise Me!" So there I was, lying on my side, one naked breast pointing out into the world for all to see, and I asked, "Can I put my iPod in?"

"Yes," they agreed. I sang at the top of my voice. Only the doctor and nurse and heaven heard, but I felt nothing but the love of God as they taped me up, and off I went.

I found myself trawling through all the information people have sent me and wondering how I would know what God wanted me to do. Then I remembered that every time I have asked for God's leading, He has led. So why not ask Him now? So for everything that has come across my path, I have asked God if He wants me to do this at this time. And I appreciate that I have had yes or no answers very quickly.

Why am I sharing this story? Because God is *the* God of love—yep, God is love. My learning has been that I was praying so feverishly that I wasn't being quiet so as to hear from my God. Once I listened, I heard. When I heard, I had peace. Healing is in His hand: physical, emotional, and spiritual.

Julie Nagle

Answers Before Prayers

Before they call, I will answer; and while they are still speaking, I will hear.
Isa. 65:24, NASB.

THIS IS ONE of a hundred Bible verses that my friends and siblings have memorized through the years. But I didn't feel the significance of this verse until 23 years ago. And for 23 years it has been one of my favorites.

At 24, and two years after my graduation from college, I had yet to find a job. So when a secondary school teacher transferred to another school and a vacancy was created, I immediately applied. I submitted my application on a Friday and came back the following Wednesday for the interview. The superintendent told me to report to the school the following Monday.

Three days before my actual day to report for duty, I made a familiarization visit to my first school as a public secondary school teacher. I was accompanied by Judy, a cousin. With a 60-peso budget (about $1.50 then), which was borrowed from my sister-in-law, we left around 9:00 a.m. We learned from my conductor friend that we had to transfer at the next town and take another jeepney ride to our destination. I mentally computed our money. It was enough for the return trip. When we reached the next town, however, my conductor friend told us we had missed the last trip. We had to go to the airport, about three miles (five kilometers) farther, to catch the jeepneys waiting for passengers there. While waiting, Judy inquired whether we had enough money.

"Let's pray; the Lord will provide," I had just finished saying when my friend returned to inform us that the Philippine Airlines service vehicle was leaving for the airport, and he had asked the driver to take us for free. Judy and I looked at each other. We had not yet started to pray, but here came the answer. The Lord really hears when we call—even before we call.

Had we paid for the extra trip, we wouldn't have had money for lunch. We wouldn't have had even enough for the return fare.

God is so good. He knew what we needed before we ourselves knew it. He gave my sister-in-law just enough money. He assigned my conductor friend to be scheduled that day. He caused the airlines' service vehicle to be delayed so we could ride for free. I'm sure He even made the vehicle's driver act favorably toward my conductor friend. I sincerely believed He did it all for Judy and me. I sincerely believe He will do it for you, too.

Hedy F. Fontamillas

You Will Be a Blessing

I will make you into a great nation and I will bless you; I will make your name great, and you will be a blessing. Gen. 12:2, NIV.

I HAVE LIVED with women who simply exist, and with others who really want to live. But there are also some women who not only exist and live, but insist on making their lives a blessing to others. I'm grateful to God that He has allowed me to live with some of these women.

For several reasons I couldn't finish my studies—financial, health, and the separation of my parents. The last reason was the strongest, because when my parents separated, my sister, brother, and I went with our mother. As our mother was a woman of little culture, she thought that her daughters did not need to study. For her, only knowing how to read and write was enough. But we learned how to sew, wash, iron, take care of the house, catch a husband, and get married. Studying in the evening was unthinkable.

When I was 19 years old, I met a young man who was active in church. We began dating, and when I was 21 years old we got married. We were blessed with a couple of children. Life was difficult. I didn't have a profession, but helped supply the needs as I could. I cleaned, taught literacy to old people, sold Tupperware, and was a companion to old people.

Then we went to live near a couple whom I had met many years before. My life changed. Sonia Regina, who had already finished the nurse-assistant course, encouraged me to do the same. Her incentive wasn't only verbal; she did everything she could, including lending me her notes, books, and even her short coat, because it was mandatory to use a short coat in class. I still remember how funny the coat was. I'm just a little more than five feet (1.6 meters) tall, and Sonia is about 5 feet 9 inches (1.75 meters) tall. Well, you can see that her short coat was almost a dress for me.

I finished my course with a lot of difficulty. God used other people to help me. Even the woman whom I accompanied paid some monthly payments without deducting them from my salary. At the conclusion of the course I began to work in the new profession. I participated satisfactorily in two tests, with God's help. Today I am a federal and state employee.

I am very thankful to God for women who put themselves in God's hands to be a blessing to everyone near them.

Vilmêdes Goese

Healed by Faith

Just then a woman who had suffered for twelve years with constant bleeding came up behind him. She touched the fringe of his robe, for she thought, "If I can just touch his robe, I will be healed." Jesus turned around, and when he saw her he said, "Daughter, be encouraged! Your faith has made you well." And the woman was healed at that moment. Matt. 9:20-22, NLT.

SHE WOULD HAVE had soiled garments, and not been able to be included in society. She had been to doctors, and none of them could help her. For 12 years she had lived with this affliction. The amount of faith it must have taken to make her way through the crowds just to touch the hem of Jesus' robe would have been immense. Jesus knew this, and that's why she was healed. She knew the instant that she touched His hem she had been healed.

We women go through our lives bleeding every month. It can impact our lives and what we might want to do. I began to understand her better when I experienced bleeding for 18 weeks. I still went to work, still saw friends, and attended church. Even so, I felt a little isolated, and I wished to be healed.

But like the woman whose story is told in the Bible, I have to keep my trust in God. When I start losing my faith in God, I remember that woman. She had such amazing faith that she would be healed, and she was. If only I could have the same amount of faith. Is it because of my doubt that I didn't get healed as I had hoped? Jesus told the woman, "Daughter, your faith has healed you. Go in peace, and be freed from your suffering" (Mark 5:34, NIV). I think He is saying that to each of us today as well.

This is a story about love and faith and acceptance. We are so unworthy of love and acceptance from God. Yet He gives us love and accepts us just as we are. I am in my soiled dress of sin and know that just touching His hem will heal me. As long as I have faith and trust in God's promises I will be healed from this world of sin and be part of God's family.

He came to heal the world, and He also heals us. He makes us clean and heals us from the sin of the world we live in. In Isaiah He is described this way: "Surely he took up our infirmities and carried our sorrows, . . . the punishment that brought us peace was upon him, and by his wounds we are healed" (Isa. 53:4, 5, NIV).

Melanie Carter Winkler

Cattle on a Thousand Hills

*If ye abide in me, and my words abide in you, ye shall ask
what ye will, and it shall be done unto you. John 15:7.*

EVERYONE GATHERED FOR the women's ministries meeting was filled to over-flowing with joy and words of praise for the leader and her associates. They had succeeded in providing a weekend filled with moments of deeply spiritual significance. After the opening remarks and prayer, the leader invited us to share a testimony or ideas regarding the activities of the weekend. Several persons expressed their concern for families who were having problems because of the existing economic conditions in the country. One testimony related by the woman sitting next to me especially surprised and excited me. This was her story:

The burden of an unpleasant and failed job weighed heavily on her, but her trust in God permitted her to keep doing what was expected of her. She worked with a home health agency as a registered nurse. For nine months she received just a small fraction of her wage, and when a new owner took over the agency, he paid her for three months—and after that he paid nothing.

With no money to pay her bills, she talked to the Lord. "You say I must cast all my cares upon You; and if I ask, I will receive; so I am going to venture out on Your word. You have cattle on a thousand hills; You can just sell any one of them and send me the money I need."

Soon after her talk with the Lord she went to the bank to take care of a utility bill. She was shocked when the ATM revealed a sizable balance on her account. She rushed into the bank to find out where the money had come from. She was told that the money was put there by the Social Security Administration. Needing to be reassured that the money was rightly hers, she called them and was informed that because of an accounting error she had been underpaid for three years. She could hardly believe what she was hearing. Furthermore, the money was deposited to her account on the second of the month, the same day on which she needed to pay her monthly bills, instead of the usual deposit date. In faith she had claimed God's promise, assured that she would be rewarded, and rewarded she was with $6,000.

The request was so simple, as that of a trusting child making a request of a loving earthly father. God, our loving heavenly Father, had fulfilled for her a covenantal promise: "Ask, and you will receive" (see Matt. 7:7).

Quilvie G. Mills

God's Selection

Behold, I send an Angel before you to keep you in the way and to bring you into the place which I have prepared. Ex. 23:20, NKJV.

I WAS DRIVING to my daughter's home when steam began pouring out of the engine. Seeing an off-ramp, I sent up an urgent prayer that I would be able to get off the freeway safely. There was a park 'n' ride area nearby, and after reaching it I offered a prayer of thanks. Then I called my daughter, Jennifer, to let her know I was having trouble. Following that, I made a call to my auto club. Again I recognized God's blessing as the automobile dealer where I routinely had my car serviced was within the club's range of free towing.

The service manager called me the next day with the bad news. "Because you have had your car for several years, and recently you've had to put out a lot of money on it for repairs, I suggest you look for a newer model." I knew he was right, but financially what was I to do? However, I needed a car.

Meanwhile, my son-in-law, Harry, graciously lent me one of his two cars, giving me time to think. After praying about it, I felt it would be wise to apply for a low-interest bank loan on my own rather than using the dealership's financing. When I went to the used-car lot, a salesman showed me two cars that I felt I could afford. "But this one is the one I think you should choose," he suggested.

It's black, and I don't want a black car! I thought silently. Yet it did seem to be the better of the two automobiles, and the salesman seemed honest.

It took the bank a whole month to process my loan, and I was concerned that someone else would see the car and buy it. But God saved it for me. The day I took the check to purchase it, they had washed and polished it. And in the bright sunlight I realized it was not black, but a beautiful charcoal gray. *Thank You, dear Jesus!*

God selected my vehicle for me. He forced me to get another car before the financial crisis when it would have been more difficult for me to get a low-interest loan. I am reminded that even when life seems to be going bad, God is still in control. As it says in Nahum 1:7, "The Lord is good, a refuge in times of trouble. He cares for those who trust in him" (NIV).

Mildred C. Williams

A Lull in the Storm

So do not fear, for I am with you. Isa. 41:10, NIV.

ALL OF A SUDDEN the huge plane began jumping, creaking, and bouncing like a kite on a windy afternoon. The captain had announced that we were approaching an area of strong storms, but nothing had prepared us for the violence of the ordeal just ahead. Overhead bins opened, bags and other contents fell on passengers' heads, hot liquids and food flew all over the place. One of the flight attendants had been thrown on the floor and couldn't find the strength to get up. A state of panic developed as the pilot shouted orders. People screamed and children cried as the winds raged amid lightning and all the dangerous signs of a powerful electrical storm. Having traveled countless times before, I had experienced turbulence, but never anything comparable to this terrible night. Trying to land somewhere wasn't an option—we were flying over an area of huge mountains and extensive forests. The crew was as terrified as we were.

I always pray a lot on planes, not because I'm afraid, but because there is privacy. Somehow, though, now I wanted to pray. The terror was so raw, so overwhelming, that I couldn't put my thoughts or words together. My numb brain couldn't respond. My heart cried, "Lord, Lord!" but I couldn't formulate a prayer.

When I was growing up, I'd always been uncomfortable with amusement park rides and altitude. This was certainly a "ride" that I hadn't signed up for. Now I needed to ask God to take away my fear so that I could think and communicate with Him. And all of a sudden, for no apparent reason, I felt that I wasn't so afraid any longer. God had taken away my fear; I could ask Him for the assurance of salvation, for forgiveness of my sins, for my family, for rescue for all of us, if that was His will.

A few minutes later the storm was over. The captain told us in an emotional speech that he had been flying for more than 25 years and that this had certainly been his worst flight ever.

Since then I've thought that sooner or later the storms of life will come. Sometimes our fear separates us from our Lord, numbing us and preventing our communication with Him. I now know that He will take away my fear precisely when I think that I can no longer cope. I do believe Jesus when He says that He will not let us suffer beyond what we can stand. What a wonderful blessing in a world so full of struggles and dangers!

Odette Ferreira

God Never Gives Up on Us

For I am convinced that neither death nor life, neither angels nor demons, neither the present nor the future, nor any powers, neither height nor depth, nor anything else in all creation, will be able to separate us from the love of God that is in Christ Jesus our Lord. Rom. 8:38, 39, NIV.

WHEN I WAS a young girl, I didn't go to any church, but my friend took me to her church, Vacation Bible School, summer camp, and Pathfinders. I found Jesus at Camp Au Sable, a youth camp in Michigan. I became very involved and went on a teen mission trip to Haiti with Pathfinders, took Bible studies, and told my parents I wanted to get baptized. Unfortunately, my parents weren't thrilled with this and told me I had to wait until I was 18 years old.

When I reached high school age, the world had a very strong hold on me. In high school the teachers taught evolution, which I thought made sense at the time. I completely stopped going to church and Pathfinders with my friend. I was confused, ran with the wrong crowd, started smoking, drinking, and doing drugs.

In my late 20s I went through a divorce, and during that time I quit smoking. Being a single mom, I did my best to be in control of my life and the situations around me, but I didn't realize that Jesus was working on me even then.

In my 30s I found out that the Pathfinders were having a 25-year reunion for anyone who had gone on the teen mission trip. I went with my 5-year-old son. This was the first time I had been to Camp Au Sable in 20 years. I soon realized that being back up there at the youth camp made me miss Jesus. I hated how far away I was from Him. It hit me like a ton of bricks: I didn't want to raise my son alone anymore. I saw how much I needed Jesus in my life, and with Him I would never be alone again.

One year later I had decided to go back to church when I got a phone call saying that the company I worked for was going bankrupt and not to report to work. I attended some evangelistic meetings and was baptized. I truly accepted Jesus Christ as my personal Savior. Two weeks later the state church headquarters offered me a job. God's blessings continued to flow as there I met the love of my life, my husband, in whom my son sees Jesus every day. I praise God that He never gives up on any of us!

Cynthia Stephan

Bonsai

I am the vine; you are the branches. Whoever abides in me and I in [her], [she] it is that bears much fruit, for apart from me you can do nothing.
John 15:5, ESV.

A FRIEND SENT me an e-mail attachment of pictures of bonsai trees in bloom. Plums, peaches, wisteria, even a hibiscus—a colorful variety. I've seen bonsai trees at various exhibits and nurseries. I've admired the artistry of the tiny trees, but never before had I seen these singular plants in bloom.

Like any other tree, bonsai trees start out from a seed. From there on the treatment they receive makes each one unique. The bonsai grower chooses a pot of the exact size to force the plant to grow into the form he dreams. He chooses and maintains the soil with the end product in mind. Leaves, twigs, branches, and roots are pruned according to his dream.

Does the bonsai plant hurt? Is it uncomfortable? Does it wish the designer would try something else, perhaps a less-painful intervention? Does it have any pleasure from the admiring stares of exhibit goers? Who gets the glory—the plant or the designer/grower?

This has led me to think of myself. If I were a bonsai tree in the hands of the Master, what would I become? The big difference, of course, between Nancy and a bonsai tree is that Nancy has her own ideas of what she wants to be. She usually has no idea how beautiful she could become in the hands of the Divine Designer. She has never seen the bonsai in full bloom, much less burdened with luscious fruit.

From a flowering bonsai tree my imagination travels to a fruited vine. Its grapes are dark, sweet, and juicy. A hungry person is satisfied with a handful of them. Jesus told His disciples that He was the vine, and they were the branches. Their job was to produce fruit. They could do that only if they remained in Him and allowed the needed pruning (see John 15:1-8).

Jesus wants me to become that kind of vine. And He knows how to help me become that fruit-laden vine. He even knows best what kind of pruning—ouch!—I will need. And when the hungry are satisfied, He will get the glory!

Rather than being a flowering bonsai tree, I want to be a productive vine—regardless of the cost to myself. To the glory of God!

Nancy Jean Vyhmeister

The Presence of an Angel

Though I walk in the midst of trouble, you preserve my life; you stretch out
your hand against the anger of my foes, with your right hand you save me.
Ps. 138:7, NIV.

EVERY MORNING I pray to my precious Redeemer, praising His name and giving
thanks for the infinite mercies He has showered upon my life even though I don't
deserve them. I ask His blessings and the presence of the Holy Spirit to help me
against the temptations of Satan, the destroyer and seducer. This is the support I
need all day long so that I can walk and do all my errands with confidence, knowing He is by my side.

One Sabbath afternoon in November I was driving my car to attend choir rehearsal. That night we were going to present the annual Christmas concert. The
weather is very hot here in Brazil at this time of year, so I took a bottle of fresh water
with me. Two girls were walking in the same direction on the road, so I stopped to
give them a lift. When I stopped the car, the water bottle fell down. While I continued to drive, I asked one of the girls to pick up the water bottle. As I brought my attention back to my driving, I realized that the car was off the road and I had no
control. I didn't know what to do. In front of us was a brick building, and the car
was headed toward it. I didn't even have time to ask Jesus' help. Even now I don't
know how I drove the car back onto the road and continued on as if nothing had
happened. The girls were very afraid, and I was shaking a lot.

Before leaving home, I always ask for God's guidance to protect me. So I believe
that my guardian angel helped me drive the car back onto the road. This experience
taught me a lesson, one that I had heard before: when you are driving, never take
your eyes away from the road, because in a second a tragedy may occur.

I thanked God for keeping the girls, me, and the car safe. We could have
crashed against that brick building. How sweet and comforting to know that He is
always leading us every step of our lives. Truly His love is shown to us in all our surroundings as we pass on life's way. Let us not forget to take time for Jesus every
morning. Praise His name! Let's fill our heart with His joy so that our whole day
will be a praise song to Him. When we start the day with Jesus, we feel His love and
joy all day long.

Ani Köhler Bravo

The Wristwatch

Therefore I say unto you, Take no thought for your life, what ye shall eat, or what ye shall drink; nor yet for your body, what ye shall put on. Is not the life more than meat, and the body than raiment? Behold the fowls of the air. . . . Are ye not much better than they? Matt. 6:25, 26.

I HAPPILY WAITED for my uncle to return to Nigeria with the wristwatch I wanted him to get for me. The day came, and he had me choose a lovely wristwatch from a collection he'd brought. I was able to choose the one I loved the most and flaunted it in front of everyone who cared to look with admiration at my wrist.

Two weeks later a friend in the neighborhood and I went to visit someone, only to find that they weren't home. I wasn't happy, after going on that long ride, when I later discovered that the person we went to check on hadn't been gone after all. As if that wasn't enough unhappiness for me, my friend's grandson, unknown to me, had tampered with the hook of my wristwatch while fondling it when I carried him, and by the time I got back home I discovered that my lovely wristwatch was gone. I searched my room and went back to the path I had taken to and from my friend's house, but I couldn't find it. However, instead of brooding, I slept fine.

The next morning, when I was ready for work, it dawned on me again that the wristwatch was missing. I feel my dressing isn't complete without a wristwatch. Sometimes when I forgot to wear it I've even gone back home to get it. It's not an obsession, but just part of me. Surprisingly, this time it didn't bother me. I prayed that I'd find the missing wristwatch, and I went on with my normal life as if nothing had happened. What I didn't know was that God had something wonderful in store for me.

Exactly a week later a friend's brother walked into my office and placed a cute little white box, wrapped inside black nylon, on my table. I asked him, "What's this for?"

"It's a gift from your friend to show his appreciation for your support."

I was so curious! When I opened the box, there lay a beautiful gold wristwatch! I saw that as God in action.

Are you a woman who always worries about things, about food, what to wear, money? Don't! God owns everything, and He will take care of everything. You only have to trust.

Temitope Joyce Lawal

An Unforgettable Trip

Do not be like them, for your Father knows
what you need before you ask him. Matt. 6:8, NIV.

THE YEAR 1998 had just begun when I received a phone call from Alessandra, my daughter-in-law, who lived in the United States. She called me to give the address of a travel agency in São Paulo, Brazil, where I should go to pick up a ticket that would take me to her home in Indianapolis to visit my granddaughter, Isadora, who had just been born. I was very happy because I could meet her and also have a beautiful trip, for I always liked to travel. After thinking about it, however, I got a little worried because I didn't know a word of English. But soon I calmed down because I knew that I could count on my best friend Jesus. He has always been by my side.

The expected day came, and my husband took me to the airport. After waiting some time, I learned that the flight had been transferred to another airline and that the departure gate had been changed. It was obvious from the beginning of the trip that I could already count on Jesus' help.

During the flight I asked many people if they were going to Indianapolis, but I didn't find anyone. But in the morning, before we arrived in Atlanta (where we would make a connection), I found a Brazilian woman who had been living in the United States for some years. She offered to help me through immigration. We weren't going to the same place, but she explained how I should take the subway that would take me to the other end of the airport, where my flight to Indianapolis was already waiting for me.

On the next portion of my trip nobody spoke Portuguese, but everything was all right, and I could pray thankfully. I was almost to my destination. Soon I would see my family who was already waiting, bringing my dear little granddaughter, Isadora. What a wonderful trip!

I spent several days with them, and when I came back to Brazil I thanked God for having been with me during this time. As we read in today's text: "Do not be like them, for your Father knows what you need before you ask him."

I'm thinking of another trip that I'm really looking forward to taking! There will be nothing to worry about—no tickets, no immigration, no transfers, no language barriers, no money worries! Everything will already have been taken care of. Please join me!

Neide Balthazar de Oliveira

An Unanswered Prayer?

And it shall come to pass, that before they call, I will answer; and while they
are yet speaking, I will hear. Isa. 65:24.

The steps of a good man are ordered by the Lord,
and He delights in his way. Ps. 37:23, NKJV.

EVERY TIME I get into a car I pray, "Lord, protect me as I (we) drive. Don't let
there be any accidents. Keep the car running safely." It's a habit, but it's also calm-
ing to know that God is now in control of my safety. So on August 3, 2007, I prayed
my usual prayer as I got into my foster daughter's Mercedes. Christina followed me
in her RV as we started off to find a restaurant for a victory celebration.

At the corner of 17th and Figueroa, I stopped at a traffic light. In seconds one
of those oversized pickup trucks ran the red light at freeway speed, hitting me and
totaling both his vehicle and the Mercedes.

I was taken to Los Angeles' only trauma hospital, where my left ankle's double
compound fracture was operated on and pinned back together. I was still in the
hospital five days later when, on my sixty-ninth birthday, I had a mysterious
"episode." The trauma hospital's usual caseload was gunshot wounds and drug
overdoses, so personnel there had no idea what was wrong with me. It was entered
in the records as "a possible anxiety attack." I was put into an induced coma until
they could figure out how to treat me.

A visiting cardiologist, Dr. Faye Lee, saw my file. Although I wasn't her patient,
she read the file and called Christina to tell her, "You might want to transfer your
mother to Good Samaritan Hospital, where we can give her an angiogram."

Christina transferred me immediately. The angiogram was administered, and
three days later I had triple bypass heart surgery.

When I came out of the coma the heart surgeon told me, "If you'd had the heart
attack anywhere but in the hospital, no one would have been able to save you in
time."

Although I had prayed that we would have no accidents, He had allowed me to
be injured in a head-on collision so that I would be *in* the hospital when I had a life-
threatening heart attack. God knows our needs, and when we give Him control of
our lives He does just that—He controls what happens to us to our advantage, even
if it means a head-on collision.

Darlenejoan McKibbin Rhine

Flour in the Pot:
A Modern-Day Miracle

"O man of God, there is death in the pot!" And they could not eat it. He said, "Then bring flour." And he threw it into the pot and said, "Pour some out . . . that they may eat." And there was no harm in the pot. 2 Kings 4:40, 41, ESV.

I PLAYED THE phone message again: "Rita, I don't want to alarm you, but instead of 300, you need to plan for 450, maybe 500, for lunch on Saturday." I deleted the message and went back to the lab. *Don't panic! It will work out. Just a few more hours at work, then I will have time to adjust the menus and plans,* I thought.

I had asked Lee-Roy a few months before if anyone had been asked to prepare food for the church leader's meeting for our region. I was told no. I had said that if that was the case then I would like to do it, because I had told a group of pastors' wives that I would raise half of their funds to do a mission trip in about 18 months. This could be a real help! Now I'd just been told that instead of the 200 to 300 for each meal, I should plan for 300 to 500. This was Tuesday, and the meetings were to begin on Friday evening.

Fortunately, my friend Ann came to help on Thursday evening. All of a sudden Ann shouted, "Oh, no! The beans have burned!"

That was $40 worth of beans! Even though Ann said she would pay for them, I replied, "That isn't the problem. I don't have time to go get the supplies to make more."

Quickly we removed the big pot from the stove. "Wait!" I said, as I ran to get another big pot. Ann helped me lift the pan of burned beans, and we poured them into another container. Yes, the beans were definitely burned. "Stop! Before we taste them, let's pray," I suggested.

With the aroma of burned beans in the air, we bowed over the pot, and I began to pray, reminding the Lord of the time He had taken the death out of the pot when a young man had placed poisonous gourds in the soup. Remembering that Elisha had added a little flour to the pot and declared the soup edible, I thought that surely it would be easier for the Lord to remove the burned taste from the beans than poison from the pot. After the prayer we both took a spoon to taste the soup. "Delicious!" I declared.

"It's fine!" said Ann. The soup had been saved. God did it! A modern-day miracle.

Rita Kay Stevens

Blessings, Anyone?

Open your mouth wide, and I will fill it. Ps. 81:10, NKJV.

THE OTHER DAY I ventured into a department store to do a bit of shopping. I needed to buy a few tops—blue, red, and a print. So I began my pilgrimage through the store where I saw myriads of blue, red, and print tops. But none appealed to me. They were either too small, too big, too unsuited to my taste, or, most of all, too expensive. After roaming the store in futility for more than an hour, I was ready to give up.

Suddenly my husband appeared, grinning boyishly behind an armload of clothing. I eyed him enviously. He had actually found some treasures. "Where are the things you came to get?" he questioned in disbelief.

"I—I couldn't find anything that I liked that much," I replied sheepishly.

"Do you mean that you found nothing in this huge store?" Typical male response!

I decided to make another attempt. In less than five minutes I discovered a beautiful print blouse on the bargain rack. Then after a few paces, there was a stunning blue top, begging for my attention. Suddenly I was finding things! My heart danced with glee.

Many times we walk aimlessly in our world, almost without a dedicated purpose. We take a fleeting glance at life as a whole and miss the unique and singular blessings that are scattered here and there in our path. We see this big world as a place of stress, disarray, and disappointments. What is there in it for us? With this mind-set we miss the lessons, and even the bargains, of experiences that are all around us. Then we give up in despair. We even convince ourselves that we don't need the blessings after all, and deprive ourselves of joy and satisfaction while others are enjoying God's blessings and happiness. If only we would look we would find a blessing here, and a lesson there, tucked away on the rack of our experience.

Today is another day of opportunities. This new day presents itself to us with a chance to search for opportunities and blessings to enjoy. Good things are all around us. Jesus wants us to seek so that we may find. He wants to fill our mouths with blessings. He is waiting to shower us with His blessings, not just to sprinkle mercy drops upon us. Our God is abundant. "Oh, taste and see" (Ps. 34:8, NKJV). I urge you to face today with determination to celebrate God's blessings.

Gloria Lindsey Trotman

Hope and a Future

"I know the plans I have for you," declares the Lord, "plans to prosper you and not to harm you, plans to give you hope and a future." Jer. 29:11, NIV.

MATTHEW 6:34 STATES, "Therefore do not worry about tomorrow, for tomorrow will worry about itself. Each day has enough trouble of its own" (NIV). For as long as I can remember, this verse from Matthew has been my favorite Bible verse. As a teenager and young adult who had suffered from depression for many years, as well as obsessive compulsive disorder (OCD) and separation anxiety, this verse was my rock. It helped me remember that I needed to take only one small step at a time, one day at a time, and that in small doses I could handle anything through Christ.

After years of loving this Bible verse and, in effect, having it as a goal for me to remember how to deal with difficult life circumstances and challenges, I often still felt dismayed and a little frustrated with how I pictured my time here on earth. It wasn't until recently when reading a Christian novel series that I came across today's Bible verse: "I know the plans I have for you," declares the Lord, "plans to prosper you and not to harm you, plans to give you hope and a future." That's when I really understood what God had been trying to tell me all these years. Not only do I need to take each day at a time, slowly but surely surviving my depression, but I can take *on* each day, knowing that God has a plan for me and that these plans are to prosper me, to give me hope and a future, and not to harm me in any way.

Since realizing these truths and forming a deeper understanding of God's character and will for my life, my depression, OCD, and separation anxiety have all reduced until they have only a minimal impact upon my life. There are still days when I am down and life seems hopeless, but remembering these two verses has always helped bring a smile back to my face and a glimmer of hope within my heart, in even the darkest hours. Not only do I see that the Lord has plans for me here on earth, but I can look forward also to the day my Lord returns and that time when I can spend eternity with Him in heaven.

Through surrounding yourself with Christian support networks, reading His Word daily, and seeking the Lord in prayer, it is my hope that you will come to know the character and grace of God that I have, knowing and understanding that He has great plans for you.

Billie Jo Whitehurst

Teacups Over the Pacific

Great peace have those who love Your law, and nothing causes them to stumble. Ps. 119:165, NKJV.

RECENTLY MY HUSBAND attended an event at the Library of Congress in Washington, D.C., where he received a book featuring stories of men and women who served during recent wars. The Veterans' History Project amassed an archive of more than 35,000 individual stories. However, only 37 made the final cut and are published in *Forever a Soldier!*

When my husband left for work the next morning, I picked up the book; I was transported back to memories of my childhood. It was during this time that my father said goodbye to us and left to serve his stint in World War II. This was a very sad and challenging time for my family, but because my brother and I were very young at the time we understood very little. Our happiest days were when we received a letter from him, letting us know he was safe.

One summer day I remember the mailman stopping by our house with a package. This brought great excitement to my brother and me, as we were filled with anticipation. We soon discovered the package was from our father and had come all the way from the Philippines. With great eagerness we waited while our mother slowly opened it. Little by little we uncovered a box filled with delicate, hand-painted plates with matching cups and saucers. Our mother told us the china was as thin as an eggshell and neither of us could imagine how it had made the long journey unscathed!

Today I am the guardian of the contents of this precious box from my father. Almost 70 years have passed since that day, but I've not forgotten the first sight of the delicate china and the smile on my mother's face as she opened the box. Love had found its way from the other side of the world in the form of teacups. We also reasoned that our father must be safe if he could take the time to remember our mother with such a treasured gift.

Our dad came home in the spring of 1945 when I was 5 years old and just completing kindergarten. Reading *Forever a Soldier!* brought back these memories as if they had happened yesterday, along with the realization that not all families of soldiers were as lucky as we were. We felt grateful to God when we said our prayers that not only did the teacups make a safe journey as a signal that our father was safe, but we could continue leaving Dad in God's hands.

Rose Otis

Too Fat and Too Old to Be Beautiful?

But when you give a feast, invite the poor, the maimed, the lame, the blind. And you will be blessed. Luke 14:13, 14, NKJV.

MY 12-YEAR-OLD granddaughter is hooked on the television show *America's Top Model*, and I didn't realize until recently the extent of the show's influence on her thinking. While watching the show at our home, she asked that I bake her some chocolate-chip cookies. I refused with the excuse that I was dieting. "You shouldn't be dieting," she scolded, "because grandmothers are *supposed* to get fat when they get old!"

I laughed and said, "Poppa wouldn't like it if I got fat!"

"Why would Poppa care?" she asked. "Only young, thin girls are beautiful, and you're *way* too old to *ever* be beautiful—so you might as well bake me some cookies!"

Needless to say, she was shocked when I told her that Poppa thought I *was* beautiful!

But weren't her remarks indicative of how the world values beauty? We value beauty because it often brings rank, power, money, and prestige. How many of us look at models and actresses and yearn to look like them? Then we feel that we must work very hard to measure up—or else we feel totally unworthy! And let's face it, our self-confidence and our self-worth often are tied to our looks. We women seem to place a higher value on people who look sharp. How do we grow to the point that we stop measuring each other by looks, rank, power, money, and prestige, and start measuring ourselves and our value by God's standard?

Some years ago a school of theology was seeking a new president. More than 100 candidates applied for the position, and the search committee narrowed the list to five equally qualified persons. Then somebody suggested that they send a person to the institutions where each of the five finalists was employed and interview the janitor at each place, asking him what he thought of the person seeking to be president. This was done, and one janitor gave such a glowing appraisal of William McElvaney that he was selected president of St. Paul's School of Theology. Somebody on that search committee understood, in a flash of genius, that those who live close to Christ become so secure in His love that they no longer relate to other people according to their looks, rank, power, or money. Janitors and governors are treated with equal dignity. And they *never* care that they don't meet the television industry's idea of beauty!

Ellie Green

Salt Is Healthy

It is not the healthy who need a doctor, but the sick. Mark 2:17, NIV.

PLAIN TABLE SALT is an important element for our bodies. I visited my husband every day during one of his hospitalizations. Our son and our nephew were visiting and decided to get something to eat. As they left I rose from the chair to join them. Without any symptoms or warning, the next thing I knew I was stretched out on the sofa with many medical personnel surrounding me. Realizing I hadn't suffered a stroke, they took me to the emergency room against my will. After many tests I was admitted to the hospital on a different wing but the same floor as my husband.

I was given more tests to get a diagnosis. It was the "table tilt" test that revealed the problem. For this test the patient is strapped flat to a table and gradually raised upright to a standing position.

I fainted on the second elevation. The physician then knew the problem.

My prescription was to add salt to my food and drink plenty of water. You see, my husband had been diagnosed with high blood pressure years before. To help him, I no longer used salt while cooking, and as much as I could, I eliminated salt from my food. I could eat an egg without salt. I never did drink a lot of water, so coupled with loss of sodium in my body, it took its toll. Now when I eat and people see me sprinkling salt, they want to chastise me. I just kindly say, "Doctor's orders."

The Lord has promised to restore our bodies and heal our wounds. However, we have a responsibility to do what we can to keep our bodies in a healthy condition as much as we can. I thank the Lord that I didn't have any serious problem. Now when I feel a bit faint, I know it's because I haven't followed the prescription.

In the age in which we live, with so many aches and pains caused by diseases and maladies, we should eat to live. The Lord has given us a book of prescriptions: the Bible. All we have to do is follow it. Nevertheless, I look forward to the day when Christ comes and there will be no more sickness, no more disease. There will be no need for physicians or hospitals, for we will eat from the tree of life, bearing 12 crops of fruit, yielding its fruit every month, and the leaves will be for the healing of the nations. I want to be there. What about you?

Marie H. Seard

Trust in Jehovah

Trust in the Lord with all your heart and lean not on your own understanding; in all your ways acknowledge him, and he will make your paths straight.
Prov. 3:5, 6, NIV.

I AM THE oldest sister of six siblings. Since I was very young I wished to study in a Christian school. However, for my primary and secondary school years I studied in government schools. I lived out in a province, and when I heard of the Peruvian Union University in Lima, the capital of Peru, I wanted to go there. I read a leaflet in the adult Sabbath school Bible study guide about the school and thought, *This university is only for young people who have a lot of money.* And that was not me. Nevertheless, God had dreams and plans for my life.

Thus, through God's leading, a year after I finished high school I entered the Peruvian Union University and worked one entire year before I could begin my university studies, for my family didn't have the economic means to pay for my studies. During this time there were sad and discouraging moments, as well as happy and motivating moments. But Jesus was always by my side, guiding me, encouraging me, covering my needs one way or another. I began some semesters with no money to cover even the registration, but somehow I was still able to study.

As I write this I am now in my tenth and last semester of college. One of the ways in which God helped me cover part of my account is through the women's ministries scholarships from these devotional books sold in South America. Of course I am very grateful to the women who write these devotionals and support this scholarship program—it has made such a difference for my life.

Now, after seven years, I am one month from my graduation in December. I still do not have money to cover the final costs of this education and graduation, but I have faith in God that He will continue to provide the resources. And thus I know I will conclude my studies and will go on to serve and fulfill the mission that Christ has given to me on this earth.

Something beautiful that I have learned in this university is to trust, believe, and depend on Jehovah. I, of course, thank God who has been so faithful to me. "O Lord, you are my God; I will exalt you and praise your name, for in perfect faithfulness you have done marvelous things, things planned long ago" (Isa. 25:1, NIV). Do you also have things for which to praise God?

Olinda Milagros Rojas Valle

Crooked Pinkies

So God created man in his own image, in the image of God he created him; male and female he created them. Gen. 1:27, NIV.

"DOES SHE HAVE crooked pinkies?" I asked my oldest son, Greg, a few hours after his wife delivered their first child. I could hardly wait for his answer. We had talked many times before about our family trait—crooked pinkies—and chuckled about how people had reacted to them over the years. Maybe Avery had crooked pinkies too.

"I don't know, Ma," he answered. "Her hands are so tiny, I was afraid to touch them. But she's got big dimples, like me." As I held the phone and heard more about my newest little granddaughter, I could picture Greg's deep dimples and his winning smile.

The next day Greg called again. "Yep, she has my crooked pinkies," he said proudly.

I saw them for myself a few days later. How cute they were, and so curved. One curved considerably more than the other, just like Greg's fingers, and just like mine. I immediately thought back to Greg's birth and how I discovered his pinkies as I held him a few hours after he was born. And now Avery, a beautiful baby created in the image of her father, grandmother, great-grandfather, and many other ancestors who had perhaps inherited them too. I was ecstatic knowing my newest granddaughter had the family trait, even though Greg had told me a year before that he had researched crooked pinkies and found out that it was a birth defect, a minor congenital malformation caused by underdevelopment of the middle bone in the finger. It was called clinodactyly, curving of the little finger toward the ring finger.

How ecstatic God must have been—creating man and woman in His own image—knowing that they would be like Him in mind and character, His perfect creations. And how sad when the beauty of His handiwork was marred by sin, and the resulting evil passed down to every generation since—God's characteristics masked by wicked thoughts, words, and actions. I see it every day in the attitudes of my three older granddaughters whose sweet and adorable innocence is being replaced with mean-spirited behavior. I see it in my own unChristlike attitude and deeds as I encounter work colleagues, grocery store clerks, or unkind neighbors. I see it in church members who profess the love of God and greet each other with a hug but turn away to gossip or stir up controversy. God's family traits, part of our DNA, are missing.

Iris L. Kitching

Finding a Pearl

Again, the kingdom of heaven is like a merchant looking for fine pearls.
When he found one of great value, he went away and sold
everything he had and bought it. Matt. 13:45, 46, NIV.

I ACTUALLY DID find a pearl at sea. This is how it happened. About 10 years ago my husband and I went to Australia to visit my son. This was our first visit, and David had planned all sorts of nice things for us. One of these nice things was a trip to a subtropical island for a two-night stay. This was to be a trip of a lifetime for us, something that was only in my dreams.

We set off from Brisbane with about 150 people on a boat. We all settled down on deck, in rows; it seemed packed. It was a lovely day, and everyone was set to enjoy the experience. At sea my eyes were drawn to a woman sitting opposite me. She was looking at me, too, and our eyes locked. We each knew the other was praying. We were drawn to each other in such a strong way that it could only be God. When someone vacated a chair, this dear woman came over to sit beside us. And this was the beginning of the "David and Jonathan" friendship with Pearl.

When we reached Tangalooma Island, we went to our separate rooms. All the people had breakfast in one big communal dining room, but the hours were staggered, and we didn't meet. Pearl, however, wanted to meet us again. As some of the people stayed only one night, Pearl didn't know whether or not we'd be leaving by evening ferry. That dear woman walked all the way to the ferry to watch the passengers boarding. We were not there, so her hope revived.

The next morning, when we entered the large dining room, Pearl spotted us and quickly came over to us. We had such a bear hug, right in the middle of the dining room! Later we were thrilled to spend time together. Although from different countries and not having known each other before, we felt so close to each other in Jesus.

When we left the Island we bade a fond farewell. She gave me her address, and we wrote to each other. We exchanged books and loved hymns, Bible verses, and so many stories of God's goodness. We were able to share so much. My daughter makes beautiful "promise boxes" with more than 100 Bible verses. The exquisite embroidery makes each a real treasure. Pearl just loves hers. We thought we would never meet again, but we have met several times since, and each time has been as precious. I thank God He allowed me to find a Pearl! A special friend can be your pearl as well!

Monica Vesey

Love Begets Love

For consider him that endured such contradiction of sinners against himself, lest ye be wearied and faint in your minds. Heb. 12:3.

MANY TIMES WE meet people who are pretty difficult to love. There are those who seem to drain us of all our energies not because they are particularly unlovable, but because to love them is a sacrifice that comes from within oneself. They don't give of themselves—they don't know how. We think that sometimes the easier way to deal with these individuals is to simply present them with a "form of love" a "form of caring." We think we love them, care about them, show concern for them, but at the same time we build fortresses around ourselves to protect us from the arrows that they too often shoot at our hearts. We choose the offensive strategy that works to protect us from hurt before it can be fostered. We don't give. We're simply posed to defend ourselves. This, however, isn't God's design of love.

The Bible says that we aren't to be weary in well doing, but in due season we shall reap our reward. For if God could be so merciful to give His only Son for our good then should we not be willing to give of ourselves to others? Our heavenly Father doesn't show love to us because He pities us or wants to feel better about Himself. He is the I Am that I Am. He is our God all by Himself; He doesn't need to love us. He just loves. He doesn't change when we do not love Him back. He doesn't change when we disregard His ultimate sacrifice for our sins. He doesn't change when we turn our backs in anger against Him. He just loves us. He accepts us, and sees it fitting to make us a part of His family. He loves us even when we choose not to love Him back. He just loves, and loves, and *loves!*

What an amazing God! He is a God who is the same yesterday, today, and forever. He is the only God who accepts our brokenness and our shortcomings. He is the one who sees the ugliness in us and still chooses to embrace us as the precious jewels of His kingdom. He loves us unreservedly, unconditionally. We can feel safe under His wings. Let us choose to accept God's love today and reflect His love to those who come into our lives—the good, the bad, and the ugly. Accept everyone as a child of the King. Love because He loves. Don't give up. He will help us love others as He loves us!

Shanter H. Alexander

Cry Out to Him

Pour out your heart like water in the presence of the Lord. Lift up your hands to him for the lives of your children. Lam. 2:19, NIV.

HAVE YOU BEEN in anguish because of concern for your children? Have you felt that you need to intercede for them? This is what Jeremiah advised if you read all of verse 19: rise up and cry out at night for your children. In the book *Handle With Prayer* Charles Stanley states, "Remember that the shortest distance between a problem and its solution is the distance between our knees and the floor." We can pray for our children, or children of our church and community.

Do you believe this? Our children need our prayers and our intercession. *Lord, thank You because You are omniscient, omnipresent, and omnipotent. You always know what is best for us.* The Lord tells us to ask, seek, and knock because the Lord loves us and supplies all of our needs (see Matt. 7:7).

Our need at this time is to pray for our children. *Please, Lord, place a protection around them. Have mercy according to Your lovingkindness.*

We ask the Holy Spirit to work in their lives and implement all that they have learned from God's Word. Guide them in the paths of justice for Your name's sake.

Lord, deliver them from unhealthy friendships; protect them from the bad influences of people. Accomplish Your will in their lives today. May they know how to distinguish right from wrong and have the courage to choose what is right. Bless them in their work and in their studies. Lord, there are no limits to what can be accomplished by these dedicated youth, gifted with the power of the Holy Spirit and supported by the prayers of their mothers.

Jesus prayed for His disciples and we mothers pray for our children. *Keep them from sinning against You. May the fruit of the Holy Spirit be manifest in their lives. May these children become generators of power, capable of transforming the world. Among them will be workers who will help to lead toward the salvation of the world.*

The Lord is searching for people through whom He can change the world, and He wants to use all the children around us. We can thank Him who will supply all of the necessities of each child according to His glorious riches in Christ Jesus (Phil. 4:19).

Susana Faria

A New View

We will all be changed. 1 Cor. 15:51, NIV.

THIS WEEK I saw something new at my house. We have a chair sitting in the entry of our home. For months it has been near the tower facing the door, but this week I placed a plant on the tower, so I moved the chair across the room. Then I opened the door so the sun could shine in. Later I sat down in the chair and looked out. Framed by the doorjambs, the front yard blazing with fall colors, presented a whole new scene. A red tree behind the evergreen magnolia glistened above the junipers in the morning light. I had seen all those plants before, but never from that perspective. What a difference a new outlook can make!

At the risk of sounding preachy, I'd like to present an old story I love even though it's not true; it makes my point. An early winter storm swept through the Swiss Alps. It was unexpected, but the monks had learned never to be surprised by such weather. All the dogs dozed peacefully on the floor except Barry. He was the largest and most noble of the Saint Bernards. Now he fretted at the door, pawing.

Finally Brother Philip unbarred the door, and Barry disappeared into the darkness. "It may be that a traveler has been caught on the mountain. Barry will find him."

There was a traveler caught in the storm. Young Franco Martin had struggled on for a few miles, but now he was sinking into a freezing stupor. As the bulky shape of the big dog approached, Franco aroused. *An enemy is trying to harm me,* he thought. With his final strength he drew his knife and plunged it into the big body hovering over him.

With a sharp yelp of pain, Barry stumbled back up the mountain. The monks had been watching and were already prepared to follow him. No one noticed the dog's wound as they followed Barry closely. In the darkness they didn't notice his blood dripping on the snow.

They found Franco and wrapped him warmly in the heavy blankets. As they began the return, Brother Philip turned to praise Barry. But it was too late. The great form lay still.

Now move the chair and look at the scenery from a different angle. In the familiar scene we are encouraged in our Christian experience to get involved with soul winning. Everyone has a certain degree of commitment to the Lord and His work. But move the chair. Am I involved, or am I committed? Am I a monk, or the dog? To use a nonvegetarian illustration, it's like ham and eggs. The chicken is involved, but the pig is committed.

Beth Wells Carlson

So Many Blessings!

He will bless them that fear the Lord, both small and great. The Lord shall increase you more and more, you and your children. Ye are blessed of the Lord which made heaven and earth. Ps. 115:13-15.

SOME TIME AGO during our morning devotion we read about a woman who in times of great distress had made a decision to begin a "Blessing Journal." This got me thinking about the many blessings in my life, wondering if there was a way I could record them so that they'd be there to remind me of God's goodness when I lapse into a state of ingratitude and complaining.

There is the blessing of my husband and son. There are times when things are difficult in the day-to-day existence and the realities of marriage stare me in the face, and my beautiful child gets on my last existing half a nerve. Then I remember how aimless my life was without them, and how they are a direct answer to many prayers I've prayed.

I thank God for my mother who is such a blessing to me and my family. At times she wants me to take her places with no regard to my agenda, and I am tempted to fuss. Then I'm reminded of those who have no mother to visit or even call on the telephone. I also remember how much help she is to us in raising our son and doing all the cooking in our home.

I thank God for the blessing of good health and the ability to work. More often than not I complain about how busy I am and how tired I feel; then I am reminded of those who would like to get up and move around and cannot. Or those who want employment and can find no work.

I thank God for using me in His work, even though I may be a reluctant subject and complain bitterly about how hard it is. I thank Him that I can be a blessing to someone else.

My in-laws are another great blessing in my life. I often hear folks around me complaining about their in-laws, but I can do nothing but sing their praises. My father-in-law likes to say, "I have run out of receptacles to collect all the blessings the Lord is sending to me. I need to find some more." That quotation always encourages me and halts my complaining spirit.

Let's daily reflect on the little things that show us how blessed we are: the ability to breathe and get out of bed, the ability to walk, talk, work and get tired; mercies as we go about our daily activities; a loving and caring family.

Raylene McKenzie Ross

Ever Thankful

In everything give thanks. 1 Thess. 5:18, NKJV.

THERE ARE TIMES I wonder if etiquette and good manners are still with us. Some folks I've talked to say, "It seems that some young people—and even some older folks—rarely say 'Thank you' these days when you give them something, or when you've done them a favor."

Have we really become a thankless generation? After reading Tom Brokaw's *The Greatest Generation,* I was convinced that the stories were of folks who were thankful and appreciated the values of their society so that they accomplished so much with so little.

What is it about good manners that can never be considered outdated or old-fashioned? First of all, who doesn't want to be liked and have friends? Who doesn't want to make their world a more pleasant place to live in, or be a more pleasing person to live with? We therefore have a time-tested code of behavior akin to the Ten Commandments.

When I was about to leave home for college thousands of miles away, my mother asked me to say goodbye to all our close neighbors as I might not see them again for some time. I wouldn't be able to fly home every year, because airfares were expensive in the 1950s, and my father couldn't afford it. As I bade my neighbors goodbye, I was touched by their good wishes, and so many gave me monetary gifts, as well. I didn't expect this generosity and thanked them so much for their kindness. I also wrote them thank-you notes, and I'm glad I did, because when I returned home three years later, some had passed away or moved away.

The Bible has given us many examples of people who were thankful. In the book of Psalms David wrote prolifically of blessings, praises, and thanksgiving for all the glorious things God had done not only for him, but for all humanity. Daniel thanked and praised the Lord for revealing to him the dream of King Nebuchadnezzar. We also have an example of thankfulness—and unthankfulness—when Jesus healed the 10 lepers but only one of them was thoughtful enough to thank Him. We could cite many examples of thankful men and women in the Bible, but our greatest example is Jesus, who always thanked His Father, as recorded throughout the Gospels. He even said grace before partaking of any food.

With Jesus as my example, I pray that thankfulness will never go out of style for me.

Aileen L. Young

A Harvest of Gratitude

For as the soil makes the sprout come up and a garden causes seeds
to grow, so the Sovereign Lord will make righteousness and praise
spring up before all nations. Isa. 61:11, NIV.

THE GRAINS ARE harvested. Our garden produce has been gathered in and stored for use during the winter months. The fields are cultivated and ready for winter. The whole scene is almost like we have tucked the fields and gardens into bed for a good rest. From the earth we have received grains and vegetables to nourish our bodies and sustain us from day to day. The harvest has been bountiful this year, and for this harvest our hearts are filled with gratitude.

The early settlers of Massachusetts had hearts filled with gratitude as they celebrated the first Thanksgiving feast to commemorate their survival through their first year in this new land. Tribulations had been a great part of their experience. The hardships had increased their heartfelt belief that only God could have guided them in knowing how to survive. They were truly thankful for this and for the friendship of the Native American people who taught and helped them.

Thinking of the history of the Thanksgiving holiday and our planned celebrations, it's good for us to think of the gratitude we have in our hearts. Through the years, how have we reaped a harvest of gratitude? Each of us will have a long list of things for which we are thankful. Most of us would begin our list by saying we are thankful for our spouse, our children, extended family, our homes, our health, and the success we are enjoying in our careers.

I would challenge you to think of those things that go deeper. My list keeps growing as I contemplate those things for which I am thankful. Peace of mind is high on my list. Knowing that I am content with who I am and sharing that sense of contentment with family and friends has been a blessing to me. Living in our wonderful country is also something which fills me with gratitude. The blessing we have of living in this part of the world and in our community has given our family a multitude of friends. Individually, we can add to our personal list as we search our hearts and find the reason for our own harvest of gratitude. Each day we can add another reason for gratitude to our list. Enumerating our blessings will enhance our joy and thankfulness.

Those who have an attitude of thankfulness, in spite of trials and tribulations, will have an abundant harvest of gratitude.

Evelyn Glass

Seeing the Fallen Sparrows

What is the price of two sparrows—one copper coin? But not a single
sparrow can fall to the ground without your Father knowing it.
Matt. 10:29, NLT.

The small tan dog darted between cars near a busy intersection. Drivers swerved to
avoid it. "Melissa, jump out and try to get her out of the road, and I'll pull into that
lane ahead," I urged my daughter, who was already halfway out the car door.

Melissa managed to steer the confused and frightened dog off the road and into
the lane. It was then we noticed its pitiful condition. Its thin body and grimy, matted fur spoke of neglect. Its evasive reaction whenever we would reach down to pet
it was a sure sign of abuse. We also noticed its swollen mammary glands. "She must
be nursing puppies," Melissa said. "If we take her to the animal shelter and she has
puppies somewhere, they'll likely die."

A woman driving a van then pulled into the lane and stopped next to us.
"That's my dog," she said. "Is there a problem?"

Melissa explained that we had rescued the dog from the busy road and thought
it might be a stray. "Well, the dog is mine," the woman said, "but I don't want her.
Just take her." She told us she had thrown the dog out of the house and hadn't been
feeding her, hoping she would just go away. She then added, "She has an 8-week-
old puppy. You can take her, too."

What else could we do? We drove off with two additional passengers sitting on
my daughter's lap. Melissa and I just looked at each other in disbelief over what had
just happened.

Melissa works part-time at a veterinary clinic, and posting pictures of mom and baby
brought quick results. Both are now enjoying comfortable lives with loving owners.

This story has a happy ending, but countless others do not. Some might ask, "In
the midst of tragedies and wars in which countless human lives are lost, does God
still care about neglected pets and other abused animals, even the fallen sparrows?"
I have to believe that He does.

"Animals see and hear and love and fear and suffer," Ellen G. White wrote in
The Ministry of Healing (p. 315). And in *Patriarchs and Prophets* (p. 443) she adds,
"He who will abuse animals because he has them in his power is both a coward and
a tyrant . . . and a day is coming when judgment will be pronounced against those
who abuse God's creatures."

Sandra Blackmer

Angels in Waiting

And it shall come to pass, that before they call, I will answer; and while they are yet speaking, I will hear. Isa. 65:24.

IN LIFE WE are all bound to have trials, but God in His infinite wisdom has already put a plan in place to help us. God loves us so much that He sends the right people at the right time to help us.

My husband, James, was rushed to the hospital. As I had done so many times before, I made the 90-minute drive to be with him. During the next two months that James would be in intensive care, I would need somewhere to stay and a way to get to and from the hospital daily. It never occurred to me that I would need more money to purchase food. God knew that I would be in need of help and He prepared an "angel in waiting" in the form of Sister Whatley. This special woman opened her home to me, providing me with a place to sleep, breakfast each morning, and even a ride to and from the hospital each day. She even washed my clothes. I still had more needs to be met, so the Lord brought into my life another special woman. Dr. Callins provided me with food, cash for future meals, encouragement, and the pleasure of her company.

Having just started home schooling our five adopted children for the second year, I realized I couldn't be in two places at one time. God knew this day would come, and He prepared another "angel in waiting" in the form of Sister Miller. This very special woman worked with all five of our children for an entire semester. When a storm knocked a tree down on her home and she had to move out during the repairs, she continued to faithfully work with the children.

I've learned how to take care of Jim's medical procedures. During the long hospital stay, transition home, and getting used to doing so many different things for him, I needed help caring for my children and home. The "angels in waiting" this time were my parents, Dortha and Theodore Swanson, and my adult children, Shayna and Willie Brantley. There were others who helped in various ways, and all of these "angels" helped at their own expense and received no compensation.

Caring for James, the children, and the house is very stressful. When I'm about to snap, God sends "angels in waiting" to help and encourage me. Let us trust God—He is ever faithful.

Theodora V. Sanders

My Blunt Knives

Till we all come in the unity of the faith, and of the knowledge of the Son of God, unto a perfect man, unto the measure of the stature of the fulness of Christ: that we henceforth be no more children, tossed to and fro, and carried about with every wind of doctrine, by the sleight of men, and cunning craftiness, whereby they lie in wait to deceive; but speaking the truth in love, may grow up into him in all things, which is the head, even Christ. Eph. 4:13-15.

FOR MONTHS I'VE been shopping for a good sharp knife. I have so many knives in my drawer, but they are all blunt. My search for a good knife began when a friend invited us for a weekend. I volunteered to prepare the salad, and as I chopped the parsley the knife just went very smoothly, no effort needed. "Wow!" I exclaimed. "This is a good knife!"

I bought several knives after that, but I wasn't satisfied. They weren't sharp like my friend's knife, and not sharp enough for my salads.

One day as I helped a friend in her kitchen, I noticed that before she used the knife she had a long iron-looking thing she called a sharpener that she used to sharpen the knife. I asked if I could try it, and after using it, I was amazed. It worked! The knife became so sharp!

The next day at home I decided to try it. I don't have a sharpener, so I used another knife on my favorite knife. And it worked! I couldn't believe how sharp my knife became. My searching was over. I have all the knives I need—all I have to do is sharpen them.

As I contemplated this, two things came to mind: First, we have all that we really need to be good, sharp Christians: Christians whom people would like to have around, Christians who lead people to exclaim, "This is good!" Yes, we have everything within our reach and at our call. Our Bibles are there to guide us and to sharpen our faith. God is just a prayer away from us; He is the one who can make us good and sharp.

Second, it tells me that we are God's knives, His tools to penetrate into the hearts of people. But before He can use us effectively He first sharpens us that we may be knowledgeable about His will for us and His people. So as we go through the "sharpening" process, as we go through hardship and trials in life, know that we are being sharpened for His service. Only after the sharpening do we become polished, loving, and lovable Christians.

Jemima Dollosa Orillosa

A Face to Remember

For now we see in a mirror, dimly, but then we will see face to face.
1 Cor. 13:12, NRSV.

MY TRIP TO Italy was a memorable experience. However, the first five days were a little more memorable than I would have wished for.

I was scheduled for the 12-day trip to conduct workshops. I left Washington, D.C., at 3:00 p.m. on a Wednesday afternoon, and arrived at my final destination in Italy (after four different flights) Thursday afternoon. Unfortunately, I got only a couple hours' sleep on the plane. I collapsed in my bed at 7:00 p.m., eagerly anticipating a solid night's sleep. I awoke at 10:30 p.m., wide-eyed and far from falling back to sleep.

This pattern occurred for five nights. The stress on my body from lack of sleep, lack of exercise, a change in eating habits, and conducting back-to-back workshops while having to be translated, took their toll. By Sunday evening the cortisol levels in my body were so high that I experienced an eczematic reaction. Half my face was red, swollen, and itchy. In addition to the physiological effects of the flare-up were the psychological effects: I looked about 10 years older—and my ego was not handling this well. I don't feel the need to look 20 years old when I'm in my mid-40s, but I also don't like the idea of looking like I'm in my mid-50s, either!

After another flight and suffering the loss of my luggage, I settled in at Villa Aurora, the college in Florence, where I was to teach a couple of classes for the seminary students for several days. It was here that I began to heal. But healing isn't always confined to the physical.

At breakfast one morning I sat with Laura, one of the seminary students. I knew very little Italian, and she very little English. But through helping each other we were able to communicate well. At one point in our conversation she looked at me, used her hand to make a circle in front of her face, and said, "You have a peaceful face."

At that moment I came to see my vanity for what it was. I had been feeling anxious because my face looked older than it should. But now I realized that in spite of all that stress and anxiety—possibly even because of it—God could work to allow others to see what really mattered: the fruit of His Spirit. This experience made me realize that when all is said and done, the memorable moments for those with whom we come in contact will be when we have allowed God to work through us so others can see *His* face. His face is much more memorable than mine.

Bonita Joyner Shields

A Night Meeting With Prayer

*Before they call I will answer; while they are still speaking I will hear.
Isa. 65:24, NIV.*

I'D BEEN WORKING so hard for two weeks that nothing seemed clear anymore, and nothing seemed to be going right. During the first week I felt as if I experienced more confusion than anything. Adding to an already stressful week, my computer, my printer, and my mouse—all of which were only 2 months old—decided they weren't going to work. And my 2,000-word essay was due the next day.

At this point my spiritual state seemed to be diminishing by the moment. Nevertheless, I decided to open my Bible for guidance, and the Lord led me to this text: "And being in anguish, he prayed more earnestly, and his sweat was like drops of blood falling to the ground" (Luke 22:44, NIV). This Bible text, referring to Jesus, brought something to my attention that I had never noticed before. Even though Jesus was the Son of God, He still had to cry out to His Father in prayer, with great intensity.

My silent prayer to God that evening was for Him to move me to pray as Jesus had. I continued asking Him to have mercy on me, to allow me to witness a miracle. What I wanted and needed intensely was for my electronics to work—and for His glory alone. Continuing my Bible study through the evening and early hours of the morning, God led me to read the entire Gospel. I wanted a deeper experience of prayer, to see God move. He led me to these words from Jesus: "If you believe, you will receive whatever you ask for in prayer" (Matt. 21:22, NIV).

At 6:00 a.m. a fresh awareness of God overwhelmed me, and sleep never seemed so peaceful. I awoke after just a couple hours of sleep. Furthermore, my computer was working, as were the mouse and the printer. Let's just say I received more than I could have ever imagined. God taught me that night how easy life is when we stop looking at our situation and return our focus to the One who can overcome anything. Even though my recent attitude didn't deserve any mercy from Him at all, let alone a miracle, His love for me, His child, brought the answer to my humble prayer.

My prayer today for everyone who reads these words is that no matter what life brings to you during your journey with Christ, always remember the power of His name.

Deon Dill

God's Word Preserved

And the angel of the Lord appeared unto him in a flame of fire out of the midst of a bush: and he looked, and, behold, the bush burned with fire, and the bush was not consumed. Ex. 3:2.

DUSK WAS APPROACHING. The evening was quiet, the neighborhood tranquil. The occupants of the house were all out. All of a sudden a scream was heard: "Fire! Fire!"

The fire was of mysterious origin that quickly enveloped the entire building. Neighbors formed bucket brigades and doused the building with water, but to no avail. By this time the fire engine arrived on the scene. The firefighters got their hoses attached to the water supply in the area but only could prevent the fire from spreading to houses nearby. The house was burned flat.

The family members got word of the raging fire and returned home, only to view the embers and remains of the house that was once their home. Everything they owned was lost to the conflagration—or so they thought. The owner of the house, who migrated overseas, had left four of her children living in the house. The building was cared for by one of her siblings who lived two houses away.

The following day, after the fire department gave approval, family members combed through the debris to see what valuables could be salvaged. To their amazement, there was one item they had not lost. The *Holy Bible*, God's holy Word, which had been laid on the head of a bed in one of the bedrooms, was found intact, though the bed had been completely consumed. No trace of the other furniture could be seen. Only the ashes were left, but the Word of God was preserved.

While those of us who were members of the church were aware of the fire that destroyed the home, we didn't know of the miraculous preservation of God's Word. The following Sabbath our church pastor shared the testimony of the Bible that was removed from the ashes of a house that was burned flat; and the evidence of that miracle was brought to church for all to see—the Bible that had been pulled from the ashes.

The experience of Moses at the burning bush comes to mind. The fire burned, but neither the bush nor the Bible was consumed, testimony to God's awesome supremacy and presence in our circumstances. God allows these experiences to draw our attention to Him and to remind us of His awesome might and power.

Ruby H. Enniss-Alleyne

He Carries You and Me

And in the wilderness, where thou hast seen how that the
Lord thy God bare thee, as a man doth bear his son, in all
the way that ye went, until ye came into this place. Deut. 1:31.

ONE OF MY favorite poems is "Footprints in the Sand" in which the writer re-
counts a life with the Lord. In the "sands of life" could be seen clearly two sets of
footprints, representing a life lived with God. As the writer looked on in her dream
there were instances when only one set of footprints was present. She later discovered that God had not left her, as she thought, but rather He had carried her.

We are God's little children, and just the way we carry our own children and
offer comfort and support to them is how God takes care of us. It is so comforting
to know that we have such a loving heavenly Father who knows exactly what we
need and supplies those needs. The portion of Scripture for today's meditation is an
excerpt from the experience of the children of Israel as they journeyed through the
wilderness on their way to the Promised Land. God led them for 40 years and provided for them. They had no pharmacy, no shopping malls, no grocery stores, no
schools, no telephones, and no computers. How, then, did they survive? God was
their leader. He provided food (manna), shelter (the pillar of cloud), and warmth
(the pillar of fire). He kept them healthy, and when they sinned and got sick, God
provided healing. God fought their battles and provided their water. The Israelites
had one thing to do: trust God completely.

We are spiritual Israel because we are Abraham's seed, heirs of the promise. We
too are on a journey; our destination—our heavenly home. On this journey we are
faced with many challenges, some overwhelming at times. We have enemies on
every hand trying to destroy us. Even though most of us have a comfortable life,
many are dissatisfied. We tend to murmur and complain as did Israel of old. Have
we also forgotten that Jesus is our Supreme Leader? Have we forgotten that God
loves us? Do we believe that everything belongs to the Lord? God wants us to trust
Him, He wants us to look to Him, and He desires that we live holy lives.

God is faithful; all His promises are sure. There is absolutely no need for worry,
fear, or doubt. When the journey gets difficult; God will send the help we need. And
when human help is not enough, Jesus will carry us as parents carry their sons and
daughters. Let us trust Him!

Jacqueline Hope HoShing-Clarke

The Gift of Life

Greater love hath no man than this, that a man
lay down his life for his friends. John 15:13.

MY HUSBAND AND I are the proud parents of two girls. Shortly after our second daughter, Shelley, was born, we learned that she had cystic fibrosis. Nevertheless, Shelley lived through her childhood and early adulthood as a healthy, active, happy child. But at the age of 24, one year after she was married, she became very ill with a flu virus that collapsed both lungs, leaving her with only 17 percent lung capacity. The doctors then felt that it was the time for a lung transplant, and she was placed on the transplant list.

After a few months it was realized that cadaver lungs couldn't be obtained in time, and the doctors suggested that she have a live donor transplant. Feeling that this was the answer to our prayers, all of the family and her husband were tested to type our blood. To our dismay, all of us had different blood types than Shelley. We thought that her chances were gone.

As we discussed our situation, our other son-in-law said, "I have her blood type: I'll donate." Tears rose in my eyes as I said, "Darin, do you realize what this means?"

"Of course," he stated. "But she's my sister."

A second donor was needed. News quickly spread of our need, and 29 others were tested. After extensive testing a donor was found: Kevin, a friend Shelley had played softball with.

The day finally came, and as I stood in the pre-op area, I looked over the three gurneys that held three people I loved very much. All three would be in surgery at the same time; two would be the givers, and one the receiver. Each of the three had the chance of not making it through surgery. It was then that today's text ran through my mind. I loved my daughter so much that there wasn't anything I wouldn't do to save her. These two men who were prepared to give a part of their bodies also loved her. I wondered, how many people would do this?

I then thought about our heavenly Father and how much He loved His Son Jesus, and of the decision that they made. This world is full of people who are selfish and self-absorbed; most would deny His gift of love and tender mercy to them. But to the few who would accept Him, He gave His life so that they could escape Satan's hold and could go to live with Him forever. For the few, He told His Father, "I will go; I am the only one who can pay their price."

Pamela McPherson Ross

Chemistry

Thou shalt therefore obey the voice of the Lord thy God, and do his commandments and his statutes, which I command thee this day. Deut. 27:10.

WHEN I WAS in high school, we were required to take a chemistry class. I loved science and looked forward to the class. If we had a project during the class, we'd be assigned a lab partner and be given the specifics to follow. It reminded me of a recipe. There was a list of ingredients that were to be used in order in a particular way to receive the desired outcome. The problem I faced was that I'm not a good cook; first, because I don't follow recipes very well, and second, I'm just not a good cook.

One day my lab partner and I were assigned a science project, and we were eager to begin: our instructions in hand, supplies on the lab table, and safety goggles firmly in place. The instructions specified what chemicals to mix with other chemicals. I started off in the right direction, but then the different-colored chemicals piqued my curiosity, and I decided to mix one with another. That was not part of the instructions! Immediately a purple-like haze developed and seemed to surround my lab partner. I was so amazed by the purple color that I didn't notice that my lab partner had passed out.

I never did find out what I had created because the instructor had had enough of my creativity and kicked me out of the chemistry class, and I was sent to art class. (They must have thought there was nothing I could harm with paintbrushes.)

As I think of this funny story (well, not for my lab partner), I have to laugh. I have fond memories of the incident, and it reminds me of how many times I don't listen to the still, small voice. It is to our benefit to follow the Lord's direction through His Word. He knows the beginning from the end. How awesome is that!

I would imagine many of you are like I am, learning to follow His directions. As the old hymn says it so well: "When we walk with the Lord in the light of His word, what a glory He sheds on our way! While we do His good will, He abides with us still, and with all who will trust and obey."

That is my challenge for this day—and maybe for you, too?

Mary Wagoner-Angelin

Always Be Prepared

Trust in the Lord with all your heart; do not depend
on your own understanding. Seek his will in all you do,
and he will show you which path to take. Prov. 3:5, 6, NLT.

YOU HAVE TO be careful what you say and to whom you say it! While spending time in Spain with friends, my husband, David, was asked to tell their congregation all about the church we belonged to in Southampton, England, and the sorts of things we did. He would have preferred more notice than the 18 hours he was given, but like most men, I suspect, he was up for a challenge.

We sat quietly that Friday evening while I helped him with the task of writing about our church, including the fact that it was the first Adventist church in England, founded in the 1800s. We finally put together a nice piece to give to the church the following morning, but he was worried. "I'll be speaking in front of about 600 people," he said.

So I gave him wifely advice to buoy up his confidence. "As a lay preacher you've done this sort of thing before, maybe to a few less than 600, but just keep focused, and you'll be fine, darling!" His face told me he wasn't so sure of either my answer or my confidence in him.

Sabbath came, and we sat in the front row of a beautiful white marble church that the congregation had lovingly brought back to life, flanked by friends on either side. "You'll be great!" I whispered to my husband.

And he was. Once you give a lay preacher a pulpit, nothing will stop him. I was so proud of him! After David finished his talk and returned to his seat, a young man stopped by our pew and whispered to me, "Would you please tell a children's story for us?" My face must have been a picture—in an instant I learned that giving advice and taking it are two different things. Naturally my dutiful husband said, "Go on! You'll be great—you do them all the time at home!"

Both David and I spoke in a Spanish church to a Romanian congregation—in English! Our translators were great, and it was a Sabbath day never to be forgotten. My advice in giving someone your full support is to know that you may just get caught yourself! In giving advice and encouragement, remember: God can help you do things you've never tried before—beyond your understanding, even. But if you're depending on the Lord, He will direct you—always!

Wendy Bradley

Life With Bud the Cat

Let us therefore follow after the things which make for peace. Rom. 14:19.

I WOKE UP one morning to the sound of persistent yowling and followed it directly to our front door. There sat a little black-and-white cat that I recognized immediately. It was Bud, one of the feral cats my late neighbor had been keeping. Apparently he'd somehow escaped the clutches of ASPCA (American Society for the Prevention of Cruelty to Animals) when they came for all the neighbor's cats after she died.

As the cat kept meowing I had a sudden urge to douse it with water (which I knew must have been devil-inspired), but God squelched the urge with gentle words I could almost hear: *This is My creation too. Treat him kindly.*

I remembered a passage Ellen G. White once wrote about Jesus when He was here on earth. "His life flowed out in currents of sympathy and tenderness . . . the little creatures of the groves, the patient beasts of burden—all were happier for His presence. . . . There was nothing beneath His notice, nothing to which He disdained to minister" (*The Desire of Ages,* p. 74).

Chastened—and more sympathetic—I sought ways to help the cat. I knew he needed food, but I also knew I had nothing suitable in the house. Opening the refrigerator, I spotted some meat analog, which I put in an old plastic butter dish. Setting it on the porch outside, I watched as the cat sniffed the unfamiliar food then ate it gingerly. He finished all the food I gave him that day, and the day after that. Soon Bud became a regular addition to our household, though he was never allowed in the house. But the cat seemed to know he belonged regardless.

Now he seems to act as my protector. My neighbors tell me that whenever we are away, Bud stretches out on the front step to prevent any stranger from going into the house. My husband said he did the same thing when I had knee surgery and had to be hospitalized.

Whenever I think about Bud, I realize that God doesn't throw us away just because we aren't perfect or because we have problems or challenges. He watches over us, and even brings others—even if they are stray cats—into our lives to help us when we're in need.

And that knowledge brings me peace. I believe that Jesus used a creature of the grove to underline His love for me, for us.

Inez Payne

Mother's Answered Prayer

If ye shall ask any thing in my name, I will do it. John 14:14.

THE WINTER MONTHS in Woodland Park, Michigan, can be very cold. Sometimes the temperature drops to 20 degrees below zero, and the snow is often more than three feet deep. My nine siblings and I were raised in Woodland Park, and because our father worked in another state to support the family, our mother raised us mostly alone.

The following is a true account of an incident that happened when we were children. It happened on one of those cold days when the snow was too deep for anyone to come to our house to bring the wood we burned to heat our house.

"I had put the last pieces of wood in the stove," Mother recalled, "and I prayed, 'Lord, this is the last of the wood. When it's gone, my children and I could freeze. Please help us. In Jesus' name.'"

"Then," Mother said, "I sat in a chair, looking out the window, meditating. Seemingly out of nowhere, a wagon, drawn by two red horses, came up to the house. A young man wearing a red cap was riding on the wagon that was loaded with wood. It seemed as if the horses pulled the wagon over the snow with no effort at all. The young man unloaded the wood, returned to the wagon, and left without a word. I never saw him again. The wood lasted until the weather broke."

God answers prayers in many ways and in His own time. Sometimes He answers immediately and miraculously in dire situations, such as was experienced by our mother.

Every time I think about this incident my faith is renewed, knowing God's promises are true and faithful. He can, and will, do anything if it is His will.

I thank God for a mother who believed in prayer and who taught us to pray. Until she passed away at the age of 91, she was a faithful prayer warrior and loved studying the Bible.

We can know that God is always there for us, especially in times of need. Just trust His Word, which promises, "The Lord is good, a refuge in times of trouble. He cares for those who trust in him" (Nahum 1:7, NIV).

Moselle Slaten Blackwell

God's Mercy and Forgiveness

Forgive us our debts, as we forgive our debtors. Matt. 6:12.

SOMETIMES I FEEL so unworthy of God's wonderful grace and forgiveness. I reflect on all my bad choices and the effect they have on my life and the lives of others. When that happens, I pray and open my Bible to David's experiences. The Lord calls him a man after His own heart. But David lied and practiced deception. The psalms are replete with his pleas for mercy and forgiveness.

Then there was Jonah who rebelled against God's instructions to go to Nineveh and warn the inhabitants of the results of their sins. His story of being swallowed by a large fish, then coughed up, and taking the Lord's warning to Nineveh is certainly a striking example of God's mercy. However, the last picture we have of Jonah is of him sitting under a tree, moaning because Nineveh wasn't destroyed! What a merciful God—not only to Nineveh but to Jonah.

Let's not forget Peter. After spending three years on a day-to-day basis with his Master, at a time when Jesus needed a friend the most, Peter said, "I never knew Him." Jesus not only forgave him but gave him a profitable ministry. Peter's message is still blessing us today.

I reflect on my own experience. I married a man who was a Bible worker for the evangelistic meetings in which I learned the truths of God and joined the church. Then I learned that he was a pedophile. It was a very hard experience and took a lot of God's grace to get me through it. Later I married an unbeliever. On her deathbed his mother, who had taken care of my two children, wished for me to marry her son. I watched the Lord work on my husband's heart to convert him into a faithful follower of Jesus. Afterward I watched the devil tempt him on a weakness, causing him to lose his hold on the Lord and leave me after 28 years of marriage. It was a heartbreaking episode that drove me to my knees, once again pleading for God's mercy and comfort.

And now that I am beyond the threescore and 10 years that David writes about, I find that I need God's grace and mercy more than ever. I praise Him each day for His patience and longsuffering with me, and I am looking forward to the day I can see Him coming in the clouds of glory. I pray that somewhere along the road of my travels through life I've been able to influence someone to join me on that glad morning.

Rubye Sue

God Listens! Always!

I waited patiently for the Lord; he turned to me and heard my cry.
Ps. 40:1, NIV.

THE YEARS 2001 through 2006 were a very difficult time in my life. My relationship with my ex-husband was unbearable, filled with physical and emotional abuse. I lived an empty life day after day; the only thing that it was full of was anger—anger toward the world, and questions for God. My life was a disaster, and all I could hope for was death. Little did I know of God's plans for me.

Every time my ex-husband beat me I asked God. "Why do You let this happen to me?" I couldn't understand how this Supreme Being full of love could allow these things. I had never stolen anything, much less killed anyone, or done anything to indicate that I deserved such humiliating treatment from a person who claimed to love me.

When I thought things couldn't get worse, in 2003 I discovered that I was pregnant. This time I knew there would be no way out; I was going to have to learn to deal with it. My hopes were completely destroyed, but under such circumstances I knew, deep in my heart, that my son would give me the strength I needed, and I'd have to have pride and just leave such a life!

The real answers didn't come until January 2010, when I began my first Bible study, "The Faith of Jesus." I finally understood that God had always heard my cries of anguish and pain, and that He was always with me during this time.

God was the one who got me out of the deadly pit. He sent me far away from my ex-husband and blessed me with a wonderful new husband who worships God unconditionally. He set my feet on solid rock; He made my lips sing a new song. My heart praises God! Many people have witnessed these wonders in my life, and now they have put their trust in God. My testimony has allowed others who are living what I experienced in the past to have hope and never lose faith in God our Lord.

His promises are faithful and will be implemented fully! One such promise is recorded by David, the psalmist: "For he has not despised or disdained the suffering of the afflicted one; he has not hidden his face from him but has listened to his cry for help" (Ps. 22:24, NIV). He has held my hand in times of anguish and has never let go of me. No matter how bad or how long it has been—God listens. Always.

Vanessa Velasquez de Mejía

I'm Baptized Too

But Jesus said, Suffer little children, and forbid them not, to come unto me: for of such is the kingdom of heaven. Matt. 19:14.

IT SEEMS LIKE only yesterday, but it was really a few weeks ago that I received a very energized phone call from my niece, who is 10 years old. She stumbled over her words in excitement to tell me that she was getting baptized and wanted to know if I would be there.

"Slow down and tell me again," I replied.

"Auntie, I'm getting baptized next week by my pastor, and I want you to be there!"

Now, if there was ever a time to move heaven and earth, it was now. God had done just that when He called His precious child, at the Holy Spirit's prompting, to join His army of believers. I assured her I would do all within my power—God's power, really—to be there in support and celebration. As we talked, in the near background I could hear her 6-year-old sister who clearly wanted to do, or even outdo, what her older sister did. On the phone she proclaimed her plans to get baptized, as well. "Is that right?" I replied rhetorically.

"Yes!" she exclaimed. "It's me, my best friend, Maya, and my sister! We're all getting baptized."

It was good news all around, although I wondered if she understood the significance of the service, or if she was just following the crowd. Before long, her mother clarified the number of baptismal candidates: only one—the 10-year-old.

By the grace of God, I found myself present, supporting and celebrating the baptism. What a high day that was! It continues to resonate in my heart, mind, and soul. Not to be outdone, the 6-year-old exclaimed with assurance, "I'm baptized too!"

"When did you get baptized and by whom?" her mother wanted to know.

"I baptized myself in the bathtub," she responded.

"Who was there with you during the baptism?" Mother asked.

"God the Father, the Son, and Holy Ghost," the little girl said.

I could only envision this 6-year-old self-dunking in the name of the Father, the Son, and the Holy Ghost. But Jesus did say, "Suffer little children . . ." Oh, that we may have the same eagerness to be, or remain, one in Him as do these precious children of the Lord.

Lady Dana Austin

Serving With Love

Those who know your name will trust in you, for you, Lord, have never forsaken those who seek you. Ps. 9:10, NIV.

I'M THE OLDEST daughter in our family, and I have two brothers. We were raised by our mother. Today I am a psychology student in my eighth semester of college. I come from a family that always looked for ways to overcome obstacles in every way, thanks to God's power, because we didn't have our earthly father's support.

I came to the Peruvian Union University to study education because I wanted to be a teacher. I began motivated, but there came a time when I didn't have the money to pay for my studies. And there God helped me, making it possible for me to work and study simultaneously. It was a sacrifice, but I had to do it. In this way I was able to keep studying and advancing toward my degree.

Then I left the university for a while and began working as a literature evangelist, selling religious books and literature while also working in a school. When I returned to study, I couldn't continue in the linguistic school because there were no other students who wanted to study this course. That's when I began to study psychology, and I was excited about it. Being a student of this school gave me the opportunity to strengthen my personality and prepare myself for service to other people. Through that program and a project in the community I found that I enjoyed giving seminars on self-esteem and personal overcoming. I discovered that it is very rewarding to live by giving. You and I can be happy if we ask God to strengthen our faith, and then we can be a blessing to other people with everything the Lord has given us.

Serving God should not have limits. If we wish to do it, we will look for ways of working, even when nobody asks us. Do you know why I'm telling this to you? It's because today I am supporting the work of my church organization in several ways. It's a pleasure to do this for God out of gratefulness for all that I have received from Him.

I feel as if Paul were speaking to me when he wrote: "May our Lord Jesus Christ himself and God our Father, who loved us and by his grace gave us eternal encouragement and good hope, encourage your hearts and strengthen you in every good deed and word" (2 Thess. 2:16, 17, NIV). Has God blessed you too? Now it is our turn to encourage and strengthen others.

Amparo Silva Ascona

In God's Care

*In the same way your Father in heaven is not willing
that any of these little ones should be lost. Matt. 18:14, NIV.*

SHE LOOSENED HER belt and rearranged the pleats of her robe to hide her thickening waistline. It was important to keep this pregnancy quiet if at all possible. Especially important if she should have a boy! Hadn't the king decreed that every son born to a Hebrew mother must be killed? That was the instruction he had given the Hebrew midwives, so Jochebed determined to have a quick and quiet delivery, not even calling a midwife.

Sure enough, the birth of this baby was a private affair, and the brave mother knew as soon as she saw him that there was something special about this son. (But then isn't that how all mothers are—proud of their babies, knowing that they're special?)

By the time Jochebed's baby was 3 months old he was getting more vocal and interactive. Her creative mind had been scheming for a way she could protect and save her son. So she took a large basket, that she even may have woven herself, and covered it with tar. She must have taken it to the river a few times to check for the tiniest leak.

Then the dreaded morning came. Early before sunrise, as Jochebed nursed that precious baby, she must have held him close to her heart and softly hummed a familiar tune as she kissed him all over and cradled him back to sleep. With an aching heart she snuggled him down on the soft pillow inside the basket, woke big sister Miriam, and together they slipped through the morning shadows to the edge of the river. Finding a place to secure it in the reeds, she quietly reviewed Miriam's instructions before hurrying home with an expectant prayer in her heart.

Jochebed must have whispered to God, "I'm sure You want to save my baby even more than I do. I've done everything I could to be a good mother; now, God, it's up to You."

It doesn't matter what age they are, if you're a mother I know you talk to God about your children. We look back over the child-training years, and even though we've made mistakes and would do some things differently, we can remind God that we've done—are doing—our best to be good mothers. Just as Jochebed had to leave her baby in God's care, so we can also trust our children to the care of their heavenly Father; Jesus said He "is not willing that any of these little ones should be lost." Neither am I!

Roxy Hoehn

Winter Versus Spring

And the dead in Christ shall rise first: then we which are alive . . .
shall be caught up. 1 Thess. 4:16, 17.

WINTER IS CERTAINLY not my favorite season, especially when the days are dull and overcast. I usually feel lonesome and a bit depressed. Except for the evergreens, everything seems lifeless. This winter's view brings to my mind the story of Lazarus, when Jesus said he was asleep. But then the evergreens remind me of the saints who have been translated, not tasting death. And those who will be alive when Christ comes will have weathered the storms of sin and persecution and will come forth triumphantly.

Except for the occasional auto, it's quiet where I live, so it's easy to get depressed when everything is so still. Then I reflect on my life and realize that's what the devil wants.

When the sun comes out—what a difference it makes! My spirit is lifted, and I feel like singing. Just the same, the Son of Righteousness makes a big difference in our sinful lives as we reach out to Him.

One morning I looked through my window to see that everything was covered with snow. So fresh and untouched! Icicles hung from the trees and eaves of the houses. What a wonderful God we serve! I was awestruck at the beauty—everywhere so clean and white.

Then cars came through, and before long everything was all messed up and ugly-looking. This is what the devil does to us, so we have to keep going to our Father for cleansing.

Thanks for that precious blood.

When spring comes, the crocuses start to poke their heads out, the trees begin to bud, and the world that has been sleeping comes alive again. It's a wonderful sight! The plants regain their green appearance, flowers bloom, and all the beautiful colors are back. I listen and hear the birds singing praises to God. What a wonderful day it will be when the Son of Righteousness appears to call His sleeping saints to join with those alive to enjoy an everlasting spring!

I'm looking forward to that bright morning. Let's keep looking forward in faith and not let anything get us down, knowing that our redemption draws near, when we will be alive for evermore to praise God.

Ena Thorpe

Blessings in Disappointment

Commit thy way unto the Lord; trust also in him; and he shall bring it to pass.
Ps. 37:5.

EVERY YEAR WE look forward to doing something special on our wedding anniversary. We usually go on a cruise, and that's what we planned for our forty-seventh anniversary in January 2009. We always place our plans in God's hands and ask for His leading.

The usual anticipation and planning began: the clothes I would take, the trip to the port, the embarkation procedure, getting to the cabin, relaxing, and all the other exciting experiences that go along with cruising. Although we'd been on many other cruises, we were just as excited as if this were our first.

Then nine days before the cruise the unforeseen happened. My husband awoke with a severe bout of coughing, later accompanied by some shortness of breath. We headed immediately to the emergency room, which was 18 miles from home.

After various blood tests, chest X-rays, a lung CT scan, and an echocardiogram, it was discovered that he had a DVT (deep vein thrombosis) in his left leg and pulmonary emboli. Immediately continuous anticoagulant therapy, oxygen, and other medication therapy were begun.

When asked about going on the cruise in nine days, the doctor replied emphatically, "You cannot go. This is serious business!"

All the excitement, planning, and cruise anticipation came to a sudden halt. In fact, the dream died immediately. However, I soon recognized that God had intervened, since He'd been asked to be in our plans. If this situation had occurred while we were on our cruise, it's likely I would have returned home a widow, because limited medical care is available on a cruise ship.

We may have lost financially because of the no-refund policy, but I'm thankful to God that my husband's life was saved.

We cannot see ahead when we plan, but God can. We can safely trust Him with those plans. He will do what is best for His children. He has said, "I will instruct you and teach you in the way you should go; I will counsel you and watch over you" (Ps. 32:8, NIV).

Missilene B. Edwards

God Talked to Me

Trust in the Lord with all thine heart; and lean not into thine own understanding. In all thy ways acknowledge him, and he shall direct thy paths. Prov. 3:5, 6.

"WHAT WILL YOU do in Thailand for one long month?" the woman with the high-pitched voice at immigration questioned. I tried to find the right words to answer her query, telling her that I'd be visiting my friend in Thailand and would be touring around the country. I thought that was the best answer and the quickest way to get my boarding pass stamped. Unfortunately, she didn't stamp it, and asked me to talk to the boss. The boss asked me the same question, and I answered with respect. When she asked if my friend had invited me to go there, I said yes. She then asked me to show her the invitation letter stating that she really had invited me.

I had nothing to show, for Joana, my friend, didn't send me any letter. She had just called me and asked if I was interested in working in Thailand. So now I texted her and told her that she must send an invitation letter by fax to the immigration office or they would send me back home. I felt a bit downhearted and closed my eyes and prayed, *What's going on?*

I was startled when a woman beside me began to cry. Evidently she was facing the same situation as I. The boss was watching the two of us.

Joana texted that she was sending the invitation, encouraging me not to worry. Wait and relax, she said. I took a deep breath and got out my Bible, opening it to the book of Proverbs. I read today's text, thinking and praying about what it meant. As I opened my eyes, I saw the boss watching me. She came slowly toward me and asked if my friend was sending the letter. I replied that she was.

It's a good thing I arrived at the airport three hours before my flight, I thought as the waiting continued. I asked God again, *Lord, if it is Your will for me to be in Thailand, help me meet this challenge.*

Finally the boss told me to go to the counter, and the agent stamped my boarding pass. I thanked the boss and headed for my plane. I texted my friend again, telling her that I was boarding. She misunderstood my text and told me to plead with immigration to allow me to go without the letter. I then realized that God had intervened. Joana hadn't been able to fax the letter. As I took my seat, I closed my eyes and thanked Him for a miracle.

Edna S. Buenaventura

The Lucia Day

In him was life, and that life was the light of men. The light shines in the darkness, but the darkness has not understood it. John 1:4, 5, NIV.

I REMEMBER THAT in 1955 my mother and I were looking at the Stockholm newspaper and admiring the many beautiful girls who wanted to be chosen as the Lucia of the year. That lucky girl would head the procession through the city, wearing a long white robe and a crown of candles on her head. When the day arrived, we even went to town and stood in the bitter cold along the route to see the beautiful "Lucia" pass through the streets with her attendants. What Swedish girl hasn't longed to be chosen to be Lucia?

In school December 13 began with a special celebration. In the darkness of the early morning the Lucia passed through the unlit corridors to the assembly hall, dressed in a long white robe with burning candles on her head, a blood-red sash around her waist, followed by other girls similarly attired, each carrying a candle in her hands. The other pupils followed the impressive procession to the assembly hall. This tradition is celebrated everywhere in Sweden, in schools and at the workplace. The Lucia Day has been celebrated for centuries and has become a nationwide tradition.

Lucia of Syracuse was born in Sicily, where she became a Christian while she was still very young. She decided to dedicate her life to Jesus. When her father wanted to give her to a heathen man in marriage, she refused. Such a refusal meant the death penalty. December 13 is traditionally considered the day of her death. The blood-red sash is a symbol of her martyrdom; the burning candles on her head are a symbol of her love for Christ and others.

Today not many people think about the spiritual dimension of the Lucia Day. Everybody knows the story, but people tend rather to think more of the delicious buns served for breakfast than about the meaning of the symbols. Likewise, people celebrate the Christmas season without really knowing what it is all about. Many Christmas customs have lost their original meaning.

It's nice to enjoy the season's traditions, but we should also reflect on the real light of the world as we watch the flickering candles. Let's not lose sight of what is essential and remember that Jesus said "I am the light of the world" as well as "You are the light of the world" (Matt. 5:14). So let your light shine in this dark world.

Hannele Ottschofski

Kindness Rendered Is Always Remembered

If you make the Most High your dwelling—even the Lord, who is my refuge—then no harm will befall you, no disaster will come near your tent. For he will command his angels concerning you to guard you in all your ways.
Ps. 91:9-11, NIV.

THERE WAS A CRACK in my windshield. It happened to be located directly in front of my face when I drove, and during the last cold snap we had, it cracked about four inches further. It bothered me. So I decided to have the windshield replaced.

I called the Glass Shop, and Brandy, the woman in charge, told me the cost and asked when I would like to have it done. We settled on a day, and since I worked she suggested that I bring it after work. They would be closed, but they had a truck that they used as a loaner, and I could bring my vehicle in, leave it there, and take the truck. I could then bring the truck back the next evening and pick up my vehicle. That sounded like a plan.

The next day I began following the plan. My grandson was with me when we picked up the truck and started on our way home. There was a bit of traffic, but we were going along nicely, following an 18-wheeler. Suddenly an object dropped out from under the 18-wheeler. There was no time to avoid it before it went under my loaner truck, and I heard the *thump, thump* of a flat tire. As we looked for a way to get to the side of the highway, the car in the next lane saw our dilemma and slowed down so that I could get off the road.

In no time at all a truck pulled up behind me, and the driver came up to my window. It happened to be Nathan, who had gone to school with my oldest son. I hadn't seen Nathan in 20 years, and he didn't know who I was until he came up to the window. We assessed the damage: the tire had a huge hole in the side. It took some doing, but we finally got the spare on.

I called the Glass Shop and explained what had happened. When I returned the truck the next day, Brandy was so nice and very thankful that no one had been hurt. "That's the breaks," she said. "We have a friend who sells tires, and we'll have one on there tomorrow. Everything will be fine."

What could have been a tragedy wasn't. I'll always remember God's watchcare and the kindness rendered by Nathan and Brandy.

Donna Sherrill

Do Not Worry

Behold the fowls of the air: for they sow not, neither do they reap,
nor gather into barns; yet your heavenly Father feedeth them.
Are ye not much better than they? Matt. 6:26.

MY FATHER DIED when I was only 7 months old, and when I was 10 my mother died of a terminal disease. I was afraid to think about my future. *How will I be able to get an education? Who will help me finish the degree I dream of? Where will I get clothes, and money to cover other expenses?* This was really hard, but I never gave up on what I wanted to become.

When I became a Christian and was baptized, things changed for the better though life was still hard, but I got the chance to continue my college studies. This was a real privilege, but it was very difficult getting through every semester. I decided that, with God's help, I must finish a degree.

So for six years I was a working student, even working overtime to cope with finances, but God did help me. There was a time I couldn't enroll for a term because I didn't have enough money. I worked until 11:00 at night as a full-time worker in the cafeteria. When the supervisor in the food factory needed my service, I worked there as well. I never went home for vacation, and during breaks I worked full-time or sold religious literature for scholarships.

During my senior year I was off campus for an internship in a nearby church school (this was a requisite for graduation). Working for my school fees during that time was impossible. Worried again that I might not to be able to reach my dream, I was again reminded of God's promise: "Therefore I say unto you, Take no thought for your life, what ye shall eat, or what ye shall drink; nor yet for your body, what ye shall put on. Is not the life more than meat, and the body than raiment?" (Matt. 6:25). But a life filled with deeper happiness and contentment with God is what counts for me. God sent a friend to supply my needs until I finished my degree.

During my last two semesters in college I had many sleepless nights thinking about my situation, but I never stopped dreaming. I was convinced that God would use my problems as a blessing to make me strong. My work supervisor encouraged me not to worry. Unknown to me, she mentioned my need in the administrative committee. The next day I received a memo from the registrar's office stating that my debts were all paid. The God who feeds the birds is the same who answers our pleas!

Evelyn G. Pelayo

Small Things, Tiropita, Truffles, and Flowers

Praise ye the Lord. Praise the Lord, O my soul. Ps. 146:1.

THE LAST FEW weeks had been oh, so cold. The early-morning temperatures flirted with minuses. Then the sun came out with its brilliant, warming rays. The weatherman promised us another day of warmer temperatures. My husband, Bart, and I decided this was the day to do our errands, which included returning some shoes to L.L. Bean—a bit of a drive.

Now on our way, he asked, "Do you mind if we stop at the nursery? I want to see their flowers." I agreed, knowing full well this was one of his great treats. And what an array of pretty blooms for winter-weary eyes—begonias, pansies, and orchids smiled at us on every side.

The lunch decision was quick; it would be at the Mediterranean Grill, one of our favorites. The special of the day was spinach tiropita with mushroom sauce, which was as delicious as the news clippings posted on the wall attested. Mr. Aker, the proprietor, even remembered us and stopped by for a quick hello.

After lunch we dashed over to our real destination, L.L. Bean. We divided up the list and separated to shop. I was to purchase a birthday gift for our daughter, Janna, and found just what I had in mind: a knit top set in the grand color of maroon. When we met back in the store foyer, the shoes had been returned and socks bought.

Back in the car Bart mentioned that he'd like a truffle. I wasn't surprised, as a special candy store was in the next block. We made a quick stop for the delicious treat then drove out to the Adventist Book Center, each of us looking for our own certain book. At checkout, as we chatted with the clerk, we found that we have mutual friends, and so now we have made a new friend.

It was 5:30 when we drove into our snow-covered driveway, tired but pleased by what we had done along the way that day. Was it the sight of the spring blossoms, the tiropita, the truffle, the perfect gift, the new friend, or what?

It's a good day to take time to enjoy the good things in life, be they small or large. We know Jesus wants us to be happy, and we can find so much to cheer our days. Do we take time to thank Him for these blessings surrounding us?

Dessa Weisz Hardin

December 17

I Wish You the Best,
I Wish Jesus in Your Heart

For to us a child is born, to us a son is given. Isa. 9:6, NIV.

I LIE ON a sofa in front of a huge window that offers the most beautiful view! Everything looks so clear. Maybe it's the combination of the white snow and the light of the moon. A table behind the sofa is covered with presents. And presents is what Christmas is all about, right?

When my brothers, sister, and I were little we loved waiting for our parents to bring the presents. We'd have a night vigil, taking turns to stand watch. Things have changed now. These days we torture each other by putting the presents under the tree (sometimes even two weeks before Christmas Eve).

This morning I peeked a little bit and found one present—one out of a thousand presents. (OK, I'm exaggerating. Maybe there were three for me—the rest were for my nieces and nephew.) So I began thinking about my presents from last year. Work presents, birthday presents, souvenir presents, Valentine's Day presents, "just because" presents, cheer-up presents, goodbye presents, welcome presents. And, believe it or not, I even got a gift for Mother's Day from the two "host" daughters I had. I felt so much better for remembering this, but there is more to say.

Some of those presents have been lost, and others broken. Some have lost their "wow" moment. Yesterday my friend Nick reminded me of something: temporary things can give us only temporary happiness. I've been so happy opening presents, just knowing that I'm appreciated enough to be given a present. It truly is the thought that counts. And yet, sadly, even the thought can be temporary sometimes.

Truly, the greatest and most permanent gift we have ever been given is Jesus! Always present—yesterday, today, and tomorrow. Yesterday a present who came as a baby and brought us salvation. Today a present of faithfulness, mercy, care, forgiveness, and unfailing love. Tomorrow a present of eternal joy. I wish I could give the best gift-wrapped present you've ever seen. But if the invisible could be seen today, then you would see Jesus holding in His nail-pierced hands a ribbon, for He is the gift I wish for you today and always. I wish for Jesus to live permanently in your life. May you truly find this unwrapped present, the gift of joy, peace, faith, hope, and love: Jesus!

Sayuri Ruiz Rodriguez

His Watchcare

Fear thou not; for I am with thee. Isa. 41:10.

IT WAS MY first year of teaching in the isolated coastal community of Gibson's Landing, in British Columbia, Canada. There was no Adventist church, so I had spent the Sabbath alone.

After lunch I felt adventuresome. A walk would be what I needed. There was still much snow on the ground and it was very cold, but the sun was shining. So, bundling up in warm clothes, I took the main road leading to Grantham's Landing, the next community, an area unfamiliar to me.

At the first road leading left, I changed direction and began ascending a hill. Tall evergreen trees crowded the narrow road, and not a house was in sight. The thought crossed my mind that maybe I should return home, but I felt like exploring farther.

Suddenly, a loud *crack* sounded among the trees on the right side of the road. A creepy sensation came over me that I was being watched. Glancing around, I saw no one. "Something" had obviously stepped on a fallen branch! My mind raced—bears were still sleeping in their dens; deer wouldn't travel in such deep snow. Only one animal remained during this season—a cougar! They were plentiful this year, and something was in the bush following me.

Reason told me not to run, to walk as I had been doing. Oh, how I felt like running, though! There were still no houses in sight. I had no choice but to keep walking and praying. "Something" was still following me, for I could feel I was being watched.

As I came over a slight rise, I saw a crossroad leading in the direction of the school. Mrs. Brown lived on that road and, thankfully, she was home. I collapsed in a chair and told her about my walk. After a hot drink and conversation, I knew I must leave because it was getting dark, and I was still far from home. I covered the "Rocky Road to Dublin," as we called the shortcut to town, at a great speed. Upon reaching home, I had a long prayer of thanks for a safe return.

As a 19-year-old I had claimed today's text that afternoon. This verse has been a guide wherever I have lived or traveled, worked or vacationed. Beyond a shadow of a doubt, our heavenly Father keeps watch over His children wherever we are. We need never fear, for He keeps His promises.

Muriel Heppel

The Proposal

For you bless the godly, O Lord; you surround them with your shield of love. Ps. 5:12, NLT.

I SNICKERED TO myself when Linda asked Sonny, "What shall we have for supper?" Then she answered her own question: "I know; we'll make pierogies, because today is Ukrainian Christmas, and we'll celebrate it—yeah!"

For the past six years Linda and her husband, Jesse, have been coparenting Sonny together with Ron and me, his biological parents. Because Sonny has profound developmental disabilities, requiring 24/7 support for life, our family qualifies for government assistance that provides respite care through a service-provider and host-family arrangement. This works well for all of us who are committed to meeting Sonny's needs on this journey.

I love to laugh, and I wasn't about to miss the opportunity to tell Linda my story. Ron and I began dating while we were still students in a Christian high school in Idaho. We both attended the school's homecoming the first year after our graduation and spent most of the weekend together. It was during that weekend that Ron proposed to me in the parking lot on a glorious Sunday morning. He said, "Debbie, you buy a cookbook and start practicing!"

I replied, "OK," and a kiss sealed the deal! We were married the following December. That was 38 blessed years ago.

Ron should have specified what type of cookbook the soon-to-be American bride needed to purchase! Upon my arrival in Canada he showed me how to make pierogies, since I didn't have a clue what he was even talking about. He wanted me to cook "Ukrainian-style," like his mom and grandma. I wanted to please Ron, so after just one lesson I prepared supper all by myself. When he came home, he got a big surprise when he took the lid off the kettle.

I couldn't be bothered making dozens of little pierogies. *This will take forever,* I thought. So I made two giant ones, his and hers. "These look like moccasins—size 13!" he said.

For 30 years I cooked to please Ron and did a fine job of it. Eight years ago he assumed this job, because he likes to cook. Christmas Eve day 2008 Ron spent the entire day making a feast fit for a Ukrainian king and his family: pierogies and cabbage rolls, plus another lovely gift easily seen—patience.

Deborah Sanders

The Nightmare Before Christmas

Thou wilt keep him in perfect peace, whose mind is stayed on thee. Isa. 26:3.

WE HAD COME to Omaha, Nebraska, to spend Christmas with our daughter Sandi and her family. Two days before Christmas we went shopping at the West Roads Mall, which had just reopened for shopping following the shooting incident that had occurred at the Bryn Mawr store. A young man had apparently come to the end of his rope and went on a shooting spree early in December and killed or injured many people. Since that shooting, the mall had been closed for investigations. Now, of course, so close to Christmas, it seemed as if every shopper in Omaha was making up for lost time.

Neither my husband, Ted, nor I are in the best of health, but we still wanted to join in the fun. Ted has had multiple sclerosis for 40 years, but is still able to walk slowly; however, he has suffered much cognitive damage. He recognizes people, memories are good, but figuring out what to do in any given situation is difficult. Because of this, we planned to stick close to him.

I paused a few seconds to look at something in a center aisle. When I turned around, Ted was gone! Sandi and I both set out to look for him. I was horrified, realizing that I was carrying all of his identification cards.

We talked with two security police, describing him. I waited where I had a good view of a large area and prayed for his safety. Sandi went up and down each hallway through the mobs of shoppers, looking into entrances of every store. Ted was nowhere to be found.

I caught the strains of "Silent Night" and "Joy to the World," but couldn't help thinking that things were certainly neither silent nor joyful. I continued to pray. An hour and a half went by, and still no Ted and no word from security police. I began to worry this would be another nightmare at this mall. What if someone brought him to the police station, or he had wandered to an outside exit looking for us. It was freezing cold outside.

Suddenly there he was, standing right near us. I thanked the Lord right there in the midst of all the commotion. Oh, for a nice quiet place away from the hustle and bustle just to think about that silent night so long ago!

Darlene Ytredal Burgeson

December 21

The Battle Is Not Yours

Fear not: for I have redeemed thee, I have called thee by thy name;
thou art mine. When thou passest through the waters,
I will be with thee; and through the rivers, they shall not overflow thee:
when thou walkest through the fire, thou shalt not be burned. Isa. 43:1, 2.

I AM A businesswoman in Jamaica who has been in business all my adult life in the capital city of Kingston. Several years ago, because of expediency and a desire to expand my business, I made a decision to relocate to a more recently developed section of Kingston. As I had to construct a new building on two vacant lots, I was assigned a government street number for each lot.

However, to my surprise, an influential, high-ranking official objected quite strongly to my assigned numbers. Although the numbers were legal and correct, they apparently clashed in some way with his numbering. So strong did this objection become that the matter went to litigation, resulting in my being asked to alter the street numbering on my building and display the new number that had been assigned.

Before I got around to removing the old numbers, two police officers came into my office with a warrant for my arrest for noncompliance. I was devastated. I went momentarily into an adjoining room where I prayed for the Lord's intervention. Immediately I was impressed to call a friend who was a retired trial judge. The judge spoke to the police officers, then also advised me to display the street number as the court had directed me to do. This I did, and the law officers left without executing the warrant.

I give thanks to this day that the Lord intervened, and that I was neither arrested nor put into prison. I trust in God, and I know He cares for me so that I will eventually live for Him. My sisters, let us be faithful and never cease to pray. God has many promises of deliverance. In Psalm 32:7 we read, "You are my hiding place; You shall preserve me from trouble; You shall surround me with songs of deliverance" (NKJV), and in Philippians 1:19, "For I know that this will turn out for my salvation through your prayer and the supply of the Spirit of Jesus Christ" (NKJV). It certainly proved true for me.

Ethlyn Thompson

We Can Have a Perfect Christmas

Glory to God in the highest, and on earth peace, good will toward men.
Luke 2:14.

DO YOU HAVE a Christmas dream? Do you wish for Christmas to be extra-special this year? Do you have a wish list? If so, perhaps it includes the gifts that you'd like to receive, as well as those you want to give. How would you describe the perfect Christmas? Is it snowy weather? Is it a tree decorated with the brightest star and lots of handmade ornaments? Do you want family members gathered around the tree singing Christmas carols? Are there gifts of every size, color, and shape? a table full of goodies? While these may contribute to a perfect Christmas, even all of them together cannot guarantee that we will have a perfect Christmas in such a needy world.

Have you considered Jesus' wish list for this Christmas? He has a dream, and you and I can help it come true. He says, "I'm dreaming of a starlit Christmas. Will Bethlehem's star shine bright in every person's heart, embellishing My people? I'm dreaming of a warm Christmas. Will you extend the blanket of love and lend a hand to cover the countless needy souls? I'm dreaming of a white Christmas; let peace and understanding wipe away glooms of conflict and hatred. Let hearts be conquered by caring.

"I'm dreaming of a joyful Christmas. Will you leave resentments behind and instead be gentle and kind to those who have wronged you? I'm dreaming of a special Christmas. Let your heart be a manger, let your soul be a throne for the Child God, the Savior. I'm dreaming of a beautiful Christmas as it is meant to be—hearts united, rejoicing, living lives that reflect Me! I'm pleading while dreaming of Christmas. Will you make My dream come true? Sincerely, Jesus (the reason for the season)."

Most certainly, each of us can make a difference this Christmas season—and every day. Let our hearts be a vessel, a recipient of heavenly peace that overflows to others in blessings of joy and understanding.

"For unto us a child is born, unto us a son is given: and the government shall be upon his shoulder: and his name shall be called Wonderful, Counsellor, The mighty God, The everlasting Father, The Prince of Peace" (Isa. 9:6). He's counting on you and me to make His dream come true. Are you up to the challenge? Let's do our part so that He, too, may have a perfect Christmas. It'll make your Christmas the happiest ever, I'm sure!

Rhodi Alers de López

Touch of a Dove

Look, I am making everything new! Rev. 21:5, NLT.

I'VE BEEN CAPTIVATED by pictures in storybooks that depict the beauty and peace in the Garden of Eden. How wonderful it must have been for Adam and Eve to be part of God's perfect creation, to live in complete harmony with all the creatures!

We can only imagine what it would be like to stroke a leopard or walk with a wolf without feeling fear. Sin certainly did its work in changing the relationship not only between man and beast, but also creature against creature. How very sad.

Many animal stories are told, but occasionally there is one about a creature that has acted totally out of character with its nature. I remember hearing a story about an Arctic mail carrier whose dogs had died of poison. He was 100 miles from any post, and temperatures were 40 degrees below zero. Brokenhearted, lonely, and in despair he drew his sled after him and began the long trek home. After spending the first night in his fur bag, he awoke to find a huge bear lying close to him. The man shared his fish with the bear, who then trotted along with him, day after day, and slept close to him at night. Five miles from the post the bear disappeared. God is certainly in control of His creation.

I wonder if I could have been as brave as Dian Fossey, the woman who ventured into the realm of the mountain gorilla in the rainforests of Rwanda. As an American ethologist she worked many years studying closely the lives of these wild creatures. In time she was privileged to touch them. What a wonderful thrill!

My small experience came one Christmas morning. As I chatted with the children, and now the grandchildren, my thoughts were interrupted when a beautiful little Barbary dove flew down and sat on the trellis close to where my husband and I were preparing for the family Christmas lunch. It stayed for hours and amazed everyone when it flew to the table among us all. Eventually it sat on my hand, accepting food, before hopping onto my shoulder where I could feel the warmth of its feathers against my ear.

The experience made my day one of special meaning, giving peace and reassurance that the God of creation will restore once again the perfection of Eden. It was a glimpse of heaven.

Lyn Welk-Sandy

Grace

For by grace are ye saved through faith; and that not of yourselves: it is the gift of God. Eph. 2:8.

Grace to you and peace from God our Father, and the Lord Jesus Christ. Rom. 1:7.

GRACE HAS BEEN mine for so long that it's a bit like love—at moments taken for granted. Something happens, and it shakes you to the core, and you know that grace, like love, needs to be held gently in the "palm" of your soul and given much attention.

The first time I realized the ultimate grace of God was as a small child. It was Christmas morning and church morning as well. We'd had a great time at home opening packages, eating breakfast, talking. Usually my older sister took me to church. But this wonderful day I got to wear a pretty new dress from my grandma, and my sister made my hair look pretty. The best part was that Mom and Dad and most of my brothers and sisters went with us! For that little while I felt like a princess.

Then I heard it for the first time, that song that majestically fills my heart with the Lord's greatness: "The Lord in Zion Reigneth!" That moment I knew ultimate God love, family love—little-girl stuff that stays in the heart forever. Daddy placed a bright shiny quarter in my white-gloved hand for me to put in the offering. He smiled at my wide-eyed "Thank you!" (I usually got a dime.)

As I think of it now, it was a very simple weekly occurrence for some people, but that's where my Jesus spark got started. At that time I knew that God loved me and decided that I was His, and I wanted Him to be mine.

At times others have asked, "Why did God let this or that happen?" I knew simplistically that He's stuck with what I'm stuck with—human freedom of choice, and, unfortunately, human nature. I love Him all the more for it. That little spark that began that Christmas has grown into a steady stream of heat between heaven and here.

Through trials, even the really hard ones so far, I've known without doubt that my Lord and Savior is with me, holding me, helping me, molding me, and mending me—and someday soon He will return to make me forever new!

May that grace be yours as well this Christmas Eve.

Sally j. Aken-Linke

December 25

Joy to the World

They will call him Immanuel—which means, "God with us." Matt. 1:23, NIV.

JOY TO THE WORLD, the Lord is come!" Ever since I first learned these words that phrase has bothered me! Now, I love the song, but "the Lord *is* come" sounds wrong to me! Grammatically wrong, that is. Maybe it has something to do with Isaac Watts having written it in 1719, I don't know. How about: "Joy to the world, the Lord *has* come." Doesn't that sound better? Or what about the good news: "Joy to the world, the Lord *will* come!" The teacher in me had to type the original phrase into a Word document and press grammar check to see if "*is* come" was correct. It was. It is. I guess it always will be. H'mmm . . .

When my boys were younger, we had a Nativity set made of unbreakable soft plastic. Day after day shepherds, animals, and Baby Jesus would travel throughout the house, childhood innocence lending its own special flavor to the story being repeated by my two little wise men. One night as I straightened up the house before going to bed I noticed that Baby Jesus was missing from the stable. I knew He would show up again—He was probably safe in some boyish hiding place. Though we had long since tucked the boys in for the night, I slipped into their room one last time and a precious sight met my heart. There, on the bed by my eldest son's pillow, lay Baby Jesus, swaddled in a cozy Kleenex as carefully as little boy fingers could manage. Baby Jesus hadn't been there earlier when I tucked my boy into bed. I knelt down beside my son, and in that treasured moment he stirred and opened his eyes. Smiling at me, he whispered, "Jesus with me, Mommy," then drifted back to sleep secure, content, and confident. In one tiny, holy spark of time, heaven's presence—*Jesus with me*—pressed deeper into my heart.

Many circumstances and events have touched my life since that night. On occasion I have foolishly let them overshadow His presence, forgetting that He *is* with me, no matter the situation. Perhaps you have too. So today, Christmas Day, won't you join me? I choose again to believe the reality of a little boy's faith, symbolized in a small, Kleenex-swaddled Savior . . . *Jesus with me.* Joy to the world, the Lord *has* come! Joy to the world the Lord *will* come! But best of all, Joy to the world, the Lord *IS* come! He *is* here, right now, *with* you, *with* me. *Joy!*

DeeAnn Bragaw

Wedding Bonanza

Ask, and it will be given to you; seek, and you will find; knock, and it will be opened to you. Matt. 7:7, NKJV.

IT WAS ALMOST year-end when my son told me of his intention to marry his girlfriend of six years. I was happy for him, but I began thinking about the financial implications. I asked him if he had saved enough money to pay *lobola* (bride price) and also to plan a wedding. He told me that his savings would be enough just for the *lobola* deposit but not for the wedding. We decided to make it an issue of prayer. We asked God to provide the money for preparing the wedding.

My son paid the *lobola* as planned. A few months later his workplace was laying off workers through a voluntary retirement package. Only a few selected positions were eligible for this offer. When we calculated the money needed for the wedding preparations, the amount that my son would get, should he get approval for retirement, was going to be enough to cover the wedding preparations. Once again we decided to make it an issue of prayer.

Then my son got a job offer from another company; they would pay double his present salary. Daily we prayed earnestly as a family, because this seemed to be God's hand already preparing another job. God answered our prayers positively. My son got the voluntary retirement package that was just enough to cover the wedding preparations. He also got the new job.

In our culture the parents of the groom are expected to give their son money as a wedding gift so that he will have funds to help him as he starts the new home. I wanted to give my son 1,500 U.S. dollars. With my present salary, it was going to take me almost a year to save up that much. So I asked him to ask his fiancé if they could set their wedding date for the following year. They set their date to exactly the time that I needed. I praised God again! But for some strange reason I began to have more obligations than before. As the wedding date drew near, I hadn't saved enough. It became very clear that I wasn't going to make the amount I desired unless some miracle was performed by God.

I didn't give up. I took God at His word, and daily I kept my desire before God. Shortly before the wedding I got a salary increase and was able to give exactly the amount for which I had been asking God! We receive not because we ask not (see James 4:2).

Alice Mafanuke

December 27

A Sister's Love

By this all will know that you are My disciples, if you have love for one another. John 13:35, NKJV.

LIVING IN a refugee camp couldn't be called either easy or fun. No matter how hard you look, there is nothing positive about the situation. Very rarely is anybody kind to you in a place like that. It's hard to show kindness when nobody shows kindness to you. There are none of the comforts that so many of us take for granted. I know, for I lived in such a camp as a child.

My mother was dead, and my father had been taken captive by the Communists. My sisters and I lived with our older brothers and their families in what was basically a large tent city. If you've read about the children of Israel living in the wilderness after their escape from Egypt, you have an idea of how we lived. I'm sure there were many similarities.

Food was very scarce in the camp, barely enough food to survive. I was 6 years old, and I had a 12-year-old sister who had been sick for a long time with a terrible, racking cough. Very few doctors were available to help those of us who became ill. I didn't know about God's love at that time, but I did love my sister very much, and I would have done anything to help her get well. I hoped she wouldn't die as my mom had.

I remember being given food to eat—good, soft white rice—and I was very happy and thankful for the food. But when I asked for food for my sister, I wasn't given the good rice that I had received. Do you know what burnt rice looks like? Brown, crisp, yucky stuff! That was the kind of rice I was given for my poor, sick sister, and it made me very sad to think that people would treat her that way. I thought, *How can I give this horrible food to my sister, who feels so bad? How will she ever get well eating terrible food like this?*

Since I was only 6, I didn't understand about nutrients, but I was sure that kindness and good food could help make her well. I decided that I would give her the good rice, and I would eat the burned rice. And with the better food, she slowly began to regain her strength.

Even though I didn't really understand God's love at that time, I later realized that I was showing His love to my sister. I don't know why my sister got better; it's a mystery to me to this day, but God's love is also a mystery. Someday, when He comes to take us to heaven, we will understand that mystery.

Yer Moua

370

Speak Through Me

You did not choose me, but I chose you and appointed you to go and bear fruit—fruit that will last. John 15:16, NIV.

WHEN I ARRIVED at Machilipatnam, Andhra Pradesh, India, there were 82 young men enjoying the waves rolling in at the Bay of Bengal. With each wave they attempted to jump over or into it amid much shouting and laughing. What fun they were having!

These seminary students were enjoying some free time at the beach. Their spiritual retreat had started on Wednesday evening, and on this Friday afternoon they were enjoying the cool water of the bay, an adventure they would remember forever. When they saw me, they waved and motioned for me to join them. The coolness of the water was a welcome relief after a long, two-hour drive from the airport. It was very hot in Andhra, as is normal. We spent an enjoyable hour in the water before returning to the Quiet Corner camp to prepare for the Sabbath.

In just two weeks, these men would be graduating from the seminary. Some were very young, and some showed signs of graying hair. Several months each year for the past three years they had left their homes and families and churches to participate in an intensive study program. Many had left lucrative jobs to receive only $30 per month as a Bible worker in their village. One would wonder how these men could be so happy with so little. They each had their own story, and yet they were all the same—God changed their lives, and they were working in His vineyard.

What a blessing it was for me to speak to and encourage these men of God! Out under the trees, the songs they sang in Telugu warmed my heart. Together their voices praised God. Their prayers were heartfelt and sure. The Holy Spirit was present! During their time at the seminary, I had addressed them many times. Each time I would pray the Lord would give me the words and speak through me. Each time I received such a blessing. What a privilege to be invited to share in their lives, and what an education for me!

Many times we wonder why God chooses us. But at times like these I can only thank Him for the blessings He showers on me. He knows just what I need, and I needed this spiritual retreat as much as anyone. God is here; God is alive; and God loves me!

Candy Zook

The Table

All you who remain of the house of Israel, you whom I have upheld since you were conceived, and have carried since your birth. Even to your old age and gray hairs I am he, I am he who will sustain you. I have made you and I will carry you; I will sustain you. Isa. 46:3, 4, NIV.

SOMETIME AGO I read a memorable story of a young couple who was deeply in love as they arranged their small apartment. The basics were in place; however, there was no kitchen table. Finally, an uncle offered them a used, expandable table.

On the first day that they had breakfast at the table, holding hands, the young man said, "How wonderful that this table is small, because we are close and I can look into your eyes and see how beautiful you are."

Time passed. Children came, two boys and a beautiful little girl. As the children grew, it became necessary to add one of the table leaves so that the family could fit around the table and also include the little friends who visited.

The children grew. Now, besides the friends who came, places were set at the table for the boyfriends and girlfriends, so they added the last leaf. Now it was a large table. The wife sat at one end of the table, and the husband took his place at the other end. Around the large table they experienced the happiest times of their life: laughter, happy stories, even secrets. It was there that they gave the best advice, cleared up doubts, and settled disagreements among siblings.

The house filled with the delicious smell of bread baking, the sound of the piano playing, the voice of a brother singing in the bathroom or a sister complaining for silence because she needed to study. Happy times!

One by one the children married. Then the grandchildren came. What joy! The table was almost too small for everyone, and hearts too small to hold such joy.

Then the children moved far away, and there was no longer any need for such a large table. So the last leaves were removed, and the table became small again.

Once again the man held the hand of his beloved, and with tears he said, "After these 50 years you continue to be as beautiful as on the first day that we sat at this table."

A table is being prepared for us. How wonderful it will be to sit at that table with Jesus and family and friends. May God grant us this grace.

Eunice Michiles Malty

I Know Somebody

For I know whom I have believed, and am persuaded that he is able to keep that which I have committed unto him against that day. 2 Tim. 1:12.

THE PHONE RANG one cold winter morning. My cousin's wife had exciting news. A young man I had known years before was the chiropractor for the soon-to-be first lady, and he had given my cousin two tickets to the upcoming presidential inauguration. But all the hotels within a 100-mile radius of the Washington, D.C., area were full, so the young chiropractor and his wife were going to stay with my cousins.

My cousin's wife was delighted. This was a historic occasion. Now I, too, knew someone who knew the man who would be president of the United States. I told my friends and relatives about it. And the story spread as those friends told others.

Looking back on that moment, I see what it meant to know someone powerful. I also realized that I know an even more powerful Someone, and that Someone knows and cares about me. Furthermore, He is coming back to take us to heaven to be with Him. Then I wondered why we don't share that even more exciting news of Christ's second coming. We know that will be an incredibly glorious day. Ellen G. White describes that day this way: "As the nations of the saved look upon their Redeemer and behold the eternal glory of the Father shining in His countenance . . . , they break forth in rapturous song: 'Worthy, worthy is the Lamb that was slain'" (*The Great Controversy*, pp. 651, 652).

We have a personal relationship with the God who is at the center of this much-longed-for event. We know that we won't need tickets to view the event, because every eye will see Him (Rev. 1:7). We know that we need not worry about accommodation since Jesus is currently building mansions for us (John 14:2, 3). We also know that we have a special God-urged mission to perform: to tell others (Matt. 28:19). Now we have a commission to act upon. We must share the good news. We *know* Him!

Then I wondered, Do we really know Jesus as well as we know those around us and those in positions of trust? Thank God, we still have a little time to know, love, honor, and obey the King of heaven. I want to live and dwell with Him forever. Don't you?

Carol J. Greene

Outside Appearance

The Lord does not look at the things man looks at. Man looks at the outward appearance, but the Lord looks at the heart. 1 Sam. 16:7, NIV.

TO LOOK AT my car, a 2007 Hyundai Accent, you'd never guess that it could have a problem. It looks new, as I have kept it clean, and it has been regularly serviced. From outside appearances, my car looks perfect. But that changed one day when my son drove it to school. A yellow light came on: "Check Engine." Because the car never before had such a problem, my son thought it wasn't a big problem. He pulled off the road, switched off the engine, and restarted the car, thinking that the light might go off. It did not.

Upon returning home from school, he said that the car was now shaking every time he tried to accelerate. Both my husband and I were surprised. Because the car was still under warranty, my husband decided that we should take it to the dealer where we had bought it.

It didn't take long for them to pinpoint what was wrong. "We know the problem. As a matter of fact, you may have just missed our letter to you in which we indicated that we were recalling all 2007 Hyundai Accents to adjust the computer system that coordinates the running of the vehicles." That morning the car was fixed and back to normal.

As I drove home that night, today's Bible text came to my mind: "Man looks at the outside appearance, but the Lord looks at the heart." On the outside, my car looked excellent; but inside it had a problem. God our Maker knows us from the inside out. He sees what is truly there. When people look at us they may be deceived by external appearances that hide the real condition of our hearts, but God sees the truth. Our hearts may be in need of healing from Him, and when He who sees the inside looks at us, He knows exactly what He needs to fix.

God gently calls us to go to Him and ask Him to fix us so that we may be healed from our weaknesses and failures. Even when we're trying to help other people, let's not always think that what we see from the outside is what they are inside. Only God knows the inside. We should, instead, encourage them to surrender to Jesus, who alone provides the needed healing.

As we go into a new year, may God give each one of us that special touch so that we can operate to the fullest potential He has set for us in this world.

Judith M. Mwansa

AUTHOR BIOGRAPHIES

Jodie Bell Aakko lives in Colorado. She has served as a teacher and principal in Seventh-day Adventist schools for 16 years. She enjoys hiking, cooking, and family nights. She has two daughters (a teenager and a toddler), and is married to an amazing athletic husband. **Aug. 6.**

Marjorie Ackley lives in Paradise, California, where she is a nurse, dietitian, and health and wellness coach in private practice. She's working on a program to train individuals in local churches to coach others in health improvement. **Feb. 5.**

Betty J. Adams, a retired teacher, lives in California, where she is a mother of five, grandmother of seven, and great-grandmother of eight. She has written for *Guide* magazine and her church newsletter, and is active in community services. She enjoys writing, her grandchildren, scrapbooking, and traveling—especially on mission trips. **Apr. 9, July 14.**

Sally j. Aken-Linke lives in Nebraska and is married to LifeNet pilot/husband, John. She writes stories for women and children, as well as contributing to the church newsletter and various magazines. She and John have five children and four grandchildren. Sally enjoys reading, music, and traveling. She is active on FaceBook, MySpace, Twitter, and Skype—especially to keep in touch with family. **Mar. 31, Dec. 24.**

Shanter H. Alexander hails from the beautiful island of St. Lucia and has served as teacher and school counselor with the mission's department of education since 1997. She is passionate about ministry and is currently pursuing doctoral studies at Andrews University. She enjoys reading, writing, public speaking, travel, cooking, and quiet time. **Nov. 17.**

Maxine Williams Allen resides in central Florida with her husband and two fast-growing sons, Brandon and Jonathan. She's a licensed real estate professional who enjoys reading, writing, and traveling, and has a special interest in family life ministries. She endeavors to discover and live God's plan for her life. **Apr. 22.**

Jacqueline V. R. Anderson writes from Canada, where she has lived most of her life. She has a Bachelor of Theology and B.A. degree. After university she worked three years as a volunteer service worker. She now works full-time at an assisted living facility and has published her first book, *Modern Day Psalms.* She has an active worship life, and cooks for the homeless. **Mar. 17.**

Mirlène André, who lives in Baltimore, Maryland, has made some life adjustments. She worked as a computer specialist and computer trainer for the federal government for 15 years; was a Peace Corps volunteer in The Gambia, West Africa, and a systems programmer for the state of Maryland. She is now working full-time for the Lord as a literature evangelist. **Feb. 28.**

Raquel Queiroz da Costa Arrais is a minister's wife who has developed her ministry as an educator for 20 years. Originally from Brazil, she now works as associate director of the General Conference Women's Ministries Department. She has two sons and two daughters-in-law. Her greatest pleasure is to be with people, sing, play the piano, and travel. **Jan. 20, July 19.**

Amparo Silva Ascona is a first-time contributor to this devotional book series. She writes from Peru, where she is a student at Peruvian Union University. **Dec. 8.**

Lady Dana Austin writes from the north Georgia mountains in Ellijay. She enjoys the outdoors, and loves to white-water raft, cycle, swim, and run. She is a women's and youth ministry leader at church. Her passions are writing and tea—she recently opened a tea house to minister to the souls that thirst, while serving up the love of Jesus. **Dec. 7.**

Edna Bacate-Domingo has three daughters and is a member of Loma Linda Filipino church (LLFC) in Loma Linda, California. She has served LLFC as an elder. She is also on the church's nurture council and the women's/family ministries council. Edna is a nursing professor at National University. She retired from California State University, College of Nursing. **June 25.**

Yvita Antonette Villalona Bacchus is from the Dominican Republic and is finishing a degree in graphic design. She is a member of Central Quisqueya church, where she is active in the music department and the Pathfinder Club. This is the second time she has submitted a devotional, hoping that another young girl or woman may find comfort as she has in devotionals past and present. **Feb. 18.**

Darlen Cibeli Martelo Bach lives in Brazil, where she is a bank employee. She is the church secretary and conductor of the choir. She enjoys painting and reading. She's been married for five years. **Feb. 6.**

Carla Baker is women's ministries director for the North American Division of Seventh-day Adventists in Silver Spring, Maryland. Her special areas of interest in women's ministries include reclaiming inactive members, ministries to teens, and abuse prevention and education. Carla enjoys traveling, reading, walking, and spending time with her granddaughters. **Feb. 21, July 26.**

Jennifer M. Baldwin writes from Australia, where she works in risk management at Sydney Adventist Hospital. She enjoys church involvement, travel, crossword puzzles, and writing, and has contributed to a number of church publications. **Oct. 9.**

Tammy Barnes-Taylor lives in Pell City, Alabama. She is the assistant women's ministries leader and a women's ministries council member. She's been married for 25 years and has three sons and one daughter. Her hobbies include writing, scrapbooking, and photography. **Apr. 12.**

Mary Barrett, who lives in England, is a pastor who is married to a pastor. They have two adult daughters. She has written several books and numerous articles. She likes to spend her spare time with family and friends and in her garden, attempting to grow produce for her family. **Jan. 14.**

Dana M. Bean is an educator who lives in Bermuda with her husband and two children. Dana enjoys traveling, telling children's stories, photography, and writing spiritual lessons for others. **Aug. 19.**

Lisa M. Beardsley is director of the Education Department of the General Conference of Seventh-day Adventists. She works with the Adventist Accrediting Association and is editor in chief for *Dialogue* journal, which is published in English, French, Spanish, and Portuguese for Adventist university students around the world. **Feb. 2.**

Ginger Bell resides in Brighton, Colorado, with her pastor husband. Their two married children and their families live in the area. Ginger is active in women's ministries at her church and for the Rocky Mountain Conference. Her hobbies include gardening, crafts, antiquing, and being in the beautiful Rocky Mountains. **Aug. 18.**

Flora F. Beloni is a nurse working for the government in Martinique, French West Indies, and is in charge of women's ministries in her local church. Her husband, Pierre A. Beloni, is first elder of their church. Their two daughters are studying and living in the United States, and their son is studying at Northern Caribbean University in Jamaica. **Sept. 12.**

Sylvia Bennett lives in Suffolk, Virginia, with her husband, Richard. They have two adult children. She enjoys her position as a fiscal accountant and likes to spend quality time with family and close friends. She is a member of the Windsor Seventh-day Adventist Church. Her hobbies include reading, traveling, music, writing, witnessing, and caring for the elderly. **Feb. 13.**

Annie B. Best, a retired teacher in Washington, D.C., is a widow, mother of two adult children, and has three grandchildren. She enjoys reading and listening to music. She is a leader in the children's departments of her church, which inspired her to compose a song published in *Let's Sing Sabbath Songs.* **June 14.**

Cynthia Best-Goring lives in Glendale, Maryland, where she is the principal of a pre-K–6 elementary school. Her passion lies in helping children learn, teachers teach, and all to become acquainted with our heavenly Father. She is a wife and mother of two adult children. Cynthia's hobbies include writing, playing the piano, and reading. **Mar. 6, June 4.**

Selena Blackburn, who lives in Washington State, is a wife, mother, grandmother, nurse, and so much more. Most days she feels she comes up short, and the only balance to this life is God's grace, which covers her. She was thrilled to write for the devotional book as she longs to share the sweetness of the grace heaven blesses her with again and again. **June 15.**

Dinorah Blackman lives in Panama with her husband and young daughter, Imani. **Feb. 23.**

Sandra Blackmer is features editor of *Adventist Review* and an assistant editor of *Adventist World.* An advocate for humane animal treatment, she and her family rescue and foster many of God's four-legged creatures. She and her husband, Larry, who is a vice president of and the education director for the North American Division, live in Maryland. Their daughter, Melissa, is a graduate student. **Nov. 23.**

Moselle Slaten Blackwell is a retired widow in Michigan who has two adult children and one granddaughter. In her church she serves as deaconess, Sabbath school teacher, and choir member. Her favorite interests are working in the yard, listening to religious music, beautiful sunsets, and a clear moonlit night sky—all of which speak of God's sovereignty of the universe. **Dec. 4.**

Cintia García Block, originally from Argentina, was raised in different parts of Africa, where her parents worked as missionaries. Years later she went back to Argentina to study psychology and marry a good Argentine husband. She was successful on both counts. Presently she lives in Canada, where she is a homemaker and the proud mother of an 11-month-old baby. **Mar. 25.**

Juli Blood, who lives in Pennsylvania, is happily married with two sons and a desire to stay in God's plan for her life. Hebrews 6 speaks to her heart when it emphasizes the need to dig deeper into the Scriptures for a greater understanding of God. It is her prayer that every woman will find her worth, strength, and joy in her personal relationship with Jesus. **Aug. 7.**

Julie Bocock-Bliss is pursuing her master's degree in library and information sciences (MLISC) at the University of Hawaii at Manoa. She is an active member of the Honolulu Japanese Seventh-day Adventist Church in Manoa. She is the "mommy" to three cats, and loves reading, traveling, and crafts. **May 3.**

Fulori Sususewa Bola writes from Papua New Guinea, where she is a lecturer in the School of Education at Pacific Adventist University. She loves to contribute to the women's devotional book and help out with women's programs. She also enjoys going out with her students for outreach and ministering to the marginalized and needy. **Mar. 15.**

Evelyn Greenwade Boltwood is a mother of two young adults and grandmother to two grandsons. She is the Pathfinder and Adventurer coordinator for western New York. Her passions are youth ministries, camping, reading, inspirational writing, and traveling. She is a member of the Akoma women's community gospel choir, which raises scholarships for young women. **Apr. 16, June 9.**

Ingrid Bomke writes from Germany. She is married and has three sons and two grandchildren. She was a leader in a nursery school for many years. Since 1997 she has had a ministry counseling teens and young people. She presents seminars on Christian education. Her second audiobook will be presented soon. **July 25.**

Tamar Boswell is a registered nurse residing in Bermuda. She loves to pray for others and gets excited when she sees answered prayers, especially in the lives of unbelievers. Her interests include travel, reading, experimenting with vegetarian recipes, and participating in community-outreach programs. **Feb. 11.**

Althea Y. Boxx, a Jamaican, is a registered nurse. She has published her first book, a devotional entitled *Fuel for the Journey,* an inspirational nugget for life's uphill climb. Althea believes that nothing is as contagious as enthusiasm. Her hobbies include reading, writing, traveling, and photography. **Mar. 18.**

Elizabeth Boyd, a physical therapist, served as a traveling therapist in the early days of the traveling health-care industry. She founded the company Traveling Medical Professionals, Inc., based in Maine. Now retired at her farm in Harpswell, she enjoys horses, writing, hospitality, and music. Weekends are filled with coaching young people in Bible study and prayer activities. **Jan. 28, June 10.**

Wendy Bradley lives in a small town near the New Forest in Hampshire, England. Her husband, David, passed away in 2007, and now she has taken up her writing again. God has put around her the most wonderful set of friends who have encouraged her back to driving after a gap of 12 years. **Dec. 2.**

DeeAnn Bragaw joyfully lives in Colorado and serves as an educator, author, speaker, and trainer. DeeAnn's hobbies include climbing mountains, biking, snowshoeing, finding new wildflowers, feeding hungry teenagers, and eating chocolate. A retreat speaker and trainer, she can be reached at deeannbragaw.com. **Dec. 25.**

Ani Köhler Bravo is a retired secretary who worked at the Brazil Publishing House and wrote the 2007 daily devotional book for juniors. She lives with her husband and son in Engenheiro Coelho, Brazil, and serves her church by leading women's ministries. She enjoys reading and says that a day doesn't have hours enough to read all the books she wants. **Nov. 4.**

Sherrie Anderson Bryant lives in northwest Indiana, where she is an herbalist, gardener, and a member of the Prairie Writer's Guild. She married her husband, Ralph, in 1973. They have two children and three grandchildren. **Apr. 18.**

Edna S. Buenaventura writes from the Philippines, where she graduated from Adventist University of the Philippines with a BSE-English. She was a scholarship recipient from the General Conference Women's Ministries Department, partially funded by the sale of these devotional books. **Dec. 12.**

Darlene Ytredal Burgeson is a retired sales manager, and caregiver for both herself and her husband in Michigan. Although they are not well, they spend much time with their great-grandchildren. They thank God they have time to take them to many interesting places, even some lengthy car trips. Their family is their hobby, and Darlene also loves to write. **June 1, Dec. 20.**

Maureen O. Burke is a busy retiree in New York, serving her church as an elder, interest coordinator, and Sabbath school teacher. She enjoys giving Bible studies, reading, music, writing, entertaining, and helping others through what she calls the "ministry of encouragement." She also volunteers at the central public library. **July 11.**

Jennifer Burkes loves the Lord, first and foremost! She was baptized in 2006 and is the women's ministries leader of the Grants Pass Seventh-day Adventist Church. She lives in Grants Pass, Oregon, with her husband, James, and 10-year-old daughter, Krista. She works at the community college as a department secretary. **Mar. 29.**

Nancy Buxton is the women's ministries director for the Mid-America Union of Seventh-day Adventists in Lincoln, Nebraska. She has been married to Bob for 42 years, and they have two married children and six grandchildren. She has a blog at nancyoutlook.wordpress.com, where you will find stories, women's ministries ideas, inspirational thoughts, and other fun things. **Apr. 15.**

Elizabeth Ida Cain writes from Jamaica, West Indies, where she works at a new motor vehicle dealership as a human resources assistant. She attends the St. John's Seventh-day Adventist Church, where she is a member of the women's ministries association and also serves as Sabbath school teacher. She enjoys writing and is a floral arranging art designer and instructor. **Jan. 29.**

María Gabriela Acosta de Camargo writes from Venezuela, where she is a pediatric dentist with a private practice, and also works at the University of Carabobo teaching dentistry. At church she is in charge of the music department. She has written for journals in dentistry and is writing a book to help students. She is married and has two boys. She plays tennis and enjoys playing the piano. **Mar. 11.**

Beth Wells Carlson and her husband, Jim, are retired in Ardmore, Oklahoma, where they have lived for about 40 years. Beth is a mother and grandmother, and she volunteers at their Community Services center. **May 28, Nov. 19.**

Tina Carriger, 27 years old, lives in Lincoln, Nebraska. She is an active member of the Allon Chapel Seventh-day Adventist Church and is a full-time employee of AdventSource. She is a part-time student at Union College as a theology major. Her passion is preaching, evangelism, and music. She is currently training women (ages 17-40) how to be spiritual leaders in their church. **Feb. 25.**

Antonia Castellino is married and lives in the English Midlands. She has two grown children and two grandchildren—her pride and joy. She is a retired teacher who with her husband founded the Harper Bell School, an elementary church school in the Midlands. She enjoys walking, nature, listening to music, visual arts, and Bible study; she is active in her local church. **July 30.**

Priscilla Charles and her husband, Keith, live in Suffolk, Virginia, and have two adult children and three grandchildren. She is active in her church as women's ministry leader and Sabbath school leader, and assists in health ministries. When she is not on the job as a registered nurse, her hobbies include cooking, reading, and gardening. **Mar. 5, Aug. 17.**

Suhana Chikatla is a doctor who was born in India. She attends the church in Mobile, Alabama, where she lives with her husband, Royce Sutton. Suhana serves as an executive counsel member for the Gulf States Conference Women's Ministries Department. She has a zeal for working with youth to help them love the Lord. Her passion is recycling. **Feb. 14.**

Caroline Chola is the women's/children's ministries director for the Southern Africa-Indian Ocean Division of Seventh-day Adventists. She lives in Pretoria, South Africa, with her husband, Habson. They have five adult children and one granddaughter. **Aug. 9.**

Birol Charlotte Christo is a retired teacher. During her active service she also worked as an office secretary and statistician. She lives with her husband in Hosur, India. The mother of five adult children, Birol enjoys gardening, sewing, and creating craft items to finance her projects for homeless children. **Apr. 2, June 26.**

Rosemarie Clardy and her husband enjoy the blessings of country living while raising their three boys in North Carolina. They volunteer at church and school. **Mar. 8.**

Jayne Strickland Colby is married and the mother of one delightful special-needs son (age 37). From her home in Maine, she finds gardening and spending time fellowshipping with fellow believers and those interested in learning more about God's plan pleasant ways to occupy her time. She is an attorney with her own general civil litigation practice. **Mar. 23**

Rose Constantino is associate professor at the University of Pittsburgh School of Nursing. She lives with her family in Pittsburgh, Pennsylvania. **Oct. 7.**

M. J. Corrales has been writing for many years with a concentration in biblical studies and devotionals. She can be contacted through her Web site www.TheGloryFoundation.com or by e-mail to director@thegloryfoundation.com. She lives in Oklahoma. **Apr. 4.**

Daphnie Corrodus has her own business in Jamaica. She has a passion for sharing the love of Christ and promoting healthy living. **Sept. 6.**

Elizabeth Grécia Coutimho writes from Brazil, where she is married and has two children. She is an English teacher who works with children. She likes to read and make handicrafts (tapestry and loom). She works in the children's department of her church. **Aug. 14.**

Patricia Cove, who writes from Canada, celebrated her fiftieth wedding anniversary in 2008. She is a mother of five, grandmother of 17, and great-grandmother of one. She is head elder of her church, a freelance writer, does substitute teaching, and spends much time in her gardens. Her hobbies are sailing with husband, George, outdoor pursuits, and reading. **Jan. 26, Aug. 4.**

Celia Mejia Cruz lives with her pastor-husband in the highlands of Tennessee, where she owns her own business of providing innovative office solutions to small businesses. She is also a freelance writer and public speaker, and serves as a church elder and local women's ministries leader. She enjoys camping, reading, writing, and teaching. **Aug. 30.**

Betty Cummings is a registered nurse who works as a public health nurse (BSN) in Washington State, where she is involved with depression recovery programs and brain development. She has three children: Ron, a pastor; Jeanine, disabled, who lives with her; and Gina, a medical doctor. Betty is the daughter of Esteban and Olivia Lopez, who were missionaries for 50 years. **June 6.**

Carol J. Daniel is the director of the Career Development Services at the University of the Southern Caribbean in Trinidad and part-time lecturer for the School of Education. Carol holds an M.A. in educational psychology and is pursuing a terminal degree in industrial/organizational psychology. She enjoys counseling students and preparing them for the world of work. **Oct. 12.**

Avery Davis, originally from Jamaica, lives in England, where she is actively involved with both children's and women's ministries in her local church. She is the mother of Theresa, Sarah, and Grace, and is currently working on a collection of family stories and a book of conversations with women. **Jan. 25.**

Wanda Grimes Davis, the senior chaplain at Florida Hospital, East Orlando, Florida, is a sought-after speaker for women's ministries. She and her husband have three young adult children who are frequently the source of her stories and inspiration. She enjoys sewing, travel, and "adventures." She enjoys preaching, teaching, and sharing the good news of Jesus. **Feb. 17.**

Fauna Rankin Dean lives in Tonganoxie, Kansas, with Bill, her husband of more than 30 years, and a houseful of golden retrievers. They have three adult children, two still in college. She enjoys photography, writing, and gardening in her spare time. **Apr. 13, Sept. 3.**

Deon Dill is a 20-year-old Bermudan studying at the University of Wales in England for a degree in secondary teaching. After her first missionary trip to Haiti at age 19, she plans on making missionary work her main focus after graduation. Her creative passions include writing poetry and abstract thoughts, scrapbooking, reading, traveling, and photography. **Nov. 27.**

Sinikka Dixon is retired on Prince Edward Island, Canada, with her husband. She is an Adventist sociologist with a Ph.D. from the University of California, Riverside. She is multicultural and multilingual, with publications in her professional field of social inequalities, aging, and community studies. She loves to read, travel, and participate in water and snow sports. **June 2.**

Leonie Donald thanks God every day for the beauty of Queen Charlotte Sound, New Zealand, where she lives. She enjoys long walks, "devours" books, and admits to spending more time in her garden than doing housework. Leonie and her husband of 43 years attend the Blenheim Adventist Church. **Apr. 10, Sept. 5.**

Louise Driver, now retired, lives in Idaho, where her three sons and four grandchildren also live. She is the librarian at the Caldwell elementary school, where two of her grandchildren attend. Her hobbies are singing, music, reading, gardening, and traveling to historical places. **Oct. 8.**

Joy Dustow, recently widowed at the time of writing, lives in a retirement village in Queensland, Australia. She had a varied career in education and now enjoys volunteer work in the spiritual and social activities in the village. She still enjoys playing tennis. **Mar. 19.**

Pauline A. Dwyer-Kerr, a native of the beautiful island of Jamaica, lives in Florida. She has served the church as an elder, in Sabbath school, in communication and family life, on social committees, as receptionist, and as a church clerk. She has sung in the church choir and led their singing group. She has a doctorate and is a professor. She loves travel and the outdoors. **Sept. 21.**

Valsa Edison writes from India, where she served as a secondary school teacher for 35 years and in 1991 was awarded the Best Teacher Award. Now retired, she serves as an honorary director of women's and children's ministries. She teaches the teenagers' classes in the church. She and her husband have two daughters. Her hobbies include reading, writing, listening to music, and cooking. **Oct. 14.**

Missilene B. Edwards, a registered nurse, lives in Hogansville, Georgia, with her husband of more than 47 years. She has two adult children and three grandchildren. Missilene is a third-generation Adventist and has served the church in many capacities, including 15 years as clerk and as Investment leader. Her hobbies include gardening, cooking, and bird-watching. **Dec. 11.**

Ruby H. Enniss-Alleyne writes from Guyana, South America, where she is the assistant treasurer for the Guyana Conference of Seventh-day Adventists. In her local church she is the family ministries leader and a church elder. Ruby is the mother of three adult children and a partner in ministry for more than 28 years with her husband, Ashton. **Nov. 28.**

Doreen Evans-Yorke is the Jamaican-Canadian mother of three young adults. She spent 16 years living and working in three countries in Africa. She says that her experiences there were the source of many blessings. She now lives in Montreal, where she works as a child life specialist. **Mar. 3.**

Fartema M. Fagin is a retired social worker and is now an adjunct instructor in development writing at a community college in Tennessee. She graduated from Georgia State University, and received a master's degree in English from the University of Tennessee at Chattanooga. She and her husband have three sons, two daughters, and four grandchildren. Fartema enjoys singing, reading, and writing. **June 12.**

Dorcas Modupe Falade is a vice principal and her school's guidance counselor. She has served as the women's ministries secretary for the South West Nigeria Conference of Seventh-day Adventists. Her husband is the conference stewardship, communication, and trust services director. They are blessed with children, and her highest interest is engaging in Bible studies. **Aug. 20.**

Susana Faria writes from Brazil. She enjoys volunteering her time with children's ministries at her church. She has been married to Marco Faria for 23 years, and they have two sons, Marco 22, and Jorge, 20. Susana has worked in a hospital for 21 years, and enjoys reading, embroidery, and walking. **Nov. 18.**

Gloria Stella Felder lives in Atlanta, Georgia. She and her retired pastor-husband share a family of four adult children and five grandchildren. Gloria enjoys music, writing, speaking, playing Scrabble, and spending time with family—especially her grandchildren. She has written magazine articles and a book of poetry, and is working on a second book. **Mar. 12, Aug. 1.**

Odette Ferreira lives in Burtonsville, Maryland, with her husband, Teofilo. They have two children, Paulo and Elia, and five grandchildren. She serves as director of Adventist Colleges Abroad. She enjoys reading, music, and interacting with family and friends. She also loves foreign languages and believes that fluency, as well as exposure to other cultures, is important. **Nov. 1.**

Carol Joy Fider is chair of the Department of English and Modern Languages at Northern Caribbean University in Jamaica. She serves as women's and prayer ministries director for her church, as well as church elder and Sabbath school teacher. She enjoys cooking, gardening, and mentoring young people. She and her husband, Ezra, have two adult daughters, Carla and Carlene. **Mar. 26.**

Edith Fitch is a retired teacher living in Lacombe, Alberta, Canada, and volunteers in the archives at Canadian University College. She enjoys doing research for schools and churches, as well as individual histories. Her hobbies include writing, traveling, needlework, Sudoku, and cryptograms. **Apr. 11.**

Lana Fletcher lives in Chehalis, Washington, with her husband. They have one married daughter; their younger daughter was killed in a car accident in 1993. Lana is the church clerk. She loves gardening, does the bookkeeping for her husband's business, makes Creative Memories albums, helps with a Loss-of-a-Child support group, and journals her prayers. **Jan. 24, May 18.**

Helen Lennear Florence is a native of Bird Song, Arkansas, and is married to P. M. Florence, who is a pastor in the LaGrange/Greenville, Georgia, district. She is a graduate of Oakwood University and the mother of two adult children. She enjoys traveling, sewing, and ministering to the sick. She is a retired educator, and is now active in her local church. **July 16.**

Hedy F. Fontamillas writes from the Philippines, where she is a secondary public school teacher. She has served her church as a Sabbath school superintendent, and currently is the music ministries leader. Her hobbies are crocheting, gardening, amateur cooking, and cross-stitching. **Oct. 27.**

Carol Wiggins Gigante, a former day-care provider, is a teacher at heart. She is an avid reader, photographer, and flower and bird lover. Carol resides in Beltsville, Maryland, with her husband, Joe, their dog, Buddy, and cat, Suzannah. They have two grown sons, Jeff and James. "Even so come, Lord Jesus!" **June 5.**

Prasedes Gillett writes from Belize, where she is an educator at Canaan Adventist High School. She is a pastor's wife and the mother of two daughters. She and her husband work together with several congregations. She enjoys writing; loves cooking, gardening, and crafts; and speaks five languages. Since the death of her first husband, she has tried to "seize the moment." **Mar. 21, Apr. 26.**

Evelyn Glass and her husband, Darrell, live in northern Minnesota on the farm where Darrell was born. They have three grown children and two grandchildren. Evelyn writes a weekly column for the local paper and is active as a speaker and a community volunteer. Evelyn recently authored a series of Bible studies, *Women in the Bible and Me*. **Aug. 15, Nov. 22.**

Vilmêdes Goese was born in Espírito Santo, Brazil. When she was small, she moved to Rio de Janeiro, where she still lives. She has two children, Angelo and Agnes, and two beautiful granddaughters. She was born into an Adventist family, and participates in many church departments. Her hobbies are reading, listening to music, walking, and taking care of plants. **Oct. 28.**

Hannelore Gomez, from Panama, teaches Spanish in a high school in Virginia. Her hobbies are reading and traveling. Knowing the gospel since she was born has been her greatest blessing. **May 4.**

Kimberly Goodge lives in the beautiful Northwest of the United States. She enjoys reading, swimming, biking, and travel. She says spending time with God, family, friends, and neighbors is the highlight of any day. **Apr. 28.**

Beverly P. Gordon lives with her husband and two sons in Downingtown, Pennsylvania. She is a professor of psychology, a registered nurse, and family ministry coordinator for her church. She has presented seminars, sermons, and keynote addresses for various academic and religious settings. Her hobbies include gardening, music, reading, word games, and chess. **Mar. 27.**

Mayla Magaieski Graeps writes from Brazil, where she is a first-year high school student. She had been involved in Missionary Pairs with her mother, Helena. She spends most of her time studying, but in her free time she crochets, knits, embroiders, paints, gardens, and reads. Her biggest goal is to leave marks of Christ in the life of others through published articles. **Aug. 12.**

Cecelia Grant is a Seventh-day Adventist medical doctor, now retired from government service, and living in Kingston, Jamaica. Her hobbies are traveling, gardening, and listening to good music. She has a passion for young people, to whom she often gives advice. **Sept. 1.**

Stephanie A. Grant is an information systems program manager living in Beltsville, Maryland. She loves being a member of the Emmanuel Seventh-day Adventist Church in Brinklow, Maryland. She loves to sing, take great photographs, and travel. **Sept. 26.**

Mary Jane Graves lost her husband, Ted, in January 2009 after more than 58 happy years of marriage. She continues to live in their retirement home in western North Carolina. She is involved in women's ministries and the church library, and enjoys gardening, reading, writing, family, and friends. **July 31, Oct. 6.**

Chrisele Green accepted the Lord as her Savior in 1985. She and her husband of 23 years have two children. In her church in Michigan she teaches a Bible class, sometimes preaches, is a women's ministries leader, sings in the choir, and serves on the hospitality committee. Her passion in life is to help bring Christ's healing to women, encouraging them to live a life deeply dedicated to Him. **Aug. 21.**

Ellie Green is a retired registered nurse and serves as the Sharon church head elder and as a lay pastor's assistant in the Carolina Conference of Seventh-day Adventists. Evangelism is her passion, and she has conducted 16 evangelism series. Her husband is retired from NASA. They have two children and three grandchildren. **Nov. 12.**

Carol J. Greene has been a Florida resident for the past two decades. She is the proud grandparent of four and is settling into her golden years looking forward to the coming of the King of kings. **Dec. 30.**

Eilean L. Greene is a member of the Sligo Adventist Church in Takoma Park, Maryland, and is an ordained elder in the African Methodist Episcopal Church. In her retirement she is pursuing a double master's degree in public and health services administration. She enjoys intercessory prayer, writing, and speed walking. **Feb. 24.**

Glenda-mae Greene, a retired university educator, writes from her wheelchair in central Florida. Her passion is helping other women write their stories of God's grace. **Apr. 1, Sept. 27.**

Gloria Gregory is a minister's wife and the mother of two young adult women. She works as director of admissions at Northern Caribbean University in Jamaica. She believes that each person is precious in God's sight and is born to fulfill a special mission. She is convinced that her mission is to help others unearth their full potentials and use them to honor God. **Mar. 24.**

Bertha Hall is an elementary teacher who lives in Mississippi with her husband, Curtis, and teaches in Louisiana. Her hobbies are reading and traveling; she likes to read religious books on the power of prayer. Bertha likes to participate in outreach activities and is currently in a pastors' wives' (Shepherdess) prayer group. **Mar. 1.**

Dessa Weisz Hardin lives in Maine with her husband. She enjoys the ocean, is teaching herself the piano, and is interested in traveling, writing, art, and music. Grandparenting has added a new dimension to her life. She enjoys the women's devotional book and hearing from friends who have been blessed through it. **Sept. 25, Dec. 16.**

Marian M. Hart, a retired elementary teacher and nursing home administrator, works with her husband in property management. A member of the Battle Creek Tabernacle in Michigan for 35 years, she has served in many different capacities. Six grandchildren make her a proud grandmother. Marian enjoys knitting, reading, growing flowers, and spending winters in Florida. **Jan. 22, Oct. 22.**

Janet Hatcher is a retired licensed practical nurse (LPN). Her daughter lives in Worchester, Massachusetts, and her son lives in Texas. She has five grandchildren. **July 27.**

Bessie Russell Haynes is an English professor in Korea and has served across America as a teacher and principal. She has edited several books while living abroad. She is the mother of three adult children and loves to spend time with them. Her hobbies include traveling, gardening, music, reading, meeting people all over the world, and mission trips. **Mar. 16, Aug. 2.**

Hortense Headley lives in Trinidad and Tobago, and is retired after spending 35 years as an educator in government service. She serves her church as women's ministries coordinator and is an elder. A widow for eight years, she has two adult sons. She enjoys reading and traveling, and now tutors at the University of the West Indies. **Oct. 17.**

Irisdeane Henley-Charles is a nurse consultant working in Washington, D.C. She is married to Oscar, and they have three children. She has worked in many areas of the church over the years and enjoys serving the Lord. Some of her hobbies include arts and crafts projects, sewing, playing the guitar, and reading. **Jan. 19.**

Muriel Heppel, who writes from Canada, has taught for many years. She and her husband were missionaries in the Philippines when he retired. She is active in their local stroke support group, and volunteers at Pleasant Valley Manor, the local assisted living facility. Now a widow, she enjoys bird-watching, reading, knitting, and traveling. **Dec. 18.**

Denise Dick Herr teaches English at Canadian University College in Alberta, Canada. She loves to read and to travel, especially with her family. **Mar. 28, July 10.**

Vashti Hinds-Vanier was born in Guyana, South America, and is presently retired in New York after a nursing career that spanned 40 years. This story was edited from Vashti's published work, "School Daze and Beyond." Her hobbies include travel, cake decorating, gardening, and crocheting. **Jan. 27.**

Patricia Hines was born in Jamaica and has lived in Florida for 14 years. She is a member of the South Orlando Adventist Church, where she is the women's ministries director. Patricia has a great passion for saving lost souls and is hoping that her devotional writing will touch many lives. **June 30.**

Roxy Hoehn writes from Topeka, Kansas, where she is retired after happy years as a teacher and women's ministries director for the Kansas-Nebraska Conference of Seventh-day Adventists. She is the mother of three and grandmother of 11. She has written many stories for children, as well as material for Sabbath school and Vacation Bible School. **Dec. 9.**

Jacqueline Hope HoShing-Clarke has been an educator since 1979 as principal, assistant principal, and teacher. She now serves Northern Caribbean University in Jamaica as the head of the Teacher Education Department. She and her husband have two adult children. Jackie enjoys writing, flower gardening, and housekeeping. She is in love with Jesus. **Nov. 29.**

Annette Howell is an insurance underwriting assistant in Toronto, Canada. She lives with her husband, Michael, and two sons, Brandon and Adrian. In her church she is a Sabbath school superintendent. She enjoys reading in her spare time. **Oct. 1.**

Bonnie Hunt is a retired associate professor of the School of Nursing at Southern Adventist University in Tennessee. She stays active in the School of Nursing coordinating an "academic assistance" program. Life is good, with opportunities for travel, reading, writing, and interacting with family and friends who live close by. **Apr. 14.**

Shirley C. Iheanacho is retired in Alabama and thoroughly enjoys traveling with Morris, her soul mate of 41 years, speaking, writing, visiting, and singing to the sick and shut-in, helping and encouraging fellow travelers, sending e-mails to friends, playing handbells, and singing in the choir. She is grateful to God for His gift of her daughters, Ngo, Chi, and Aku, and her two grandsons. **July 4.**

Shizuko Ikemasu has worked as a pastor's wife for 31 years. She has been appointed director of children's and women's ministries and Shepherdess coordinator for the Japan Union Conference of Seventh-day Adventists. **Apr. 19.**

Rebecca Ishii writes from Yokohama, Japan, where she lives with her husband, Pastor Chris Ishii, who is director for the Adventist Development and Relief Agency. She works at Japan Union Conference of Seventh-day Adventists as English secretary and assistant English Language School coordinator. She and her husband have four grown children and six grandchildren. **Aug. 29.**

Avis Floyd Jackson is the mother of five and lives in Pleasantville, New Jersey. She runs a party planner business out of her home. Avis has been the women's ministries director in her local church for the past five years. She says she is an Adventist by calling. **Sept. 15.**

Joan D. L. Jaensch and Murray, her husband of more than 60 years, live in South Australia. They have two sons, two granddaughters, two grandsons, and two pet stray cats. Joan has served in the Adventist church for 71 years. **Oct. 23.**

Donette James is a staff nurse who lives and works in the United Kingdom. She studied in the West Indies College (now Northern Caribbean University). At church she is involved in the health department and sings in the choir. She especially enjoys working with the youth and the elderly. Instrumental music and reading give her much comfort. **Apr. 30, Oct. 11.**

Velda M. Jesse is director of women's and children's ministries in the Belize Union of Seventh-day Adventists. She works tirelessly in this capacity because of her love and commitment to the work of the Lord. She is the wife of Pastor Luis Jesse and the mother of three (two boys and one girl). A business administrator by profession, she has worn the hat of a teacher for more than 12 years. **Apr. 20, Sept. 17.**

Greta Michelle Joachim-Fox-Dyett, from Trinidad and Tobago, is a wife, mother, artist, writer, teacher, blogger, radio announcer (with Resurface Radio on the Adventist Internet radio station), and member of the women's ministries council. Most important, she's a child of the most high God. **Feb. 19.**

Emily Felts Jones began Bring Forth Ministries in 1996. Through music, writing, and speaking she loves to share God's infinite power to work in and through each one of us, whatever our age. Emily lives in Tennessee. **Jan. 18.**

Nadine Joseph has a Web site (www.nadinejoseph.com) on which she shares her writings, poetry, devotionals, thoughts, and quotes. She hopes to publish a book, and is a devotional writer for an online radio station. Nadine contributes to the *Collegiate Quarterly* and prepares monthly devotions for the East Caribbean Conference Youth Department. **Apr. 21.**

Barbara Ann Kay, writing from Alabama, enjoys spending time in nature, listening to her Father's messages. She has combined writing and nature photography on a Web site (gardenofgraceandhope.com) as her ministry of encouragement. Her book *God's Character From A to Z* shares stories from the Bible and personal experiences about God. **Sept. 7.**

Lynette Kenny is a wife, mother of four school-age children, business partner, Sabbath school teacher, and registered nurse. Most of all, she is a daughter of the King. She writes from rural Australia. When time allows, she enjoys painting, writing, photography, and being out in nature. She has been published in *Signs of the Times*. **Feb. 12.**

Marília Macieira Kettle has worked as a Bible instructor and secretary in Brazil. She and her pastor-husband are both now retired. They have three adult children and two grandchildren. She likes to cook, read, and spend time with her family. She lives in Sumaré, São Paulo, Brazil. **May 5.**

Bridgid Kilgour is a registered nurse specializing in aged care. She writes from Sydney, Australia. Her passion for writing was born when she started writing scripts for puppet plays while she, her husband, and two sons were leaders in children's ministries. **Jan. 21, May 14.**

Janette Kingston has been both a primary and high school teacher and a chaplain in Adventist schools in three states of Australia. She is married to Andrew Kingston, president of the Solomon Islands Mission. They have five children, all married, and 11 grandchildren. Janette's passion is teaching adults to read Pidgin English so they can absorb God's Word. **July 13.**

Iris L. Kitching enjoys every day of life with her husband, Will. She works in the presidential section of the General Conference of Seventh-day Adventists. She is communication secretary at her church in Maryland, edits her church newsletter (including layout and design), and learns interesting life lessons from four very special granddaughters. **Mar. 10, Nov. 15.**

Glena Knopp lives in Grande Prairie, Canada. On July 8, 2009, Glena's beloved husband, Doug, lost his courageous battle with abdominal cancer at the age of 53. Glena and daughter, Cheri, eagerly await Jesus' soon return to be reunited with him. She has served her church as head deaconess, head of the social committee, and head of the fellowship committee. **June 21.**

Linda Mei Lin Koh is the director of children's ministries at the General Conference of Seventh-day Adventists. Originally from Singapore but now living in Maryland, she enjoys helping women develop their talents and gifts in service to the church and the community. She is married with two grown-up sons. Her hobbies include baking and playing basketball. **Aug. 25.**

Hepzibah Kore writes from Hosur, India, where she is the Shepherdess coordinator of the Southern Asia Division of Seventh-day Adventists. Her husband, Gnararaj, is a minister. Her passion is to open the eyes of the women in her country to read the Word and see the world through adult literacy programs. **May 9.**

Betty Kossick, writing from Georgia, is a freelance writer-journalist, and the author of an autobiographical book, *Beyond the Locked Door* (2006), and *Heart Ballads,* a potpourri of poetry (2009). Both are available via amazon.com and other Internet book sites. Regardless of growing older, retirement from her craft and writing ministry is not in her vocabulary. **May 26.**

Patricia Mulraney Kovalski, a widow, lives in Collegedale, Tennessee. She enjoys traveling and visiting her children and grandchildren in Michigan and her sisters and brother-in-law in Sun City, Hilton Head, South Carolina. **Apr. 29.**

Mabel Kwei is a retired university-college lecturer. She served in Africa for many years as a missionary with her pastor-husband and three children. She reads, loves to paint, write, give talks, and spend lots of time with very little children in church and in the community. **Jan. 17.**

Sally Lam-Phoon serves the Northern Asia-Pacific Division of Seventh-day Adventists, headquartered in Korea, as children's, family, and women's ministries director, and Shepherdess coordinator. Her passion is helping people unleash their potential as they seek to live out God's purpose. Married for 39 years to Chek-Yat, a gospel minister, she has two married daughters and one granddaughter. **Apr. 7.**

Barbara Lankford recently retired from work for the state of Idaho to care for her two youngest grandchildren. She and her husband, Jerry, have two married daughters and six grandchildren. Her hobbies include quilting, any kind of needlework, gardening, reading, singing, and playing with the grandchildren. **Apr. 23.**

Iani Dias Lauer-Leite, a college professor, lives in Bahia, Brazil. At church she likes to help with music and prayer ministries. **Jan. 6, Apr. 27.**

Temitope Joyce Lawal is a pastor's daughter and the Sabbath school secretary for her local church. She has been working for nine years as a payroll officer-administrative secretary at the Adventist Hospital in Ile-Ife, Nigeria. She loves singing. **Nov. 5.**

Loida Gulaja Lehmann sold religious books in the Philippines for 10 years, then went to Germany. She and her husband are active members in International church in Darmstadt. For years she worked in the U.S. Military Service Center in Frankfurt/Main. Her hobbies include traveling, collecting souvenirs, nature walks, and photography. **June 19, Sept. 19.**

Sharon (Brown) Long, originally from Trinidad, West Indies, resides in Edmonton, Canada. She has worked with the Alberta government for 30 years as a social worker. She and her husband, Miguel, have four adult children and two granddaughters. They attend the West Edmonton Adventist Church. Sharon enjoys entertaining, shopping, and serving others. **Aug. 13.**

Rhodi Alers de López is a bilingual writer living in Massachusetts. Her ministry as a singer, speaker, and songwriter inspires others in their walk with God. She leads an active team of prayer warriors, "El Escuadrón de la Victoria." Her bilingual Web site is ExpresSion Publishing Ministries. She has recorded two CDs. Rhodi is a wife, mother, crafter, and church leader. **Mar. 13, Dec. 22.**

Erika Loudermill-Webb lives in Oakland, California, and is a graduate of San Francisco State University, where she majored in television production. She is a wife and the mother of two beautiful girls. She loves to write. **Apr. 24, Aug. 3.**

Emma Lutz is a retired pastor's wife who has degrees in education and office administration from Southwestern Adventist University. She works for the Department of Health in Washington State, where she lives with her husband. She has two daughters, two sons-in-law, and five grandchildren. She likes to play the piano and crochet doilies. **Mar. 4, Aug. 31.**

Alice Mafanuke is the audit manager at Camelsa Chartered Accountant Zimbabwe. She has four children. She enjoys preaching, teaching, reading, and sharing God's Word, and has been women's ministries and personal ministries director at her local church. She is now the Voice of Prophecy director and Sabbath school teacher at Harare City Centre Church, Harare, Zimbabwe. **Dec. 26.**

Georgina Maglis moved in 1997 from Melbourne, Australia, to Greece. Her husband is the president of the Greek Mission, which is part of the Trans-European Division of Seventh-day Adventists. They are Greek by origin. They have two married sons and one granddaughter, 14, who live in Melbourne. **July 9.**

Rhona Grace Magpayo is a third-generation Adventist from the Philippines who lives in Maryland. She is married to Celestino Magpayo, Jr., a retired master chief in the U.S. Navy. They have two children, Celesti Marie and David Allen. She has been a licensed optician for more than 20 years, and has taken mission trips to South and Central America. **Mar. 14, Aug. 22.**

Fe C. Magpusao, who writes from the Philippines, has a bachelor's degree in elementary education. She's a church school teacher, pastor's wife, and the mother of two. She enjoys reading books, listening to religious music, traveling, and adventure. **July 17.**

Eunice Michiles Malty writes from Brazil. A congresswoman for 16 years, she was the first female senator in Brazil. She actively participates in women's ministries in the Central church in Brasilia. She and her second husband, Gerson Malty, participate in senior citizens' ministry. She enjoys traveling, reading, social work, and making flower arrangements. **June 23, Dec. 29.**

Cassandra Marquez de Smith is a gifted second grader at Redeemer Christian School in Ocala, Florida. She loves to read, swim, and play the piano. Cassandra is an active member of the primary division in her local church. **July 12.**

Lillian Marquez de Smith is an eighth grader at Redeemer Christian School in Ocala, Florida. Lillian is a cheerleader, a volleyball player, and an avid reader. Lillian is a junior deaconess at the Belleview Seventh-day Adventist Church. **May 6.**

Tamara Marquez de Smith writes from Ocala, Florida, where she is teaching exceptional students from kindergarten through fifth grade. The family has moved from New York, and with her husband, Steven, and daughters, Lillian and Cassandra, they have become members of the Belleview church. Tamara is currently the primary division leader and the head of the social committee. **Sept. 8.**

Marion V. Clarke Martin, a physician who writes from Panama, is the immediate past dean of the faculty of medicine of the University of Panama and full professor of medical microbiology. She enjoys reading, playing the piano, and interior decorating. She considers herself greatly blessed with two adult sons and one granddaughter. **May 30.**

Melissa Harumi Acosta Mau, 22 years old, works in the Anne Sullivan Center of Peru as a psychologist-teacher for people with special needs (autism, mental retardation, and Down syndrome, among others). She divides her free time between talking with friends and family and being the assistant secretary of personal ministries of the Spain church in Lima. **Aug. 10.**

Ivani Viana Sampaio Maximino is the mother of three daughters: Camila, Caroline, and Catherine, and is married to Roberto. She has a new son, Sandro Roberto. Ivani loves family gatherings on Sabbaths, and likes to read and jog. She is a deaconess and helps in the decoration of the church of Brazil Adventist University Academy, São Paulo, Brazil. **Sept. 11.**

Mary L. Maxson is an associate pastor in Paradise, California. Her responsibilities include seven ministries and discipling young adult women. For creativity, she makes sure her landscaping isn't demolished by the deer or squirrels that often pass through her property. She loves flower gardening and creating computer cards to send to church members. **Jan. 5.**

Nakku Mbwana, from Tanzania, recently moved to Silver Spring, Maryland, where her husband serves as a vice president of the General Conference of Seventh-day Adventists. They have two daughters, Orupa and Upendo, and her hobbies are listening to Christian music, cooking, reading books, visiting new places, gardening, and learning to swim. **July 8.**

Retha McCarty, who lives in Missouri, has been the treasurer of her church since 1977 and the editor of the church newsletter for three years. Reading, writing, poetry, crocheting, and bird-watching are her hobbies. Her latest interest is sewing quilt tops for her daughter's "bags of love" ministry project. **May 7, Sept. 10.**

Vidella McClellan is a married senior and a caregiver of the elderly in British Columbia, Canada. She is a mother of three with seven grandchildren, one great-grandchild, and seven stepgrandchildren. Her current hobbies are gardening, crosswords, Scrabble, and writing. She loves cats, reading, and instrumental music. She often speaks in nearby churches. **Jan. 15.**

Melissa (Missy) Daughety McClung is a National Board Certified school counselor in a public school in North Carolina. She is married to David, her husband of 20 years. They have one son, Spencer, 16. She attends the same church, Kinston, in which she was reared, and is church pianist there. She enjoys baseball, writing, and traveling with her family. **July 21.**

Mary McIntosh is a writer, poet, and freelance editor who lives in Vancouver, Washington. She holds a Ph.D. degree in English from Suny/Buffalo, has taught at Pacific Union College and Weimar College, has published several of her poems, and teaches creative writing workshops. She has been women's ministries leader at her church in Washougal for five years. **Oct. 5.**

Ruth Esther McKinney is a retired educator whose last appointment was chairperson of the office administration department at Northern Caribbean University in Mandeville, Jamaica. Ruth and her husband, Pastor Silas N. McKinney, live in Nassau, Bahamas. She enjoys distributing inspiring e-mails, visiting the sick and shut-ins, gardening, and giving plants away. **June 18.**

Gay Mentes writes, does her art, and works with flowers in Kelowna, British Columbia, Canada, where she happily resides with her artist husband. Together they are enjoying being grandparents to a granddaughter, Callah Anada Sharlet Tataryn, the "best Christmas Eve gift I ever received." Gay has two grown children and a son-in-love. **May 11.**

Annette Walwyn Michael writes from St. Croix in the U.S. Virgin Islands. She is a retired English teacher who has replaced the classroom with many family, church, and community activities. Her husband, Reginald, daughters, and grandchildren continue to enrich her life. She has written and published Caribbean literature. **Feb. 22, June 7.**

Sharon Michael is a family physician practicing in Pennsylvania. She is one of three daughters born to Dr. and Mrs. Michael. Scrapbooking, gardening, traveling, and writing are her hobbies. **July 18.**

Quilvie G. Mills is a retired community college professor. She lives with her husband, Pastor Herman, in Port St. Lucie, Florida. She serves her church as Bible class teacher, board member, minister of music, and member of the floral committee. She enjoys traveling, reading, music, gardening, word games, and teaching piano. **July 23, Oct. 30.**

Cheryol Mitchell is an assistant high school principal to eleventh-grade students in the second-largest school district in St. Louis, Missouri. She has been an educator for 22 years in both parochial and public school systems. She is an avid reader and enjoys spending time with friends and family. **Oct. 10.**

Susen Mattison Mole´ grew up as a missionary child in India and enjoyed moving around. She has two girls who are both in college. She enjoys hiking, writing, reading, painting, playing her cello, and eating food from different cultures. She travels around with her Navy doctor-husband, as she has for the past 28 years. **Apr. 25.**

Marcia Mollenkopf, a retired teacher, lives in Klamath Falls, Oregon. She enjoys church involvement and has served in both adult and children's divisions. Her hobbies include reading, writing, music, and bird watching. **May 23.**

Natacha Moorooven, born in Mauritius, completed a B.A. in information management and theology in Cameroon. After graduating, she was employed as a pastoral intern in Mauritius, then as a Bible/English teacher in Korea while doing an M.A. in religion at Sahmyook University. After working in Maryland, she is back in Korea working toward a Ph.D. **Sept. 23.**

Lila Farrell Morgan is a widow with five adult children and five grandchildren, ranging in age from 3 to 19 years old. She serves as an assistant Sabbath school superintendent in the church in North Carolina where she and her husband were charter members 49 years ago. She enjoys her grandchildren, reading, walking, bird-watching, baking, table games, and e-mailing family and friends. **Aug. 23.**

Yer Moua was born in Laos and lived there until she was 13. Then she came to America, which she now calls home. She and her husband, Thomas, have six children. Her hobbies include hiking, gardening, and raising animals. She is happily employed by McKee Foods in Gentry, Arkansas. **Dec. 27.**

Bonnie Moyers lives with her husband and three cats in Staunton, Virginia. She has two adult children and two granddaughters. She is a musician for a Methodist church and a Presbyterian church on Sundays. She writes freelance, and has been published in many magazines and books. She is a volunteer musician in her local church. **Jan. 3.**

Ethel Doris Msuseni is a single parent, professional nurse and teacher, and a member of the Ngangelizwe Seventh-day Adventist Church in Umtata, South Africa. She has two adult children and loves to listen to gospel music, enjoys cooking, sewing, baking, and gardening. **Mar. 20.**

Judith M. Mwansa comes from Zambia and currently works for the Women's Ministries Department at the General Conference of Seventh-day Adventists in Maryland. She and her husband have been blessed with four children. Her joy is spending time with her family, reading, listening to music, taking walks, and being a part of the great Adventist family. **Dec. 31.**

Joelcira F. Cavedon Mÿller was introduced to Adventists through the Hong Kong Adventist Hospital. She lived and worked in Southeast Asia for 18 years, but was baptized when she returned to her roots in Brazil. She has four grown children. Jo divides her time between Brazil and Germany, and she and her German husband are working hard to open an international church in Stuttgart. **Apr. 5.**

Julie Nagle is a wife, a mother of three, and a professional who works for the Australian Public Service. An ordained elder, she is dedicated to service for God and with God. Her motto is "In His Service." Julie is an indigenous Australian involved in many ministries that benefit women and the general public. She enjoys public speaking and continual learning. **Oct. 26.**

Anne Elaine Nelson is a retired teacher who works with testing for schools. She has written the book *Puzzled Parents.* Her four children have blessed her with 14 grandchildren and three great-grandchildren. Anne lives in Michigan, where she stays active in her church. Her favorite activities are sewing, music, photography, and creating memories for her grandchildren. **June 3, Sept. 9.**

Ashley Anne Nelson is a first-time devotional contributor who is studying to be a photographer. She is an only child who lives in Michigan, where she spends her spare time training her palomino quarter horse mare, Abby, to jump and do Western pleasure. She is the assistant in the children's department of her church. **May 25.**

Ivy Ng is married to G. T. Ng. Prior to their coming to the United States they served as missionaries to the Philippines and to war-torn Cambodia. Ivy holds a master's degree in education. She was a university admissions officer and chair of the fund-raising committee. Her new post is at the Hope Channel Television Network in Silver Spring, Maryland. The Ngs have two children. **May 19.**

Angèle Rachel Nlo Nlo is a pastor's wife and missionary. She and her husband have served for 17 years at the Seventh-day Adventist church headquarters in Abidjan, Ivory Coast. She has degrees in family law and public law. Angèle is a Shepherdess coordinator and works in the church's publishing department. Her hobbies are reading, traveling, conducting evangelistic campaigns, meeting friends, and cooking. **Oct. 13.**

Elizabeth Versteegh Odiyar of Kelowna, British Columbia, has managed the family chimney sweep business since 1985. She has three adult children. Beth enjoys mission trips and road trips. She loves being creative, sewing, cooking vegan, and decorating. She has filled many positions in her local church and is still a Pathfinder at heart. **July 2.**

Lourdes S. de Oliveira has been married for 37 years and is the mother of three and grandmother of one. She is a retired civil servant and lives in Hortolândia and Serra Negra, São Paulo, Brazil. She likes to read and listen to music. She is learning how to deal with the computer. **July 15.**

Neide Balthazar de Oliveira was born in Brazil and is writing for the first time. For several years she has been coordinating the primary Sabbath school class in the Central church of Cotia, São Paulo, Brazil. She likes to walk, listen to music, read, cook, and enjoys her family. **Nov. 6.**

Jemima Dollosa Orillosa lives in Maryland with her husband, Danny. Originally from the Philippines, they have two married daughters and two sons-in-law. Her passion is organizing mission trips. Her greatest happiness comes from experiencing the joy of people accepting Christ as their personal Savior, and seeing the joy of service and the changed lives of team members. **Nov. 25.**

Sharon Oster lives near St. Louis, Missouri, with her pastor-husband, Jerry. They have three grown children and six grandchildren. Diagnosed with multiple sclerosis several years ago, Sharon has taken medical retirement from the special school district. She enjoys reading, cross-stitch and embroidery, and spending time with her family. **Jan. 1.**

Rose Otis was the first director of the General Conference Women's Ministries Department. Now a full-time grandmother, she and her husband, Bud, live in Middletown, Maryland, near their children and grandchildren. Rose enjoys her flower and potting gardens and eating the lush vegetables her husband grows. They travel, like visiting friends and family, the ocean, and some golf. **Apr. 17, Nov. 11.**

Brenda D. (Hardy) Ottley lives with her husband on the island of St. Lucia. A teacher at heart, she teaches both secondary school and university students. She is engaged in a radio ministry with her husband, Ernest, at Rizzen 102fm/Rizzen102.com, specializing in family, couples, and communication. **May 8, Sept. 13.**

Hannele Ottschofski is living in southern Germany. She has four daughters and three grandchildren. She has helped to organize women's ministries events and has put together two devotional books for women. **Jan. 7, Dec. 13.**

Ofelia A. Pangan lives with her husband in central California. She enjoys her retirement, teaching a Bible class at church, her children and their spouses, her grandchildren, and playing Scrabble. She and her husband love gardening. **Mar. 9, July 1.**

Revel Papaioannou works with her retired-but-working pastor-husband of 54 years in the biblical town of Berea. They have four sons and 14 grandchildren. She has held almost every church position and now is Sabbath school superintendent. She teaches the adult Bible lesson, cleans the church, and cares for a tiny garden. Free time is filled with visiting, Bible studies, and hiking. **May 10, Aug. 11.**

Claudia Parks, a breast cancer survivor, lives in Nebraska with her husband, Nicholas. They have a daughter, a son, and many others they claim for the family of God. Claudia is a grandmother and a woman who is passionate about life and people. She has worked with refugees, hosted international students, and enjoys using her time helping people for Jesus. **July 29.**

Mary Paulson-Lauda lives in Gladstone, Oregon, and is retired after 47 years in health-care work. She has served on various church and community committees, and was involved with children's ministries in Pathfinders and summer camps. She tutors first-grade reading, handcrafts greeting cards, and enjoys visiting her family. **Sept. 30.**

Inez Payne, a retired nurse, writes from central Florida, where she is active in the Palm Bay Seventh-day Adventist Church. Her husband, with whom she worked in the Adventurer and Pathfinder clubs of the area, died in 2010. She has an adult daughter. **Dec. 3.**

Evelyn G. Pelayo writes from Madagascar, where she is an assistant librarian. She and her husband have two sons, a daughter-in-law, and a granddaughter. She enjoys reading, baking, and entertaining people. **Dec. 15.**

Naomi J. Penn is the proud parent of two adult children, Cherise and Shenita. She attends the Shiloh Adventist Church in St. Thomas, Virgin Islands. An accountant by profession, she served in women's ministries for several years at her former church. She enjoys reading, baking, and gardening. **Sept. 4.**

Judi Penner resides in Kelowna, British Columbia, Canada, with her family. She is an active member of Son Valley Fellowship. Judi, an elementary teacher, is on sabbatical and hopes to return to the classroom next year. **Oct. 15.**

Ester Loreno Perin lives in Mato Grosso, Brazil. She is married and has two children whom she loves as jewels that God gave her. She likes to read, walk, and take care of her dogs and birds. She serves her church as the leader of a small group and a deaconess. In 1972 she had a prayer published in a book. She enjoys reading. **July 6.**

Betty G. Perry lives in Fayetteville, North Carolina, with her semiretired pastor-husband. They have two adult children and five grandchildren. An anesthetist for 34 years, she too is now semiretired. Hobbies include sewing, trying new recipes, playing the piano, interior decorating, and arts and crafts. **Jan. 8.**

Angèle Peterson lives in Ohio, where she works as an administrative assistant and serves her church in several capacities. She enjoys spending time with her family, especially her niece and nephew, and looks forward to Christ's soon return. **Feb. 20.**

Margo Peterson writes from Eagan, Minnesota. A former financial analyst, she is now a substitute special education teacher. She spends her free time volunteering as an English as a second language (ESL) teacher, reading, walking, traveling, working with the young people at her church, and spending time with her family. **Jan. 30.**

Karen Phillips is a single mother of four children and works as a human resource/safety manager in Omaha, Nebraska. She is active in her church choir, teaches young children, and serves as an elder. She devotes time to prayer journaling, walking her two dogs, traveling, and ministering to others. Spending time with her children is her favorite pastime. **May 15, June 17.**

Birdie Podder, a retiree, came from northeast India and settled in south India. She has two adult children and four grandsons. Her hobbies are gardening, cooking, baking, telling stories, writing articles, and composing poems. She has a card ministry for encouraging those in need of comfort and encouragement and to glorify God's name. **Mar. 7, Aug. 24.**

Marcia R. Pope is a registered nurse living in Westminster, Colorado. She has three sons and one daughter-in-law, and attends Chapel Haven Adventist Church in Northglenn. She is active in her church, teaching a Sabbath school Bible class and directing the choir and praise singers. She enjoys music, teaching, writing, crocheting, and drawing, and has written several health-care study courses. **May 31, Aug. 16.**

Judith Purkiss is a secondary school teacher living and working in London, England. She loves reading and working with words. Judith serves in Sabbath school and women's ministries in her local church. **July 3.**

Leslie R. Quiroz is a cancer survivor mom of a premature baby. Leslie enjoys working, cooking, practicing yoga, praying, and living one day at a time with her husband and son. She lives in Texas. **May 12.**

Sylvana Ramhit is a third-year student in religious education at Adventist University Zurcher in Madagascar. She says, "It's so amazing how the Lord has called a young woman such as I for His purpose." She wishes that all young women who are receiving His call will help to hasten His second coming. **Mar. 30.**

Darlenejoan McKibbin Rhine was born in Nebraska, raised in California, schooled in Tennessee, and lives in Washington State. She holds a B.A. in journalism and is retired from the Los Angeles *Times.* She attends the new Anacortes Adventist Fellowship on Fidalgo Island, on which she lives. **Jan. 10, Nov. 7.**

Susan Riley, born in Trinidad and Tobago, lives in England. She is a mental health nurse who works on a child and family unit. She loves corresponding, walking (especially along the river near her home), and writing poems. One of her dreams—her aim—is to be a freelance writer. **Feb. 29, June 11.**

Sweetie Ritchil writes from Bangladesh, where she is the treasurer for the union mission and has served the church in different financial areas. She has been involved with children's Sabbath school, and is women's ministries and Dorcas director. She loves Bible reading, composing religious songs, writing articles, and finding ways to help the helpless. **Oct. 4.**

Charlotte Robinson was born in Arkansas, where she has lived for 48 years. She and her husband, David, have sent three children through Adventist schools, the youngest now in academy and the older ones in college. Charlotte works for the postal service and for McKee Foods in Gentry. She would love to write more! **Sept. 14.**

Avis Mae Rodney is a justice of the peace for the province of Ontario, Canada, where she resides with her husband, Leon. Avis is the mother of two young adults and has five beautiful grandchildren. She enjoys early-morning walks, gardening, reading, and spending time with family and friends. **Feb. 15, May 13.**

Sayuri Ruiz Rodriguez lives in San Jose, California, where she enjoys working with youth and women's ministries. She has a heart for missions: "Once a missionary, always a missionary." Sayuri and her husband lead a sign language choir, S.L.A.M. (serving God, loving others, and making a joyful noise unto the Lord!), and both enjoy serving God, knowing that the best is yet to come! **Dec. 17.**

Pamela McPherson Ross and her husband, Allen, moved to a small ranch in Nebraska when he semiretired from Colorado, where they raised their two girls. She has been a registered nurse for 29 years. She loves being with her daughter and four grandchildren and going on mission trips. She enjoys her dogs, horses, crafts, singing, and being outdoors snowmobiling and four-wheeling. **Nov. 30.**

Raylene McKenzie Ross is a labor and delivery nurse who works in Newark, New Jersey, but lives in Spanish Town, Jamaica. She and her husband, Leroy, have a son, Zachary, who makes her life very interesting. She serves her church in Spanish Town in the health ministries department. When Zachary allows her the time, she likes to sew, scrapbook, and read. **Nov. 20.**

Peggy S. Rusike was raised in Zimbabwe, but now lives in England. She is divorced and the mother of two young men and an adult daughter. She worships at Luton Central Seventh-day Adventist Church. **June 22, Sept. 16.**

Leah A. Salloman is a pastor's wife who works in the East Visayan Conference, Tacloban City, Philippines, as a church school teacher. She just graduated, earning a master's degree. She enjoys women's ministries, reading, baking, and producing programs in the church. She and her husband have two grown children. **Oct. 19.**

Deborah Sanders lives in Alberta, Canada. In 2007 Deborah and her husband, Ron, wrote the book *Our Journey Through Time With Sonny*. Sonny has significant developmental disabilities. The book is a collection of sacred memories shared in hopes of spiritually encouraging others in the family of God until Jesus comes for His people. **Feb. 4, June 21, Dec. 19.**

Theodora V. Sanders is the mother of seven and the grandmother of eight. She is married to James, and they are members of the Mount Calvary SDA Church in Huntsville, Alabama. She holds a B.S. degree in elementary education, and in her spare time she enjoys reading, writing, playing Scrabble, traveling, singing, and making memories with family and friends. **Nov. 24.**

Patrícia C. de Almeida Santos is a pastor's wife from Brazil and has a son named André. She earned a degree in pedagogy and likes to read, write, cook, and wander in nature with her family. **Mar. 22.**

Susana Schulz is from Argentina. She has three adult daughters and three grandchildren. A missionary spouse, she has studied people and languages and cultures. She was the first women's ministries director for the South American Division of Seventh-day Adventists, and director of the Adventist Colleges Abroad at the River Plate University. She works in the General Conference Education Department in Maryland. **June 27, Oct. 18.**

Jennifer Jill Schwirzer wears many hats, including running a private practice in mental health counseling in Philadelphia, conducting a music and speaking ministry, and cooking a mean gourmet vegan meal. **Jan. 2.**

Marie H. Seard is a regular contributor to the women's devotional project. She and her husband of more than 50 years have relocated from Washington, D.C. (after 48 years), to Hendersonville, Tennessee, where they are continuing to enjoy retirement. She enjoys keeping in touch with family and friends and looks forward to spending time with her grandchildren. **Nov. 13.**

Donna Lee Sharp enjoys using her music in care homes, Christian women's clubs, local churches, and more distant places. Gardening, flower arranging, bird-watching, and traveling to visit her far-flung family bring her pleasure. She lives in California. **July 28.**

Donna Sherrill has lived in Jefferson, Texas, for 35 years. Most of her time is spent managing the Academy Health Store and caring for an invalid husband. She loves to read, has a multitude of cats, and loves being with her grandkids. **Dec. 14.**

Bonita Joyner Shields is an editor at the General Conference of Seventh-day Adventists. In her spare time she likes to read, write, organize closets, and ride her go-cart. She lives in Brookeville, Maryland, with Roy, her husband of 28 years. **Nov. 26.**

Bessie Siemens, who passed away in 2011, had remarried her sons' father, John; they were very happy together again in their old age and enjoyed being near their oldest son, grandchildren, and fast-growing great-grandchild. She was a retired librarian who worked overseas and at home. **Aug. 26, Oct. 16.**

Rose Neff Sikora and her husband, Norman, call the beautiful mountains of North Carolina their home. She retired three years ago from a 45-year career as a registered nurse. She enjoys walking, writing, and helping others. Rose has one adult daughter, Julie, and three lovely grandchildren: Tyler, Olivia, and Grant. **Feb. 3, July 7.**

Heather-Dawn Small is Women's Ministries Department director at the General Conference of Seventh-day Adventists. She has been children's and women's ministries director for the Caribbean Union Conference, located in Trinidad and Tobago. She is the wife of Pastor Joseph Small and the mother of Dalonne and Jerard. She loves air travel, reading, and scrapbooking. **Jan. 4, Apr. 8.**

Yvonne Curry Smallwood lives in Maryland, where she is a wife, mother, and grandmother. She credits God for each opportunity afforded her to share His Word. Her stories have appeared in various publications. **May 16.**

Thamer Cassandra Smikle writes from Jamaica, where she is an auditor at Jamaica Customs Department. She has completed an M.A. in business administration (specializing in financing) at the Northern Caribbean University. She is an active member of Portmore church. Her hobbies include reading, singing, relaxing, and laughing. **Oct. 3.**

Lynn C. Smith was born on the beautiful island of New Providence, Bahamas. She has been a teacher and principal for many years and has been married to a pastor/conference administrator for the past 28 years. They have three young adult daughters. Lynn loves to read, cook, travel, shop, sing, play the piano, conduct choirs, and spend time with family. **Feb. 16, May 29.**

Heidi R. Snow was born in Honduras. She is a teacher for the Montessori School in the U.S. Virgin Islands. Her husband is a physician's assistant who works at the St. Croix Hospital. They have three beautiful children: Emily, Faith, and Jay. In 2006 Heidi won second place in a marathon, running 26 miles in four hours. She loves nature and listening to good music. **May 20.**

Érica Cristina Pinheiro de Souza, a native of Rio de Janeiro, Brazil, is a teacher and a pastor's wife. They have two children, Gabriel and Lílian Raquel. Érica loves working for God and with children. She likes very much to read. **Feb. 27.**

Marcilene Kapich Souza is a 27-year-old young woman who writes from Brazil. She is married, and she serves her church as a children's teacher. **Oct. 2.**

Ardis Dick Stenbakken lives in Loveland, Colorado, where she spends most of her time editing these devotional books. She enjoys working with her husband, Richard, and spending time with her children and four grandchildren. Her passion continues to be empowering women for personal and spiritual growth and ministry, and encouraging women in serious Bible study. **Jan. 11, May 1, Aug. 27.**

Cynthia Stephan works for the Wisconsin Conference of Seventh-day Adventists. She attends church with her husband, Brian, and her son, Dalton. Her hobbies include singing, ceramics, birding, and enjoying God's nature. **Nov. 2.**

Saramma Stephenson writes from India and is the wife of R. Stephenson, a mission president. She works as a department director of women's and children ministries and family ministries, and is Shepherdess coordinator. Her hobbies are sewing, embroidery, crafts, and gardening. **June 29.**

Keisha D. Sterling is from Jamaica and by training and practice is a registered pharmacist. Since age 16 she has served her church in areas of youth, health, education, church building, and women's ministries. She likes avocado, pineapple, ackee, and breadfruit, and always enjoys a good sleep and music. **Sept. 29.**

Rita Kay Stevens, a church administrator's wife, lives in New Mexico, where she works as a medical technologist. Rita enjoys traveling. She is a liaison for women's ministries and sponsor for the ministers' wives in the Texico Conference of Seventh-day Adventists. She is the mother of two grown sons and is thankful for a daughter-in-law and two grandchildren. **Sept. 22, Nov. 8.**

Rubye Sue and her husband, Bill, enjoy living on the campus of Laurelbrook Academy in Dayton, Tennessee, in the summer. In the winter they appreciate the sunshine in their home in Avon Park, Florida. They enjoy traveling, seeing old friends, and meeting new ones. **Dec. 5.**

Carolyn Sutton lives with her husband, Jim, on a small farm in Tennessee. They are field representatives for Adventist World Radio as well as being involved in their local church, prison ministry, and community events. Carolyn enjoys grandparenting, writing, speaking, music, and herb gardening. **Feb. 9.**

Kimberly N. Sutton, Ph.D., is a clinician, educator, and administrator in Georgia. She is the mother of one daughter, and enjoys traveling, reading, cooking, and dining out. **Mar. 2, May 22.**

H. Elizabeth Sweeney-Cabey is a retired widow in Florida. She has worked as a school teacher, sample maker for party frocks, and a mental health worker. Since retiring she has homeschooled many of her grandchildren. Her hobbies include reading, writing, sewing, carpentry, and especially in-depth Bible study. She has published one book, *'Twas Worth It All.* **Feb. 10, Apr. 6.**

Loraine F. Sweetland is retired in Tennessee. She coordinates an Adventist Food Buying Club for her church and community. She is now training to be a CASA (court-appointed special advocate) volunteer for neglected and abused children. She lives alone with her two dogs. **June 16.**

Anna (Ivie) Swingle has been an administrative specialist at a government facility for more than 10 years and a church clerk for more than 20 years. Music is her passion—she plays the organ and piano for church and coordinates a women's singing group that ministers to small churches in the Texas panhandle. Hobbies include family camping, birding, cross-stitching, and music. **June 8.**

Frieda Tanner is a retired nurse who turned 91 in August 2009! She still helps her husband make lovely visual aids for children around the world from her home in Eugene, Oregon, near her older daughter and two grandchildren. **Sept. 28.**

Neusa Bueno Targas is a retired teacher and pastor's wife in Brazil. She has three children and six grandchildren. She likes to conduct weeks of prayer in schools, give Bible studies, read, and solve crosswords. **Feb. 26.**

Arlene Taylor is risk manager and director of infection control for three Adventist Health hospitals in northern California. A brain-function specialist, she does research through her nonprofit corporation Realizations, Inc., and presents a variety of seminars internationally. Web site: www.arlene-taylor.org. **Jan. 23, May 24.**

Patrice Hill Taylor is a speech/language pathologist. She attends Church of the Redeemer, Presbyterian in Washington, D.C. She has served as chair for the forty-ninth Anniversary Committee of her church and is a member of the education committee and pastoral nominating committee. She loves to read devotionals and sing in the choir. **June 28.**

Rose Joseph Thomas is the mom of Samuel Joseph and Crystal Rose. She lives in Altamonte Springs, Florida, with her husband. She works at Forest Lake Education Center (FLEC). **Jan. 9.**

Sharon M. Thomas, a retired public school teacher, and her husband, Don, a retired social worker, are enjoying retirement in Louisiana. Sharon likes quilting, reading, walking, and traveling. She is grateful for the omniscient, omnipresent, and omnipotent God of love that we serve. **Oct. 24.**

Stella Thomas is an administrative secretary in the Global Mission Office at the General Conference of Seventh-day Adventists in Silver Spring, Maryland. She enjoys working for God and is longing for His second coming. **June 20.**

Bula Rose Haughton Thompson is a dental assistant who works at the Bellefield, Cross Keys, and Pratville health centers in Manchester, Jamaica. She also works at the Mandeville Comprehensive Clinic. In addition, she is a *couturière par excellence* whose other hobbies are singing, reading, and meeting people. **Sept. 2.**

Ethlyn Thompson, from Kingston, Jamaica, recently retired from a career in real estate and food service. (She started the first, and largest, restaurant in Jamaica.) Married, with four children and four grandchildren, she is the music director at her church in Constant Spring, an elder, organist, and pianist. Her hobbies are gardening, cooking, and floral arranging. **Dec. 21.**

Ena Thorpe lives in Hamilton, Ontario, Canada. She has three grown children and four grandchildren. She loves to play Scrabble and enjoys doing Sudoku and puzzles. She is an elder in her church and a member of the women's ministries for many years. **Dec. 10.**

Gloria Lindsey Trotman, Ph.D., is a commissioned minister of the church she has served for 40 years. Until her recent retirement, she was director of women's and children's ministries, and Shepherdess coordinator of the Inter-American Division. Gloria is also an author. Her motto is "Making a Difference." She now lives in Texas. **Aug. 8, Nov. 9.**

Olinda Milagros Rojas Valle writes from Lima, Peru. This is her first contribution to a women's devotional book. **Nov. 14.**

Nancy Van Pelt is a certified family life educator, speaker, and best-selling author of more than 40 books. For 25 years Nancy has traversed the globe, teaching families how to really love each other. Her hobbies include getting organized, entertaining, having fun, and quilting. She and her husband live in California and enjoy a highly effective marriage. **July 22.**

Wanda Van Putten-Allen, originally from St. Thomas, U.S. Virgin Islands, writes from Maryland. She is a wife, mother, and educator. Her hobbies include reading the Bible, sharing testimonies, writing, illustrating, singing, and listening to music. She also enjoys travel and fellowship with family and friends. **June 13.**

Gisselle Lavandier de Vásquez lives in the Dominican Republic with her husband, Pastor José Enrique Vásquez. She serves God in the offices of the North East Dominican Mission and loves writing and counseling youth, women, and couples through therapy and seminars in the district in which she works with her husband. **May 27.**

Vanessa Velasquez de Mejía, born and raised in Tela, Honduras, is an English teacher. She has been married to Héctor Manuel Mejía for one year and says that he is an "inspiration toward my spiritual growth." Vanessa is a member of the Adventist church of Tela. She loves cooking and enjoys time spent with her husband and children. **Dec. 6.**

Monica Vesey writes from Berkshire, England. She is the daughter of Leonard Edmonds, a pioneer missionary in Aba, Nigeria. A retired teacher, she started working in 1949 at age 17 and retired when she was 75. She enjoys writing about how wonderfully God has led, and she has a passionate interest in helping dyslexics. She is involved in prayer ministries. **Nov. 16.**

Carmem Virgínia is a community health agent and Portuguese teacher in Brazil. She loves to read and to praise the name of the Lord with beautiful hymns. She uses her work as an instrument of evangelization. At her church she serves in the areas of music and women's and children's ministries. **May 2.**

Heidi Vogt, a recent transplant to the alpine high country of Colorado from her beloved Pacific Northwest, praises the Lord for her lifelong blessings of God's natural world. Learning, research, reading, writing, and hiking are hobbies. Whether as a wildlife biologist, author, paralegal, community volunteer, or accountant, she lives for the Lord each day. **Feb. 1.**

Nancy Jean Vyhmeister's career has included a half century of teaching (mostly of ministers) in formation, and writing and editing various projects. In retirement she is busy in her local Yucaipa, California, church and finds all kinds of teaching, writing, and editing projects that land in her willing lap. **Nov. 3.**

Lilya Wagner, director of Philanthropic Service for Institutions, has spent years working and writing in the field of philanthropy as a vice president for philanthropy at Counterpart International in Washington, D.C., the Center on Philanthropy at Indiana University, the Women's Philanthropy Institute, the Fund Raising School, and the Center on Philanthropy's philanthropic studies. **July 20.**

Mary Wagoner-Angelin lives in Ooltewah, Tennessee, with her husband, Randy, and their two daughters. Mary is a social worker at a psychiatric hospital. She volunteers for Make-A-Wish Foundation, at her local library, as a field leader for MOPS (Mothers of Preschoolers), and as a young adult leader at her church. She enjoys humor therapy, exercise, and vegan recipes. **Oct. 21, Dec. 1.**

Cora A. Walker is a retired nurse, editor, and freelance writer who lives in Fort Washington, Maryland. She is an active member of the church she attends in Charles County, Maryland. She enjoys reading, writing, swimming, classical music, singing, and traveling. She has one son, Andre V. Walker. **Feb. 7.**

Dolores Klinsky Walker (and her husband), having launched her three children into adulthood, is finding great satisfaction in mentoring released prisoners and tutoring English as a second language students. A prolonged convalescence temporarily switched her from "doing" to "being," and revealed the treasure of time alone with God. The Walkers live in Washington State. **Jan. 12.**

Cathy Roberts Ward writes from Lincoln, Nebraska, where she and her new husband, Mike, work in church ministry through DivorceCare, sharing God's goodness in the healing process after divorce. Blending two families with nine children, 14 siblings, and aging parents will bring years of new life experiences to Cathy's writing. Cathy enjoys writing, gardening, and friends! **Oct. 25.**

Naoko Watanabe lives in Kobe, Japan, where she graduated from the nursing school of Japan Missionary College. She is a third-generation Adventist pastor's wife, and one of her four sons has continued the tradition—he is serving as a pastor with his wife in Australia. **Sept. 18.**

Anna May Radke Waters, who lives in Washington State, is a retired administrative secretary from Columbia Adventist Academy, and served for many years as an elder and greeter at church. She has too many hobbies to list, but at the top of what she enjoys are her four children, eight grandchildren, two great-grandchildren, and her husband of 58 years. **Jan. 31, Apr. 3.**

Dorothy Eaton Watts, who retired in 2009 from administration responsibilities for her church head-quarters in India, passed away November 8, 2009. She was a missionary in India for more than 28 years; she founded an orphanage, taught elementary school, and wrote more than 25 books. In 2007 the Association of Adventist Women gave her its Woman of the Year award for entrepreneurial church leadership. **Jan. 13, May 21.**

Lyn Welk-Sandy lives in Adelaide, South Australia. She works as a grief counselor and assists Sudanese refugee families. Lyn has spent many years as a pipe organist and loves church music and choir work. She enjoys nature, photography, and caravanning around outback Australia with her husband, Keith. Lyn is a mother of four and has 12 grandchildren. **Aug. 5, Dec. 23.**

Penny Estes Wheeler has been blessed by a family she treasures and work she enjoys in Maryland. She loves "scrapping," growing flowers, and travel. She says that there will never be enough time to do all she wants to do, read all she wants to read, and see all the places she wants to see—perhaps in the new earth. She and her husband have four adult children and three grandchildren. **Aug. 28.**

Billie Jo Whitehurst was born in Texas but has lived in Australia since 1990. She is a high school math teacher who is happily married to Karl, her high school sweetheart. She loves animals, writing to pen pals, reading, and traveling the world with Karl. In 2003 Billie Jo became actively involved with the Adventist Church; she works with women's ministries and is bulletin editor. **Nov. 10.**

Sandra Widulle is married and has two children. She loves to express her thoughts in writing. In her local church in Germany she is engaged in the children's division and uses her creativity to decorate the church showcase. **Jan. 16.**

Vera Wiebe is the women's ministries leader for Saskatchewan, Canada, where her husband is the conference president. She enjoys traveling and visiting the churches with him. She has two adult sons and four grandchildren, who bring a lot of joy. Her hobbies include organizing music for her church and for camp meeting, and sewing and knitting for the grandchildren. **July 24.**

Mildred C. Williams is a widow and retired physical therapist living in southern California. She enjoys studying and teaching the Bible, writing, gardening, public speaking, sewing, and spending time with her grown children and granddaughter. She also likes writing for this devotional book series, as it gives her a chance to share God's love with others. **Oct. 31.**

Patrice Williams-Gordon is a Jamaican motivational speaker and seminar presenter who enjoys writing, speaking, reading, and a good laugh. She shares ministry with her husband, Pastor Danhugh Gordon, who currently serves in Nassau, Bahamas. Mother of Ashli and Rhondi, Patrice is excited about reaching anyone for Jesus. **July 5.**

Melanie Carter Winkler writes from Western Australia. She is a wife and author who sings and praises God. Her loves are music, reading, writing, and finding treasures from God. Her aim is to make a difference in at least one person's life, to bring them to God. **Oct. 29.**

Barbara Wyman and her late husband, Frank, completed 40 years of ministry in Burma and in the Pacific Northwest. After retirement they spent three years in volunteer assignments in South Korea and Russia. They retired to Washington State to be near their daughter and her three children. They were also blessed with a son. **June 24.**

Aileen L. Young, writing from Hawaii, enjoys art, music, and three grandchildren: Spencer, Ashley, and Liliane. She is a retired teacher, church and community helper, and has traveled extensively. Her current occupation is e-mailing, reading, writing, singing, and playing the organ. She enjoys board games. **Nov. 21.**

Shelly-Ann Patricia Zabala writes from Puerto Rico, where she is a registered nurse. A minister's wife, she is a stay-at-home mom for their two sons. She enjoys children's and women's ministries, and her hobbies include singing, gardening, and entertaining. Together with her husband, Florencio, she serves in the East Puerto Rico Conference of Seventh-day Adventists. **Feb. 8, Sept. 24.**

Leni Uría de Zamorano is the mother of two adult children who have given her and her husband, Luis, two granddaughters. She is a member of the Florida Adventist Church in Buenos Aires, Argentina, where she plays the piano and the organ and teaches a Bible study class. She likes to travel, do handwork, play the piano, and translate from English to Spanish. **Sept. 20.**

Kathy S. Zausa writes from the Philippines. She was 23 years old at the time of writing and a fresh magna cum laude graduate from Adventist University of the Philippines. She was a women's ministry scholarship recipient, partially funded by the sale of these devotional books. Kathy is currently looking for work. **Oct. 20.**

LaToya V. Zavala is a mother and military wife living in Virginia. She is also a seminary student, entrepreneur, and lay preacher. She enjoys reading, writing, public speaking, and playing the cello. **May 17.**

Candy Zook, is a mother of three and grandmother of six. She recently returned to Nebraska from the mission field in India. She is currently writing her first book about India. **Dec. 28.**